Saxifrages

Saxifrages

A Definitive Guide to the 2000 Species, Hybrids & Cultivars

Malcolm McGregor

Timber Press

Portland | London

Frontispiece: *Saxifraga callosa* subsp. *callosa* by the waterfall at Notre Dame des Fontaines near La Brigue in the Maritime Alps.

Published in 2008 by Timber Press, Inc.

The Haseltine Building   2 The Quadrant
133 S.W. Second Avenue, Suite 450   135 Salusbury Road
Portland, Oregon 97204-3527   London NW6 6RJ
www.timberpress.com   www.timberpress.co.uk

ISBN-13: 978-0-88192-8808

Designed by Dick Malt
Printed in China

Library of Congress Cataloging-in-Publication Data
McGregor, Malcolm, 1947-
  Saxifrages : a definitive guide to the 2000 species, hybrids &
cultivars / Malcolm McGregor. – 1st ed.
      p. cm.
  Includes bibliographical references and index.
  ISBN-13: 978-0-88192-880-8
  1. Saxifraga. I. Title.
  QK495.S3M34 2008
  635.9'3372–dc22
                              2007038593

A catalogue record for this book is also available from the
British Library.

Contents

Acknowledgements

This book is dedicated to all those who have contributed to its making: photographers, gardeners, writers, guides, nurserymen, botanists, librarians, friends and growers; to Dick Malt, Penny David and Anna Mumford at Timber Press; to the memory of those whose enthusiasm led me to write about saxifrages: Winton Harding, John Byam-Grounds and my father Ken; and to all my family, and in particular to Daniel and Maureen, Matthew and, above all, Monica.

Foreword

It is surprising that, since the monumental account of the genus *Saxifraga* by Engler and Irmscher in *Das Pflanzenreich* between 1916 and 1919, there has been no full treatment of such a widely grown genus that contains so many attractive garden plants.

While there have been excellent publications on European saxifrages and on section *Porphyrion*, which includes the well-known *Kabschia* saxifrages, and section *Ligulatae*, the silver saxifrages, as well as a revised botanical classification of the genus by Richard Gornall in 1987, the lack of a complete overview of the genus has been a very noticeable gap in garden literature.

Malcolm McGregor, Editor of the *Saxifrage Magazine* from 1993 to 2003, is very well qualified to fill this gap through his studies of the genus that have already resulted in publications for the Saxifrage Society of *Saxifrages: the complete list of Species* (1998, with Winton Harding) and *Saxifrages: the Complete Cultivars & Hybrids* (2nd edition 2003), which is the International Register of Saxifrages.

This blend of botanical and horticultural studies is particularly welcome in such a complex genus (or, as discussed in this book, probably two genera, *Saxifraga* and *Micranthes*), as there is considerable confusion in groups where much hybridization has taken place in gardens.

The chapters covering garden hybrids from different sections of the genus are also extremely valuable in helping to unravel the confusion and misnaming that exists among the "mossy saxifrages" and also those of the "London pride" persuasion, all of which are excellent garden plants.

While Malcolm has spent many years delving deeply into literature about the genus and examining specimens in herbaria, this very readable and thoroughly researched book is also based on his extensive travels during the last fifteen or more years in many parts of the world, where he has searched for and studied saxifrages in their natural habitats. In addition, he cultivates many species and cultivars in his own garden, has produced some intriguing hybrids, and from first-hand experience provides, in the chapter on gardening with saxifrages, much information on all aspects of cultivation, propagation and siting the different species, hybrids and cultivars in the garden.

I have no doubt that this much-needed and very informative account of this popular genus of garden plants will find favour not only with specialist alpine growers but with a wide range of gardeners who appreciate the charms and garden adaptability of this large and diverse genus.

Chris Brickell CBE, VMH
President, Saxifrage Society and former Director of Wisley Garden and Director General Royal Horticultural Society

Part 1 · An Overview

1 · On the Road

Saxifrages are wonderful garden plants. They come in all sorts of shapes and sizes, there are plants for all the different parts of the garden, the flowering season is from January through to the frosts of autumn, and they come in every colour except blue. White, yellow, buff, orange, red, mauve, purple and pink are all in the saxifrage palette, in a variety of mixtures, with petals, nectary ring and stamens each having the possibility of being a different colour. The result is a myriad of delicious combinations—like the fondants from a Parisian pâtissier.

Saxifrages have inhabited large parts of my garden, have dictated where I've been on holiday, and have generally absorbed an awful lot of my spare time: watering the plants in the alpine house, tending the rock garden and taking cuttings; writing, editing and giving lectures; learning botanical Latin, travelling to increasingly obscure places to find and photograph plants in the wild. As with all enthusiasts, the subject of an enthusiasm can become an obsession.

I didn't get hooked on saxifrages until the end of the 1970s when my father asked if I could get him *Saxifraga* 'Tumbling Waters', a particular saxifrage he had read about and become intrigued by. He had just retired from his job as a marketing manager to live in rural mid-Wales, where he and my mother were to spend the next ten years keeping geese, chickens and a few goats, growing vegetables, and just getting by. He had few opportunities to visit nurseries while I had plenty. It took me quite a long time to get hold of 'Tumbling Waters'—although it is so spectacular that any wait only sharpens the appetite—but in the meantime I got hooked. One day in March I was visiting the local market in Beverley, in East Yorkshire, when I found the stall of a local nurseryman who was selling tiny *Porphyrion* saxifrages in flower. I'd never seen such plants before: exquisite flowers on tiny domed cushions no bigger than a large coin. I bought three—'Myra', 'Sulphurea' and 'Gold Dust'—and they are still among my favourites: first loves. When I next

Fondant dreams: *Saxifraga* hybrids from section *Porphyrion*.

Top three rows (from left to right): 'Peach Melba', 'Bohemia', 'Allendale Amber'.

Bottom row (from left to right): 'Vladana', 'Jupiter' and 'Mrs Gertie Prichard'.

visited my parents I took the plants with me, and we tried to take cuttings, and over the next few years we managed to keep them alive, and they flowered, and we read and learnt, and bought more plants. It was a hobby we shared, buying plants and propagating them, and maintaining and documenting our collections.

I have been interested in wild flowers since I was a boy. Perhaps it was the sheer magic they represented when we moved from a basement flat in Fulham in bomb-damaged London, where we had no garden, to the outer fringes of London, and I was suddenly, at the age of nine, free to tramp the Kentish woods, finding flowers, watching woodpeckers, catching fish, and over the next few years exploring further on my bike, finding orchids in the chalk meadows, crayfish in the chalk streams. I can still feel the same joy in my searches for saxifrages, kneeling in a stream or edging along a rocky ledge—even if today caution occasionally takes over.

Starting Work

The greatest work on saxifrages is *Das Pflanzenreich: Saxifraga*, the monumental work of Adolf Engler and Edgar Irmscher. This was published in two parts in 1916 and 1919 and contains detailed approaches to every species then known, describing them and their distribution in great detail. Engler's approach is very much founded in the tradition of exhaustive scholarship of the late 19th century which led in Britain to such productions as the Ninth Edition of the *Encyclopaedia Britannica*. That all human knowledge could be encompassed was still at the heart of these late 19th-century compilers. Engler undertook this for plants—with massive works—and his account of the *Saxifraga* remains fundamental today, as I am sure do his accounts of other groups of plants, despite the revisions of a number of later authors. Since then there has been no equivalent, although Webb & Gornall's *Saxifrages of Europe* (with the American edition titled *A Manual of Saxifrages*) is wonderfully useful and Horný, Webr and Byam-Grounds's *Porophyllum Saxifrages* is one of the great books if you are a specialist.

By 1994 I was already well advanced in compiling the *International Register of Saxifraga Cultivars*, and I decided to try and make sense of all the newly described species that had appeared and publish a full list of them and their synonyms. When I started on this I was lucky enough to find that Winton Harding, then President of the Saxifrage Society, for whom I was the Editor, had already done a lot of preparatory work. As generous as ever, Winton handed me all the work he had done, explaining that with the explosion of new Chinese species he felt that younger eyes and new enthusiasm were needed to bring the project to completion. A little later he passed on to me his copy of *Das Pflanzenreich*, which had been owned by W. R. Dykes, famous for his work on irises, before it had come to him. The result of this relay of work was that by 1998 we were able to publish our *Saxifrages: the complete list of Species*, clarifying much of the synonymy of otherwise obscure species. And so, for a time it was left, although I continued to annotate my own copy and accumulate papers describing new species.

Over time I have grown many hundreds of cultivars and every species I have been able to get my hands on. I have been part of two International Seminars of the Saxifrage Society, one in Loenen in the Netherlands in 2000, and a second in Beroun in the Czech Republic in 2004, and I've travelled to a long list of places to find saxifrages in the wild. Three societies have provided me with financial support which has been very much appreciated and I hope those involved will feel that this book pays back their support: the North American Rock Garden Society (NARGS) Norman Singer Endowment Fund generously supported my trip to Alaska, the Olympic Mountains and the Rocky Mountains; the East Surrey Group of the Alpine Garden Society gave me a generous grant from the Hendry Bequest towards the costs of our search for Andalucian saxifrages and for a follow-up trip to the Rif Mountains of Morocco; and the Scottish Rock Garden Club has given me grants towards the photographic costs of my trip to Tibet and to my costs in Morocco.

Occasionally I have been on my own on these trips but much more often I've been with other people and I want to thank all of those. I hope everyone who has been along on trips, and all those who have found plants for me, will accept these accounts as a small symbolic token of the part that they have played, and that this book goes some way to nail down our shared enthusiasms. Sometimes they have been local people, sometimes travelling companions. So many people in England, Scotland, Wales, the Czech Republic, the United States and Canada have helped me, but Paul Kennett, David Victor and John Howes are the only people I am going to single out here for special thanks. They have shared my enthusiasm and have long played a part in discussions, in photography, and in reading parts of this book as it progressed. John was my Illustrations Manager while I was Editor for the Scottish Rock Garden Club, as well as being Slide Librarian for the Saxifrage Society. He has visited numerous shows and nurseries with me, and grown plants in parallel with me. Paul is the webmaster for the Saxifrage Society, of which David has been Chairman and is now President. They have all contributed photographs to this book, many in the cases of Paul and John, and they have all been good companions on many trips to the mountains.

Over the years I have now been to a lot of places in search of wild saxifrages: northwest India, Tibet, Nepal, Turkey, Austria, Slovenia, France, Italy, Spain and Morocco. In North America I have visited the northern and central Rocky Mountains, the Cascades, the Olympic Mountains, the Appalachians and Alaska. So I have lots of memories of places and the people I was with.

On top of the world—
Malcolm McGregor
looking at *Saxifraga
oppositifolia* on Ankögel
in Austria. Photograph
David Victor.

Malcolm McGregor
photographing *Saxifraga
reuteriana* in the Sierra
del Valle, Andalucia.
Photograph Paul Kennett.

Andalucia

My Spanish was limited to what I had been able to learn in one term's evening class—Paul Kennett and John Howes had far less—but it had seemed a useful piece of preparation for the trip. I had learnt enough to allow me to ask for vegetarian food for John and to discuss what degree of vegetarianism was required. I had learnt vocabulary about mountains, and fuelling the car, and explaining that we had a reservation, and I'd learnt the numbers and the alphabet. When we lost the sump of our hire car it was just enough for me to understand the recorded message on the emergency service that redirected me to another number and to decipher that number.

As far as saxifrages are concerned the mountains of Morocco and eastern Spain are an archipelago with successive groups functioning as biological islands developing individualized flora and fauna. They are not separated from one another by sea like the Galapagos Islands or the islands of the eastern Mediterranean, but they are isolated from one another by a number of natural barriers. The sea itself forms one of these barriers, and the hot dry interior of the country another, so that the ranges along the Mediterranean coasts have populations of plants that are susceptible to fragmentation. The higher mountain groups, with very divergent geologies, function exactly like islands, with some progressively differentiating plants unable to jump the gap from one suitable habitat to the next.

We had spent ten days visiting a succession of these saxifrage islands in Andalucia: the Sierra Bermeja for *Saxifraga gemmulosa*; the Serrania di Ronda and Grazalema for *S. bourgaeana*, *S. haenseleri* and *S. globulifera*; El Torcal for *S. biternata*, and the Sierra del Valle for *S. reuteriana*. In the Sierra Nevada the snow was still too low for us to find *S. nevadensis* although we were able to sit by the roadside and watch ibex licking salt from the roads, and lower down we found *S. carpetana* and *S. erioblasta*. Our last stopover was in the Sierra di Cazorla to look for *S. rigoi*.

We stayed in a small hotel in the hills which had been a monastery and still maintained the tradition of religious pictures, with the Sacred Heart overlooking us at dinner. While the family and the other guests watched the Spanish Royal Wedding, we tried again for *Saxifraga rigoi*, encountering a wild boar and young trotting across our path. Despite our efforts—including a thirty-kilometre traverse in our hired Renault on a rock-strewn track to get us to Los Pontones, where we scoured the tops and edged down a remarkably steep gulley—we failed to find a site for *S. rigoi*, although we found other endemics such as *Viola cazorlensis* and *Orchis cazorlensis*.

On our last day we had to drive out through the northeastern end of the Sierra de Cazorla and on to the airport in Murcia and although *Saxifraga rigoi* eluded us to the last we were entranced to find cushions of *S. camposii* strewing the rocks. If we'd had a little more petrol or had known that there was a garage only another twenty miles down the road we'd have been more relaxed, but it was still a treat … .

New Jersey

My love of saxifrages spreads out across the whole saxifrage family, so trips to North America in the spring and early summer are always exciting. I had to do a presentation to the local NARGS chapter, but apart from that it was a lovely pause in the middle of a hectic schedule—lecture tours can be like that. I'd been to North Carolina, first Raleigh and then Asheville, then on to Washington DC, and New York to talk on Saturday morning and again in the afternoon to the three local chapters, and I would be going on to Pennsylvania and then back to DC for a second presentation. Rural New Jersey does not sound like the opportunity to find many saxifrages. Ruby and Martin Weinberg were hosting me in their Lloyd Wright-inspired home with bird feeders outside the window attracting indigo buntings, woodpeckers and American goldfinches. Most days we had something planned but on one clear afternoon I took off on foot, crossed Beaver Creek Road and explored

Micranthes virginiensis in glorious profusion by a New Jersey roadside.

the wooded lane. Spring in woodland is always good on a sunny day with the dappled sunlight lighting up anything that is in flower—four species of violets, a stand of anemonellas on the roadside bank—but suddenly in the sun the bank was a mass of saxifrages: *Micranthes virginiensis* as a host of bloom. Any other time, perhaps even three weeks later, it would have been interesting but not spectacular; that day it was the most glorious sight … .

Colle Berici

The three of us had been on the Saxifraga Society trip to Austria for a week but we had flown into, and were flying back from, Italy. Paul Kennet and David Victor were flying out on separate flights from Venice and I was flying three days later from Bergamo. We only had about an hour before we had to set off to get David to the airport.

The turning would be obvious, Paul assured us, but it was far from that, with all the obvious turns proving fruitless. We were trying to get up to the slopes of the

Saxifraga berica growing in pockets in the soft limestone of the Colle Berici, near Vicenza, Italy.

Colle Berici just south of Vicenza—we were looking for *Saxifraga berica*. The turn when we found it was at a traffic lights, the fourth and almost squeezingly narrow of the four arms of a crossroads. At what appeared to be a dead end there was a very tight sharp right which led up past the little church.

Italian weddings are major events in small communities and everyone dresses accordingly. Normally it would have been intriguing to stop for a moment and watch the guests arriving at the church. But we were in a hurry. The steep narrow lane, and its sharp bends were made much less manoeuvrable by the large cars parked along the side. Our hour had diminished by more than half when we managed to park on the inside of a hairpin bend and set off along a shaded hillside track.

Saxifraga berica grows on the bare dusty limestone deep in the shade of the scrubby woodland obviously stranded here after the last great glaciation and doomed to a lingering heat death if temperatures rise. So we had fifteen minutes with the plants, before stumbling back along the path, back to the car, to get out down the road before the wedding guests started to leave … and then on to Venice to get David to the airport for his flight.

Paul wasn't flying out till the evening so we had a few more hours and we went up to the foothills of the Alps where we found stands of *Saxifraga hostii* by the roadside and then stopped at a hillside farm selling its own cheese and wine, facing south across the plains of the Veneto.

Having dropped Paul at the airport I got back to the hotel where I watched the World Cup Final with the family—Italy beating France—and in the morning I drove westward to the west side of Lake Garda to look for *Saxifraga arachnoidea* on Monte Tombea. Stopping at a small petrol station in Capo Valle for fuel, I asked whether there was an albergo and the woman serving went through to the bar and brought back the owner of the only albergo in the community.

Here looking out down the narrow village street from the balcony of the small, spartan, but spotless room, I could see the narrow three-storey houses opposite with wooden balconies that would have looked at home in the Himalayas. I was the only guest and my fragment of Italian did little more than allow me to complement mama on her homemade mushroom soup, the veal cutlet and the beans and salads from the tiny vegetable garden.

Next morning after breakfast I drove to the head of the road and trekked up the steepest of tracks past the farm dogs up to the lower slopes of Tombea. On the shady bank of the path there was a little bit of *Saxifraga petraea* but it was a little further up, out of the woodland, that I found what I was hoping for. The cliffs were rather soft, dusty limestone with *Physoplexis comosa* finding sites in pockets on the vertical surfaces. In the lee of the cliffs nestling under the overhang in the dusty rubble was *S. arachnoidea* with its pale yellow flowers floating in the soft hairy mass of stems and leaves … .

Baralacha

The high passes of the Himalaya are generally reached after long hard treks up from lower levels, gradually gaining altitude and acclimatizing as you go. But here and there are high passes which can be reached by road, and the Baralacha Pass in northwest India, on the road from Manali to Leh, is one of these. It is a bleak but beautiful place, with views out across Himalayan peaks. It's a wonderful place on a good day, but being driven up to a 5000-metre pass is not an ideal way to acclimatize to the altitude, even if you have camped the night before at 4500 metres on

The Baralacha Pass: Monica, and in the distance (from left to right) Daniel, our guide Kuchal (orange jacket), and Matthew (with the white hat).

Herdsmen in the early morning. Himachal Pradesh, India.

a moraine surrounded by 6000-metre peaks. I don't sleep that well at this sort of altitude, and Monica and our sons Daniel and Matthew, and Alastair McKelvie and Joel Smith, were doing little better. At these altitudes the thin air holds little heat once the sun goes down and even in August the early morning was still sharply cold. These conditions were obviously very much to the taste of the snow pigeons showing in the early morning sun against the still-shaded cliffs, and of the horned shore larks, only occasional winter visitors to British coasts, which picked their way through the gravel between the tents. After a typical camp breakfast of porridge and tea we drove on up to the top of the pass where Monica, the boys

The teashop on the top of the Rhotang Pass.

and I were meeting up with the guides and ponies who we were going to trek with, while Alastair and Joel were taking the jeeps on, over the pass toward Leh. The altitude would catch up with them and force them back to meet us again a week later back at the Rhotang Pass, where we found them camping on the dry side of the pass in a field full of *Geranium cashmerianum* back at an altitude where shepherds would bring their flocks of sheep and goats.

We had driven up to the Rhotang Pass from Manali and spent time searching the lower meadows, and at the top we had stopped to search again and for a cup of tea in the fog. Lower down we had found *Bergenia ciliata* on shaded cliffs, and in the meadows below the Rhotang Pass there were *Saxifraga parnassifolia* and *S. brachypoda*, and *Micranthes pallida* was flowering at the roadside.

Up at the Baralacha Pass, a day's driving later, we found another three species of saxifrage—*Saxifraga jacquemontiana* and *S. stenophylla* from the archetypal Himalayan section *Ciliatae*, and the *Mesogyne* species *S. sibirica*. Each of these three species is highly adapted to the extreme conditions they have to face. Here the snows start to fall in late September and only melt again in June, so the Baralacha Pass seems an unlikely place to find many flowering plants, but for those that are sufficiently adapted this is a marvellous spot since there is not a lot of competition. Small drifts of *Polygonum* with pink-flowering pokers, deep-rooted corydalis, dwarf arenarias and asters are scattered among the rocks. In flatter, damper areas there is a continuous weaving of *Primula reptans* and small potentillas. No grass grows here—conditions are too hard. Winter is too long, with snow cover for more than six months, but those plants that can survive benefit from fantastically high light levels, since the atmosphere is only half the density of that at sea-level and consequently filters out only a fraction of the ultraviolet.

As we waved goodbye to Joel, Alastair and their guide Roop, to set off across the high slopes with Kuchal, I did wonder what I'd done in planning the trip for the whole family. It was desperately hard trekking but stunningly beautiful … .

Ultima Thule

If you've never been to Alaska, it might not strike you as one of the world hot-spots for saxifrages (*Micranthes* and *Saxifraga*), but very few places rival it for sheer variety of species. I had written to Verna Pratt when first planning my ten-day visit to Alaska, and as well as sending me precise details about where I could find the plants I was looking for, she and Frank had also offered me a bed while I was in Anchorage and their company in Nome. We spent a couple of days around Anchorage in the Chugach Mountains and at Hatcher Pass, enjoying success with *Micranthes lyallii*, predominantly found in British Columbia and southern Alaska, and *M. nelsoniana*, found from Washington up into Alaska and on across into Siberia. We also found a number of other members of the saxifrage family: *Leptarrhena pyrolifolia*, *Mitella pentandra* and *Chrysosplenium tetrandrum*. But my final destination was the *ultima Thule* for any saxifrage enthusiast: the far west of Alaska, the Seward Peninsula, on the Bering Sea coast. As if this were truly the end of the world, any farther would have meant crossing into Russia, and I would be on my way home to England. Certain places have this quality of being a destination rather than a transit point on the road: high places, remote places. I've never been to the Antarctic, but the far northwest of Alaska ranks for me along with Tibet and the mountains of the Continental Divide in equatorial Africa. This is what makes people climb the highest mountains or try to reach the poles: not because they're there, but because of this sense of final arrival. But this remoteness, which makes western Alaska a true wilderness, was not what I came for; it was the saxifrages that brought me.

Nome is one of those few places in the world that make you feel you have finally got to where you were going, that you are not just stopping off on the way to somewhere else. It was established in the gold rush of 1898, and there are still gold panners spending the summer in huts scattered for many miles along the beach, and in the surrounding area abandoned workings and the rusting remains of a failed railway venture. On the tundra, long-tailed skuas hawk across the hills, and loons, like the spirits of loneliness, are found on the coastal lagoons. In high summer, when the tundra is in bloom at the beginning of July, you can be writing postcards home about the herd of wild musk oxen you watched that afternoon, saying it has been a beautiful sunny day, and that it still is beautifully light—at midnight. Make the best of it. After three days penetrating the surrounding tundra we were being blasted by continuous drear, wintry gales, with the temperature in town down to forty-one degrees Fahrenheit, surrounded by thickly fog-bound hills where it was quite a lot colder than that. We took refuge in the Russian store and browsed among the stock. Walrus ivory carvings, baleen brooches, a carved seal skull, red and Arctic fox furs were all part of the native population's allowable harvest; videos and tapes of native song and story; Russian fur hats of almost any fur you could imagine, ex-Soviet army hats including the pointed hats beloved of Cossacks; newly produced Orthodox ikons alongside pieces of old Russian porcelain. The store reflects its owner, Victor Goldsberry, and talk is as important as selling. Finding that I was in Nome to photograph saxifrages, and particularly *Micranthes nudicaulis*, he dragged me out to the tiny patch of garden flanking the wooden steps up to the front door. In these two small beds, Victor and his wife Nadejda grow a collection of food plants. Not much of a vegetable garden, too small for that, but a special garden nonetheless—and in it a patch of *M. nudicaulis*.

Victor told me about the continuing use of native plants for food. Later he wrote to me: "Last night (folks visiting) was bowhead whale—*mangtak* (from Saroonga so Coastal Siberian Yupik—*maktak* in Inuit), walrus meat, bearded seal meat, and greens in seal oil for supper. Folks outside don't realize how many greens, berries, vegetables—*masu* (Eskimo potatoes)—roots, wild chives, occasionally mushrooms are eaten in northern people's diets …".

Victor Goldsberry and his wife Nadejda Soudakova in front of their garden and shop in Nome, Alaska.

Outside his store he talked about the way in which the leaves of the saxifrage are eaten fresh or kept for the winter in jars of seal oil. For Nadejda the saxifrage was *sitngegh-haq* in the language of the Naukan Yupik, the root of the word, *site-*, meaning the leaf is shaped like an ear. Victor also came up with the name *azigaq* from the Central Siberian Yupik. In 1990, Naukan Yupik was confined to fewer than a 100 speakers, almost all in Chukotka, the region of Siberia where they were resettled from coastal Naukan, and Central Siberian Yupik was spoken by around 800 speakers in Alaska and a further 300 in Chukotka. Of all communities split by the Cold War the native people of this region have a claim to be most affected: extended families separated for fifty years by the US–USSR border, and entire villages in the USSR relocated inland where their language and culture declined in urban settings, a process of acculturation paralleled, although not forcibly, in Alaska.

Eric Hultén in his *Flora of Alaska* notes that *Micranthes nelsoniana* subsp. *nelsoniana* was used by native people as a food plant, and Verna Pratt believes it was used by the Aleuts, but we only found small numbers of this species in the Nome area. That *Micranthes nudicaulis* has names in both Naukan and Central Siberian Yupik as well as being a food might seem unlikely to the outsider, as surely it too is rare. In fact we found it in three different places; in two, it grew in large quantities surrounded by running water, rather like an arctic version of an English watercress bed ...

... And there are still wild places to go: Yunnan, the Ozarks, the Elburz mountains of Iran. And there are always new plants to grow. And you don't need to go to remote places to find beautiful plants. So often they are on our doorsteps ...

Over the years I've been shown round gardens, have been allowed to poke around and take cuttings, have received gifts of rare and obscure species, sometimes in person, sometimes through the post. Most of all I've visited dozens of collections and nurseries as individual as the people running them—friendly and welcoming; unnervingly tidy; chaotically charming. Some nurseries are packed with the latest prizes, some with historic treasures. Some have plants organized alphabetically—*Satureja, Sauromatum, Saxifraga*—but in others any original logic has long been overtaken. Some are in old walled gardens, warm and sheltered; others bleak and exposed to the winds. Some open all week, some only two days, some only in summer; some do mail order, some only do mail order, some hate mail order or set their minimum order at something like the price of a couple of dozen decent trees. Sometimes you are welcome, sometimes you are turfed out so the owner can close for lunch. Yet it's through these people's efforts that garden saxifrages come down to us—a box of delights.

Micranthes nudicaulis growing in sphagnum by the Nome–Council Road, Seward Peninsula, Alaska.

2 · The Saxifrage Family

There are 33 genera in the saxifrage family, the Saxifragaceae, including *Astilbe*, *Bergenia*, *Heuchera*, *Rodgersia* and *Tiarella* alongside the range of *Saxifraga* proper. At the heart of our approach to the family, whatever the refinements since 1753, lies the insight of Linnaeus that plants can be classified according to the numbers of their floral parts. The saxifrage family consists of a group of plants which have five sepals, five petals, two carpels and five or ten anthers. Alongside this recognition of the importance of floral structure was his revolutionary system of naming all living things with just two Latin words, one for the genus and one for the species. With these tools he gave us an elegant way of looking at the natural world which has served us ever since. But it is not the elegance of Linnaeus's approach which makes it so durable, it is the fact that his analysis, based on floral structures, has proved to be correct: plants that have the same floral structure are genetically similar.

Of course, as time has gone by it has been possible to look at organisms in more detail. At the first level the study of the form of organisms relies on physical characteristics which can be observed with the naked eye, but progressively smaller characteristics need a hand lens or even a microscope. The use of electron microscopes allows this approach to be extended to the study of the surface of pollen grains, but still, essentially, it has been a study of external physical characteristics.

Heuchera bracteata. Echo Lake, Mount Evans, Colorado.

The Saxifragaceae

Taxonomy is of enormous interest to taxonomists but to many gardeners it is just an excuse to change the names of plants well-known, well-established and well-loved. Saxifrages have not escaped this process but compared with many groups they have survived pretty much intact from Linnaeus's 1753 *Species Plantarum*. Saxifrages belong to a family of herbaceous perennials, biennials and annuals which are predominantly plants of the northern temperate and subarctic zones and *Saxifraga* is by far the largest genus in the family. The name, from Latin, means "rock-breaker" because ancient traditions ascribed medicinal properties to them—the treatment of urinary stones—rather than because of their supposed habit of growing in and fragmenting rocks. As Webb & Gornall point out, the species to which the name was given by Dioscorides was *S. granulata*, a meadow plant, not one which usually grows on rock. It is worth noting that while *Saxifraga* derives from the Latin for "rock-breaker", the name of another genus in the family, *Lithophragma*, means almost the same, "stone-breaker", but is derived from Greek.

In the past the Saxifragaceae has included various plants which have now been found new botanical homes. The shrubby genera such as *Ribes* and *Escallonia* now belong to the Grossulariaceae, the gooseberry family, which is the family most closely related to the Saxifragaceae. Other shrubby genera such as *Hydrangea*, *Philadelphus* and *Deutzia* are now placed in the Hydrangeaceae, which is closer to daisies (the Asteraceae) than saxifrages. Some non-woody genera such as *Parnassia* and *Lepuropetalon*, formerly included in the family, have also been excluded.

In the case of the Saxifragaceae, as with so many plants, the great discoveries about relationships are now being made by using DNA analysis, and it has become

Lithophragma parviflorum.

Micranthes tolmiei running along a crack in a boulder at Crater Lake, Oregon. Saxifrages may not break rock, as the derivation of the name suggests, but they can exploit any fissures.

clear that our central genus *Saxifraga* should be split between a new narrower *Saxifraga* and a new genus *Micranthes* (consisting of what were previously two sections of the genus *Saxifraga*). With this split about 33 genera are generally accepted as belonging in the Saxifragaceae and they can be grouped into eight groups split between three broad branches (A, B and C in the list below). The grouping of 29 of these genera is fairly clear, but four other genera have not been genetically analysed as yet: *Saniculiphyllum*, a monospecific Chinese genus, which probably belongs in the Darmera group, two South American genera *Saxifragodes* and *Saxifragella*, and the North American monospecific genus *Cascadia*.

Groups of genera in the Saxifragaceae

A. 1. Astilbe/Saxifragopsis group (*Astilbe*, *Saxifragopsis*)
   2. Boykinia group (*Boykinia* plus *Bolandra*, *Jepsonia*, *Suksdorfia*, *Sullivantia*, *Telesonix*)
   3. Leptarrhena/Tanakea group (*Leptarrhena*, *Tanakea*)

B. 4. Darmera group (*Darmera* plus *Astilboides*, *Bergenia*, *Mukdenia*, *Oresitrophe*, *Rodgersia*)
   5. Chrysosplenium/Peltoboykinia group (*Chrysosplenium*, *Peltoboykinia*)
   6. Heuchera group (*Heuchera* plus *Bensoniella*, *Conimitella*, *Elmera*, *Lithophragma*, *Mitella*, *Tellima*, *Tiarella*, *Tolmiea*)
   7. Micranthes group (*Micranthes*)

C. 8. Saxifraga group (*Saxifraga*)

It is with the last two of these genera that the present book is concerned.

Ribes griffithianum in the Langtang Himal, Nepal. Of all the shrubby genera, *Ribes* is the closest to the Saxifragaceae.

Geographical Perspectives

The saxifrage family looks very different depending on where it is viewed from. In Europe there are about 124 species, of which 112 belong to the *Saxifraga* with the others belonging to the *Micranthes* (seven species) and *Chrysosplenium* (five species). With such a preponderance of *Saxifraga* species and the early systematic botanists being European, it is not surprising that the fundamental view in traditional western botany is of a family of saxifrages to which a few other plants were appended, as a retinue of hangers-on.

A similar situation is found in Asia, with the *Saxifraga* outnumbering all the other Saxifragaceae genera put together. In China, for example, there are about 270

Bergenia ciliata growing on cliffs above Manali, northwest India.

species in the family; over 200 of them are *Saxifraga*, 25 *Chrysosplenium* and 15 *Micranthes*. The remainder come from a variety of smaller genera, only three of which have more than two species in them: *Astilbe* and *Bergenia* each with seven, and *Rodgersia* four. Beyond these are a range of small endemic genera: *Tanakea, Astilboides, Mukdenia, Oresitrophe, Peltoboykinia* and *Saniculiphyllum;* and a few which also have members in North America: *Boykinia, Tiarella* and *Mitella*, as well as *Astilbe*. But even with all these other genera represented, more than two-thirds of the Asian Saxifragaceae belong to genus *Saxifraga*.

Anyone surveying the saxifrages of North America will end up with a very different picture of the family. They will see the fantastic diversity of the Saxifragaceae, with representatives of all eight groups listed above being part of the North American flora. There is also a very different balance between *Saxifraga* and the rest of the family, with a whole back-story of *Micranthes*, foamflowers or sugar scoops (*Tiarella*), woodland stars (*Lithophragma*), alumroots and coralbells (*Heuchera*), Indian rhubarb (*Darmera*), fringecup (*Tellima*) and others. As much as in the eponymous genus, it is in these others that the glory of the saxifrage family is found in the Americas.

From Mexico to Alaska, from Greenland to damp lands in the South, in every US state and every Canadian province, there are members of the saxifrage family to find and grow. There are even species found down the Andes all the way to Patagonia. Of the 23 genera which make up the saxifrage family in North America, 16 have fewer than five North American species in them. These smaller genera represent a great diversity of form and include some that have a well-established place in the garden—*Astilbe, Darmera, Elmera, Leptarrhena, Telesonix, Tellima, Tiarella* and *Tolmiea*. The remainder are perhaps less obviously plants that most gardeners might try—*Bensoniella, Bolandra, Cascadia, Conimitella, Jepsonia, Saxifragopsis, Suksdorfia* and *Sullivantia*—although they include some intriguing plants. Among the larger genera *Chrysosplenium, Boykinia, Lithophragma* and *Mitella* have five, six, nine and eleven species respectively. There are only three genera in North America with more than a dozen species in them: *Saxifraga, Heuchera* and *Micranthes*, and these have 25, 36 and 45 species. Of these only six or seven of the *Saxifraga* are endemic to North America, but most of the *Micranthes* are endemic, and *Heuchera* is purely North American.

Telesonix jamesii. Pike's
Peak, Colorado.

Boykinia richardsonii.
Anvil Mountain, Nome,
Alaska. Photograph Ian
Bainbridge.

3 · Survival Strategies and Speciation

Two characteristics, life-cycle and reproductive strategy, are crucial in determining the general habit and structure of living things. In animals most reproduction is sexual, particularly in higher animals, but their life-cycle may be confined to a single reproductive cycle, as in many insects, or may offer the opportunity of repeated reproduction, as in most mammals. In plants there is rather more variety, with many plants having asexual reproductive strategies, either in place of or alongside sexual ones. They may have life-cycles offering just one reproductive opportunity, or they may have repeated opportunities. Single-reproduction life-cycles may be limited to a single year, as in annual plants, but they may be longer, taking several years before they produce seed. It might seem that a long life-cycle offering multiple opportunities for reproduction is the most efficient—after all, it is what occurs in humans and other higher animals—but a moment's reflection on the success of hoverflies, mosquitoes, chickweed and bittercress indicates that these are very effective alternatives for the species even if the individual is shorter-lived.

Animals and plants both show a variety of strategies, but they differ in some fundamental areas and how they cope with seasonal variation is one of these. Many animals stay in one place all year round and are active throughout, but others minimize the impact of adverse seasons. Hibernation and migration are two strategies by which animals boost their survival rates by avoiding the worst of the weather—either by hunkering down, as do many bears, or by moving away, as do swallows, wildebeest and monarch butterflies. For most animals the season when survival is hardest is winter, but for those that live in areas with very hot dry summers and cool damp winters it may be the summer that has to be escaped through migration. Plants do not have all these options. They do have different ways of surviving from year to year, but one of those that can be used by animals, migration, is off the agenda for most plants. The great majority of plants are essentially committed to one location for the lifetime of an individual: where the seed first germinates and roots is life-determining. Some plants will spread vegetatively: forming a mat, using runners or stolons to creep sideways, or climbing up or through other plants

Saxifraga tridactylites is a winter-annual species. Pen-y-ghent, Yorkshire.

to find new places to root. Some may dry up and roll away, being bowled along by the winds, like tumbleweed, or parts may break off and roll or blow away, but in general it is only with the production of seed that plants can find new locations. So, plants are forced to face the seasonal variation in the weather in different ways to animals and there are many adaptations which enable them to do this. One of the most obvious ways of looking at year-to-year survival is to consider the lifespan of a plant: annual, biennial or perennial.

Saxifraga cymbalaria. This is a very easy-going annual species which will self-seed in the garden.

Annuals complete their life-cycle within a single year: from seed germination through growth to maturity, flowering, and seed production. Then they die. They are monocarpic. This strategy enables them to pass though the worst of the seasons as seed. In northerly latitudes this is likely to be winter, with its cold icy weather, but farther south, where the winter is mild and pleasant, the adverse season is the summer when temperatures can rise dramatically. In such conditions there will be species such as *Saxifraga tridactylites* which complete their life-cycle as "winter annuals", germinating in autumn and seeding in spring. There are quite a few other annual saxifrages, including species such as *Saxifraga cymbalaria*.

Biennials, like annuals, are monocarpic and have a life-cycle which is time-limited. However, in their case, the seeds germinate in one year, growing to reach a size that enables them to survive the winter. They then flower in the second year before dying. Two examples of biennial saxifrages are *Saxifraga latepetiolata* and *S. petraea*.

Saxifraga petraea is an intriguing biennial species. Monte Baldo, Italy. Photograph Paul Kennett.

Perennials do not have a time-limited lifespan: they survive from year to year. They may take some time to attain flowering size, but once flowering—and hence fruiting and seed-production—has started, they typically produce flowers and seed every year. Most saxifrages are perennial (although some are longer-lived than others), and most of the saxifrages that gardeners deploy are perennial.

This picture is, however, too simple on its own. Annuals and biennials, both with life-cycles limited by seed production, are obviously monocarpic (or semelparous), dying once they have flowered and set seed. The same can happen with plants that are longer-lived; some might take a number of years to reach flowering size, but die once they have flowered and produced seed. These monocarpic perennials are often plants which will flower only in years in which conditions are particularly favourable, and may sit waiting even decades for just such conditions. In a good year all the plants in a generation may flower simultaneously. It is flowering that sets in train the death of the plant. In saxifrages there are some notable examples of this, in particular *Saxifraga longifolia* and *S. florulenta*.

Other things also come into play here. Perennials take many different forms, from woody plants in the form of trees and shrubs, through evergreen non-woody perennials (represented in saxifrages by the *Porphyrion* saxifrages among many others), herbaceous perennials which die down in the adverse season to survive as dormant shoots (as do many of the *Ciliatae* species such as *Saxifraga hirculus*), through to those which survive the winter in the form of underground storage organs such as tubers, corms or bulbs. Among saxifrages the nearest approach to this last is among some of the section *Saxifraga* species such as *S. granulata*, in which the herbaceous growth dies completely and perennation is through the production of basal bulbils.

Combining life-cycle and reproductive strategy shows the range of possibilities:

annuals   monocarpic seed producers—*S. cymbalaria, S. tridactylites*
biennials   monocarpic seed producers—*S. latepetiolata, S. petraea*
perennials monocarpic seed producers—*S. longifolia, S. florentula*
       repeat seed producers—evergreen—most of section *Porphyrion*
       repeat seed producers—herbaceous perennials which lose their
         leaves and have a dormant period—most of section *Ciliatae*
       repeat seed producers— "bulbous"—*S. granulata*

There are exceptions even to this schema, since some species such as *S. mertensiana* and *S. cernua* generally survive without any seed production.

Reproduction in Saxifrages

Another area of interest in looking at survival strategies is in the way in which the plant reproduces itself. Saxifrages exhibit variations in both sexual and asexual reproduction.

Sexual reproduction

Sexual reproduction is essential to animals and plants to ensure that there is sufficient genetic diversity to provide for the differing demands which may face populations. In plants sexual reproduction involves the production of seed. A few plants can produce seed by apomixis, whereby seed produced does not require fertilization from pollen by the male gamete. This is well known in some species in genera such as *Viola*, with pods of viable seed being produced without flowering or fertilization. But no saxifrages use such a strategy: seed production involves pollen being transferred to the stigma and hence to the unfertilized ova. In saxifrages it is noticeable that although most species are monoecious, having female and male parts in each flower ("perfect" flowers), there is often a time lag between the stigma becoming receptive to pollen and the anthers producing pollen. This delay allows the female part of the flower to receive pollen from another plant. However, if no pollen arrives, then most saxifrages are efficient at self-fertilization, with the stamens curving inwards to bring the pollen-laden anthers into contact with the stigma. Cross-fertilization is clearly of evolutionary benefit and degrees of self-incompatibility among saxifrages mean that although flowers are perfect, the ova are not fertilized by pollen from the same plant, or at least are less readily pollinated by their own pollen. But this can lead to what might be construed as potential evolutionary dead ends. Both *Saxifraga cernua* and *S. mertensiana* use

asexual mean of reproduction through the development of bulbils in the axils of the inflorescence branches. In both cases this means that most of the plants in any particular locality are genetically identical and there is clearly a fairly high degree of self-incompatibility, since viable seed appears to be extremely scarce in either species. Very few *Saxifraga* species are dioecious, having separate male and female plants, but one such is *Saxifraga eschscholtzii*, and once flowering is completed it is easy to identify the female plants since only these carry seed capsules.

Hybrids, of course, can only be produced by cross-fertilization, with the transfer of pollen from a plant of one species to the stigma of a plant of another species. Hybridization is one mechanism of sexual reproduction which can lead to speciation, and the study of hybridization in the wild and in cultivation is of value. Among the *Saxifraga* there are many hybrids in the wild, some of which are intersectional.

Saxifraga eschscholtzii is dioecious and only female plants carry seed capsules. Kigluaik Mountains, Seward Peninsula, Alaska.

Asexual reproduction

Unlike sexual reproduction, asexual means of ensuring survival involve the production of genetically identical individuals down through time. Alternative terms are vegetative or viviparous propagation. Of the many ways in which this can occur, only those that are found in the *Saxifraga* and *Micranthes* are discussed here.

1. The most obvious way in which saxifrages maintain themselves asexually is through adventitious rooting. Such rooting extends a cushion into a mat which need have no definite limit, rooting as it extends. When the original rooting point dies, parts of the plant which have rooted survive. This is the predominant mode in sections *Porphyrion* and *Trachyphyllum*.

2. An extension of this is the production of side rosettes which root at or before the death of the parental rosette after it has flowered. In such cases this is central

Saxifraga callosa. The developing side rosettes can easily be seen in this section.

to the survival strategy, and it distinguishes species such as *Saxifraga callosa* from the monocarpic species *S. longifolia*, in which such side rosettes are not formed.

3. Runners, or stolons, are found in species from section *Irregulares* and section *Ciliatae* subsection *Flagellares*, and in both cases these function in exactly the same way as strawberry runners, with long stems forming embryo plants at their tip. Once rooting occurs and the plantlet becomes independent, the stolon can die away.

Saxifraga stenophylla on the Baralacha Pass with stolons and plantlets.

4. Embryo plants, or plantlets, are also found at the base of the leaf blade in *Saxifraga epiphylla* from section *Irregulares*. Again, these can root and form independent plants around the parent plant.

Leaf of *Saxifraga epiphylla* showing developing plantlet on upper surface (left).

5. Basal bulbils are developed in the subsection *Saxifraga* species such as *S. granulata* and *S. bourgaeana*. They are formed in the axils of the basal leaves at or just below ground level and allow the plant to die down in summer after flowering, remaining summer-dormant through the dry summer months.

Bulbils of *Saxifraga granulata* in among the grass sward. Photograph Paul Kennett.

Bulbil of *Saxifraga carpetana*.

6. Aerial bulbils are also formed in the axils of leaves, but in this case they are the leaves on the flowering stems. This is seen in *Saxifraga bulbifera* from section *Saxifraga* and *S. cernua* from section *Mesogyne*, while in *S. mertensiana* from section *Heterisia*, bunches of such bulbils are found in the axils of the inflorescence branches. Similar aerial bulbils are found in a number of *Micranthes* species. In some cases seed production is extremely limited, and it may cease completely in some populations.

7. A further development is the production of leafy buds, rather than just leafy bulbils, in place of flowers. These detach either before or after the stem withers. This is seen most clearly in some forms of *Micranthes* species such as

Leafy buds in
Micranthes stellaris
var. *prolifera*. Koralpe,
Kärnten (Carinthia),
Austria.

M. stellaris var. *prolifera*, and intermediates between aerial bulbils and leafy buds can be seen in *M. foliolosa*.

8. A method of propagation in genus *Saxifraga* previously unrecorded is the "break-out" of shoot tips in *Saxifraga georgei*, which I have observed in late summer in cushions which have been kept in the open. During heavy rain, drops will break out the tips of the opposite-leaved shoots, and these will root readily in surrounding compost. The effect can also be seen by watering this species from a watering can held high above the plant. It happens at no other time of the year than late summer and is presumably an adaptation to monsoon conditions. The same may be true of *S. quadrifaria*, but this has not been observed.

What Makes a Species?

It is obvious that different people approach the issue of species definition in very different ways. Some of the reasons for this are based on differences in tradition, some on advances in science. The definition of species based on recognizable morphological differences has given way to approaches based on breeding incompatibility and then to genetic separation. Various species concepts include:

typological species—conforming to a type specimen
morphological species—physical (and recognizable) similarity
biological species—breeding compatibility
phylogenetic species—genetic similarity representing evolutionary closeness

The basis for separation into species is not dealt with in any of these approaches; they are descriptive of the separation rather than of the reasons behind it. These in turn are the subject of much debate. The major types of separation are dealt with through the concepts of sympatry, allopatry and parapatry.

Sympatric species are ones growing in the same locality in the wild which do not interbreed. In such a situation it is clear that some other mechanism for reproductive isolation other than mere physical separation must exist. These reproductive barriers may be morphological, with some change in flower form ensuring different pollinators; they may involve separation in time so that one species flowers some time after the other (allochrony); or it might be that some other change such as chromosomal doubling ensures separation. If the changes in form do not ensure breeding separation, then taxonomists will probably treat them as subspecies or varieties.

The *Trachyphyllum* saxifrages exemplify the different approaches to species definition. This is *Saxifraga funstonii* in the narrow species tradition, or *S. bronchialis* subsp. *funstonii* in a broad species approach. Kigluaik Mountains, Seward Peninsula, Alaska.

Allopatric and peripatric species are ones in which separation by geography, over a sufficient period of time, allows the accumulation of sufficient difference, morphological or genetic, to justify allocating species status to these geographically separated populations. This is very much the situation observed in the speciation which occurs on islands. Allopatric speciation occurring between two more or less equal-sized populations is sometimes called dichropatric or vicariant, while the situation where there is a small peripheral population is known as peripatric.

Parapatric species are ones in which separation is by ecological or geographical niche. In this case the separate niche in itself could be evidence for the separateness of two taxa.

The approach of botanists in the Russian and western traditions treats geographical separation, whether allopatric or parapatric, in very different ways. From the western point of view, Russian botanists are far too willing to ascribe specific status to plants whose differences are merely adaptations to local conditions. This is particularly relevant in the study of circumpolar flora, such as the *Trachyphyllum* saxifrages which are essentially a pan-Arctic section and which may therefore be found in the homelands of botanists with very different persuasions. There may be agreement on the various groups of plants which should be accorded some sort of taxonomic status, but just what that status is may be much disputed. Botanists brought up with a narrow species approach, which includes those Russian botanists who have turned their attention to saxifrages, will have a much longer list of species than those western botanists who take a much broader approach to species.

In the Russian tradition, taxa which are allopatric (and which a western European botanist might recognize as subspecies because of their distinguishing characteristics) would be recognized as species rather than subspecies precisely because they are allopatric. This approach operates in such a way as to generate "narrow" species. Nowhere among the saxifrages is this more obvious than in section *Trachyphyllum*, where successive treatments by Russian botanists have led to some 27 species being recognized—most of which would certainly be given a much lower taxonomic status by European botanists.

To sum up: the approach used by Linnaeus was that of the morphological species which, along with the use of the "type", has been the basis of field botany ever since. But concepts of biological species and genetic species are supplanting these. Much confusion arises from eliding these different concepts. There will be readers who find that there is confusion at places in this book, but my approach has been to try and ally the latest recognitions of genetic analysis with the more traditional approaches.

4 · The Taxonomy of *Saxifraga* and *Micranthes*

Since the time of Linnaeus there have been various schemes in which the species of genus *Saxifraga* have been split into sections. Some of the more notable have been those of Haworth (1812), Engler & Irmscher (1916) and Gustav Hegi (1975), but the taxonomy which has become most widely accepted is that of Richard Gornall's revision in 1987. This represents the pinnacle of the morphological approaches to the *Saxifraga* with the genus divided into 15 sections, but the upheaval in taxonomy since then has meant that this broad genus has now been split, by Brouillet & Gornall and Gornall & Ohba, into *Saxifraga* and *Micranthes*. It is also clear from the combined results of research by Soltis, Conti and others that within this new narrower genus *Saxifraga* the boundaries of Gornall's sections *Ligulatae*, *Porphyrion* and *Xanthizoon* need revision. The new taxonomy based on such approaches means that genus *Micranthes* has five sections and it seems probable that genus *Saxifraga* will have twelve sections in five broad groupings:

Genus *Saxifraga* Linnaeus

A. Section *Ligulatae* Haworth
   Section *Porphyrion* Tausch
      includes section *Xanthizoon* Grisebach and section *Ligulatae* subsections
      Florulentae (Engler & Irmscher) Gornall and *Mutatae* (Engler & Irmscher)
      Gornall
   Section *Gymnopera* D. Don
   Section *Mesogyne* Sternberg

B. Section *Cymbalaria* Grisebach
   Section *Ciliatae* Haworth
   Section *Trachyphyllum* (Gaudin) W. D. J. Koch

Saxifraga cespitosa and *S. bronchialis* subsp. *austromontana* among a mass of other alpine plants on Hurricane Ridge in the Olympic Mountains, Washington.

C. Section *Saxifraga*
   Section *Odontophyllae* Gornall

D. Section *Cotylea* Tausch

E. Section *Irregulares* Haworth
   Section *Heterisia* (Rafinesque ex Small) A. M. Johnson

Genus *Micranthes* Haworth

   Section *Merkianae* (Engler & Irmscher) Gornall
   Section *Intermediae* (Engler & Irmscher) Gornall
   Section *Micranthes* (Haworth) Gornall
   Section *Calthophyllum* (A. M. Johnson) Gornall
   Section *Arabisia* (Tausch) Gornall

Two areas of uncertainty remain in this scheme. The first is the position of section *Odontophyllae*, which has yet to be fully clarified and may be closer to section *Mesogyne* than to section *Saxifraga*. The second is rather more complex. In Gornall's 1987 revision, section *Porphyrion* had three subsections, *Kabschia*, *Engleria* and *Oppositifoliae* (itself subdivided into series *Oppositifoliae* and *Tetrameridium*). Research shows that the *Kabschia*, *Engleria* and *Tetrameridium* (together equating to section *Porophyllum* Gaudin) are very closely related, with the *Oppositifoliae* being slightly less closely related along with groupings containing *Saxifraga caesia* and *S. squarrosa* (section *Porphyrion* series *Squarrosae*), *S. florulenta* (section *Ligulatae* subsection *Florulentae*), and *S. aizoides* and *S. mutata* (section *Xanthizoon* and section *Ligulatae* subsection *Mutatae*). These four groups are clearly more closely related to the *Kabschia*, *Engleria* and *Tetrameridium* than they are to any other grouping and I have treated them in this way. If they were treated as separate sections, then the core section (*Kabschia*, *Engleria* and *Tetrameridium*) would revert to section *Porophyllum* Gaudin, since *S. oppositifolia*, the type of section *Porphyrion*, would be excluded from such a grouping.

Beyond the genetic work, major contributions on the Chinese *Saxifraga* and *Micranthes* have been made by the appearance of the *Flora of China* treatment of the genus by Pan Jintang, Richard Gornall and Hideaki Ohba. The treatments in the *Flora of North America* initiated by Patrick Elvander and completed by Luc Brouillet will also be very helpful. Another important area of study has been among Spanish botanists, in particular Vargas, of the proper taxonomy of the section *Saxifraga* species, the wild mossy saxifrages, with some revision of Gornall's 1987 taxonomy.

Outline of *Saxifraga* and *Micranthes* Sections

Genus *Saxifraga*

1. Section *Ligulatae* (8 species)

Evergreen perennials with rosettes of lime-encrusted leaves. The lime is secreted by pores (hydathodes) near or in the margin of the leaves; in some species lime encrustation is confined to margins, in others it spreads across the whole leaf surface. The inflorescence is a panicle, and may contain hundreds of flowers. The flowers are generally white but they may be cream, pink or red, and petals may be spotted. The ovary is more or less inferior and there is often a prominent nectary ring. Predominantly European with outlying populations in North America, the Caucasus and north Africa. Gornall's 1987 view of the section had three subsections, *Aizoonia*, *Florulentae* and *Mutatae*, but the single species in each of the last two are both more appropriately considered as part of section *Porphyrion*. The *Ligulatae* are the silver or encrusted saxifrages and are popular as rock-garden plants. Most of the species are cultivated and there is a range of hybrid cultivars.

2. Section *Porphyrion* (over 100 species)

A complex group of evergreen perennials. The leaves have hydathodes, usually lime-secreting, along the leaf margins or singly at the tip. Flowers may be solitary or in an inflorescence of up to about a dozen flowers, or many more in *Saxifraga florulenta* and *S. mutata*. The ovary is more or less inferior and there is often a prominent nectary ring.

In general terms plants in this section form small cushions of quite hard-leaved rosettes with flowers borne on stems up to a few centimetres tall. In the *Tetrameridium* and *Oppositifoliae* leaves are opposite, but in the remainder leaves are alternate and usually form rosettes. Approaches to this new broad grouping have yet to be resolved, but one would be a new broad section *Porphyrion* divided into subsections along some lines such as:

Porophyllum (*Kabschia*, *Engleria* and *Tetrameridium*)
Oppositifoliae
Squarrosae
Xanthizoon (including *Mutatae*)
Florulentae

Of the species about half are being maintained in cultivation, often in a number of distinct variants. However, there has been considerable hybridization of the *Porophyllum* species since the end of the 19th century, particularly in England, Germany and Czechoslovakia, and there are now well over 600 hybrid cultivars. Flowers may be white, yellow, orange-yellow, deep purple-red or pale mauve-violet in the species; in hybrids this has been extended to deep purples, pale reds, orange and beige. Flowers are often enhanced by contrasting anthers and nectary rings. Species are European, circumpolar, Caucasian, Iranian or from the mountain ranges of Asia: the Pamirs, Karakorum, Hindu Kush, Himalaya, and the mountains of Tibet and Yunnan.

Among this group are some of the most exquisite of alpine plants which flower from January through till April (or occasionally May). The group contains quite easy-going, long-lasting plants which will adorn any rockery, but at the other extreme there are exquisite treasures which need the care of a specialist—but most of even these can be grown in troughs or in tufa without any need to be covered in winter.

3. Section *Gymnopera* (4 species)

Perennial species forming mats of evergreen, broadened, leathery-leaved rosettes connected by short ground-level rhizomes. There are hydathodes on the leaves but these are not lime-secreting. The inflorescence is a panicle of small flowers with white or pale pink petals, often with small yellow and red spots. The ovary is superior. They are European and three of the four species hybridize in the wild. They are quite widely cultivated, most commonly as hybrids.

This group of saxifrages is usually known by the name of one particular plant, the ubiquitous London pride which is so very well known that it has acquired a common name. With leathery leaves these are widespread and easy-going, forming mats of rosettes which can be covered in soft clouds of dainty white or pink flowers in early summer. Most the plants of this type are very tough, surviving poor conditions and long-term neglect. London pride itself, so named because it came from George London's Nursery in the late 17th century, is a hybrid and will flourish in dry shade as well as sun and moister soils.

4. Section *Mesogyne* (10 species)

Small perennials, not usually evergreen, with tufts of palmate leaves with a broadly lobed or toothed blade which is usually about as long as broad. There are hydathodes but they do not secrete lime. Bulbils are formed in the axils of basal leaves and sometimes in the axils of stem leaves. Flowers are white or pink, usually solitary, with an ovary which is more or less superior. Not easily cultivated. Circumboreal.

5. Section *Cymbalaria* (4 species)

Annuals or biennials with palmate leaves but no hydathodes. Flowers yellow or white with a superior ovary. *Saxifraga cymbalaria* can be a self-seeding plant in a shaded spot in the garden. Southern Europe and northern Africa and Ethiopia.

6. Section *Ciliatae* (over 250 species)

Perennials which may be evergreen. Leaves are simple and usually entire although in some cases they may be slightly toothed on the margin or toward the apex. The overwhelming majority of species have yellow flowers, a few have red flowers, and a handful white, the petals often spotted with orange or red dots. The ovary is superior.

This is a diverse section, by far the largest in the genus and it is divided into seven subsections:

Hirculoideae
Gemmiparae
Cinerascentes
Serpyllifoliae
Rosulares
Hemisphaericae
Flagellares

The *Hirculoideae* and *Rosulares* are by far the most numerous. In general terms the *Hirculoideae* form tufts of erect stems (sometimes very short) with relatively similar leaves up the stems, usually with curly brown (crispate) hairs in the leaf axils if nowhere else, and a solitary flower or small cyme. The *Rosulares* form a basal rosette, sometimes small rosettes making a mat, from which a flower stem may arise—usually solitary, but often with a cymose inflorescence of up to thirty flowers. Very few species are cultivated except for one or two from subsection *Flagellares*. Only two species out of over 250 in this whole section are found in Europe; a handful are found in North America, and the vast majority are from China and the Himalaya.

7. Section *Trachyphyllum* (up to about 27 species)
Mat-forming perennials, mainly from the Arctic and subArctic regions. Most species have small linear or lanceolate leaves, although a minority have broader or apically toothed leaves. The leaves usually have regularly spaced, stiff, bristle-like hairs along the leaf margins. Flowers white or very pale creamy-yellow, and usually with small yellow and red dots on the petals. Ovary superior. Approaches to this section vary widely, with many authors recognizing far fewer, but more widely defined, species. Europe, North America, Russia and Pacific coasts of Asia. Cultivation is straightforward.

8. Section *Saxifraga* (around 80 species)
Most species are perennial, although a small minority are biennial or annual. Species may form tufts, mats or cushions, and most are evergreen although a few are summer-dormant and form basal bulbils. Leaves are often deeply divided into a number of main divisions which are themselves divided. Flowers are white, cream, greenish-yellow to red. The ovary is at least one-third inferior and often wholly so.

Saxifraga globulifera growing on fractured needle-like shale in the Central Rif Morocco.

This large section is divided into four subsections:

Saxifraga
Triplinervium
Holophyllae
Tridactylites

Primarily European but with a few outlying species in North and South America, in Africa, and in the Caucasus. In Europe there is a concentration in the Iberian Peninsula. Quite a number of species in the first two subsections are cultivated; the species of the last two subsections are generally ignored. A very large range of artificial hybrids has been produced, many of them excellent garden plants.

Widely available through garden centres in unnamed thousands, the original mossy saxifrage hybrids arose at the end of the 19th century, and remain the most widespread of saxifrages in cultivation. They form soft leafy cushions, in some cases spreading up to a metre or more in diameter. They are generally easy-going if the ground is reasonably moisture-retentive. They do not have to be grown in shade but often are put out of full sun because of the need for a slightly moister soil. There are also intriguing species, much more varied in form than the hybrids, mainly from Europe, which can be very effective in the garden.

9. Section *Odontophyllae* (1 species)

A little-known perennial species from the Himalaya, not in cultivation, and not so far investigated genetically to determine its immediate relatives. The single species, *Saxifraga odontophylla*, is rhizomatous, has hairy circular crenate leaf blades, hairy petioles, and an inflorescence of white flowers, often with red veins. The ovary is superior and it lacks bulbils.

10. Section *Cotylea* (2 species)

Perennial species from southern Europe. They have underground rhizomes. The flowers are white with the petals spotted similarly to those of the section *Trachyphyllum* and *Gymnopera* species. *Saxifraga rotundifolia* is easy to grow.

11. Section *Irregulares* (about 16 species)

Perennial species, with zygomorphic flowers with one or two petals dramatically longer than the others. Most species are tufted although they may become large plants over time. Some are evergreen and they vary from a few centimetres to half a metre or so tall. Two species propagate themselves vegetatively—*Saxifraga stolonifera* with aerial stolons, and *S. epiphylla* with foliar embryos.

They are all Asian, primarily Chinese or Japanese. Although some of the species flower in early to mid-summer, most of the plants cultivated originate in Japan and many are very late-flowering. They have an important place in the late autumn border but are susceptible to early frosts.

12. Section *Heterisia* (1 species)

The single North American perennial species, *Saxifraga mertensiana*, is more closely related to the species of section *Irregulares* than to any other. Unlike them it has actinomorphic flowers with all the petals equal and it has clusters of pink-red bulbils in the axils of the inflorescence branches. It is easy to grow in a pot or in a shady border.

Genus *Micranthes* (about 80 species)

Recent work has now split *Micranthes* from *Saxifraga*. The species in genus *Micranthes* are divided into five sections, although the position of about a dozen remains unclear. Very few are grown in the garden, but many of them are straightforward to grow and make charming additions to the wild garden.

1. Section *Merkianae* (1 species)

The single species, *Micranthes merkii*, is found in far-eastern Asia. It forms mats of foliage with solitary white or cream flowers. Not in cultivation.

2. Section *Intermediae* (1 species)

The single North American species, *Micranthes tolmiei*, forms mats of small fleshy leaves and has solitary white flowers with very noticeable clavate filaments. Not in cultivation.

3. Section *Micranthes* (about 35 species)

The largest section in the genus, with only three or four species found outside North America. Tufts or rosettes of leaves which usually have a blade but no obviously separate petiole. Flowers usually numerous, small and white, sometimes in very diffuse inflorescence but often tightly clustered. There are three series, with the first having just a single species *Micranthes micranthidifolia*:

Aulaxis
Dermasea
Micranthes

Most of the saxifrages of the Appalachians, the Rocky Mountains and the Cascades belong to this section. Many species can be grown.

4. Section *Arabisa* (9 species)

Species are quite varied. Rosettes of foliage, leaves often toothed but not toughened, sometimes making mats. Inflorescences varied with leafy bracts (sometimes large), usually small flowers, usually with two distinct types of petal, three clawed and having coloured spots, two normal and unspotted. Species are found in Europe, North America and Asia. Some species grown.

5. Section *Calthophyllum* (about 30 species)

Rosettes of toughened or thickened leaves with cuneate or circular blade, usually toothed, often with distinct petiole. Generally fairly small plants with few but quite large and showy flowers with large coloured ovaries. Predominantly Asian with only a handful of species spreading into North America. Difficult in cultivation.

The twelve sections of genus *Saxifraga* are the subject of Part 2 (Chapters 5 to 16); the five of genus *Micranthes* of Part 3 (Chapter 17). Each of the chapters has a similar overall structure. The first part of each chapter is a narrative, telling the story of that group of plants. This narrative may involve the botany, taxonomy, geography and history of the plants and in all cases there will be some consideration of them as garden plants. The second part of each chapter is a more formal alphabetic list, briefly describing all the species, hybrid crosses or cultivars within that section. In this way the listing of each section is kept with the narrative discussion of that section rather than separated in an aggregated listing at the end of the book. In some of the larger sections the lists have been subdivided and in these cases the subdivision is described and the plants in each separate part of the list are in alphabetic order. In the case of subtaxa the typical subtaxon is listed first and the remainder are listed alphabetically. All taxa, whether botanical or horticultural, are also listed in the Index.

Part 2 · *Saxifraga*

5 · Silver Saxifrages
Section *Ligulatae*

In the mountains of Europe the silver saxifrages are a central element of the alpine flora, huddling in rocky fissures or embossing the rock face with their encrusted rosettes and drenching the early summer cliffs with fountaining sprays of white flowers. And they will do the same in the garden—they are plants with a wild charm, easy and robust enough to survive alongside ordinary garden plants, and in the rock garden they have few rivals.

Saxifraga longifolia on the cliffs of the Cirque de Troumouse in the French Pyrenees.

Rosettes, Leaves and Lime Pores

The section *Ligulatae* species form evergreen rosettes of thick, stiffened leaves with lime-secreting pores (hydathodes) on or near their margins. The lime they secrete encrusts the leaves and it is this that gives them the name of encrusted or silver saxifrages. In some cases the leaves are leathery; in others brittle, breaking if flexed (*Saxifraga cochlearis* and some forms of *S. callosa*); and the margins of the leaves may be toothed.

The position of the hydathodes varies between species. In those with a toothed margin (*Saxifraga cotyledon*, *S. hostii* and *S. paniculata*), the lime pores are on the upper surface of the teeth, one on each tooth. In the other species the pores may be in a line along the edge of the upper surface of the leaf (*S. hostii* and *S. crustata*); they may be set into the edge rather than the top of the leaf (*S. longifolia*, *S. callosa* and *S. cochlearis*), or they may even be scattered across the surface of the leaf (*S. valdensis*).

The smallest rosettes are those of *Saxifraga valdensis* and small forms of *S. paniculata* and *S. cochlearis*, where the rosettes may be as small as 1 cm in diameter; the largest are in *S. longifolia*, where rosettes can be up to 30 cm across. Apart from the size of the rosette, the overall appearance is determined by the width of the leaves and whether the leaves are curved or straight. In *S. longifolia* the leaves are straight, so that the rosette is more or less flat; in *S. paniculata* the leaves curve upwards, or inwards, so that the rosette forms a bowl or cup of leaves, but in many of the other species the leaves are recurved. In *S. cotyledon* and *S. crustata* they may gently recurve along their length; in *S. hostii* they recurve gently at the tip, and in *S. callosa* var. *australis* they are strongly recurved at the tip.

The flower stems are terminal, erupting from the heart of the rosette. After flowering, the flowering rosette shrivels and dies and the long-term life cycle of the plant is determined by whether small side rosettes have been produced. In *Saxifraga longifolia* no side rosettes are produced and the individual plant/rosette dies once seed is set. The remaining species do develop side rosettes and thus form mats or cushions, with the individual rosettes replaced as they in turn flower. In some cases (particularly *S. paniculata*, *S. crustata* and *S. hostii*), rooting occurs adventitiously as new rosettes are produced and large mats can form. *Saxifraga callosa* behaves similarly, although rarely making such large mats, but in *S. cotyledon* the few side rosettes usually develop only at flowering and large mats are rare. In *S. cochlearis* and *S. valdensis* the only root system is usually that established by the seedling and in such cases only small cushions develop.

Flowers and Inflorescence

Silver saxifrages usually have white flowers, pure white in some cases, but off-white or cream in *Saxifraga crustata* and sometimes in *S. paniculata*. In some forms of *S. paniculata* and the associated taxa from the Caucasus, the colour range is extended, with some having red or pink flowers, and there are pale pink and pale yellow cultivars ('Rosea' and 'Lutea') which probably derive from the eastern and Italian Alps respectively. In many species the white or cream petals have very small crimson or carmine spots, usually along the lower part of the main veins, but in some cases, such as *S. paniculata* 'Punctata', these may be much more abundant, and the hybrid 'Canis Dalmatica' demonstrates this very well. *Saxifraga cotyledon* may have much more dramatic markings, with blotches rather than spots.

The petals may be quite rounded, as in *Saxifraga paniculata*, or much more elongated in, for example, *S. cochlearis* and *S. callosa*. The ovary is more or less inferior and there is a nectary disc often emphasized by being shiny and bright yellow.

The inflorescence is a panicle, because the lowest flowers open first, but the shape of the inflorescence is determined by the length of the side branches and by the point along the main stem at which branching starts. In *Saxifraga longifolia* and *S. cotyledon* the inflorescence has side branches all the way up the stem with the lower ones being the longest, so that the overall shape is pyramidal. There are fewer individual side branches to the inflorescence in *S. cotyledon*, but each of these side branches has more flowers and in both this and *S. longifolia* the whole inflorescence can have many hundreds of flowers. The only other species in which branching occurs well below the middle of the flower stem is *S. callosa* and here the branches tend to be much more equal in length. In the other species, which have from a handful to around fifty flowers per stem, branching is only from the mid-point of the main stem (*S. crustata*, *S. paniculata* and *S. valdensis*) or even only in the top one-third (*S. hostii* and *S. cochlearis*).

Alongside the shape of the inflorescence and the number of flowers, the overall effect is determined by the way in which the stem is held: in *Saxifraga longifolia* it is stout and stiff, in *S. callosa* an arching or drooping spray, in *S. paniculata*, *S. crustata* and *S. hostii* a rather stiff open or flat-topped stem, and in *S. cochlearis* it is stiff but delicate.

The *Ligulatae* Species

There are between eight and twelve species in the section—the number depending on your particular view of what a species is—with most botanists inclining towards the lower number. All of them have their primary home in the mountains of Europe or the Caucasus, but one species extends into Morocco and one into eastern North America. Although there are some excellent hybrids, most of the silver saxifrages in the garden are selections of species rather than hybrid cultivars. All the species are in cultivation, and only *Saxifraga valdensis* presents particular problems for the gardener.

The widespread species *Saxifraga paniculata* and *S. cotyledon*

These two species are by far the most widely distributed, being the only ones found in the Pyrenees, the Alps, Scandinavia and Iceland. *Saxifraga cotyledon* can be regarded as the more obviously arctic-alpine species, more widely distributed in Scandinavia and more restricted to higher-altitude sites in the Alps and Pyrenees. Despite this wider northern distribution of *S. cotyledon*, it is *S. paniculata*, with its main centre of population in the Alps, which has spread on from Iceland into Greenland and North America. Although in many areas of their ranges both species can be found, they are separated by different geological preferences. *Saxifraga paniculata* can be found on both alkaline and acid rocks, perhaps with a preference for limestone. *Saxifraga cotyledon* is restricted in the wild to acid rocks, but in cultivation seems much less fussy, happily growing in normal neutral or even slightly alkaline conditions.

Saxifraga paniculata
'Correvoniana'.

A small form of *Saxifraga paniculata*. Sella Nevea, northeastern Italy.

Saxifraga paniculata
on the Col de Tende
in the Maritime Alps.
Photograph John
Howes.

Saxifraga paniculata

Saxifraga paniculata is the Platonic ideal of a rock-garden plant. It comes from the mountains, makes intriguing mats of encrusted rosettes, and can survive many years without demanding any hard work on the part of the gardener. It is extremely hardy, not prone to disease, flowers well in the early summer, and the evergreen rosettes are beautifully enhanced by winter frosts.

Saxifaga paniculata makes mats of incurved rosettes rarely more than about 5 cm across, sometimes much smaller, and the leaves are broadly oblong or obovate and sometimes quite angular with quite broad "shoulders". In small forms the leaves may be more or less as broad as they are long, but in larger forms the leaves are usually lengthened rather than enlarged proportionately so that they are more linear. The leaves themselves may be quite a cheerful leaf-green but vary from yellow-green through to darker and cooler mid-green. The margins of the leaves are toothed and these marginal teeth are usually blunt, like worn-down saw blades, although in some cases they may be slightly more pointed. The lime pores are on the upper surface of the teeth, one to each tooth.

Typically the surface of the leaf is smooth, although in some cases it may be covered by fine hairs and the leaves will look much greyer. Flowering stems may be only 5 cm tall or up to about 30 cm.

In Europe, despite the variation, all the varieties belong to the typical *Saxifraga paniculata* subsp. *paniculata*, but outside Europe things are more complicated.

Saxifraga kolenatiana in cultivation. Photograph Mark Childerhouse.

Young plants of two of the Caucasian taxa grown from seed. The characteristic bright green foliage of *S. kolenatiana* (on the right) contrasts clearly with the more encrusted, darker, glaucous foliage of *S. cartilaginea*.

From Iceland through to continental North America, *S. paniculata* subsp. *neogaea* has been designated with microscopic differences in the seed coating and the seed capsules although many authors do not see this as outside normal variation.

In the far east of the range, from northeastern Turkey into the Caucasus and Iran, the plants may have more pointed leaves, sometimes broadly acuminate, and often have pink or red flowers. One approach has been to place these in *Saxifraga paniculata* subsp. *cartilaginea*, with further subdivision being recognized in var. *kolenatiana*. Many of those who have visited the area and collected material would assert that there should be species boundaries drawn here and Holubec & Křivka are an essential source in their treatment of these species as well as of the *Porphyrion* species from the Caucasus. In part, of course, people who have travelled a long way in difficult terrain simply want to find distinctive plants, but sometimes their findings represent valuable recognitions of taxonomic value. Cases for specific status are made for *S. cartilaginea* which has variable, pointed leaves and white or occasionally pink flowers, and is found on limestone; *S. kolenatiana*

Saxifraga khiakensis, Mount Khiakh, Ossetia, north central Caucasus, Russia. Photograph Vojtěch Holubec.

with broader and more sharply pointed leaves and pink or red flowers, which is found on silicaceous rocks; and *S. khiakensis* which is much smaller, has single white flowers, and is otherwise regarded as belonging to *S. cartilaginea*. Of these *S. kolenatiana* is the one which is most removed from the typical European sub-species of *S. paniculata*. It is clearly distinguished from the other taxa by having more sharply pointed leaves, sometimes broader and acuminate, sometimes more narrowly linear, but always brighter green, rather than darker blue-green, with the surface lime-free rather than encrusted and glaucous. Plants have been collected in the Little Caucasus which have sharply pointed more linear leaves and are close to 'Sendtneri'.

Saxifraga cotyledon

Saxifraga cotyledon is the other widely distributed species, but unlike other species in the section it shows a marked preference for acid rocks rather than limestone. Its largest centre of distribution is in Scandinavia, throughout Norway and into western Sweden, and with an outlying population in eastern Iceland, but it is also found in both the high Pyrenees and the high central Alps where it extends as far south as the Italian side of the border some miles east of Isola 2000. It never seems to make a large cushion although individual rosettes can be very substantial, particularly in some of the plants found in more northerly parts of its range. The rosettes vary up to about 10 cm across; the leaves are broadly obovate or oblong and sometimes slightly recurved towards the rounded or bluntly pointed tip. The leaves are smooth and quite dark green, set off by a thin line of lime along the finely and sharply toothed margin.

Saxifraga cotyledon growing with other acid-loving plants, such as *Calluna vulgaris*, in the central Pyrenees below the Cirque d'Estaubé. The petals are often tinged pink and have small spots at the base.

Saxifraga cotyledon. The delicate lime encrustation on the edge of the leaves is easily seen here. Below the Cirque d'Estaubé, French Pyrenees.

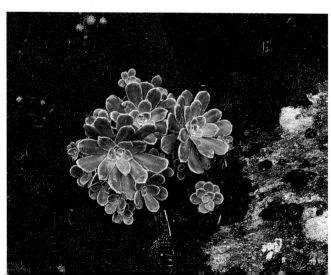

This is one of the species that can be spectacular in flower—there may be up to a thousand flowers per stem in some forms—and the inflorescence is broadly pyramidal. The petals are often elongated at the base and separated, rather than the rounder and touching petals of *Saxifraga crustata* and many examples of *S. paniculata*. The petals are usually pure white, but may have pink or red dots towards the base—most obvious in plants of the Southside Seedling Group, where the markings become much more vivid blotches.

It is often said that *Saxifraga cotyledon* is found on vertical sites, and although this is true, it also can be found on top of rocks if they are fairly inaccessible or not readily visible. It seems likely that the spectacular flower stem has led to the flowers being picked or the plant collected from more accessible sites. In the past it was apparently grown in Britain for the cut-flower market and in Lapland it had a romantic connotation as a flower for young men to give their sweethearts.

The more restricted species

While *Saxifraga paniculata* and *S. cotyledon* are very widely distributed, all the other species are more restricted. In general terms, *S. longifolia* is centred in the Pyrenees; *S. callosa*, *S. cochlearis* and *S. valdensis* are centred on the southwestern Alps, and *S. hostii* and *S. crustata* are distributed in the southeastern and eastern Alps. The isolation of these groups led to a suggestion by Conti, Soltis et al that speciation might in part have been the result of the fragmentation of populations of *S. paniculata* during Pleistocene glaciations.

The other Pyrenean species: *Saxifraga longifolia*

Saxifraga longifolia is one of the most wonderful of all saxifrages—not for its flowers, but because it has one of the most perfect of all rosettes of leaves. When flowering comes after five or six years, the vertical limestone cliffs where it is at home may be scattered with the weighty fox-brushes of white flowers. But unlike all the other species in the section, *S. longifolia* is monocarpic. No side rosettes are produced, so once flowering and seed set is accomplished the rosette dies. Like the mayfly or cicada, reproduction in *S. longifolia* is the precursor to the death of the individual.

Saxifraga longifolia is confined to limestone, and, although it is most common in the Pyrenees, it is also found scattered through the mountains of eastern Spain and across into Morocco, where it is found in the mountains of the Middle and High Atlas. Plants from the High Atlas have shorter, broader leaves and have been separated as *S. longifolia* subsp. *gaussenii*.

In the Pyrenees it can be found on limestone alongside the more cosmopolitan *Saxifraga paniculata*, and at occasional sites among the cirques of the central Pyrenees, where there are granite outcrops, it can also be found in close proximity with *S. cotyledon*, and wild hybrids between each of them have been recorded. Although a characteristic of *S. longifolia* is that it has only single rosettes, in

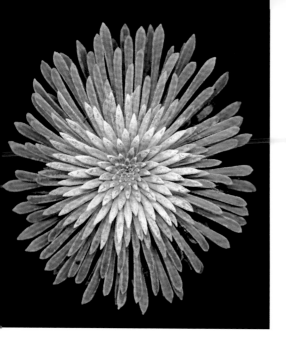

Saxifraga longifolia. Fort Portalet, Pyrenees. Photograph Carole and Ian Bainbridge. The stem in this specimen is arched but stems are commonly straighter and stiffer.

Saxifraga longifolia can take five or six years to reach flowering size by which time the rosette is up to 30 cm across, with hundreds of stiff narrow leaves.

populations growing in close proximity with *S. paniculata*, occasional plants can be found in which there are multiple rosettes and hybridity can be inferred.

Saxifraga longifolia is an easy species from seed and it is fascinating to grow on as year by year its wonderfully symmetrical rosette of leaves gradually outgrows the span of your hand. Occasionally plants with more than one rosette will appear, and these should be weeded out if a population is to be kept clear of hybrid influence. For the enthusiast it is much better to raise a batch of seedlings than it is to buy a plant under the label "*Saxifraga longifolia*" to find that it is only remotely connected to the original species.

Distinctive rosettes of *Saxifraga callosa* subsp. *catalaunica* collected by Adrian Young at Montserrat, Spain.

Saxifraga callosa

This is such a variable species that it can be difficult to believe that plants from the extremes of the different subtaxa can possibly belong to the same species. It becomes more obvious that these diverse plants belong to the same species when they are in flower, because the arching sprays of up to 400 flowers are very much the same width throughout their length, rather than pyramidal as in *Saxifraga longifolia* and *S. cotyledon*. There are two subspecies: subsp. *callosa* in France and Italy, and subsp. *catalaunica* in Spain in a small area near Barcelona. The latter has a hairy inflorescence, possibly less one-sided than in the typical subspecies, and has more obviously pointed leaves with a clearly delineated, heavily encrusted margin. Vargas distinguishes this as a species, but further work seems necessary, particularly in the light of Webb & Gornall's comment that

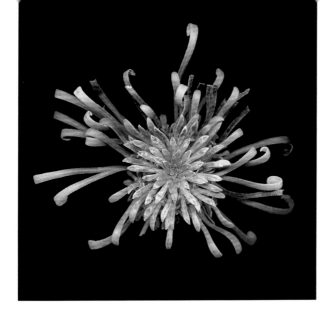

A large form of *Saxifraga callosa* var. *australis* clearly showing the recurved tips to the leaves.

The long leaves of *Saxifraga callosa* var. *callosa* tend to form strange, complex tufts

individual plants of the most westerly populations of subsp. *callosa*, although clearly belonging to that subspecies, are transitional in having sparsely hairy inflorescences.

The typical subspecies, *Saxifraga callosa* subsp. *callosa*, which has a non-hairy inflorescence, is found from Sicily and Sardinia up through western Italy into the Maritime Alps and on to mountains a little east of Marseilles. This is split into two varieties, var. *callosa* and var. *australis*, and they can be extremely different. The leaves of var. *australis* are broadened at the tip and recurve strongly but it varies quite a lot in size with small examples having neat rosettes often no more than about 5 cm and large ones up to 15 cm or more across. On the other hand, in var. *callosa* the leaves are linear and in extreme examples can be more than 20 cm long and, rather than a rosette, they form weirdly complex tufts.

Saxifraga callosa var. *callosa* on a shaded cliff where it develops the longest leaves and can be the most elegant of all the *Ligulatae* species when in flower. Photograph John Howes.

The other species of the western Alps: *Saxifraga cochlearis* and *S. valdensis*
Saxifraga cochlearis has a very limited geographical distribution in the Maritime Alps, with a small outlying population near Portofino in Italy, but it is not a rare species within this area and, where conditions are right, it can be found in large quantities on the bare limestone. The rosettes vary up to 5 cm in diameter, occasionally more, usually much smaller, and form quite small but dense hemispherical cushions. The leaves are quite brittle and very encrusted, slightly broadened toward the recurved tip which may be slightly pointed but may be roundly spathulate with the lime-secreting pores set in the margin, rather than on the upper surface. It readily forms cushions up to about 15 cm across but generally this seems to be the

Saxifraga cochlearis growing on the north face of a bridge at Le Boreon, Maritime Alps.

Saxifraga cochlearis at Tende in the Maritime Alps. Photograph John Howes.

limit of growth since the root systems remains central, with the individual rosettes remaining dependent on this central root system rather than rooting adventitiously to enable larger mats to form. The flower stems are dark red and typically have about 20 pure white flowers, often with two or three lines of small dark red spots running some way from the base of the petals, which are about twice as long as they are broad. The contrast between the pure white flowers and the thin dark red or brown stems make this a particularly pretty small species which presents no problems for the gardener.

Although there is quite a lot of variation from plant to plant in *Saxifraga cochlearis*, none warrants botanical rather than horticultural recognition. Most of the plants in cultivation are ones with smaller rosettes, the usual being the particularly charming 'Minor', but there is no particular difficulty in growing larger ones.

It is possible to find *Saxifraga callosa* and *S. cochlearis* growing together in the wild, and mixed with *S. paniculata*, but this is not common. Although a few hybrids have been recorded, they are surprisingly uncommon in the wild. The hybrid of *S. cochlearis* with *S. paniculata* is *S. ×burnatii* (now *S. ×burnatii* 'Emile Burnat'), and a similar cultivar is 'Reginald Farrer', one of the *S.* Silver Farreri Group.

While *Saxifraga cochlearis* is easy to grow in gardens, *S. valdensis*, the other species with a limited range in the western Alps, is not. This is the only one of the *Ligulatae* species that is particularly difficult to grow. *Saxifraga valdensis* is found on limestone in the mountains along the French–Italian border north of the Maritime Alps and has rosettes similar in size to some of the smaller forms of *S. cochlearis*, but the leaves are darker—although they are heavily encrusted with the lime-secreting pores across the surface of the leaves as well as in the margin. The flowers are usually off-white rather than pure white and it has fewer flowers on shorter stems. It cultivation it seems to prefer rather drier conditions than many species, particularly in winter.

The other species of the southern and eastern Alps: *Saxifraga hostii* and *S. crustata*

In the southeastern Alps *Saxifraga paniculata* is joined by two other species: *S. hostii* and *S. crustata*. *Saxifraga hostii* is the larger and it is distributed in southern parts of the Alps from northern Italy, in the Alpi Orobie, through the Trentino and Dolomites into Austria and Slovenia. It can be a very impressive plant, growing on rocky outcrops, among the rocks of roadside banks or the First World War emplacements cut into the mountainsides at such places as Monte Grappa. Unlike *S. longifolia* and *S. cotyledon*, which have pyramidal inflorescences, *S. hostii* has heads of creamy-white flowers fitting well with the umbellifers and other summer-meadow flowers which grow on the surrounding slopes. There are two subspecies: the larger is subsp. *hostii* which forms small groups of large rosettes with flower stems up to 60 cm tall. The leaves are up to 10 cm long, finely encrusted along the toothed margin, linear-oblong, and tend to recurve slightly at the tip, which is rounded or bluntly pointed. The smaller subsp. *rhaetica* is about half the size of the typical subspecies and the leaves are more sharply pointed and it usually has rather fewer flowers on each branch of the inflorescence.

Saxifraga crustata makes congested mats of narrow-leaved rosettes which vary from less than 2.5 cm to about 8 cm in diameter. The leaves are usually glossy and the lime pores are along the edge of the upper surface of the leaf, but the encrustation can be limited to a series of quite discrete small spots—although the

Saxifraga hostii subsp. *hostii* on roadside rocks on Monte Grappa, Italy.

Saxifraga hostii subsp. *hostii*. New rosettes often form at the end of short stems

Saxifraga crustata.
Karawanken, Austria–
Slovenia border.

surface can be rather more generally smeared with lime. Selections can have attractive foliage and some hybrids are very nice. The flowers are often fairly small and an unimpressive off-white or cream and the flower stem, which may be up to 40 cm, is usually rather loose with only up to 30 flowers although they may be more tightly grouped toward the top of the stem and plants at the Loibl Pass on the Austria–Slovenia border had much more robust stems and more impressive heads of flowers. The range of *S. crustata* overlaps that of *S. hostii* in the Dolomites, although it does not stretch quite as far westward, and to the east it spreads down as far as Montenegro. In parts of northeastern Italy it is not difficult to find both of these and *S. paniculata* growing together.

Cultivars and Hybrids

In most silver saxifrage species, apart from *Saxifraga paniculata*, named garden forms are the exception. In *S. paniculata*, however, variations in size, toothing, leaf shape and colour, encrustation and hairiness give rise to numerous varieties which hold their place in the rock garden on foliage interest alone. Growing several varieties in close proximity helps emphasize these qualities. *Saxifraga paniculata* has also played a part in many of the hybrids which the gardener knows: *S. ×burnatii* 'Emile Burnat', *S. ×fritschiana* 'St John's', the garden hybrid *S.* 'Whitehill', *S. ×gaudinii* 'Canis Dalmatica' and the intersectional hybrid *S.* 'Winifred Bevington'.

The garden hybrid 'Tumbling Waters' exploits the best of the qualities of both its parents. From *Saxifraga longifolia* it gets large rosettes of narrow, heavily silvered leaves and a flower spike which branches from very low down; from *S. callosa* it gets an inflorescence that is more elegant than that of *S. longifolia*. But it does pay a price: although it is perennial rather than monocarpic, as in *S. longifolia*, it does not produce large cushions of rosettes. It does produce some side rosettes, and the best approach is to remove some of these and root them separately—they tend not to root if left to their own devices, and plants can easily be lost. Plants can be very spectacular with the spray of flowers up to a yard long. The best flowering is achieved on plants where the rosettes have been encouraged to grow to a large size and this is achieved by ensuring that the plant is fed regularly and growth is not interrupted. If it is being grown in a pot it should be repotted at regular intervals, probably twice a year, so that flowering is deferred for as long as possible.

Saxifraga crustata is not particularly common in gardens and is often unimpressive but the hybrids with *S. paniculata* and *S. hostii* are often nice plants. 'Carniolica' which has particularly glossy dark green leaves with a beaded edge, and 'St John's' are both plants worth looking for.

All forms of *Saxifraga cotyledon* are attractive, but they never form large cushions. They only make a few side rosettes before the flowering rosette dies, and these often fail to become rooted and self-sufficient long before this, so it is sensible to take and root some of these small side rosettes. There are a number of named forms including 'Pyramidalis', 'Norvegica' and 'Highdownensis' which have been selected because of their large size or good flowers but 'Southside Seedling' stands alone. This is an interesting, and occasionally spectacular, cultivar derived at some point from *S. cotyledon*, with its petals more or less heavily marked with deep rich red

Foliage of some of the best garden forms of *Saxifraga paniculata*.

Top (from left): 'Baldensis', 'Venetia', 'Labradorica', 'Correvoniana'.

Middle: 'Cultrata', 'Balcana', 'Notata'.

Bottom: 'Lutea', 'Cockscomb', 'Harold Bevington'.

The flowers of *Saxifraga* [Southside Seedling Group] 'Slack's Ruby Southside'.

blotches. The original accidental seedling was found by Gerald Sutton of the Sutton's Seeds family in his Surrey garden and it was shown to the RHS in London in 1951. But it became apparent that a number of forms were going round under the same name and this led to their being part of the 2002–2004 RHS Trial of Silver Saxifrages. Among the results of this Trial was the definition of *Saxifraga* Southside Seedling Group, with two quite distinct forms given awards: 'Southside Star' and 'Slack's Ruby Southside'. Both can hold their place in the garden: 'Southside Star' is a larger plant with larger flowers, but in 'Slack's Ruby Southside' the red blotches are extremely dramatic.

Growing Silver Saxifrages

The silver saxifrages do not belong to one of the larger sections of the genus, but among the species and hybrids are magnificent plants which grace any rock garden. And yet it is not just because of their flowers that these saxifrages have such a prominent place in the rock gardener's palette—it is because of their evergreen mats of foliage. In winter, frost exaggerates the edges of the encrusted leaves, and in cold dry weather the limy surface of the leaves is enhanced; like frozen roses, the rosettes, which may be single and as large as a dinner plate, or as small as a little finger nail and clustered together in a mat, form a backbone for the winter rock garden when so much else is in retreat. In summer they erupt in splendour.

The larger species are all good on the open rock garden and the smaller species and hybrids will cope very happily here but seem more suited to growing in troughs where they look very much in scale with their surroundings. Any form of *Saxifraga paniculata* will do well in a trough, along with smaller forms of *S. callosa*, and *S.* ×*burnatii* and *S. cochlearis*, which are beautiful plants. The most common mistake among gardeners is to plant them among sun-baked south-facing rocks as they would sempervivums. This is not what most of them need in lowland gardens. In their natural habitats the night-time fall in temperature helps recovery but in lowland gardens they can suffer heat stress and scorch. They will be much more successful if given a position where they are shaded for part of the day, perhaps with the protection of a handy rock or planted on an east or north-facing slope. As with most alpine plants, a well-drained compost will help plants develop a substantial root system.

With the obvious exception of *Saxifraga longifolia*, which makes no side rosettes and has to be propagated from seed, silver saxifrages are easy to propagate from cuttings. Single rosettes are removed—in many species and hybrids they can just be pulled away—but in some cases, where the leaves are particularly stiffened, such as in *S. cochlearis*, it is usually better to use a blade. There are a number of older cultivars of *S. callosa* var. *australis* which now seem not to be securely identifiable, but 'Limelight' and the larger 'Lantoscana Superba' are both excellent plants and tend

Saxifraga ×*burnatii* 'Emile Burnat' is one of the most glorious of all saxifrages.

to survive well in sunny sites. The problem with the very long narrow-leaved forms of *S. callosa* var. *callosa* is that it is very hard to take cuttings. Detaching a rosette of leaves often results in a handful of loose leaves: putting an elastic band around the bunch of leaves before separating it from the group makes success more probable.

Despite the fact that *Saxifraga hostii* is an excellent garden plant, certainly the easiest and most permanent of the large silver saxifrages, it is far less common in cultivation than it deserves. The main reason for this is that it does not flourish in a pot and is therefore rare in the nursery trade. In the open garden it flourishes and if it is grown in a richer soil rather than confined to the rock garden it flowers quite readily. It is very successful in our heavy garden soil, which other silver saxifrages would tend to find too sticky, but also grows happily enough in the better-drained mixture I use in my rock garden—although not always flowering quite as well. Unfortunately it is not easy to find in nurseries, but it is worth pursuing—it will repay the effort.

Section *Ligulatae* Haworth

Species

Saxifraga callosa Smith (1791). Rosettes splayed rather than cup-shaped, with straight or recurved glaucous leaves. Leaves untoothed, lime pores in edge, encrustation across surface. Widely variable between subspecies and varieties. Stems to 40 cm, but often less in var. *callosa*, with side branches from below midpoint. Sprays of up to 200–300 white flowers, petals to 12 × 4 mm. Western Italy from Sicily to Maritime Alps (into France). Corsica, northeastern Spain.
  subsp. *callosa*. Inflorescence barely or not hairy.
    var. *callosa*. Tufts or rosettes. Leaves are linear with unexpanded tip, may be to 15 × 0.3 cm. Italy, France.
    var. *australis*. Rosettes. Leaf tip expanded and recurved typically to 7 cm, often shorter, with tip expanded sometimes to 0.7 cm. Italy and France. Includes the plants that used to be called 'Lantoscana'.
  subsp. *catalaunica*. Whole inflorescence glandular-hairy. Leaves broader, to 4.5 × 0.9 cm. More broadly branched flower stem. Northeastern Spain. Note that Vargas treats this as a separate species (*S. catalaunica* Boissier & Reuter). This is supported by Young, who comments on flowers being all round the stem, although this is not shown in Vargas.
Saxifraga cartilaginea. See *S. paniculata*.
Saxifraga cochlearis Reichenbach (1832). Small cushions or mats of heavily encrusted glaucous foliage. Rosettes 1–8 cm, leaves untoothed, 0.8–4.0 × 0.25–0.6 cm, tip broadened, bluntly rounded or slightly

pointed, lime pores in edge of leaf. Stems typically to 20 cm, often dark red, branched in upper half. Flowers (typically 15–25, occasionally 60) white, sometimes with rows of spots, petals to 11 × 5 mm. Maritime Alps and Portofino peninsula in Italy. Natural hybrids with *S. paniculata* (*S. ×burnatii*). Cultivars: 'Minor', 'Major', 'Probynii'.

Saxifraga cotyledon Linnaeus (1753). Small groups of rosettes with slightly recurved leaves. Leaves to 8 × 2 cm, oblong or slightly spathulate, margins finely toothed, lime pores on each tooth, only toothed edge encrusted. Flower stem to 80 cm, curving pyramidal inflorescence, side branches from base or at least from halfway. Many hundreds of white flowers (up to 1000) sometimes pink- or red-spotted or marked, petals to 10 × 6 mm, narrowed at base. Widespread in Europe: Norway, Sweden, Iceland, Pyrenees, Alps. Natural hybrids with *S. paniculata* (*S. ×gaudinii*), *S. longifolia* (*S. ×superba*).

Saxifraga crustata Lorenz Chrysanth von Vest (1804). Mats or cushions of rosettes, to 8 cm, leaves narrow, linear, untoothed, pointed, to 2.5 × 0.3 cm, lime pores along edge of upper surface. Leaves mid- to dark green, encrustation as beading along edge, sometimes glaucous across surface. Stems to about 30 cm, flowers off-white/cream, petals to 6 mm. Italy (Dolomites), Austria, Slovenia to Montenegro and Serbia. Natural hybrids with *S. hostii* (*S. ×engleri*) and *S. paniculata* (*S. ×fritschiana*).

Saxifraga hostii Tausch (1828). Small mats, large rosettes, leaves linear to 10 cm in subsp. *hostii*, toothed, lime pores along edge of upper surface, encrustation confined to edge. Flowers stems to 60 cm, fairly stiff, branched in upper third, typically 40–50 white flowers (occasionally to 80), petals to 8 mm. Much better garden plant than many, often happier in normal soil than in the very well-drained soils more typical of rock gardens. Alps: Italy, Austria, Slovenia. Cultivars: 'Altissima', 'Dosso Alto', 'Elatior'. Natural hybrids with *S. paniculata* (*S. ×churchillii*) and *S. crustata* (*S. ×engleri*).

subsp. *hostii*. Leaves to 10 × 1 cm, tip rounded. 5 flowers per inflorescence branch. Eastern part of range (east of Ortles).

subsp. *rhaetica*. Smaller, leaves to 5.0 × 0.7 cm with pointed tip. 3–5 flowers per inflorescence branch. Western part of range.

Saxifraga khiakensis. See *S. paniculata*.

Saxifraga kolenatiana. See *S. paniculata*.

Saxifraga longifolia Lapeyrouse (1801). Single flat monocarpic rosette (up to 30 cm diameter) with untoothed glaucous leaves to 15 × 0.4 cm (sometimes narrower) with lime encrustation from pores in margin. Flower stem to 60 cm, stiff, straight or arched, side branches from base. Many hundreds (400–800) of white flowers, petals to 7 × 5 mm. Pyrenees (France and Spain), scattered in eastern Spain, Morocco (High Atlas). Natural hybrids with *S. paniculata* (*S. ×lhommei*) and *S. cotyledon* (*S. ×superba*). Two subspecies have been described: subsp. *longifolia* from Spain and subsp. *gaussenii* with broader leaves from the Atlas Mountains, but the latter may be no more than a local ecotype.

Saxifraga paniculata Miller (1768). Rosettes more or less cup-shaped to 9 cm. Leaves oblong-obovate, 0.5–5.0 × 0.15–0.7 cm, margin bluntly saw-toothed, lime pores on upper surface of teeth. Flower stem to 30 cm branched from mid-point, up to 40 flowers. Petals, 3–6 × 2–4 mm, white, cream, pale yellow, pink or red. Very widespread in Europe from northern Spain to Germany, southern Poland, the Caucasus and Iran, and southern Norway, Iceland, Greenland, northeastern North America. Natural hybrids with *S. longifolia* (*S. ×lhommei*), *S. cochlearis* (*S. ×burnatii*), *S. crustata* (*S. ×fritschiana*), *S. cotyledon* (*S. ×gaudinii*) and with *S. hostii* (*S. ×churchillii*).

subsp. *paniculata*. Variable, leaves not acuminate. Flowers white, cream, pale yellow or pink.

subsp. *cartilaginea*. Leaves acuminately pointed, flowers white, or pink/red. Caucasus

subsp. *neogaea*. Variation in capsule and seed coat. North America. Probably unwarranted as subspecies.

Many authors split *S. paniculata* in the Caucasus into a number of species:

Saxifraga cartilaginea Willdenow ex Sternberg (1810). Pointed glaucous leaves. Stems to 30 cm, white or pink flowers (possibly only in *S. kolenatiana*), ovate buds. Typically on limestone.

Saxifraga khiakensis Holubec & Křivka (2006). Very compact form with small spathulate leaves. Stems to 10 cm with white, usually single, flowers, round buds, deviating from *S. cartilaginea* rather than from *S. kolenatiana*.

Saxifraga kolenatiana Regel (1865). Broader acuminate leaves, surface smooth, not glaucous, brighter leaf green. Stems to 30 cm, red or pink (rarely white) flowers. Typically on silicaceous rock and screes.

Saxifraga valdensis De Candolle (1815). Small cushions of heavily lime-encrusted foliage, rosettes 1–3 cm. Stems to 11 cm, 6–12 creamy-white flowers, petals to 5 × 3.5 mm. Alps: French–Italian border north of Maritime Alps. No natural hybrids.

Hybrids

S. ×*burnatii* Sündermann (1906). (*S. cochlearis* × *S. paniculata*). Natural hybrid. Cultivar: 'Emile Burnat'.

S. ×*churchillii* Huter (1872). (*S. hostii* × *S. paniculata*). Natural hybrid.

S. ×*engleri* Huter (1873). (*S. crustata* × *S. hostii*). Natural hybrid. Cultivar: 'Carniolica'.

S. ×*fritschiana* L. Keller (1899). (*S. crustata* × *S. paniculata*) (*S.* ×*pectinata* Schott, Nyman & Kotschy). Natural hybrid. Cultivars: 'Krain', 'Portae', 'St John's'.

S. ×*gaudinii* Brügger (1868). (*S. cotyledon* × *S. paniculata*). Natural hybrid. Cultivars: 'Canis Dalmatica', 'Iced Cream'.

S. ×*lhommei* H. J. Coste & Soulié (1912). (*S. longifolia* × *S. paniculata*). Natural hybrid.

S. ×*macnabiana* R. Lindsay (1885). (*S. callosa* × *S. cotyledon*). Artificial hybrid.

S. ×*superba* Rouy & E. G. Camus (1901). (*S. cotyledon* × *S. longifolia*). Putative natural hybrid.

There are also two hybrids which have never been validly named:

S. ×*calabrica*. Invalid horticultural name never formally published for artificial hybrid *S. callosa* × *S. longifolia*. Cultivars: 'Tumbling Waters', 'Cecil Davies'.

S. ×*farreri*. Invalid: see *S.* Silver Farreri Group.

Cultivar Groups

S. **Silver Farreri Group**. (*S. callosa* × *S. cochlearis*). Cultivars: 'Reginald Farrer', 'Snowflake', 'White Spray'.

S. **Southside Seedling Group**. (*S. cotyledon*). Cultivars: 'Southside Star', 'Slack's Ruby Southside'.

Selections and Hybrid Cultivars

'Altissima' (*S. hostii*). Leaves to 10 cm, toothed margin, narrowing toward tip. Inflorescence quite broad.

'Balcana' (*S. paniculata*). Old selection. Leaves smooth, mid-green, more pointed than many.

'Baldensis' (*S. paniculata*). Originally collected from Mount Baldo. Very small leaves and rosettes, colouring red in winter, otherwise indistinct from 'Minutifolia'.

'Canis Dalmatica' (*S.* ×*gaudinii*). Mounded cushion, oblong leaves to 4.5 × 1.0 cm, fairly blunt-tipped, silvered only at toothed margin. Stems to 45 cm, about 30 flowers, petals white with large numbers of red spots speckled over whole surface. Origin around 1930.

'Carniolica' (*S.* ×*engleri*). Mats of rosettes, leaves narrow, pointed, recurved, to 4.0 × 0.4 cm or narrower, dark green with encrusted margin. Stems to 25 cm. Flowers off-white/cream.

'Cecil Davies'. Hybrid of *S. longifolia*. Small congested cushion, rosettes to 5 cm, leaves flat, edges heavily encrusted. Stems to 15 cm, quite stiff, petals round, overlapping, pure white. Few rosettes and hence scarce. Clarence Elliott, 1910s.

'Cockscomb'. Cultivar of *S. paniculata* with raised pustulate area of lime glands down centre of leaves. Grown for foliage. Easy. Very distinctive. USA, possibly Frank Cabot, 1980s.

'Correvoniana' (*S. paniculata*). Plants under this name do not match original description (Farrer, 1919) but properly match original description of 'Lagraveana'. Rosettes about 1.25 cm diameter. Leaves encrusted at edge. Dark red stems, white flowers, very marked yellow nectary disc. See also under 'Lagraveana'.

'Cultrata' (*S. paniculata*). An old collected form.

'Dosso Alto' (*S. hostii* subsp. *rhaetica*). Collected form.

'Dr Clay'. Form of 'Hirtifolia'.

'Dr Ramsey'. Not now the original plant (Lissadell Nursery, Ireland, ca.1913). Plants today have silvery leaves, rosettes to 7 cm, slightly conical. Flower stem to 30 cm, 40–100 small white, slightly pink-spotted flowers. Not outstanding.

'Elatior' (*S. hostii*). Wild-collected form.

'Emile Burnat' (*S.* ×*burnatii*). Wonderful old hybrid, probably wild-collected, from around 1890. Silvery rosettes up to 4 cm, leaves blue-green, margin slightly toothed, to 2 × 0.2 cm, tip slightly expanded, lime glands on upper surface. Flower stems delicately arched, 40–50 flowers, pure white, larger than typical in *S. cochlearis*, branched in top half.

'Esther' (*S. paniculata*). Light green rosettes to 3 cm, leaves serrate. Flower pale yellow, red-spotted. Originally described as *S. paniculata* 'Lutea' × *S. cochlearis*.

'Flavescens'. See 'Lutea'.

'Foster's Red' (*S. kolenatiana*). Small dark red flowers. USA, presumably from Lincoln Foster.

'Gorges du Verdon'. Putatively a hybrid of *S. callosa* and *S. paniculata* but more likely an atypical form of *S. paniculata* according to Beryl Bland. Toothing on leaves rather blunt, leaves sometimes somewhat recurved. Fairly tall.

'Hare Knoll Beauty'. Seedling of *S. kolenatiana* with flowers which fade from red buds to light red to light pink. Small mat, rosettes to 2.5 cm, leaves recurved. Steve Furness, 1994.

'Harold Bevington' (*S. paniculata*). Selection. Regular rosettes to 3.5 cm, leaves incurved. Pure white flowers, larger than most forms of the species, red stems. Not as vigorous as some. Collected by Harold and Winifred Bevington, 1987, Spain.

'Highdownensis' (*S. cotyledon*). Form with broad leaves, brownish flower stem and white flowers.

'Hirtella' (*S. paniculata*). Old selection. Finely hairy glaucous leaves. Larger than 'Hirtifolia'.

'Hirtifolia' (*S. paniculata*). Old selection. Finely hairy glaucous leaves, greyer, more "silvery" than 'Hirtella'.

'Iced Cream' (*S. ×gaudinii*). Small cushion, awkward flower stems with pale creamy yellow flower.

'Kathleen Pinsent'. Hybrid cultivar, parentage unknown. A very attractive but rather difficult cultivar, small mat, rosettes to 4 cm, leaves dark blue-green, pointed, sometimes curved slightly clockwise. Flower stem curved and often slightly elbowed, flowers with distinctive oblong, cool pink petals. Not easy to keep long-term. Roy Elliot & Commander Pinsent, 1934.

'Krain' (*S. ×fristchiana*). Originally as *S. ×pectinata*. Rosettes to 4 cm, leaves toothed and heavily encusted. Flowers white, usually red-spotted.

'Labradorica' (*S. paniculata*). Selection with small silvery rosettes. Leaf margin and tip with small sharply pointed teeth. Also as 'Minima Glauca'.

'Lagraveana' (*S. paniculata*). Confusion stems from fact that plants under this name did not match original description, but plants in cultivation as 'Correvoniana' do match original description of 'Lagraveana'. Both are selections. The plant that was circulating as 'Correvoniana' is the better, with more and better flowers with marked yellow nectary discs, slightly smaller rosettes (1.5–2.0 cm rather than 1.5–2.5 cm).

'Lantoscana' (*S. callosa* subsp. *callosa* var. *australis*). Originally as *S. lantoscana* Boissier & Reuter. The use as a name for cultivated plants originated with a particular collection from Lantosque in the Maritime Alps. Small, rather short, pale green leaves. Bland named the particular small clone 'Limelight' in 1999 to avoid confusion with other plants matching the original *S. lantoscana* descriptions, and then proposed the name 'Lantoscana Limelight' for the same plant in 2000. The cultivar and name are old ones, pre-1911 and the original name 'Lantoscana' for this particular collection was given by Farrer.

'Lantoscana Limelight' (*S. callosa* subsp. *callosa* var. *australis*). Leaves to 3.0 × 0.4 cm. Flower stem only to about 20 cm, stiff, slightly curved but hardly arched, flowers white. Very good for a trough. See notes under 'Lantoscana'.

'Lantoscana Superba' (*S. callosa* subsp. *callosa* var. *australis*). Rosettes larger than 'Lantoscana Limelight', and leaves longer, outside longest, to more than 5.0 × 0.2 cm, broader at tip and base (to 0.5 cm), strongly recurved towards tip, Flower stems arching to 30 cm or more. Backhouse, 1886. Magnificent plant for raised position on the rock garden.

'Limelight'. See 'Lantoscana Limelight'.

'Lutea' (*S. paniculata*). Selection from the wild. Rosettes to 5 cm, leaves light green, narrow, incurved, serrated margin. Flowers pale yellow rather than just cream. Pre-1911. Plants circulated as 'Flavescens' are almost always the same as this.

'Major' (*S. cochlearis*). Name applied, rather vaguely today, to large forms of the species.

'Minima Glauca'. See 'Labradorica'.

'Minor' (*S. cochlearis*). Selection with rosettes no more than about 2 cm.

'Minor' (*S. paniculata*). May not be a single cultivar. Abundant creamy-white flowers on stocky stems. Rosettes about 1.25 cm diameter. White flowers, very slightly red-spotted on veins, petals to 7 × 3 mm.

'Minutifolia' (*S. paniculata*). Selection with smallest leaves and rosettes in the species. Leaves broad, very short, congested, very heavily limed. Rarely flowers well. Probably not now distinct from 'Baldensis'.

'Monarch'. Used to be under the name *S. longifolia* 'Imperialis', but clearly not very close to *S. longifolia*. Rosettes to about 10 cm, slightly yellow-green leaves oblong, acute to 5 × 1 cm. Tall upright stems to 50 cm, branches to 11 cm from low down with white flowers, pink dots particularly towards petal base. Renamed 'Monarch' by Adrian Young, 1990s.

'Norvegica' (*S. cotyledon*). Form with bluntly pointed leaves. White flowers, pink anthers.

'Notata' (*S. paniculata*). Old selection. Very broad, incurved light green leaves, shaded dark red on back. Sharp marginal teeth.

'Portae' (*S. ×fritschiana*). Rosettes to 2.5 cm, flowers off-white to cream.

'**Probynii**' (*S. cochlearis*). Old selection. Flower stems short, small foliage, small cushion, leaves 1 cm, tip rounded. Correvon, 1910.

'**Punctata**' (*S. paniculata*). Quite broad leaves. Heavily spotted petals. Not unlike 'Canis Dalmatica', although spots may be smaller.

'**Pyramidalis**' (*S. cotyledon*). Broad-leaved rosettes, foliage turning deep red in winter. May be up to 1000 pure white flowers.

'**Rainsley Seedling**' (*S. paniculata*). Flat mats of rounded rosettes, silver-grey foliage.

'**Reginald Farrer**' (Silver Farreri Group). Rosettes to 4.5 cm, leaves grey-green, lime glands in edge of leaf margin. Flower stems branched in top two-thirds, 20 cm, 65–80 flowers, white with few tiny red spots towards base. Originally collected by Farrer.

'**Rex**' (*S. paniculata*). Collected by Reginald Farrer. Plants today are of middling size, flowers creamy-white—not the plant that Farrer raved about.

'**Rosea**' (*S. paniculata*). Selection originally from Bulgaria. Pretty pink turning to pale pink flowers.

'**Sendtneri**'. Few large rosettes to 10 cm, leaves triangular-linear, slightly acuminate tip. Pink flowers with darker base, all fading. Derived from *S. kolenatiana* or *S. cartilaginea*. Used to be *S. cartilaginea kolenatiana Major*. Very distinctive, rather awkward plant. Farrer, Craven Nursery, pre-1913.

'**Slack's Ruby Southside**' (Southside Seedling Group). Rosettes typically to 5 cm exceptionally to 8 cm, leaves more pointed than rounded (compare with 'Southside Star'). Flowers to 1.0 cm diameter with heavily red-blotched (across centre, base and tip white) petals to 7 × 4 mm narrowed to claw at base.

'**Snowdrift**'. Probably not distinct from 'Snowflake'.

'**Snowflake**' (Silver Farreri Group). Foliage like that of *S. cochlearis* but not as silvered, rosettes to 4 cm, light green. Arching stems to 20 cm, typically 50 flowers, occasionally to 150, petals pure white perhaps with very few red spots at base. Reginald Kaye, 1933. 'White Spray' is effectively identical.

'**Southside Seedling**' (*S. cotyledon* seedling). Foliage very much within the range of species, flowers variously blotched with deep or bright red spots. Original plant from Gerald Sutton, 1951, now diluted by many plants and generations raised from seed. *Saxifraga* Southside Seedling Group now established to accomodate plants of this type.

'**Southside Star**' (Southside Seedling Group). Rosettes typically to 7 cm, exceptionally to 15 cm. Leaves rounded rather than pointed (compare with 'Slack's

Ruby Southside'). Flowers 1.75–2.0 cm diameter, petals white with dramatic red blotch toward base, broader and more rounded than in 'Slack's Ruby Southside'.

'**St John's**' (*S. ×fritschiana*). Sometimes incorrectly as 'Saint John's' and as *S. caesia* 'St John's'. Mats of small heavily encrusted rosettes to 2.5 cm. Flowers small, cream, red-spotted, petals to 4 mm.

'**Superba**' (*S. callosa*). See 'Lantoscana Superba'.

'**Tumbling Waters**' (*S. longifolia × S. callosa*). Can be the most spectacular of all rock-garden plants. Very large rosettes to 20 cm, leaves narrow, recurved at tip. Few side rosettes. Stems strong, arching, to 100 cm, sometimes with many hundreds of white flowers.

'**Venetia**' (*S. paniculata*). Selection. Mat of small rosettes, mid- to dark green leaves with distinctive dark red back. Flowers pure white, stems dark red.

'**Whitehill**'. Distinctive hybrid from the 1940s, probably hybrid of *S. paniculata* with *S. cochlearis*. Small cushion, rosettes to 3 cm. Toothed, heavily encrusted blue-grey leaves often stained deep red-purple at the base. Stems to 20–30 cm, white flowers.

'**White Spray**'. See 'Snowflake'.

Intersectional Hybrids between section *Ligulatae* and section *Gymnopera* species

S. ×andrewsii (probably *S. paniculata × S. spathularis*). Narrow linear, toothed leaves, encrusted along margin. Flower stems to about 25 cm. Flowers like London pride, but fewer and larger.

'**Winifred Bevington**' (*S. paniculata × S. umbrosa*). Rounded, rather incurved dark green leaves with clear lime-encusted margins. Stems to 20 cm with small, pretty pale pink flowers with pink anthers.

S. ×zimmeteri (*S. cuneifolia × S. paniculata*). Foliage similar to *S. paniculata*. Flowers white.

Others include:

S. ×jaeggiana synonym for *S. ×zimmeteri*.

S. ×pseudo-forsteri (*S. crustata × S. cuneifolia*).

S. ×wildiana (*S. hirsuta × S. paniculata*).

S. ×wisleyensis (invalid) (*S. paniculata × S. umbrosa*).

Plants have been collected of *S. callosa × S. cuneifolia* but have not yet been described.

6 · Dwarf Cushion Saxifrage Species

Section *Porphyrion* 1 – *Porophyllum* (*Kabschia*, *Engleria* and *Tetrameridium*)

Many of the cushion plants which so delight the specialist rock gardener are difficult plants to grow and maintain in the long term. In its natural habitat *Eritrichium nanum* is a glorious plant, but in cultivation only the most dedicated of growers is likely to succeed. Similarly, the cushions of *Androsace* and *Dionysia* can require great attention. Even the specialized cushion *Draba* species can be lost very easily. Compared with these, most of the saxifrages in section *Porphyrion* are remarkably easy to grow and keep, although some are sufficiently challenging to maintain the interest of the expert and some have yet to be photographed, never mind collected.

The charm of cushion plants is obvious: the rotationally perfect domes of foliage have a fascination that is writ large in the "biomes" of the Eden Project in Cornwall. The dome is an incredibly efficient form: for a greenhouse it is very strong with forces distributed efficiently; for a plant it allows every bit of foliage to be exposed to the sun without the need to maintain superfluous lengths of stem. Like jewelled pincushions or millefiori paperweights, the plants are studded with flowers which may be intensely coloured. Few plants have quite the same exquisite perfection as the best cushion plants and while it is possible to grow many of them to large size, it is not always a case of bigger is better. In some cases the optimum size for one of these domed cushions is relatively small, certainly within the compass of the average grower as well as the obsessive.

The dwarf cushion saxifrage species of section *Porphyrion* come from the mountains of Europe, the Middle East and Asia. Many of them are widely available, easy to grow in the open as well as in an alpine house, and they retain the qualities that make them so attractive in their natural habitats. Growers have been hybridizing them for over a hundred years, initially crossing European species but progressively involving new species as they have come into cultivation, a process that is still going on today and which is discussed fully in Chapter 7. The flowering

Saxifraga marginata 'Balkan' growing in a trough.

Saxifraga porophylla. Monte Greco, Italy. Photograph Winton Harding.

Saxifraga burseriana clinging to the cliffs on the Hoch Obir in Austria. Photograph Paul Kennett.

season is surprisingly long, from the very beginning of the year, sometimes as early as December, through to late spring, the last coming into flower well after Easter, with *Saxifraga andersonii* starting to flower for me only at the beginning of May.

The Botanical Perspective

Recent phylogenetic analysis has made it clear that section *Porphyrion* has been too narrowly defined and that a broader section is justified. For Engler, section *Porphyrion* contained just three species: *Saxifraga oppositifolia*, *S. biflora* and *S. retusa*. Alongside this were section *Tetrameridium* which consisted of the only other opposite-leaved *Saxifraga* species then known, *S. nana*, and section *Kabschia* in which Engler & Irmscher included 42 species. This approach remained the orthodoxy until 1975, when Hegi revised the sections and Engler's three sections became two: section *Porphyrion* and a new section *Porophyllum* with *Kabschia* and *Tetrameridium* brought together. Gornall's revision of 1987 brought these two together in a newly enlarged section *Porphyrion* with three subsections *Kabschia*, *Engleria* and *Oppositifoliae*. This now included all the opposite-leaved species previously in sections *Porphyrion* and *Tetrameridium*. However, it now seems clear that this revision was insufficient (Soltis, Conti et al) and that a new, broader, section *Porphyrion*, recognizing the findings of the phylogeneticists, will also make better sense of breeding compatibility. In such a scheme a broad section *Porphyrion* would be subdivided along lines such as:

> Subsection *Porophyllum* (*Kabschia*, *Engleria* and *Tetrameridium*)
> > Series *Kabschia*—includes *S. marginata*, *S. aretioides*, *S. lowndesii*, *S. juniperifolia*
> > > alternate leaves, cushions and mats, Europe and Sino-Himalaya

Series *Engleria*—includes *S. media* and *S. sempervivum*
    alternate leaves, small flowers, cymose inflorescence, Europe and
    Himalaya
Series *Tetrameridium*—includes *S. georgei*
    opposite leaves, cushions, white flowers, China and Himalaya
Subsection *Oppositifoliae*—includes *S. oppositifolia*
    opposite leaves, mats of linear shoots, purple-pink flowers, centred on
    Europe
Subsection *Xanthizoon* (including *Mutatae*)—*S. aizoides* and *S. mutata*
    alternate leaves, mats or rosettes, leaves fleshy
Subsection *Squarrosae*—*S. squarrosa* and *S. caesia*
    alternate leaves, small rosettes, flowers small, white, very thin pedicels
Subsection *Florulentae*—*S. florulenta*
    monocarpic rosette, cymose inflorescence

In such an approach, new combinations will need to be formally published to reflect the new level at which the *Florulentae*, *Xanthizoon* and *Squarrosae* are being applied. The changes are:

1. *Tetrameridium* and *Oppositifoliae* would once again be seen as two separated groups. This follows the recognition that although the morphology of species in the two appears very similar this is superficial, with genetic barriers to breeding between the two groups. There are no hybrids formed between any of the subsection *Oppositifoliae* species with any of the species from subsection *Porophyllum* series *Kabschia*, *Engleria* or *Tetrameridium* either in the wild or, despite repeated efforts, in cultivation. This contrasts with the *Tetrameridium*: here there is a high degree of breeding compatibility between *Kabschia*, *Engleria* and *Tetrameridium*, with barriers almost wholly being physical separation. Wild hybrids between species in *Kabschia* and *Engleria* are found in Europe, and Jan Bürgel has found what appear to be hybrids between species from *Kabschia* and *Tetrameridium* in Nepal.

2. *Saxifraga mutata* from section *Ligulatae* subsection *Mutatae* should be grouped with *S. aizoides* in subsection *Xanthizoon*.

3. The *Squarrosae* species *Saxifraga squarrosa* and *S. caesia* would be separated from subsection *Kabschia*.

4. Subsection *Florulentae*, with the single species *Saxifraga florulenta*, would be transferred from section *Ligulatae*.

5. Subsection *Porophyllum* might be subdivided into series *Kabschia*, *Engleria* and

Tetrameridium but might also have the *Kabschia* split into smaller series such as *Juniperifoliae, Aretioideae, Rigidae* and *Marginatae* as maintained by Hegi after Engler & Irmscher. Although there are benefits to this approach in that they deal well with some groups, such as the Caucasian species in series *Juniperifoliae*, there are many species which fit very uncomfortably into such a division.

Although the species of the *Squarrosae, Oppositifoliae* and new *Xanthizoon*, are morphologically very diverse there are clearly relatively low breeding barriers between them, with a number of wild hybrids recorded. Hybrids between both the species in the new *Xanthizoon* are found with members of the *Squarrosae*, and the now-stabilized polyploid species *S. nathorstii* provides an example of a species which has originated from a cross of *S. oppositifolia* from subsection *Oppositifoliae* with *Saxifraga aizoides* from the new *Xanthizoon*. *Saxifraga florulenta* is in a subsection on its own and no hybrids are recorded for this species, but it is now set alongside species with which it is more closely related than it was in section *Ligulatae*. Or, to put it another way, it is now an anomalous member of section *Porphyrion*, whereas before it was an anomalous member of section *Ligulatae*.

In this chapter the *Kabschia, Engleria* and *Tetrameridium* species and wild hybrids are discussed. The artificial hybrids are dealt with in Chapter 7 and the species of the *Florulentae*, new *Xanthizoon, Squarrosae* and *Oppositifoliae* are discussed in Chapter 8.

The Historical Perspective

The discovery and description of the *Kabschia, Engleria* and *Tetrameridium* species we recognize today mirrors the pattern that can be seen in many groups of plants in which the gardener is interested. European species were largely known by the second half of the 19th century. The boundaries of species were quite well understood and most of the species had entered cultivation. This is certainly not true of plants from the Caucasus, from which dramatic species are still entering cultivation for the first time. The *Porophyllum* saxifrage species endemic to the Caucasus still need further work and it is only since the mid-1990s that some of the most exciting species have appeared in cultivation.

Saxifraga juniperifolia (described in 1805) and *S. kotschyi* (described in 1856) occur in Turkey (as well as in the Caucasus in the case of *S. juniperifolia*) but the species which are confined to the Caucasus did not start to be described until the last quarter of the 19th century. By 1909 eleven species had been described, but after the Russian Revolution no further species were described until 1956. Since then there has been a proliferation of species described, the majority of them not in cultivation. Many of the species are narrowly defined, a feature of Russian botany, but among them there are indisputable species in any tradition.

In parallel, from Iran, *Saxifraga iranica* was described in 1906, *S. wendelboi* in 1967 and *S. ramsarica* in 1993.

The geopolitics of the mountainous countries of Asia farther east meant that it was not the great range of *Porophyllum* saxifrages from the mountains of Nepal, Sikkim and Bhutan that were first described, but those from further west. The first species was *Saxifraga ramulosa* in 1830, although this was poorly defined. In the period of the Great Game it is appropriate that the next two species to be described were *S. alberti* from the Tien Shan in 1877 and *S. afghanica*, which although widespread was originally found on the borders of Afghanistan and described in 1880. From 1883 (with Engler's description of the Chinese *S. nana*) through to 1933 nineteen further species were described. Many have never been seen in cultivation and the status of a number of them is under question today. However, there are a number of species with which we are familiar: *S. lilacina*, *S. andersonii* and the closely allied *S. stolitzkae*, and the tiny *S. georgei* and *S. quadrifaria*. No further species were described from this region until 1958 when Harry Smith published his remarkable paper on the Himalayan saxifrages in which he described 54 new species. Among these are a number of the species which we are led to believe are in cultivation today and some which are indubitably so: *S. alpigena* (the collection McB1379), *S. cinerea*, *S. lowndesii*, *S. poluniniana* (although this is in danger of disappearing from cultivation in England at least after recent hot summers), *S. matta-florida* and *S. lolaensis* (which probably belong to just one species) and *S. pulvinaria*.

An area of confusion has been highlighted in recent years by the work of Jan Bürgel. Having already looked at hybridization of *Porophyllum* saxifrages in the Balkans, his attention has turned to field studies of the Himalayan saxifrages. After a series of visits he has made a strong case that many of the species which have been described are at best confused and in some cases may be wild hybrids, and that the number of species with which we might be dealing may be far fewer than has been previously thought.

Three of Harry Smith's 54 species—*Saxifraga williamsii*, *S. brevicaulis* and *S. sessiliflora*—are very closely related to one another and appear superficially to fit well with other members of section *Porphyrion* subsection *Porophyllum*. They form small cushions which are like those of the *Porphyrion* subsection *Porophyllum* saxifrages; and they have white or creamy-white flowers with petals persisting while the capsule ripens. Harry Smith, however, pointed out some anomalies regarding their leaves, which are strongly ciliate and lack the lime-secreting pores that are a distinguishing characteristic of the section. It is now clear from genetic analysis that they are misplaced in section *Porphyrion* and should be seen as belonging to section *Ciliatae* subsection *Rosulares*. The vast bulk of the species from section *Ciliatae* are very difficult to maintain in cultivation and this helps make sense of the repeated failure of *S. williamsii* to be established in cultivation despite its obvious desirability.

This re-examination of the place of *Saxifraga williamsii* and its two close relatives is made clear in *The Flora of China* (Pan Jintang et al), which also brings to the reader of English the full treatment of all the Chinese species. Since 1978 the most important recognitions by Chinese botanists, especially J. T. Pan, but also including C. Y. Wu, T. C. Ku, C. Z. Gao, G. Z. Li and Y. Y. Qian, have been in sections *Ciliatae*, but even in subsection *Porophyllum* Pan has described *S. rotundipetala*, a yellow-flowered species from Tibet. This represents just the latest of a range of yellow-flowered eastern Himalayan and Chinese species from the section, most which have so far almost completely eluded both photographers and collectors.

Species in Cultivation

Around a hundred species have been described and around half of these are in cultivation, although many of them are in restricted circulation. However, as can be seen from the notes below, it is possible fairly easily to assemble a collection of around thirty different species, of which some, most notably *Saxifraga marginata* and *S. burseriana*, can be found in a number of very distinct forms.

One characteristic which has largely missed the attention of botanists up until this point is the colour of anthers and pollen. This is a noticeable distinguishing character among the species which have white or purple flowers. All white-flowered species from west of Pakistan have yellow anthers and yellow pollen. East of Pakistan, right along the Himalaya, all such species have orange, brown or dark red anthers and orange pollen. In collections from Pakistan, generally the SEP (Swedish Expedition to Pakistan) collections, some have yellow anthers and pollen, some red-brown anthers. The failure of botanists to comment on this must result from the traditional use of herbarium specimens for their primary observations.

In the case of the purple-flowered species the situation is very similar, with the species from east of Pakistan having dark red-brown anthers, while those from west of Pakistan may have yellow anthers. This is certainly the case with *Saxifraga dinnikii* and may also be true in some collections of *S. columnaris* but not others, but since there are no other saxifrage species in which anther colour is known to vary this is a significant observation and needs further investigation.

As far as is known all the yellow-flowered species have yellow anthers and pollen, but the yellow-flowered species from Bhutan and the far-eastern Himalaya remain relatively obscure.

Saxifraga scardica shows the typical flowers of a *Kabschia* saxifrage.

Saxifraga sempervivum in cultivation. Photograph Winton Harding.

Saxifraga federici-augusti. Like all Engleria species, this has small flowers with the petals barely visible.

Europe: *Engleria*

Within Europe there are *Porophyllum* saxifrages in the Picos de Europa, Pyrenees, Alps, Apennines, Dolomites, Carpathians and Balkans. They fall into a number of distinct groups depending on their basic structure and their flower colour. Two of the three series, *Kabschia* and *Engleria* (but not *Tetrameridium*) are represented in the European flora.

The *Engleria* have numerous very small flowers, petals often not emerging from the calyx, in a generally hairy inflorescence. *Saxifraga corymbosa* (*S. luteo-viridis*) has yellow flowers, but the others have either dark red flowers or pink flowers in dark red calyces. *Saxifraga sempervivum* and *S. federici-augusti* (which used to be *S. grisebachii*) are common in cultivation, and *S. stribrnyi* is not too uncommon. The other two species are *S. media* and *S. porophylla*, which are much harder to obtain and to keep. *Saxifraga media* tends to be monocarpic, and is best therefore maintained from seed, while *S. porophylla* needs to be kept in tufa.

Europe: *Kabschia*

While the *Engleria* species are interesting, they can hardly be called beautiful—unlike many of the *Kabschia* species, which are not difficult to grow.

European *Kabschia*: white flowers

This group includes some of the most attractive of the *Porophyllum* species: *Saxifraga burseriana* with spiny grey-green foliage, from the Alps; *S. marginata* with blunt or spathulate leaves, from Italy to Greece, and *S. scardica* with starry rosettes of pointed leaves, from the former Yugoslavia through to Greece. These are the most widespread white-flowered species in Europe and are generally easy-going in cultivation, although the flowers of *S. burseriana* tend to be more easily spoilt by rain than are those of *S. marginata*.

Variation in *Saxifraga burseriana* flowers and foliage (from left to right).

Top row: 'Cordata', 'Snowdon', 'Falstaff'.

2nd row: 'Crenata', 'Brookside'.

3rd row: 'Crenata', 'Cordata', 'Crenulata'.

4th row: 'Snowdon', 'John Tomlinson'.

Bottom row: 'Brookside', 'Falstaff', 'Gloria'.

There are other white-flowered species in various parts of the Alps: *Saxifraga vandellii* is clearly linked with *S. burseriana* with similar spiny foliage, and there are two smaller species, *S. tombeanensis* and *S. diapensioides*. Two uncommon species in the wild and in cultivation from further east in Europe are associated with *S. marginata*: a rather obscure species, *S. obtusa*, which may in fact have hybrid origin; and *S. karadzicensis*, which has been separated from *S. marginata*. Although all of these species are in cultivation, only *S. tombeanensis* is fairly straightforward.

The only other white-flowered European species is *Saxifraga spruneri*, a fairly anomalous species with glandular hairs on the leaves and differences in inflorescence and flower form from other *Porophyllum* species; it also has a different chromosome number (2n=28) from all other *Porophyllum* species for which counts

Variation in *Saxifraga marginata* and *S. obtusa* (from left to right).

Top row: *S. marginata* 'Intermedia' (3), *S. marginata* 'Lidice' (3).

Middle row: *S. marginata* subsp. *boryi* (2), *S. marginata* 'Sorrento' (1), *S. obtusa* (2), *S. marginata* subsp. *karadzicensis* (2).

Bottom row: *S. marginata* subsp. *rocheliana* (3), *S. marginata* 'Balkan' (3).

Saxifraga marginata var. *karadzicensis* is a wonderful garden plant, the flowers turning pink with age.

Saxifraga scardica on Mount Olympus, Greece. Photograph Winton Harding.

Saxifraga spruneri in cultivation.

Saxifraga ferdinandi-coburgi on a col below Vihren in the Pirin, Bulgaria. Photograph Paul Kennett.

have been done (2n=26). While the rest of the *Porophyllum* form a group with a high degree of breeding compatibility, *S. spruneri* does not hybridize with any of the other *Porophyllum* species in the wild or, despite repeated efforts, in cultivation, although there are reports of a very recent hybrid by Oldrich Maixner of *S. spruneri* and *S. columnaris*. The only reported hybrid is with *S. glabella*, a rather anomalous species from section *Saxifraga* which has flowers very similar to those of *S. spruneri*. These two species warrant detailed investigation and it may be that they will find a new position within the *Saxifraga*.

European *Kabschia*: yellow flowers

There are two groups of yellow-flowered species in Europe and both have very bright flowers. One group has larger flowers with shorter stamens: *Saxifraga ferdinandi-coburgi* from the Balkans is quite common in cultivation; *S. aretioides* from the Pyrenees is scarce; and *S. felineri* from the Picos de Europa may not be in cultivation. Although widely separated geographically from the other two, *S. ferdinandi-coburgi* does seem to be closely related to the others, and can be very similar to *S. felineri*.

The second group is very different, with two very similar species from the Balkans having clusters of much smaller flowers with prominent stamens. These species are linked very closely to the bulk of the species from the Caucasus. *Saxifraga sancta* is common and easy in the garden, and *S. juniperifolia* may also be found in cultivation.

Saxifraga aretioides
collected in the Cirque de
Troumouse. In cultivation.

Saxifraga sancta on
the rock garden.

Caucasus

A number of mountain groups are in general terms part of the Caucasian complex. The Great Caucasus, along the northern borders of Georgia and Azerbaijan; the Little Caucasus running from southern Georgia and incorporating most of Armenia, and the Pontic Mountains of northern Turkey are all included here.

Most of the *Porophyllum* saxifrages in this region have numerous small yellow flowers. One species, *Saxifraga artvinensis* from the Pontic Alps in northeastern Turkey, is otherwise similar except that its flowers are white. There is a great deal of complexity in the taxonomy of these multi-flowered species, with the narrow species concept of Russian botany adding quite substantially to the number of species recognized by most western botanists.

There are also some species that fall outside this group: two species with purple flowers, and a yellow-flowered species with single flowers, *Saxifraga carinata*. This may have links to *S. koelzii* from Iran, but neither has been brought into cultivation.

There is also some evidence, although so far unsubstantiated by any further reports, that there are white-flowered plants related to *Saxifraga marginata* in Abchasia in the western third of the range, with plants in cultivation from the Betscho Pass having white flowers, and collection JJH9309174 from Josef Halda producing some white-flowered plants. Collection JJH9309176, listed as having been collected in the same area, produced plants akin to a small *S. spruneri*. Confirmation from further collections would be welcome.

Caucasian: purple flowers

Saxifraga columnaris and *S. dinnikii* were described in 1892, but they were introduced into cultivation only after the Czech expedition in 1996 to the northern

Saxifraga columnaris on the vertical cliffs of the Skalistyj Khrebet, northern Caucasus. Photograph Vojtěch Holubec.

Saxifraga dinnikii. Skalistyj Khrebet, northern Caucasus. Photograph Vojtěch Holubec.

Caucasus. Both are found on dolomitic rock, *S. columnaris* growing on vertical cliffs often sheltered by overhangs. Neither *S. dinnikii* nor *S. columnaris*, which can be one of the most exquisite of all *Porophyllum* saxifrages, is suitable for cultivation in the open, except perhaps in tufa. *Saxifraga dinnikii* is the easier of the two and both are worth considerable effort. These two species are probably the most exciting of all the new species introduced in a long time.

Caucasian: yellow flowers

Apart from *Saxifraga carinata*, all the species are multi-flowered and their taxonomy is complex. There is a division between those with whorls of leaves, based around *S. scleropoda* and *S. subverticillata*, and those in which the foliage is more normal. There are a number of broad species in this latter group: *S. juniperifolia* and *S. pseudolaevis* are quite straightforward to grow; *S. kotschyi* from Turkey and *S. caucasica* (or the closely allied *S. desoulavyi*, which is somewhat easier to obtain) are harder, perhaps best in a pot. Russian botanists have split these into a number of narrower species. For completeness, the often very narrowly defined species asssociated with *S. caucasica* are *S. desoulavyi* and *S. sosnowskyi*; with *S. pseudolaevis* there are *S. biebersteinii*, *S. caspica* and *S. polytrichoides*; and with *S. juniperifolia* there are *S. artvinensis*, *S. grisea*, *S. ruprechtiana*, *S. kusnezowiana* and *S. charadzae*. Some of these are in cultivation from seed collections, but identification and species boundaries are often very uncertain.

The two broad species which have whorls of leaves are *Saxifraga scleropoda* and *S. subverticillata*. *Saxifraga scleropoda* is available and easy; *S. subverti-*

cillata is neither. Again, for completeness, the narrow species associated with *S. scleropoda* are *S. abchasica*, *S. sommieri* and *S. unifoveolata*; and associated with *S. subverticillata* there is *S. colchica*.

These are complex groups of plants and the treatment by Siplivinsky is invaluable. For those who want an easier approach there is discussion of this in McGregor (1997). The recent publication of Holubec & Křivka's *The Caucasus and its Flowers* provides stunning pictures and valuable notes on most of the Caucasian saxifrages, including the hybrids, and must be highly recommended.

Outside of the Caucasus, *Saxifraga kotschyi* from Turkey, *S. sancta* from the Balkans, and *S. meeboldii* from the Himalaya are clearly associated with these Caucasian species.

Saxifraga subverticillata is the most exaggerated of the yellow-flowered species from the Caucasus.

Saxifraga unifoveolata is the smallest of the yellow-flowered Caucasian species. Mount Fisht, western Caucasus. Photograph Vojtěch Holubec.

Iran

The saxifrages of Iran are often treated with those of the Caucasus but the three *Porophyllum* species with white flowers, *Saxifraga iranica*, *S. wendelboi* and *S. ramsarica*, are allied to one another but not clearly to any species in the Caucasus. All are in cultivation and are attractive. *Saxifraga ramsarica* has solitary flowers; *S. wendelboi* and *S. iranica* are very similar, but have more than one flower on each stem.

Saxifraga koelzii, which has light yellow petals, is the other Iranian species, from the Kakashan Mountains, but has not been introduced. It may well be allied to *S. carinata* from the Caucasus and it would be of real interest.

Saxifraga ramsarica has the largest flowers of the three white-flowered Iranian species.

Central Asia

None of the species from this area is common in cultivation. *Saxifraga alberti*, which can have white or pink flowers, has come into cultivation from a number of seed-collecting expeditions; *S. bryomorpha*, which was collected and named by Halda, is probably properly identified as *S. ovczinnikovii*; and *S. vvedenskyi* may only be a rather more lax white-flowered form of *S. alberti*.

Himalayas and China

This is a massive region which it might seem sensible to break down into smaller areas, but quite a number of species have very wide distributions, and it is very clear that even when different taxa are being considered, relationships only make sense across this wide region.

Sino-Himalayan: pink or purple flowers

These vary widely and do not constitute a very coherent group. Many of the pink- and purple-flowered species have more in common with neighbouring white-flowered species than they do with other more remote pink- and purple-flowered species.

    Saxifraga lilacina from the western Himalaya has long been in cultivation from a single introduction. However, many plants are now of hybrid origin, often being in fact the cultivar 'Quarry Wood', which is lime-tolerant where *S. lilacina* is very definitely not.

    Saxifraga lowndesii from Nepal is in cultivation from a collection by Ron McBeath. It varies quite a lot, the strongest-coloured forms being extremely attractive, but it should not be allowed to get too dry or too hot. According to Tim Roberts, this is typically found on steep shaded banks with water seeping through, which emphasizes its needs in cultivation. Although the foliage is unlike that of many of the white-flowered species from Nepal, the flower shape is very similar, with broad petals and a depressed central part to the flower.

    A number of other species with pink flowers have yet to become available. *Saxifraga ludlowii* from Tibet, which from photographs appears generally not unlike

Saxifraga alberti. Ulkun-Kyinidi Pass, Aksu-Dzhbageley National Park, Tien Shan, Kazakhstan. Photograph David Victor.

Saxifraga lowndesii has sumptuous flowers. In cultivation.

Saxifraga chionophila. Da Xue Shan, Yunnan. Photograph Vojtěch Holubec.

Saxifraga pulchra is an exquisite species which is new to cultivation.

S. dinnikii, would be particularly nice. *Saxifraga decora*, which probably includes *S. lamarum*, is also reported to have pink flowers. *Saxifraga chionophila*, which includes *S. schneideri*, has heads of pink flowers with tiny petals and is one of only two Asian species of *Engleria* saxifrage; the other is the yellow-green *S. rupicola*.

One enticing species which has come into cultivation from China recently is *Saxifraga pulchra*. This has very distinctive pink flowers with long stamens and is quite unlike any other other pink-flowered species.

Sino-Himalayan: white flowers and yellow anthers

The most common examples in cultivation are some of the SEP (Swedish Expedition to Pakistan) collections, such as SEP22 (others with orange-brown anthers include SEP37, SEP45 and SEP549). These have not been formally described but there are others that have: *Saxifraga staintonii* is recorded as Nepalese; *S. doyalana* as Tibetan, and *S. unguipetala* as Chinese. This last is repeatedly stated as in cultivation, but it is likely that most of the plants under this name are misidentified since other Tibetan saxifrages are not in cultivation. According to Harry Smith, *S. saxicola*, *S. saxatilis* and *S. mundula* are also white-flowered species with yellow anthers, and seem to be associated with *S. unguipetala*, *S. doyalana* and *S. staintonii*.

Sino-Himalayan: white flowers and orange–red–brown anthers

In the Himalayan region many of the white-flowered *Porophyllum* species differ markedly from those of other regions. Two characteristics mark these out: flower shape, and anther and pollen colour. That anther and pollen colour in these saxifrages has not generally been noted or investigated by botanists is presumably because it is not a characteristic which is preserved in herbarium specimens.

The flower shape of these species, whether they have white flowers (or purple, in *Saxifraga lowndesii*), is also very often, although not invariably, distinctive and quite different from that of species from elsewhere. In these, the central part of the flower is depressed in such a way that the stamens and twin stigma are more or less in a plane with the petal surface, rather than projecting out above it. At the same time the profile of the flower tends to an oval rather than a circle. This is not allied to size, as can be seen very clearly in species as diverse as *S. andersonii*, which can be fairly tall and has a flat head of flowers, and *S. georgei*, which is very small, with single sessile flowers and tiny opposite-leaved rosettes. Finally it is worth remarking that the petals of these species are often much thicker than in other species and the surface appears crystalline, with the larger tapetal cells refracting the light.

Three taller species regularly listed are *Saxifraga cinerea*, *S. andersonii* and *S. stolitzkae*, although the last two, which have multi-flowered heads, are often confused, and are not always very tall. Other species which are closely related are *S. afghanica*, *S. micans* and *S. rhodopetala*. The latter, as its name implies, is described as having pink-red petals, as may some forms of *S. andersonii*.

Saxifraga lolaensis makes cushions of tiny rosettes. Unlike the white-flowered species from farther west, those from the Himalaya east of Pakistan (*S. lolaensis* is from Nepal) have orange rather than yellow pollen, and orange, red or brown rather than yellow anthers.

Saxifraga poluniniana. In cultivation.

Saxifraga poluniniana is the most important of the shorter species here because of its impact among the producers of *Porophyllum* hybrids. An easy plant initially, it can disappear very suddenly if it suffers drought or excessive heat. When it first came into cultivation it was very widely distributed in Britain, but it is now rarely seen in England, where it seems to have been lost by most growers. It has been used extensively in many of the recent hybrids from both England and the Czech Republic. The other species which may be found in cultivation, although they will need to be searched for, include two or three species which form mats of tiny rosettes: *S. pulvinaria* and *S. lolaensis* (which is now seen to include *S. matta-florida*). *Saxifraga hypostoma*, as seen in cultivation, seems usually to be *S. ×tukuchensis*, a hybrid between *S. hypostoma* and *S. andersonii* which was found by Jan Bürgel in Nepal.

A recent collection, *Saxifraga* sp. ACE2400 from China, with red anthers and what seems to be yellow rather than orange pollen, is in very limited circulation. Other species which are generally not in cultivation, certainly not under names which are indisputable, are *S. clivorum*, *S. kumaunensis* and *S. saxorum*. *Saxifraga ramulosa* seems to be a dubious species. *Saxifraga rupicola*, one of the two Asian *Engleria* species, has very small yellowish-green petals (shorter than sepals) and *S. likiangensis*, which includes *S. calcicola*, may have yellowish petals.

Various other collections and identifications have been made, but very few of these seem to be unarguable.

Sino-Himalayan: white flowers, orange–brown anthers and opposite leaves

This small group of about seven species makes up the *Tetrameridium*, but it is clear that flower form, petal shape, and anther and pollen colour are all identical with those of the alternate-leaved species such as *Saxifraga poluniniana* and *S. lolaensis*. There are three species in cultivation: *S. georgei*, which makes a cushion of extremely small rosettes; *S. quadrifaria*, which is even smaller but is very scarce and difficult, and *S. alpigena*, which is somewhat larger and can be found under the collection McB1379 among others. This is the easiest of the three. Hybrids between these opposite-leaved species and alternate-leaved species have been produced quite easily in cultivation, and there is some evidence that some such hybrids may exist in the wild. It is worth recording that in every case the offspring of such crosses have alternate rather than opposite leaves.

Saxifraga jarmilae appears to be appropriately placed here and it is probably conspecific with one of the other species; its foliage is tiny, like that of *S. oppositifolia* subsp. *rudolphiana* or a very reduced *S. quadrifaria*, and the white flowers are in scale. It is a very difficult species to maintain through the summer. None of the other species in this group is in cultivation.

Saxifraga alpigena McB1379. The flower shape, petal texture and anther colour are all similar to *S. poluniniana*, but the leaves can clearly be seen to be in opposite pairs.

Saxifraga meeboldii CC&McK809 has very small flowers, but they are very strongly scented—a characteristic not otherwise noted among *Porophyllum* saxifrages.

Saxifraga sherriffii was grown and flowered by Willie Buchanan in Scotland in the 1960s but was lost shortly after. This historic photograph was taken in his garden. Photograph Willie Buchanan (Saxifrage Society Slide Library).

Saxifraga rotundipetala was described in 1985, and is one of the exciting yellow-flowered species from Tibet which have not reached cultivation. This photograph of *S. rotundipetala* is the first. Dashing-La, Tibet. Photograph Anne Chambers.

Sino-Himalayan: yellow flowers

None of the yellow-flowered species from this region is in general cultivation, although there are some desirable and many interesting species. *Saxifraga meeboldii*, from the western Himalaya, is closely allied to the Caucasian species such as *S. pseudolaevis*. It was collected as CC&McK809, but may no longer be in cultivation, although plants from another collection from the Czech Republic are in circulation.

Among the other yellow-flowered species from the Himalaya only the Bhutanese species *Saxifraga sherriffii* has ever been in cultivation. There are some other very appealing species with large yellow flowers still out there in the wild that would be of great interest. In Bhutan there are *S. thiantha* and *S. flavida*, while in Tibet there are *S. elliottii* (including *S. buceras*), *S. nambulana*, *S. kongboensis* and *S. rotundipetala*. These appear to represent a group of species with strong affinities.

Wild Hybrids

It was thought until quite recently that only a small number of wild hybrids existed among the *Kabschia–Engleria–Tetrameridium* saxifrages, but that view has had to be radically revised in recent years. Until the mid-1990s the only generally recognized wild hybrids between them were *Saxifraga ×luteo-purpurea* from the Pyrenees and *S. ×akinfievii* from the Caucasus. *Saxifraga ×luteo-purpurea* derives from wild crosses of *S. aretioides* and *S. media* and populations can be found in which further crossing, self-pollination and back-crossing create hybrid swarms in which very varied forms can be found. It is an important hybrid in the history of the garden hybrids, being crossed with *S. lilacina* to produce the *S. ×anglica* hybrids.

Jan Bürgel's work among the saxifrages of the Balkans has helped to reveal the extent of hybridization in the

Saxifraga ×luteo-purpurea AA12. Photograph John Howes.

Saxifraga ×akinfievii. The flower colour can vary from bright pink to orange-yellow. Verkhnaya Balkaria, Bezengi, northern Caucasus. Photograph Vojtěch Holubec.

Saxifraga ×dinninaris can be distinguished from *S. dinnikii* by its darker flowers and from *S. columnaris* most obviously by the slightly looser foliage. Verkhnaya Balkaria, Bezengi, northern Caucasus. Photograph Vojtěch Holubec.

wild. Although a number of *Porophyllum* species grow together, no hybrids had previously been found in the wild; some, however, had been produced artificially. Bürgel's finds have now made it clear that two of these artificial crosses, *Saxifraga ×biasolettoi* (*S. federici-augusti* × *S. sempervivum*) and *S. ×wehrhahnii* (*S. marginata* × *S. scardica*) also exist in the wild. There is also another wild cross, *S. ×karacardica*, involving *S. karadzicensis* and *S. scardica*.

Outside of Europe the position has changed even more radically. In the Caucasus, *Saxifraga ×akinfievii* (*S. dinnikii* × *S. scleropoda*) has long been known, but the Czech expeditions of the 1990s which collected *S. dinnikii* and *S. columnaris* also identified and collected crosses between them, now described as *S. ×dinninaris*, and crosses between *S. columnaris* and *S. scleropoda* (*S. ×columpoda*). It seems possible that other hybrids may exist, as yet undescribed.

The situation regarding the *Porophyllum* saxifrages from the Himalayas and China was thought to be one in which collections of the species defined by Harry Smith and his forerunners would gradually come back to us as collecting trips took place. Ron McBeath is foremost among those who have brought back exciting new plants, including *Saxifraga poluniniana*, *S. lowndesii* and *S. cinerea*. In recent years, however, our view of these saxifrages has had to accommodate the findings

Saxifraga ×columpoda.
Flowers in this hybrid vary
greatly in colour. Verkhnaya
Balkaria, Bezengi, northern
Caucasus. Photograph
Vojtěch Holubec.

Saxifraga ×columpoda
JJH960750.

Saxifraga sp. McB1377. Individual seedlings
from this collection varied in flower colour.
This one had pale purple-pink petals.

Saxifraga sp. McB1476. The
crystalline appearance of the petal
surface reflects a lot of light.

of Jan Bürgel and Tim Roberts, who have visited a number of the same areas as George Smith years earlier. It is now clear that hybridization in the Himalayas is extensive. Plants have been found which appear to represent crosses involving *S. lowndesii*, *S. poluniniana*, *S. andersonii* and *S. hypostoma*. These hybrids, some of which have been formally described, others provisionally named, present a new view of the Himalayan *Porophyllum*. Some of the collections can now be interpreted in this new light. Ron McBeath's collection McB1377, from which both white and pink-flowered plants were raised, some of which were incorrectly identified as *S. rhodopetala*, seem to represent hybrids between *S. cinerea* and *S. poluniniana*. Similarly McB1476, which has been labelled *S. stolitzkae*, primarily at least a Bhutanese plant, is apparently a collection of what may be a hybrid between *S. lowndesii* and *S. andersonii*. All this implies that our view of these Himalayan species may change in the next few years as such hybridization is clarified, and some of the confusion regarding previous collections which have come from the region may start to make more sense.

Growing *Porophyllum* Species

Among these saxifrages are species which will suit gardeners across a very wide range of conditions. Hot dry habitats will be best endured by species such as *Saxifraga ferdinandi-coburgi* from the Balkans. This is one of the species which is likely to figure in the ancestry of many of the bright yellow hybrids which are the best suited for full sun in a drier area. At the other end of the meteorological scale are areas of high rainfall and generally much colder winters, perhaps with extended snow cover. Here many of the Himalayan species, which the gardener in a dry area struggles to maintain, will grow well. Typically the bright pink hybrids which feature Himalayan species prominently in their ancestry, and which flower so prolifically but can be short-lived in dry areas, will be much longer-lived in cooler, wetter areas. Of the species, *S. poluniniana* and *S. lowndesii* grow far more happily, and stand a chance of a much longer life, in cooler conditions with an ample water supply in summer.

Although many species can be very successful in the open rockery, a number of different approaches might be needed to maintain a large and varied collection. As with most alpine plants, the provision of adequate drainage is vital. Composts should be well drained, with plenty of grit and sand added. Obviously some of the smaller species are best grown in pots, from considerations of size if nothing else. Pots also have the advantage that they can be moved to an appropriate site at different times of year, perhaps to a lighter position in winter, a shadier one in summer. But there are other very appropriate situations for *Porophyllum* saxifrages. Raised beds, troughs and tufa are all highly suitable for most species, although some may need additional care. With the exception of *Saxifraga lilacina*, which demands an acid compost, they are not fussy regarding pH, but they are far more demanding as far as abundant water and good drainage is concerned.

Taking cuttings is the most successful way of propagating *Porophyllum* saxifrages vegetatively. Dividing a plant is much less likely to succeed. A cushion may look very healthy, but that does not mean that it can de divided in half—you are more likely to lose both halves than to end up with two healthy plants.

Cuttings of most species and hybrids root very well, although some such as the "whorled" species from the Caucasus can be very difficult, as can *Saxifraga diapensioides* and *S. columnaris*, which are both very slow to root. One of the most difficult of all *Porophyllum* species as far as cuttings are concerned is *S. subverticillata*, but even here cuttings will root readily at the right time of year—taking only the small fresh green growth after flowering. It is always good advice to take cuttings from vigorous healthy plants, but this does not take account of the fact that many people only get round to taking cuttings when their plant starts to look rather old or poorly. It is much better to take the cuttings from young and healthy stock; cuttings from older plants will root, although in some cases a second round of cuttings from the young plants achieved in this way will result in plants with more vigorous roots.

It might seem unlikely that *Porophyllum* saxifrages could easily be raised from seed. The seedlings appear to be so small that it should take a long time to get a plant to flowering size. In fact raising these saxifrages from seed is very rewarding: most of them grow surprisingly quickly from tiny seedlings and often flower in their second year. Fresh seed can germinate very rapidly, in around two weeks, although stored seed will germinate more slowly and irregularly. The only real snags are knowing the provenance of the seed you sow, and realizing that seed of *Saxifraga burseriana* 'Gloria' which has been propagated over the decades by cuttings will give rise to seedlings which (if it has not crossed with anything else) will be *S. burseriana*, but will not be *S. burseriana* 'Gloria'.

Section *Porphyrion* Tausch

Subsection *Porophyllum* Gaudin

(including subsection *Kabschia* (Engler) Rouy & E. G. Camus, subsection *Engleria* (Sündermann) Gornall and subsection *Tetrameridium* Engler)

Saxifraga abchasica. See *S. scleropoda*.

Saxifraga afghanica Aitchison & Hemsley (1880).
  Kabschia. Cushions with flower stems to 2.5 cm, 3–4 flowers (rarely less), pedicels to 1 cm. Rosette leaves oblong-subspathulate to 7 × 2 mm, 5 lime pores. Petals usually pink otherwise white to 5 × 3.3 mm, 5 veins. Probably with depressed ovary and nectary ring like

S. andersonii. 4200–4500m, Afghanistan, Pakistan to Nepal, Tibet, Qinghai. Not in cultivation and confused by Engler and hence by many subsequent authors.

Saxifraga alberti Regel & Schmalhausen (1877).
  Kabschia. Flower stem to 2.5 cm, 4–8 narrow flowers. Rosette oblong-linear leaves to 8.7 × 2 mm, 3 –5 lime pores. Petals white or pink to 7 × 4.2 mm. Anthers yellow. 2200–2600m, volcanic rocks. Pamirs, Tien Shan. See also *S. vvedenskyi*.

Saxifraga alpigena Harry Smith (1958). *Tetrameridium*.

Small cushions or mats. Shoots to 2 cm, flowers solitary, on stems to 0.7 cm. Leaves opposite, to 2.5 × 1.5 mm, single lime pore, looking very like foliage of *S. oppositifolia*. Petals white, 6 × 4 mm. 3400–4200m. Anthers red-brown, pollen orange. Nepal. In cultivation (as McB1379).

Saxifraga andersonii Engler (1912). *Kabschia*. Shoots to 9 cm, flower stems to 2 cm lengthening, 2–5 flowers. Rosette leaves oblong to 10 × 2.6 mm, typically 3 lime pores. Petals white or possibly pink, 5 × 3.2 mm, 3–5 veins, depressed ovary and nectary ring. Anthers brown. 4100–4700m, Nepal to Bhutan, Tibet. Most plants in cultivation are very late flowering.

Saxifraga aretioides Lapeyrouse (1801). *Kabschia*. Cushions with flower stems to 7 cm, typically 1–4 flowers. Leaves oblong, very slightly mucronate, to 7 × 1.3 mm, 3–5 lime pores. Petals yellow, oblong-cuneate to 5 × 2.5 mm. Anthers yellow. Pyrenees. Rarely cultivated.

Saxifraga artvinensis V. A. Matthews (1972). *Kabschia*. White-flowered species very closely associated with *S. juniperifolia*. Flower stems to 4.0 cm, 4–5 flowers. Leaves sharply pointed to 9 mm. Petals white to 5 mm, stamens longer. Anthers yellow. 2100–2300m, volcanic rocks, northeast Turkey. Not in cultivation.

Saxifraga biebersteinii. See *S. pseudolaevis*.

Saxifraga bryomorpha Halda (1997). *Kabschia*. Cushions 1–5 flowers. Leaves broadly lanceolate up to 5 mm, apex acute. Petals to 6 × 5 mm, white or pale pink, stamens nearly as long as petals. 3000m, Pamirs: Tadzhikistan. It is extremely probable that this should be included in *S. ovczinnikovii*.

Saxifraga burseriana Linnaeus (1753). *Kabschia*. Very variable, forming spiny-looking grey-green cushions. Single flowers, stems 4–7 cm. Leaves lanceolate, to 11 × 2 mm, glaucous grey-green. Stems dark red. Petals white to 11 × 11 mm or more, margin often rhombic or crenate. Anthers yellow. 200–2200m, eastern Alps: Italy, Austria, Slovenia. Pretty and popular, foliage attractive, better on vertical slope or protected from winter wet.

Cultivars:

'Brookside'. Flowers large, flat, petals circular to 12 × 12 mm.

'Cordata'. Petals rhombic or with three large rounded points.

'Crenata'. Tight cushion. Petals with scalloped margin.

'Crenulata'. Small tight cushion and foliage. Petals with finely crenate margin.

'Falstaff'. Large, spiny, soft foliage. Often 3 flowers.

'Ganymede'. Petals with squared off apical margin.

'Gloria'. Large flowers, often 2 to stem, petals to 17 × 15 mm.

'John Tomlinson'. Neat.

'Snowdon'. Very pointed spiny but soft foliage. Large flowers, petals to 14 × 13 mm, many fine veins.

Many other forms and collections have been named, most pretty, not all very distinct.

Saxifraga calcicola. See under *S. likiangensis*.

Saxifraga carinata Oettingen (1908). *Kabschia*. Stems 1.5 cm, solitary flowers. Leaves linear-lanceolate to 5 × 1 mm, pointed. Petals to 6 × 3.5 mm, pale yellow. Anthers yellow. Caucasus: Balkaria, Ossetia, 2900m. Not in cultivation.

Saxifraga caspica. See *S. pseudolaevis*.

Saxifraga caucasica Sommier & Levier (1894). *Kabschia*. Tight cushion, flower stems to 3 cm, 3–7 flowers. Leaves oblong-linear to 9 × 2 mm, rosettes open. Flowers in tight hemispherical head. Petals yellow, to 3 × 1 mm, stamens about as long. Anthers yellow. Western Caucasus.

Associated taxa:

Saxifraga desoulavyi Oettingen (1909). Leaves to 7 × 1.4 mm, petals to 6 × 3 mm. Central Caucasus.

Saxifraga sosnowskyi Mandenova (1956). Leaves lanceolate to 5 × 1.5 mm, petals to 4 × 2 mm. Little Caucasus.

Saxifraga charadzeae. See *S. juniperifolia*.

Saxifraga chionophila Franchet (1896) [incl. *S. schneideri* Engler (1921)]. *Engleria*. Shoots to 2 cm, flower stems to 4 cm, 2–7 flowers, pedicels to 1.5 cm. Rosette leaves spathulate-obovate to 9 × 3 mm, 5–7 lime pores. Petals red, greenish or white, to 3 × 1 mm, not or barely longer than sepals. 2700–5000m, Tibet, Sichuan, Yunnan. Not in cultivation.

Saxifraga cinerea Harry Smith (1958). *Kabschia*. Flower stems dark red to 8 cm, 3–6 flowers, very short petioles. Leaves linear-lanceolate to 12 × 2 mm, 13–18 lime pores. Petals to 10 × 6 mm, pure white. Anthers and pollen orange. 2700m, Nepal. Not difficult in cultivation but not easy to propagate so uncommon.

Saxifraga clivorum Harry Smith (1958). *Kabschia*. Shoots to 2 cm, flower stems 0.4 cm, 3 flowers. Rosette leaves obovate 6.7 × 2.6 mm, 3 lime pores, apex blunt. Petals white, 4.2 × 3.6 mm, 5–7 veins. Anthers red-brown. 4700–5000m, Sikkim, Bhutan, Tibet. May be in cultivation as McB1476.

Saxifraga columnaris Schmalhausen (1892). *Kabschia*. Foliage very tight, leaves crowded on columnar shoots, flower stems to about 2 cm, single flowers. Leaves small and silvery about 3 × 1 mm. Petals silky rich purple, usually recurved, to about 10 × 7 mm. Anthers red-purple, pollen yellow. 2000–3000m, northern Caucasus: Balkaria, Ossetia. In cultivation since 1996 but difficult.

Saxifraga corymbosa Boissier (1843) [*S. luteo-viridis* Schott & Kotschy (1851)]. *Engleria*. Small group of rosettes, flower stems to 15 cm, 3–18 flowers. Leaves glaucous, obovate, to 21 × 4 mm. Inflorescence simple or broadly branched, petals yellow, just visible in globular calyx. Carpathians: Greece and Turkey.

Saxifraga decora Harry Smith (1958) [incl. *S. lamarum* Harry Smith (1958)]. *Kabschia*. Shoots to 6 cm, flower stems to 3.5 cm, 3–4 flowers. Rosette leaves subspathulate-oblong to 5 × 2 mm, 3–7 lime pores. Petals pink–purple 5 × 3 mm, 3–5 veins. 3500–4800m, Tibet, Yunnan. Not in cultivation.

Saxifraga decussata J. Anthony (1933). *Tetrameridium*. Dense cushion, solitary flowers almost sessile. Leaves opposite, obelliptic 3.4 × 2.6 mm, apex blunt, in connate pairs. Petals 4, yellowish 2.6 × 2 mm. 3000–4100m, Yunnan, Gansu, Qinghai. Not in cultivation.

Saxifraga desoulavyi. See *S. caucasica*.

Saxifraga diapensioides Bellardi (1792). *Kabschia*. Very tight hard foliage, flower stems to 7 cm, 2–6 flowers. Leaves oblong-spathulate to 6 × 1.8 mm. Flowers flat, large for foliage, petals white to 10 × 5 mm. Anthers yellow. Western Alps. Difficult to grow, very slow, rare in cultivation. Plants under this label are often hybrids (usually *S. ×malbyana*).

Saxifraga dinnikii Schmalhausen (1892). *Kabschia*. Rosettes tight and flattened, flower stems to about 4 cm, single flowers. Leaves dark dull grey-green to about 6 × 1.5 mm. Petals rich lilac-purple to about 15 × 10 mm, with distinctive longitudinal corrugation, apical margin serrate. Anthers and pollen yellow (a unique combination among the pink- or purple-flowered species). 2000–3000m, northern Caucasus: Balkaria, Ossetia. Only in cultivation since 1996; easier than *S. columnaris*.

Saxifraga doyalana Harry Smith (1958). *Kabschia*. Shoots to 2 cm, single flowers on 1 cm stems. Rosette leaves obovate 4 × 2 mm, 5–7 lime pores, apex blunt. Petals white, 6 × 4.2 mm, 6 veins. Anthers yellow. 4800m, Tibet. Probably not in cultivation.

Saxifraga elliotii Harry Smith (1958) [incl. *S. buceras* Harry Smith (1958)]. *Kabschia*. Shoots to 6 cm, flower stems to 3.5 cm, single-flowered. Leaves to 6 × 2 mm, 5–7 lime pores, apex blunt. Petals yellow, obovate to

10 × 6.5 mm, 8 veins. Anthers yellow. 2800–3600m, Tibet. Not in cultivation.

Saxifraga federici-augusti Biasoletto (1841) [*S. grisebachii* Degen & Dörfler (1897)]. *Engleria*. Small group of flat rosettes, stems to 20–25 cm, 15–35 flowers. Leaves obovate-spathulate to 35 × 8 mm, grey-glaucous with lime pores along edge of upper surface. Flowers clustered in dense head, dark red petals barely obtruding, pinched in by calyx. Whole stem densely red-hairy. 500–2600m, Balkans: Greece, Albania, Macedonia, Montenegro.

subsp. *federici-augusti*. Rosette leaves to 18 mm, widening but not spathulate. Inflorescence dark red. Typically 15 flowers. Higher altitudes.

subsp. *grisebachii*. Rosette leaves to 35 mm, spathulate. Inflorescence bright red, typically to 20 flowers. '**Wisley**' is a cultivar with tall red inflorescence, usually seed-raised today. Lower altitudes.

Saxifraga felineri P. Vargas in Castroviejo et al (1997). *Kabschia*. Typically 6–9 flowers, flower stems to 7 cm. Leaves linear-rhombic to 7 × 2 mm, 7–9 lime pores. Petals yellow, rounded, to 7 × 5 mm. Anthers yellow. Spain: Picos de Europa, 2200m. In cultivation usually as *S. aretioides*, from which it was split.

Saxifraga ferdinandi-coburgi Kellerer ex Sündermann (1901). *Kabschia*. Hard cushions. Flower stems 3–10 cm, 5–16 flowers. Leaves lanceolate-linear to 13 × 2 mm. Petals strong bright yellow, to 7 × 5 mm. Anthers yellow. Bulgaria, Greeece, 1000–2900m.

var. *ferdinandi-coburgi*. Leaves to 9 mm. Probably taller stems with fewer larger flowers.

var. *rhodopea*. Spiny lanceolate leaves to 13 mm. Probably shorter stems with more smaller flowers.

Cultivar:

'**Drakula**'. Large flowers and spiny leaves.

Saxifraga flavida Harry Smith (1958). *Kabschia*. Stems to 7 cm, flower stems to 1 cm, single flowers. Leaves obovate-linear, 5 × 2.2 mm, single pore, apex obtuse. Petals pale yellow, more or less circular 4 × 3.8 mm. Anthers yellow. 4350m, Bhutan. Not in cultivation.

Saxifraga georgei J. Anthony (1933). *Tetrameridium*. Dense cushion of tiny rosettes, solitary sessile flowers. Leaves opposite, to 3 × 2 mm, decussate pairs, single lime pore, apex blunted. In summer tip of rosettes break off during heavy rain and can root. Petals white, 5 × 3 mm. Anthers red-brown, pollen orange. 3600–4100m, Nepal to Bhutan, Tibet, Sichuan, Yunnan. In cultivation.

Saxifraga grisea. See *S. juniperifolia*.

Saxifraga hypostoma Harry Smith (1958). *Kabschia*.
Flowers single, almost sessile. Leaves obovate-linear,
4 × 1.6 mm, single pore, apex rounded and obviously
ciliate. Petals white, 4 × 4 mm. Anthers red-brown.
4300–5300m, Nepal. Rare in cultivation and difficult
to maintain. Most plants in cultivation under this
name are of hybrid *S.* ×*tukuchensis*.

Saxifraga iranica Bornmüller (1906). *Kabschia*. Hard
cushion, flower stems to 5 cm, 3–6 flowers. Leaves
oblong-ovate, slightly pointed, about 3.5 × 3.0 mm.
Flowers open flat, petals overlapping to 11.4 × 6.5
mm, white turning pink-purple. Anthers yellow. Iran:
Elburz Mountains. Plants with solitary flowers are
separated as *S. ramsarica*.

Saxifraga jarmilae Halda (1997). Dense cushion of tiny
rosettes, solitary sessile flowers. Leaves opposite, to
2 × 1.5 mm, single lime pore, apex mucronate. Petals
white, 6–9 mm long. 4300m, Yunnan (Yulongshan).
This was collected (and seed distributed) by Halda
but it is doubtful if any seedlings survived. Described
by Halda as belonging to *Oppositifoliae* and hence
closely related to *S. oppositifolia* (see Chapter 8), but
more likely to belong to *Tetrameridium* and be closely
associated with *S. georgei*.

Saxifraga juniperifolia Adams (1806). *Kabschia*.
Very spiny cushion, flower stems hairy to 4 cm, 7–12
flowers. Leaves glossy, lanceolate, pointed, to 13 × 2.5
mm. Flowers in dense head, stamens and styles
prominently exserted. Petals yellow, to 6 × 3 mm.
Anthers yellow. Caucasus, Little Caucasus, northeast
Turkey, Bulgaria. Note that *S. juniperifolia* and *S.
sancta* are interpreted differently by different authors,
Horný taking a view that Bulgarian plants belong to *S.
sancta*.
Associated narrow species:

Saxifraga charadzeae Otschiauri (1963). *Kabschia*.
Leaves whorled, 4–6 flowers in dense head, petals to
8 × 2 mm. Central Caucasus: Daghestan, Chechnya,
Georgia.

Saxifraga grisea Siplivinsky (1982). Leaves dull
grey-green, strongly recurved, petals narrower than
sepals. Central Caucasus: Ossetia.

Saxifraga kusnezowiana Oettingen (1909) (*S.
juniperifolia* var. *kusnezowiana* (Oettingen) Engler
& Irmscher). *Kabschia*. Leaves grey-green, slightly
whorled. Central Caucasus.

Saxifraga ruprechtiana Mandenova (1956) (*S.
juniperifolia* var. *brachyphylla* Boissier). *Kabschia*.
Stems to 2 cm, 4–5 flowers. Very tight foliage,
leaves oblong to 5 × 1 mm, mucronate. Central

Caucasus: Georgia, Balkaria, Ossetia, Chechnya,
Daghestan.
Note that *S. artvinensis* with white flowers from
northeast Turkey is also closely associated.

Saxifraga karadzicensis (Degen & Košanin) Chrtek
& Soják (1988). *Kabschia*. Flower stems to 8 cm, 4–6
flowers. Leaves linear-lanceolate to 4.2 × 1.8 mm,
single pore, margins long-ciliate for most of length.
Petals white, to 5.2 × 3.8 mm. 2100m, Macedonia.
Rare in cultivation; most plants under this name are *S.
marginata* var. *karadzicensis*.

Saxifraga koelzii Schönbeck-Temesy (1967).
Kabschia. Flower stems to 0.4 cm, 1–3 flowers. Leaves
spathulate-oblong, pointed to 7 × 2.5 mm. Petals
light yellow, 9 × 3.5 mm. Anthers yellow. 3000m, Iran
(Kakashan). Not in cultivation.

Saxifraga kongboensis Harry Smith (1958). *Kabschia*.
Shoots to 7 cm, flower stems to 2.5 cm, flowers
solitary. Rosette leaves to 7 × 1.9 mm, 7–11 lime pores,
apex mucronate. Petals yellow, circular, angular, to
10 × 8.5 mm, 15 veins, wavy margin. Anthers yellow.
2400–2900m, Tibet. Not in cultivation.

Saxifraga kotschyi Boissier (1856). *Kabschia*. Tight
cushion, flower stems to 8 cm, 4–13 flowers. Leaves
linear-oblong to 12 × 4 mm, pointed, stiff. Flowers
open. Petals yellow, separate to 6 × 3 mm, longer than
sepals but stamens prominent. Anthers yellow. Turkey.

Saxifraga kumaunensis Engler (1919). *Kabschia*. Single
flowers on short stems. Leaves oblong 4 × 1 mm,
apex blunt with tiny mucronate point. Petals white,
to 5 × 2.5 mm. Anthers red-brown. 3300–4800m,
northwest India, Nepal. Not in cultivation.

Saxifraga kusnezowiana. See *S. juniperifolia*.

Saxifraga likiangensis Franchet (1896) [incl. *S.
mundula* Harry Smith (1958), *S. calcicola* J. Anthony
(1933)]. *Kabschia*. Shoots to 4.5 cm, single flowers
on stems to 1 cm. Rosette leaves oblong-spathulate
to 5.6 × 2.1 mm, 3 lime pores, apex acute. Petals
white (occasionally yellowish) to 9 × 5 mm, 5–9 veins.
Anthers yellow. 3000–5600m, Bhutan, Burma, Tibet,
Sichuan, Yunnan, Qinghai. Probably not in cultivation
(possibly ACE2401).
Note: The broad view is that of *Flora of China*. In a
narrower view *S. likiangensis* has several pores, sessile
flowers, white petals to 3.5 mm long; *S. calcicola*
(Yunnan, Burma) has about 5 pores, petals to 6 × 4 mm;
S. mundula (Tibet) has linear leaves having single lime
pore, white petals up to 8 × 7 mm, and has sepals with a
single lime pore distinguishing it from *S. calcicola*.

Saxifraga lilacina Duthie (1904). *Kabschia*. Small

cushion, flowers single on stems 1–2 cm. Leaves oblong to 5 × 1.6 mm. Petals pale lilac with darker veins, 11 × 7.5 mm. Anthers dark red-purple, pollen cream. Lime-hating in cultivation. 3300–4000m, Kashmir. Most plants in cultivation are now of hybrid origin.

Saxifraga lolaensis Harry Smith (1958) [incl. *S. matta-florida* Harry Smith (1958)]. *Kabschia*. Dense cushions of tiny rosettes. Single, sessile flowers. Leaves oblong 3 × 1.5 mm, apex truncate with single pore. Petals white from 3.5 × 4.5 (broader than long!) to 5 × 4.5 mm. Anthers red-brown. 3000–4800m, Bhutan, Tibet. *S. lolaensis* was described as slightly smaller than *S. matta-florida*. Plants are in cultivation under both species names but are difficult to flower well.

Saxifraga lowndesii Harry Smith (1958). *Kabschia*. Loose cushion. Stems to 10 cm, flowers sessile. Leaves shiny green, spathulate 7 × 2.5 mm. Petals 7 × 7 mm. Colour varies from pink-purple to rich purple. Anthers red-purple, pollen orange-red. 4000m, Nepal. In cultivation from McBeath collection.

Saxifraga ludlowii Harry Smith (1958). *Kabschia*. Shoots to 4 cm, flower stems 1 cm, single-flowered. Rosette leaves oblanceolate 5.5 × 1.6 mm, 3 lime pores. Petals purple-lilac-pink 9 × 5 mm, 7 veins. 4300–4800m, Tibet. Not in cultivation but obviously desirable.

Saxifraga marginata Sternberg (1822). *Kabschia*. Very variable. Mats or cushions, flower stems straight, flowers in flat-topped inflorescence. Petals white often turning pink or purple-pink. Anthers yellow. Leaves generally oblong-spathulate. Italy, Balkans (Croatia to Greece and Bulgaria), Romania. One of the most rewarding species with all varieties, wild and cultivated, worth growing. Conservative approaches recognize just two varieties (var. *marginata* and var. *coriophylla*).

    var. *marginata*. Tall. Stems 6–14 cm, 2–8 flowers. Leaves to 15 × 6 mm. Petals to 10 × 9 mm. Italy.

    var. *boryi*. Stem 2.0–6.5 cm, 1–5 flowers. Leaves broad to 7 × 3.8 mm. Petals pure white to 10 × 7 mm. Greece.

    var. *bubakii*. Stem 2.0–5.0 cm, 3–8 flowers. Leaves to 8 × 2.8 mm, Petals white fading to pink to 9 × 6 mm. Glabrous inflorescence. Ex-Yugoslavia: Mount Durmitor.

    var. *coriophylla*. Stem 2.0–6.5 cm, 1–5 flowers. Small leaves, to 7.5 × 3 mm. Petals to 15 × 8 mm. Albania, ex-Yugoslavia.

    var. *karadzicensis*. Leaves to 2.5 × 1.5 mm.

Distinguished from *S. karadzicensis* by having 3 pores (rather than 1) per leaf. FYR Macedonia.

    var. *rocheliana*. Stem 5.0–12.0 cm, 4–15 flowers. Leaves relatively narrow to 13 × 3 mm. Flowers wide open, petals white fading to pink, sometimes reflexed, to 14 × 9 mm. Albania, Romania, Bulgaria. In a conservative approach this is contained in var. *marginata*.

Cultivars:

'Balkan'. Petals long and elegantly reflexed.

'Intermedia'. Petals rounded.

'Jaroslav Horný'. Large, thick flower stems to 10 cm. Slow.

'Lidice'. *S. marginata* garden seedling.

'Major'. Very similar to var. *rocheliana*.

'Milica'. Foliage sharp-pointed, regular, flowers flat, large, petals to 11 × 8 mm.

'Minor'. Small form of var. *coriophylla*. Stems to 5 cm, 2–5 flowers, flowers normal size.

'Popelka'. Single-flowered.

'Purpurea'. Buds bright purple-red.

'Sorrento'. A large form from southern Italy.

Saxifraga media Gouan (1773). *Engleria*. Small group of rosettes, stems to 12 cm, 3–16 flowers. Leaves oblong-linear or spathulate, pointed, often recurved, to 22 × 5.8 mm. Inflorescence one-sided with flowers on separate pedicels, flowers small, globular calyx, petals pink-red-purple barely protruding. 600–2500m, Pyrenees. Short-lived in cultivation. Hybridizes with *S. aretioides* to give *S. ×luteo-purpurea*, an important and variable plant in the production of historic hybrid cultivars.

Saxifraga meeboldii Engler & Irmscher (1913). *Kabschia*. Small cushion. Flower stems to 2.5 cm, 3–4 flowers, very short pedicels. Leaves oblong, bluntly pointed, to 4 × 1.5 mm. Petals yellow, to 4.5 × 1.5 mm, stamens projecting. Anthers yellow. One collection (CC&McK809) had fragrant flowers. 3000–4200m, Pakistan, India: Kashmir but not Nepal, China or Tibet. Very rare in cultivation.

Saxifraga micans Harry Smith (1958). *Kabschia*. Flower stems to 2.5 cm, 3–4 flowers. Leaves linear, pointed, to 8.7 × 2 mm, 7 lime pores. Petals white, may be tinged pink, 12.5 × 8.5 mm. Anthers red-brown. 3750m, Nepal. May be in cultivation.

Saxifraga mira Harry Smith (1960). *Kabschia*. Flower stems to 0.8 cm, single white or pink flowers. Leaves oblong to 6.5 × 2.5 mm, apex slightly pointed, 5–7 lime pores. Petals white, to 7.5 × 6 mm. Anthers red-brown. 4350m, Nepal. Not in cultivation.

Saxifraga monantha Harry Smith (1958).

Tetrameridium. Shoots to 7 cm, flowers solitary on stems to 1.5 cm. Leaves opposite, obelliptic 5 × 3.5 mm, in connate pairs. Petals 4, white 6.5 × 4.5 mm. 3900m, Tibet. Not in cultivation.

Saxifraga mundula. See *S. likiangensis*.

Saxifraga nambulana Harry Smith (1958). *Kabschia*. Shoots to 3 cm, flower stems to 1 cm, flowers solitary. Leaves to 5.5 × 2 mm, 5 lime pores, apex mucronate. Petals yellow, narrowly rhombic-elliptic to 7 × 3 mm, 3–4 veins. Anthers yellow. 4200m, Tibet. Not in cultivation.

Saxifraga nana Engler (1883) [incl. *S. octandra* Harry Smith (1924), *S. qinghaiensis* J. T. Pan (1978)]. *Tetrameridium*. Dense cushions, flowers solitary on stems to 0.5 cm. Leaves opposite, spathulate-oblong 4 × 1 mm, single lime pore. Petals absent or 4 (or occasionally 5), white, 2.5 × 1.4 mm, more or less equalling sepals. 4200–4900m, Sichuan, Qinghai, Gansu. Not in cultivation.

Saxifraga obtusa (Sprague) Horný & Webr (1985). *Kabschia*. Solid cushion, flower stems to 7 cm, 3–11 flowers. Leaves linear-spathulate to 10 × 2 mm. Flowers white, petals narrowly obovate to 10 × 6.4 mm. Anthers yellow. Ex-Yugoslavia. This is an obscure taxon which may be of wild hybrid origin.

Saxifraga ovczinnikovii Kamelin (1990). *Kabschia*. Stems 5–8 cm, 3–6 flowers. Leaves spathulate up to 7 mm, apex acute. Petals to 8 mm, off-white turning pink, stamens nearly as long as petals. Anthers yellow. Pamirs: Tadzhikistan. Plants in cultivation as *S. bryomorpha* match the description of *S. ovczinnikovii* and it seems probable that *S. bryomorpha* is not distinct and should be subsumed here.

Saxifraga poluniniana Harry Smith (1958). *Kabschia*. Loose cushion or mat, flower stems to 1.5 cm, single flowers. Leaves soft to 6 × 1.5 mm, 5–7 lime glands. Petals white but often turning or flushed pink, to 10 × 5 mm, margin often wavy. Anthers red-brown. 2000–3500m, Nepal. Introductions prospered initially, but now surprisingly rare in cultivation.

Saxifraga polytrichoides. See *S. pseudolaevis*.

Saxifraga porophylla Bertoloni (1814). *Engleria*. Small group of rosettes, stems to 8 cm, 3–12 flowers. Leaves oblong-obovate, glaucous, lime pores along margin, to 15 × 3 mm. Flowers singly on short pedicels, calyx enclosing flower, petals red-purple starting paler, barely visible. 1100–2500m, Italy: Abruzzi, Apennines. Difficult in cultivation.

Saxifraga pseudolaevis Oettingen (1909). *Kabschia*. Stems to 5 cm, 5–7 flowers. Rosette leaves non-spiny, spathulate-oblong to linear, mucronate, glossy, to 8 × 3 mm. Petals yellow, to 4 × 2.2 mm, longer than sepals, protruding stamens. Anthers yellow. Western central Caucasus: Georgia, Balkaria, Ossetia.

Associated narrow species:

Saxifraga biebersteinii Siplivinsky (1982). Central Caucasus: Ossetia. This is probably best treated as a high-altitude ecotype of *S. pseudolaevis*.

Saxifraga caspica Siplivinsky (1982) [*S. mandenovae* Soják (1985)]. Distinguished from *S. pseudolaevis* by having matte rather than glossy leaves. Eastern Caucasus: Daghestan, Azerbaijan.

Saxifraga polytrichoides Siplivinsky (1982). Daghestan: high altitudes. This is probably no more than a particularly dwarf ecotype of *S. caspica*.

Saxifraga pulchra Engler & Irmscher (1912). *Kabschia*. Small cushion. Flower stems to 3.5 cm, up to 6 flowers, pedicels 1 mm. Rosette leaves obovate 7 × 2.5 mm, 7–11 lime pores, apex acute. Petals pink, to 5 × 2.7 mm, 3 veins, stamens as long as petals. 2500–4600m, Sichuan, Yunnan. In cultivation from ACE2400.

Saxifraga pulvinaria Harry Smith (1958). *Kabschia*. Dense cushion of tiny rosettes. Single, almost sessile flowers. Leaves 3.3 × 1.4 mm, single lime pore, apex acute. Petals white, to 5.3 × 2.1 mm, nectary ring. Anthers red-brown. 3900–5200m, Kashmir to Bhutan, Tibet, Yunnan, Xinjiang. In cultivation, but very difficult to flower well.

Saxifraga quadrifaria Engler & Irmscher (1919). *Tetrameridium*. Dense cushions of tiny rosettes. Nearly sessile, solitary flowers. Leaves opposite, to 2.5 × 1.2 mm, single lime pore, apex acute but slightly truncate. Petals white, 4.2 × 3 mm. Anthers red-brown, pollen orange. From 3000m, Nepal (not Tibet).

Saxifraga ramsarica Jamzad (1993). *Kabschia*. Hard cushions. Solitary flowers on stems to 3 cm. Leaves oblong to 4.5 × 2.3 mm, apex blunt. Petals to 11 × 6.7 mm, undulating, white turning pink. Anthers yellow. In cultivation originally as *S. iranica*, which has very similar foliage but has 3–6 flowers per stem. Iran: Elburz Mountains.

Saxifraga rhodopetala Harry Smith (1958). *Kabschia*. Probably close to *S. andersonii* with depressed ovary and nectary ring. Pink petals. May be an example of a hybrid. 3900–4500m, Nepal. Most plants in cultivation under this name are examples of *S. andersonii* or of hybrids of that species.

Saxifraga rotundipetala J. T. Pan (1985). *Kabschia*. Stems to 7 cm, 2–3 flowers, pedicels to 0.3 cm. Rosette leaves to 7×2 mm, 3–5 lime pores. Petals yellow, more or less circular to 5.5×4.7 mm, 7–9 veins. Anthers yellow. Dense cushions to 7 cm. 3900m, Tibet. Not in cultivation.

Saxifraga roylei Harry Smith (1958). *Tetrameridium*. Flower stems to 1.5 cm, 1–3 flowers. Leaves opposite, ovate/obovate-linear to 3.5 mm. Petals white, 4.6×3.2 mm. 3750m, Nepal.

Saxifraga rupicola Franchet (1896). *Kabschia* or *Engleria*. Dense cushion, flower stems to 0.8 cm with solitary flower. Leaves obovate-spathulate 5×2.5 mm, 3–5 lime pores. Petals greenish-yellow to 2.5×0.7 mm, not exceeding sepals. Stamens as long as petals. Anthers yellow. 3500m, Yunnan.

Saxifraga ruprechtiana. See *S. juniperifolia*.

Saxifraga sancta Grisebach (1843). *Kabschia*. Cushions of sharply pointed, stiff, glossy green foliage, flower stems hairless to 5 cm, 3–12 flowers. Leaves to 12×2 mm. Flowers upward-facing. Petals yellow, to 5×2.5 mm, stamens slightly longer than petals. Anthers yellow. Northeastern Greece, western Turkey. Also see note under *S. juniperifolia*.

Saxifraga saxatilis Harry Smith (1924). *Kabschia*. Single flowers on stems to 2.5 cm. Rosette leaves oblinear 5×2 mm, apex blunt. Petals (usually white but sometimes pink) 4.5×2.5 mm, 5–7 veins. Anthers yellow. 4200–4300m, Sichuan. Not in cultivation.

Saxifraga saxicola Harry Smith (1958). *Kabschia*. Single flowers on stems to 1.5 cm. Rosette leaves linear 4×1.5 mm, 5–7 lime pores, apex blunted. Petals white, 9×6 mm. 2800m, Sichuan. Not in cultivation.

Saxifraga saxorum Harry Smith (1958). *Kabschia*. Stems to 4 cm. Flowers single, sessile. Leaves oblong 4×1.5 mm, single pore, apex blunt. Petals white, to 4×2.8 mm. Anthers red-brown. 3900–4200m, Bhutan. Not in cultivation.

Saxifraga scardica Grisebach (1843). *Kabschia*. Hard, open, regular, starry rosettes, flower stems to 12 cm, 4–13 flowers. Leaves lanceolate or slightly spathulate, pointed, 4–17×1.5–4 mm. Flowers white sometimes fading pink, petals obovate to 9×7 mm. Anthers yellow. Balkans: Greece, Albania, Macedonia, Montenegro. Attractive foliage. Pretty flowers, but not always abundant. Very small plants from Albania have been described as subsp. *korabensis* J. Bürgel but they may better treated as a local ecotype.

Cultivar:

'Olymp'. Looser foliage, irregular inflorescence, possibly *S. ×wehrhahnii*.

Saxifraga scleropoda Sommier & Levier (1894).

Kabschia. Basal rosettes, with stems and further flat-topped whorls (or rosettes) at tip and flower stems (to 4 cm) from these, 12–19 flowers. Leaves lanceolate-oblong, strongly reflexed and curved, to 10×1.8 mm. Petals yellow, to 5×0.8 mm, equal or slightly exceeding sepals, stamens longer than petals. Anthers yellow. Western Caucasus.

Associated taxa:

Saxifraga abchasica Oettingen (1907). Distinguished from *S. scleropoda* by stem leaves being straight, petals twice as long as sepals. Stems may be up to 15 cm. Leaves conspicuously "whorled". Western Caucasus.

Saxifraga sommieri (Engler & Irmscher) Siplivinsky (1982). Distinguished from *S. scleropoda* by smaller (to 4 mm) more crowded leaves with aristulate-ciliate margins. Western Caucasus.

Saxifraga unifoveolata Siplivinsky (1982). Dense cushion. Shoots columnar 3 cm long, 0.5 cm wide, leaves to 3×1 mm, grey-green. Petals about 3 mm. Western Caucasus. This species is less clearly associated with *S. scleropoda* than *S. sommieri* and *S. abchasica*.

Saxifraga sempervivum K. Koch (1846). *Engleria*. Small cushion. Stems to 20 cm usually less, up to 20 flowers. Leaves narrow, linear-oblong, more spiny than other *Engleria* species, to 20×3.5 mm. Flowers and inflorescence dark red-purple, flowers clustered, petals barely showing. Balkans: Greece, Albania, Montenegro, Bulgaria, Macedonia. Common in cultivation but not as named cultivars.

Cultivars:

'Afrodite'. Small with dark purple inflorescence.

'Zita'. Collected albino form with glaucous grey-green inflorescence and stem and greenish-white flowers. Rare and difficult.

Saxifraga sherriffii Harry Smith (1958). *Kabschia*. Flower stems to 4.5 cm, 3–7 flowers. Leaves obovate-oblong, bluntly pointed, 4×2 mm. Petals yellow, to 7×5.5 mm. Anthers yellow. 3750m, Bhutan. Was in cultivation up till about 1960 but now lost.

Saxifraga sommieri. See *S. scleropoda*.

Saxifraga sosnowskyi. See *S. caucasica*.

Saxifraga spruneri Boissier (1843). *Kabschia*. Soft foliage, flower stems to 8 cm, 4–14 flowers. Leaves soft, glandular-hairy on surface as well as margin, to 8×4 mm. Small flowers in flat-topped inflorescence. Petals white, broadly obovate to 6×3.5 mm. Anthers yellow. Greece, Bulgaria. Very distinctive. Not difficult in a pot. Reported hybrid with *S. glabella* (section *Saxifraga*) is discussed under that species. Chromosome number 2n=28 is different to all other recorded *Kabschia* species which have 2n=26.

subsp. *spruneri*. Stems to 6 cm. Leaves to 5.5 × 2.5 mm. Throughout range.

subsp. *deorum*. Larger, stems to 8 cm. Leaves to 8 × 4 mm. Greece: Mount Olympus.

Saxifraga staintonii Harry Smith (1958). *Kabschia*. Single flowers on stems to 5 cm. Leaves sublinear pointed to 9 × 2 mm. Petals white to 10 × 4 mm. 4800m, Nepal. Not in cultivation.

Saxifraga stolitzkae Duthie (1919). *Kabschia*. Flower stems to 8 cm, 4–7 flowers. Rosette leaves to 9 × 3 mm, 5–11 lime pores. Petals white or pink, to 9 × 7 mm, depressed ovary and nectary ring. Anthers red-brown. Distinguished from *S. andersonii* by having no pores on sepals, larger flowers, and more lime-encrusted foliage, but since *S. andersonii* is very also very variable this is not always easy to apply. 3000–4300m, Kumaon, Nepal, Bhutan. In cultivation.

Saxifraga stribrnyi (Velenovsky) Podpera (1902). *Engleria*. Small cushion, stems to 12 cm, widely branched, 5–40 flowers. Leaves grey-glaucous, linear-lanceolate, to 25 × 6 mm, often narrower, occasionally slightly spathulate. Flowers small, petals dark purple, larger than in most other *Engleria* species but still barely protruding.

   f. *stribrnyi*. Throughout range.

   f. *zollikoferi*. Leaves broadly spathulate, shorter hairs, pale off-white petals. Bulgaria.

Cultivars:

'Isolde'. Albino cultivar probably from f. *zollikoferi*.

'Tristan'. Perhaps rather less branched than typical form.

Saxifraga subsessiliflora Engler & Irmscher (1919). *Kabschia*. Flowers single, more or less sessile. Leaves obovate to 6 × 2.5 mm, single lime pore. Petals white, to 5 × 4.5 mm. Anthers red-brown. 3900–4800m, Sikkim, Bhutan, Tibet, Sichuan. Yunnan, Xinjiang. May be in cultivation.

Saxifraga subternata Harry Smith (1958). *Kabschia* (closely linked to *Tetrameridium* and possibly of hybrid origin). Dense cushions, flower stems to 0.3 cm, flowers solitary. Leaves in alternate decussate pairs (ternate whorls up stem), obelliptic to 4 × 2 mm, 3–7 lime pores, apex slightly acute. Petals white, 7 × 3 mm, anthers black. 3400–3500m, Tibet. Not in cultivation.

Saxifraga subverticillata Boissier (1872) [incl. *S. colchica* Albow (1895)]. *Kabschia*. Basal rosettes with elongated stems (to 4 cm) leading to new secondary rosettes and then to flowering stems to 4 cm, 6–9 flowers. Leaves linear, pointed, to 13 × 1 mm. Petals yellow, to 4 × 1.3 mm, slightly longer than sepals, stamens much longer than petals. Anthers yellow. Scarcely in cultivation; plants are very difficult to propagate (and to maintain). Caucasus—on dripping rocks.

Saxifraga thiantha Harry Smith (1958). *Kabschia*. Flower stems to 3 cm, solitary flowers. Leaves ovate-linear 7 × 1.7 mm, apex rounded, 3–5 pores. Petals light yellow, circular-obovate 8 × 5 mm. Anthers yellow. 3900–4700m, Bhutan. Not in cultivation.

Saxifraga tombeanensis Boissier (1869). *Kabschia*. Tight cushion. Flower stems to 8 cm, 1–5 flowers. Slow-growing foliage, rosette leaves oblong-lanceolate to 4 × 1.5 mm. Flowers large for foliage, petals white, to 14 × 7.5 mm. Anthers yellow. Italian Alps. Straightforward in cultivation but slow.

Saxifraga unguipetala Engler & Irmscher (1912) [incl. *S. kansuensis* Mattfeld (1930)]. *Kabschia*. Shoots 5 cm, single flowers on stems to 3.7 cm. Rosette leaves spathulate-oblong to 9.5 × 2 mm. Petals white typically 6.5 × 3.5 mm, 6–9 veins. Anthers yellow. 3200–4300m, Gansu, Hubei. Almost certainly not in cultivation (despite labels).

Saxifraga unifoveolata. See *S. scleropoda*.

Saxifraga vacillans Harry Smith (1958). *Kabschia* (closely linked to *Tetrameridium* and possibly of hybrid origin). Flower stems to 2 cm, 1–2 flowers. Leaves 5 × 2 mm, opposite at base—alternate on vigorous stems. Petals white, to 6 × 4 mm, anthers black. 4050m, Bhutan. Not in cultivation.

Saxifraga vandellii Sternberg (1810). *Kabschia*. Flower stems to 8 cm, 3–8 flowers. Very tight, spiny grey-green leaves to 10 × 2.5 mm. Petals white, to 10 × 7 mm. Anthers yellow. Italian Alps. Rare in cultivation, very slow.

Saxifraga vvedenskyi Abdullaeva (1974). *Kabschia*. Stems with 6–7 flowers. Leaves oblinear to 5 × 1.7 mm. Petals white, 5 × 5.6 mm. Anthers yellow. Tien Shan. Closely related to *S. alberti* of which it may be lax, white-flowered variant.

Saxifraga wendelboi Schönbeck-Temesy (1967). *Kabschia*. Hard cushion, flower stems to 6 cm, usually 3–4 flowers. Leaves oblong, spathulate, to 6 × 3 mm. Flowers open flat, petals often reflex slightly, white sometimes turning pink to 10 × 8 mm. Anthers yellow. Iran.

Note: *S. ramulosa* Wallich (1830). Poorly defined and

understood. Royle looked at this plant and his plant matched *S. roylei*. Note also that *S. brevicaulis*, *S. sessiliflora* and *S. williamsii* have been transferred to section *Ciliatae* subsection *Rosulares*.

Wild Hybrids

S. ×akinfievii Galushko & Kudriashova (1967). (*S. dinnikii* × *S. juniperifolia*) (*S. ×oettingenii* Galushko & Kudriashova). Flowers 2–7, pink-yellow or orange. Hybrid from the central Caucasus.

S. ×biasolettoi Sündermann (1915). (*S. federici-augusti* × *S. sempervivum*). Intermediate between parents with very small dark red flowers in a congested head of flowers. Taller than *S. sempervivum* with longer leaves, narrrower than in *S. federici-augusti*. Produced as an artificial hybrid by Sündermann in early 20th century. More recently discovered by J. Bürgel in the Macedonian–Albanian border area.

S. ×columpoda Holubec (2001). (*S. columnaris* × *S. scleropoda*). Flowers orange-pink, sometimes pale, not opening wide. Hybrid from the Caucasus first collected in 1996. 2000–3000m.

S. ×dinninaris Holubec (2001). (*S. columnaris* × *S. dinnikii*). Flowers red-pink. Petals less serrate and corrugated than *S. dinnikii*, foliage larger than *S. columnaris*. Hybrid from the Caucasus first collected in 1996.

S. ×gyoerffiana Wagner (1935). (*S. sempervivum* × *S. scardica*). There is some doubt over this hybrid.

S. ×karacardica J. Bürgel (1995). (*S. karadzicensis* × *S. scardica*). Close to *S. karadzicensis* but with larger petals and 3–5 pores (rather than 1). Macedonia. Until *S. karadzicenis* was separated from *S. marginata* plants would have been treated as *S. ×wehrhahnii*.

S. ×luteo-purpurea Lapeyrouse (1801). (*S. aretioides* × *S. media*). Very variable. Sündermann described 11 nothomorphs but collections in the 1990s showed that the hybrids in the wild display the whole spectrum of combinations from one parent to the other, often not matching any of these. Plants may have single flowers on short or taller stems or multiple flowers on taller stems, and may have yellow to orange flowers. None of these 11 appears still to be in cultivation: although plants are in circulation as *S. ×luteo-purpurea* 'Aurantiaca' and occasionally as 'Erubescens', these do not match the nothomorphs nm. *aurantiaca* and nm. *erubescens* that Sündermann

described. Collections by A. Young at Saleix in 1990 are in cultivation under collection numbers AA7, AA12 and SA17. Pyrenees.

S. ×tukuchensis J. Bürgel (1998). (*S. andersonii* × *S. hypostoma*). Common in central Nepal where the parental species grow in close proximity. Most plants in cultivation as *S. hypostoma* are *S. ×tukuchensis*, similar to *S. hypostoma* in general form, but rather larger less ciliate and certainly much easier in cultivation. Some examples of this hybrid are much closer to *S. andersonii*.

S. ×wehrhahnii Horný, Soják & Webr (1974). (*S. marginata* × *S. scardica*). Intermediate between parents. Produced as an artificial hybrid by Sündermann. More recently discovered by J. Bürgel in the wild in Macedonia. See also *S. ×karacardica*.

Other hybrids have been found but not formally described and published:

S. andersonii × *S. quadrifaria*. Nepal. Jan Bürgel equates *S. alpigena* with this cross and intends further publication on the subject, recasting this as *S. ×alpigena*.

S. cinerea × *S. poluniniana*. Stems to 5 cm, 1–5 white or pink flowers. Found by Bürgel and Roberts at 2800m, Nepal. Artificial examples of this cross have been produced by John Mullaney. Jan Bürgel suggests that both *S. staintonii* and *S. micans* are examples of this cross.

It is also probable that a wild hybrid of *S. andersonii* and *S. pulvinaria* will be named by Jan Bürgel.

Two intersectional hybrids and one intersubsectional hybrid have been described although there is some doubt about each.

S. ×degeniana Handel-Mazetti & Wagner (1935). (*S. glabella* × *S. spruneri*). If correct this is a very interesting hybrid between species putatively in sections *Porphyrion* and *Saxifraga*.

S. ×paxii Engler & Irmscher (1919). (*S. corymbosa* × *S. paniculata*). If correct this is an intersectional hybrid between species from sections *Porphyrion* and *Ligulatae*.

S. ×saleixiana Gaussen & LeBrun (1962). (*S. aretioides* × *S. caesia*). An interesting but doubtful hybrid from the Pyrenees which would be the only one between a *Kabschia* and a *Squarrosae* species.

7 · Dwarf Cushion Saxifrage Hybrids

Section *Porphyrion 2 – Porophyllum* Hybrids

The hybrids derived from various crosses between subsection *Porophyllum* (*Kabschia*, *Engleria* and *Tetrameridium*) species include some of the most charming of all cushion plants with flowers and foliage contributing to their perfect proportions. Apart from white they come in every shade of yellow through to red, purple and mauve, from the darkest of carmine to the palest blush, from strong mustard-yellow to subtle lemons, and in ranges of pastels from peach through salmon to apricot and buff. And the petal colour is often intriguingly contrasted with the colour of the nectary ring. While many cushion plants are difficult in cultivation these hybrid saxifrages present few difficulties and there are cultivars well suited to the open rock garden, as well as exquisite and tiny cultivars only in scale in a trough or pot.

The Early Crosses

It is over 125 years since the first artificial *Porophyllum* hybrids started to appear in gardens. Sometime after 1880, a seedling saxifrage which had appeared in the Melrose garden of John Brack Boyd, flowered for the first time. Its flowers were pale yellow and it became clear that it was the result of a cross between the white-flowered *Saxifraga burseriana*, which it was near, and the strong yellow *S. aretioides*, which was the only yellow-flowered saxifrage in the garden. This was the first hybrid saxifrage from this section of the genus to appear in cultivation.

There are some wild hybrids in Europe and in the Caucasus, and recent work has suggested the possibility of very extensive hybridization in some parts of the Himalaya. But, obviously, plants hybridize only when they flower at times which overlap and when they grow in close proximity, and plants may be separated by vertical distance (altitude) as much as horizontal distance. John Brack Boyd's was the

A selection of cultivars
from some early crosses.

Top row (left to right):
S. *ferdinandi-coburgi*,
S. ×*borisii* 'Becky
Foster', 'Sofia', 'Josef
Mánes', 'Marianna'.

Middle: S. ×*apiculata*
'Albert Einstein',
'Gregor Mendel', 'Alba'.

Bottom: S. ×*elisabethae*
'Vesna', 'Sylva', 'Boston
Spa', 'Mrs Leng'.

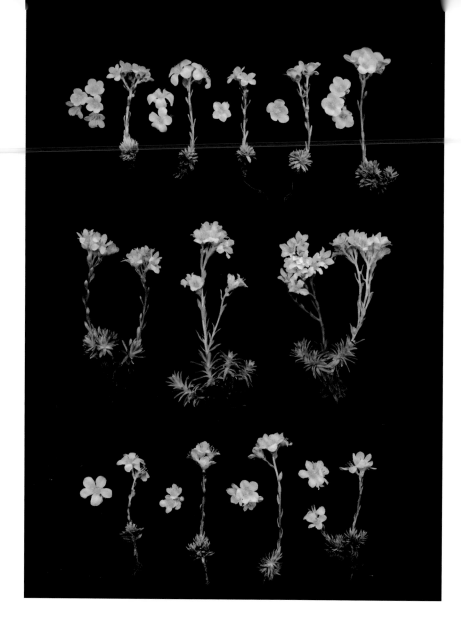

first known seedling that had appeared because of the propinquity of *Porophyllum* saxifrage species which had previously been kept apart. This Scottish hybrid, which was named *Saxifraga* ×*boydii*, was much later given the cultivar name 'Old Britain', so it is S. ×*boydii* 'Old Britain' (although, since it is a Scottish plant, 'North Britain' following the usage of Walter Scott might have been more appropriate). When it produced seed the resulting seedlings included two which were named after the houses of John Brack Boyd and his brother William Brack Boyd. These two saxifrages, 'Cherrytrees' and 'Faldonside' respectively, were put into circulation around 1890, and although 'Old Britain' is pretty scarce in cultivation, 'Cherrytrees' is still available and 'Faldonside' is a plant which looks good in any company.

The other very early cross, around 1894, was Franz Sündermann's original cross (*Saxifraga* ×*apiculata* 'Gregor Mendel') a vigorous plant which will produce large cushions and has tall stems with heads of primrose-yellow flowers. This deliberate cross was a wonderful starting point for what was to come.

Sündermann was the most important early hybridizer of *Porophyllum* saxifrages, being responsible for 25 of the 35 different crosses of *Porophyllum* species which had been produced by 1915. Of the 35 crosses some 19 involved two *Kabschia* species, resulting in over 44 different named cultivars, all of them involving at least one of just four species: *S. burseriana*, *S. marginata*, *S. aretioides* and *S. ferdinandi-coburgi*. The resulting series of classic cultivars such as *S.* ×*elisabethae*, *S.* ×*borisii*, *S.* ×*eudoxiana*, *S.* ×*grata*, and *S.* ×*paulinae* all hold their place today.

Another six of these early crosses were of pairs of *Engleria* species, with all of the possible combinations of *Saxifraga federici-augusti*, *S. sempervivum*, *S. stribrnyi* and *S. corymbosa* being created.

If the *Kabschia–Kabschia* and *Engleria–Engleria* crosses filled in what seemed to be obvious gaps between the plants available from the wild, the crosses between the two subsections really add another dimension to the framework. One hybrid between the subsections, *Saxifraga* ×*luteo-purpurea*, was already known from the wild where *S. aretioides* and *S. media* grow together in the Pyrenees. Sündermann set about the challenge of crossing *Kabschia* and *Engleria* species with much the same thoroughness that he also showed in the crosses of *Kabschia–Kabschia* and *Engleria–Engleria*. The yellow-flowered species such as *S. ferdinandi-coburgi* and *S. aretioides* were crossed with the branched *Engleria* species *S. stribrnyi*, as were the white-flowered *S. marginata*, *S. burseriana* and *S. tombeanensis*. From these he got plants with more or less branched stems of small orange, yellow or pink flowers.

Other *Engleria* species were also used: *Saxifraga media* was crossed with *S. vandellii*; *S. sempervivum* was crossed with *S. burseriana*; and *S. federici-augusti* was crossed with *S. marginata* and *S. burseriana*; and all of these give us pale pink through to darker violet-pink flowers. As well as these interspecific crosses Sündermann also made the first use of the wild *S.* ×*luteo-purpurea* as a parent. In combination with *S. stribrnyi*, it produced *S.* ×*stuartii*, one of the cultivars having pink and the other yellow petals.

Alongside Sündermann's remarkable efforts, a number of other gardeners and nurserymen produced a few crosses, but the most significant cross came from Walter Irving. In 1899 seed came back to Kew of a *Kabschia* saxifrage with pale cool violet-pink flowers. This newly discovered species, *Saxifraga lilacina*, which was not formally described and named till 1904, was crossed with *S. burseriana* and the resulting plant, which we have as *S.* ×*irvingii* 'Walter Irving', would be the first of the plants which were produced in the search for larger pink flowers. This remained alone before 1915 but would be much more significant after the Great War.

Kabschia and *Engleria* Hybrids between the Wars

The hybrids produced between the wars clearly show both the enormous influence of *Saxifraga lilacina* and the much greater role taken by English growers of saxifrages. Before the First World War the pre-eminent figure had been Franz

Saxifraga stribrnyi
(left), S. corymbosa
(middle) and
S. ×schottii 'Tabor',
a hybrid between
them.

Saxifraga ×edithae
'Bridget' (S. marginata ×
S. stribrnyi). Photograph
Winton Harding.

Saxifraga ×boeckeleri
'Armida' (S. ferdinandi-
coburgi × S. stribrnyi).

Sündermann from his nursery at Lindau on the shores of the Bodensee and
although there were contributions from others such as Kellerer, Heinrich and
Hörhammer on the Continent, and Boyd, Jenkins and Irving in Britain, these
were far more limited. In the 1920s things would change quite significantly. While
Sündermann still contributed to the new plants produced, other growers become
significant and none more than Russell Vincent Prichard through the productions
of his Riverslea Nursery until the 1930s, when he emigrated to Australia.

Walter Irving's innovative cross of *Saxifraga lilacina* with *S. burseriana* showed
what might be done. Prichard crossed *S. lilacina* with *S. marginata*, *S. obtusa*,
S. tombeanensis and *S. stribrnyi*. The cross with *S. burseriana* was not ignored, but
repeated more than once, adding to the list of *S. ×irvingii* cultivars we have today.

But the great breakthrough was the cross of *Saxifraga lilacina* with the Pyrenean hybrid *S. ×luteo-purpurea*. The oldest example of this cross is *S.* 'Myra' which
was produced rather mysteriously by Reginald Farrer. It only flowered after he
had left for the 1920 plant-collecting expedition to China on which he died. It was

Two of Russell Vincent Prichard's hybrids of *Saxifraga lilacina* and *S. stribrnyi*: *S. ×hornibrookii* 'Coningsby Queen' and 'Romeo' in Ray Woodliffe's collection, showing the extra-large flowers of 'Coningsby Queen'.

Prichard who took this cross and pursued it, crossing *S. lilacina* with different forms of *S. ×luteo-purpurea* to give a range of mauve-red hybrids which now go under the designation *S. ×anglica* and which are among the most charming and beautiful of all *Porophyllum* hybrids. Alongside these, Prichard also crossed *S. ×luteo-purpurea* with *S. ×boydii* 'Faldonside', one of Boyd's seedlings from the original 'Old Britain', and produced first 'C. M. Prichard' and then, through a slightly different cross, 'Iris Prichard'. While the former is a very rare and almost extinct cultivar, the latter is still readily available and quite delightful.

Prichard's other great productions were of 'Robin Hood' and 'Mrs Gertie Prichard' which seem to have involved the crossing of one of the *S. ×anglica* cultivars with *S. burseriana*. These two hybrids, the first of the *S. ×megaseaeflora* crosses, were the first to have four species in their ancestry—*S. aretioides*, *S. burseriana*, *S. lilacina* and *S. media*—and these same species would be combined in different ways in the future to add to this range of large-flowered hybrids.

While the English were concentrating on hybrids involving *Saxifraga lilacina*, Sündermann spent more of his time in using *S. sancta* and *S. pseudolaevis* to extend the range of yellow hybrids and, by crossing each with *S. stribrnyi*, ones with stems of small orange-yellow flowers. He also produced a handful of other crosses, the most significant being *S. ×landaueri* with tall stems of largish pale pink flowers.

The Post-War Years

The disruption caused by the Second World War to the lists of *Porophyllum* hybrids was not as dramatic as it was to those of the mossy saxifrages but it was some years before exciting new crosses were made. A handful of cultivars seem to have been lost during the war, and *Saxifraga ×anglica* 'Winifred', much used in hybridizing in recent years, was apparently reduced to a single plant of just four rosettes.

Almost all of the new crosses made till the early 1970s were complex crosses, like the later crosses of Russell Vincent Prichard, involving a previous cross as at least one of the parents. The most prolific of the producers in these years

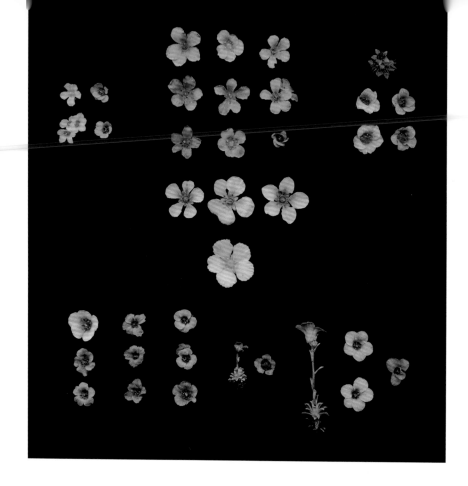

was Lincoln Foster at Millstream in Connecticut, who produced three series of hybrids: the white *S.×fallsvillagensis* cultivars and the yellow *S.×lincolni-fosteri* and *S.×millstreamiana* cultivars. Another of his crosses was 'Moon Beam' which, like 'Penelope' from Rob Dunford in England, came under the cross *S.×boydilacina*, and Czech growers continued to expand the lovely large-flowered pastels of *S.×megaseaeflora*.

A new discovery

While all these new hybrids were being produced it seemed as if this was a field that had seen its best days, or at least that it was the perfect moment to chart what had been done. In Czechoslovakia, Radvan Horný with Karel Mirko Webr were involved in producing their study of all the *Porophyllum* species and hybrids, first published in Czech as *Nejkrásnější lomikameny*. Subsequently this was published in a much-expanded form, with John Byam-Grounds, in English as *Porophyllum Saxifrages*. This stunning work has detailed descriptions of every known *Kabschia*, *Engleria* and *Tetrameridium* species and all the wild or garden hybrids between them. It is a book which any enthusiast for almost anything would appreciate, with a thoroughness that has to be seen to be appreciated—it also has the most beautifully printed cloth cover of any book I know. Among the hundreds they documented was the new cross from Lincoln Foster, *S.×wendelacina* (*S. lilacina* and *S. wendelboi*) one of his later crosses, introduced in 1974. This might not seem like much of a break, but it was the first new primary combination (one involving

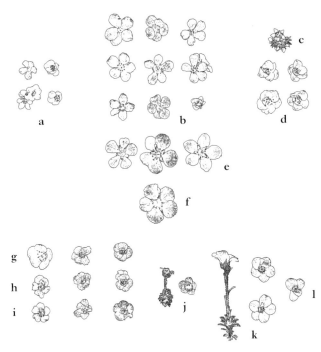

Selection of hybrids and species (left to right):

Top left group (**a**) (2 rows): 'Lužníce', 'Sázava'.

Top middle (**b**) (3 rows): 'Peach Melba', 'Bohemia', 'Allendale Amber'.

Top right (**c**): *S. retusa* top; 4 below (**d**): *S. oppositifolia* 'Greenslacks Valerie'.

Middle above (**e**): 'Vladana', 'Jupiter', 'Mrs Gertie Prichard'; below (**f**): *S. burseriana* 'Snowdon'.

Bottom left group, top row (**g**): 'Allendale Ballet', 'Maria Callas', 'Dora Ross'; middle row (**h**): 'Allendale Ruby', 'Maria Callas', 'Dora Ross'; bottom row (**i**): 'Allendale Ruby', 'Peter Burrow', 'Pearl Rose'.

Bottom middle (**j**): *S. sp.* McB1377; bottom right (**k**): 'Anne Beddall' (3 specimens); single far right (**l**): 'Nancye.

just two species) of *Porophyllum* species since the 1930s and it opened up a new route for hybridizers—the use of new species which were coming into cultivation from the Caucasus and the Himalayas. So just as the story seemed to have been told more or less for all time, the very first trickle was appearing which would lead to the deluge of hybrids seen since the mid-1970s.

One of the results of the publication of Horný's work was that during the 1980s and on into the 1990s specialists in England and Czechoslovakia built up collections of these species and hybrids about which they previously had little information. At the very end of the 1980s the Saxifraga Group was formed, later to

Saxifraga ×*boydilacina* 'Penelope'. Photograph Ken McGregor.

transmute into the Saxifrage Society under the presidency of Winton Harding. These enabled specialists to exchange a growing flow of information and plants, and a network of enthusiasts began to make information about every new development rapidly available through the *Saxifrage Magazine*.

New Species, New Crosses

The most important development since the publication of *Porophyllum Saxifrages* has been the use of a whole range of new species. Up till the late 1980s, the only Himalayan *Porophyllum* saxifrage which had been used in the production of hybrids was *Saxifraga lilacina*. Since 1990, hybrids have been produced involving *S. poluniniana*, *S. stolitzkae*, *S. hypostoma*, *S. meeboldii*, *S. andersonii*, *S. lowndesii*, *S. cinerea*, *S. georgei*, *S. pulvinaria* and *S. quadrifaria*, and in a number of cases the hybrids are much more common and easier than the parental species. While some of the crosses have been the result of calculated attempts to achieve particular sorts of plants—vigorous, free-flowering, deep pink- and red-flowered plants—others have been the result of much more scatter-gun approaches. The most significant of the Himalayan species in the production of new crosses have been *S. poluniniana*, *S. cinerea* and *S. georgei*.

Saxifraga poluniniana

This is the most obviously successful parent among the new Himalayan introductions. Its habits of rapid growth and free-flowering are qualities passed on to most of its offspring (although it can also pass on a tendency to expire in very hot weather). Winton Harding led the way when he crossed it with the old *S. ×anglica* 'Winifred' to produce 'Red Poll', the first of the easy-going, free-flowering, pink-red *S. ×poluanglica* hybrids. Others growers to make this same cross have included Brian Burrow, Jan Bürgel, Ray Fairbairn, Malcolm McGregor and David Walkey. With nearly thirty named cultivars now on the list the grower has plenty of choice, but 'Red Poll', 'Tvůj Úspěch', 'Tvůj Úsměv', 'Miluj Mne', 'Frank Sinatra' and 'Maria Callas' each bring their own charms—they are all beautiful. Others followed with crosses being made with *S. burseriana* and *S. ×luteopurpurea* and with *S. lowndesii* to give the Vanessa Group.

Saxifraga cinerea and Saxifraga stolitzkae

In the same way that he was the first to use *Saxifraga poluniniana* as a parent, so Winton Harding was the first to use *S. cinerea*. Again crossing it with 'Winifred', this time he produced 'Nancye' with flowers a cerise version of those of *S. cinerea* on the same tall thin dark red stems. Other crosses using *S. cinerea*, in particular 'Allendale Angel' and 'Orion', both from the cross *S. ferdinandi-coburgi* × *S. cinerea*, are both pretty but have had limited success.

More recently John Mullaney has produced a series of very pretty cultivars which make up the Concinna Group and come from the cross of *Saxifraga cinerea* with the Caucasian *S. dinnikii*. All are named after Scottish mountains and most have pale pink flowers, except for 'Ben Loyal' which has much stronger coloured flowers. Both the latter and any of the former should be part of any collection.

Saxifraga stolitzkae has been used less often, but again the first cross involved 'Winifred' producing the *S. ×baccii* hybrids, with both Sergio Bacci and Malcolm McGregor producing the cross. Some other crosses have involved crossing *S. stolitzkae* with *S. ×malbyana* and *S. ×borisii*.

Saxifraga georgei

Following Winton Harding's use of *Saxaifraga poluniniana*, Brian Burrow recognized the potential of the tiny opposite-leaved Himalayan species *S. georgei* as a parent. Again using 'Winifred', he produced outstanding plants (*S. ×lismorensis*) the most widespread of which remain 'Lismore Carmine' and 'Lismore Pink' with their mats of small foliage studded with small intense flowers. More recently Ray Fairbairn has favoured this cross although he has also used 'Quarry Wood' rather than 'Winifred' as the *S. ×anglica* parent in many of his crosses. His *S. ×lismorensis* 'Allendale Bravo' stands out.

Another plant that should be mentioned here is *Saxifraga* 'Gothenburg', which first circulated as *S. georgei* × *S. ×grata* 'Gratoides', apparently coming from Gothenburg Botanic Gardens. Although there have subsequently been other such crosses, such as the crosses with *S. aretioides* ('Allendale Bonny', 'Allendale Chick' and 'Allendale Czech') which are nice plants, 'Gothenburg' remains the best of the yellow-flowered offspring from *S. georgei*. It has also been crossed with *S. media* to give 'Allendale Banshee'. Among the very best new cultivars are the white 'Coolock Gem', and 'Coolock Kate' with striking pink flowers, paler at the centre. These are two seedlings of 'Myriad', itself a seedling of *S. georgei*, probably crossed with *S. poluniniana*. The brand-new 'Coolock Jean' is an attractive seedling of 'Coolock Kate'.

Equivalent efforts with other very small Himalayan species, *Saxifraga quadrifaria* and *S. alpigena*, have proved less robust. Among others *S. ×proximae* 'Květy Coventry' (translated as "Coventry Flowers") and 'Slzy Coventry' (translated as "Coventry Tears") have small pink-red flowers, and *S. ×quagrata* 'Sirius Alfa' has yellow flowers. A cross of *S. quadrifaria* with *S. ×hardingii* has been named 'Sergio Bacci'.

Saxifraga ×poluanglica 'Goldeneye'.

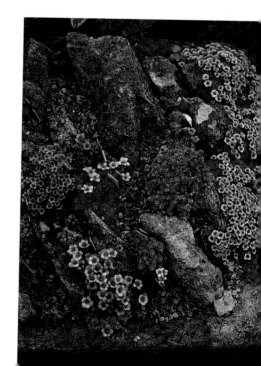

Saxifraga ×lismorensis 'Lismore Pink' is a good plant in a trough (right), with 'Lismovre Carmine' (far left) and *Saxifraga ×anglica* 'Myra Cambria' (bottom).

Saxifraga pulvinaria does not have opposite leaves but is another one of the very small-rosetted Himalayan species and it has also been used to give *S.* ×*pulvilacina* 'Niobe' with violet-pink flowers.

Saxifraga lowndesii and others

For the hybridizers, one of the great hopes from the Himalayas was *Saxifraga lowndesii*, introduced by Ron McBeath from Nepal, which has large, more or less stemless, lilac-pink to mauve-purple flowers. The foliage is soft and rather loose and it is not easy to maintain through the summer, easily succumbing to heat and even temporary drought. Despite this problem, which can make crosses involving *S. lowndesii* slightly temperamental—needing shade rather than full sun—a number are beautiful. Jan Bürgel's Beat Group and Blues Group crosses are wonderful as are 'Cio-Cio-San' and 'Marilyn Monroe', both in the Vanessa Group. All of these are in a range of rich pinks and mauve-purples, but a handful of plants such as 'Brimstone' from a cross with *S. aretioides* have rich warm yellow flowers. All the crosses have more or less stemless flowers. Other crosses include ones with *S. burseriana* ('Harbinger'), *S.* sp. SEP22 ('Antonio Vivaldi'), *S. diapensioides* ('Tahireh'), and *S.* ×*megaseaeflora* ('Johann Wol Goethe' and 'Golem').

Relatively few of the other Himalayan species have been much exploited. Sergio Bacci used *Saxifraga stolitzkae* to produce fairly robust cultivars grouped under *S.* ×*baccii*, *S.* Firenze Group and *S.* Renaissance Group. Ray Fairbairn has produced crosses using *S. andersonii*, *S. matta-florida* and *S. hypostoma* (or more probably its hybrid *S.* ×*tukuchensis*) to produce a number of Allendale cultivars such as 'Allendale Ruby', 'Allendale Garnet' and 'Allendale Vert'. One other Himalayan hybrid of note is that of *S. meeboldii*, which is barely in cultivation, with *S. poluniniana* to produce the Safran Group which carries a faint echo of the sweet lemon scent for which *S. meeboldii* is unique among *Porophyllum* saxifrages.

Other crosses involving various Himalayan species include 'Allendale Ballet', 'Allendale Dream', 'Allendale Gremlin', 'Frederik Chopin', 'Paul Rubens' and 'Theseus', all involving at least one of the Swedish Expedition to Pakistan collections, 'Allendale Fairy' (*S. lilacina* × *S. lolaensis*), and 'Marco Polo' (*S. pulchra* ACE2400 × *S.* sp. ACE2401).

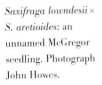

Saxifraga lowndesii × *S. aretioides*: an unnamed McGregor seedling. Photograph John Howes.

Central Asian crosses

The only *Porophyrion* species from central Asia used in new crosses has been *Saxifraga alberti* from the Tien Shan (rather than the Himalaya) which was first used to produce *S.* ×*caroliquarti* 'Ivana', and later *S.* ×*cimgani* 'Harry Smith'. Both are plants for containers; the latter is easier, but neither is indispensible.

The new Caucasians

The great concentration on new Himalayan crosses has recently started to give way to an interest in the range of trans-Caucasian and Iranian species. Up till 1975 only *Saxifraga kotschyi* (from Turkey rather than the Caucasus proper) and *S. pseudolaevis* had been used in crosses. Next up was *S. subverticillata* crossed with *S. lilacina* to give 'Radvan Horný', a pretty plant but one which can suffer badly from aphid attacks. It was the Czech expedition of 1996, which collected *S. columnaris* and *S. dinnikii* as well as a range of other species and wild hybrids, which really changed the landscape. The result of the introductions of *S. columnaris* and *S. dinnikii* has been a handful of plants with pink–mauve–lilac flowers. My favourites are John Mullaney's crosses in the Concinna Group discussed under *S. cinerea*. The best of the other crosses has to be the large-flowered white or palest pink *S.* ×*caroli-langii* 'Verona' (*S. dinnikii* × *S. marginata*) christened after the old Roman name for Beroun in the Czech Republic where the Second International Seminar of the Saxifrage Society was held in 2004. Another attractive cross from Karel Lang is 'John Byam-Grounds' from a cross of *S. dinnikii* and *S. stribrnyi*. These all suggest that *S. dinnikii* will provide us with further handsome plants.

The other great development is Karel Lang's use of *Saxifraga kotschyi* to produce a range of *Porophyllum* cultivars with brighter red flowers in the orange–vermilion–scarlet range rather than the cerise–maroon part of the red spectrum. Crossing *S. kotschyi* with *S. lilacina* (and its hybrids with *S. poluninana* and *S. subverticillata*) has given the Impressio Group, Conspecta Group and Decora Group with cultivars named after painters. Any one of these has similar qualities and Lang has many other promising *S. kotschyi* crosses among which are two crosses with *S. columnaris* ('Bohemian Karst' and 'Moravian Karst') and one with *S.* ×*megaseaeflora* 'Krákatit' ('Joyce Carruthers').

A large range of new hybrids involving either *Saxifraga columnaris* or *S. dinnikii* is likely to come into commerce. Oldrich Maixner has crossed *S.* ×*dinninaris* with each of *S. ferdinandi-coburgi*, *S. kotschyi* and *S. sempervivum* to give 'Bancis', 'Electra' and 'Kirke'; Karel Lang has produced 'Tromsø' (*S. poluniniana* × *S. dinnikii*) and 'Christian Huygens' (*S.* ×*luteo-purpurea* × *S.* ×*columpoda*). Others include Maixner's 'Merlin' (*S. scleropoda* × *S. clivorum*) and Ray Fairbairn's 'Allendale Grace' (*S. columnaris* × *S. lilacina*). Another cultivar which may be of great interest is the reported cross by Oldrich Maixner of *S. columnaris* with *S. spruneri* ('Sapho').

Top to bottom:
Saxifraga cinerea,
S. 'Nancye', *S.* [Concinna Group] 'Beinn Alligin',
S. dinnikii.

Out of Iran

There are three species from Iran which seem to have provided a small number of crosses: *Saxifraga wendelboi*, *S. iranica* and *S. ramsarica*. *Saxifraga wendelboi* was the first to be used in the 1970s in the production of *S.* ×*wendelacina* and Ray Fairbairn has used this in a number of other crosses, most notably in *S.* ×*rayei* 'Allendale Snow' which is slow, with spiny grey-green leaves and white flowers on tall stems. Other hybrids involving *S. wendelboi* include 'Donatello', 'Jocelynne Bacci', 'Allendale Billows', 'Allendale Desire', 'Allendale Envoy' and 'Allendale Epic' as well as the Swing Group.

Saxifraga iranica has also been used by Fairbairn and *S. ramsarica* has been used by Fairbairn and by McGregor but none of these has led to plants which are irresistible. The best of the plants here is 'Cumulus', a free-flowering plant from Ron Beeston with large white flowers which is probably a seedling of *S. ramsarica* rather than *S. iranica* as was first suggested.

Saxifraga [Impressio Group] 'Claude Monet' in Karel Lang's alpine house. Photograph Paul Kennett.

There have been a few hybrids involving *Saxifraga ramsarica* which have large single flowers, including 'Cumulus', 'Nimbus', 'Allendale Dance', 'Allendale Divine', 'Allendale Ghost', 'Marie' and 'Persian Primrose'.

The new Europeans

With so much attention being paid to Himalayan and Caucasian saxifrages in the new crosses it might come as a surprise to find some obvious gaps in the range of European crosses which were carried out before the First World War, with two new primary crosses being created since 1996. The first of these is the *Kabschia–Engleria* cross *Saxifraga* ×*izari* (*S. aretioides* × *S. sempervivum*) producing plants with tight rosettes and arched stems with very small dull yellow-orange petals. I have not found either of the cultivars easy to grow well. The other primary cross shows the extraordinary gaps that can be overlooked. Crossing *S. aretioides* and *S. marginata*, both of which were used extensively before 1915, produces plants (*S.* Milford Group) with solid cushions and strong stems, hanging their heads at first before raising their soft yellow flowers to the light. Sergio Bacci's 'Aldo Bacci' and Malcolm McGregor's 'Alice' are good plants.

What About the Bastards?

Throughout this account I have concentrated on the deliberate crosses with clearly established ancestries which have been carried out by British, German, American and Czech hybridizers since 1880. This helps make sense of the vast array of cultivars available today, but does not account for all the most beautiful plants. In some cases the parentage or ancestry of these other cultivars is partly known, in others there is no such knowledge—they are seedlings that have just turned up. Sometimes, like Boyd's discovery of the original yellow-flowered *S.* ×*boydii*, it is obvious what the parents were. In many cases they are unknown.

One of the difficulties associated with the creation of good hybrids is to produce a plant with clear characteristics of its own. Many are straightforward blends, retaining the clear sharp qualities of the parental species, while in others it seems as if the parents have been rubbed away, with those qualities which were loved in the first

Top to bottom:
Saxifraga [Milford
Group] 'Alice',
S. aretioides × S. cinerea
unnamed seedling,
S. 'Citronella'.

place being blurred beyond recognition. In a much smaller number the offspring go beyond their parentage creating something that is properly distinctive. This short finale looks at around a dozen hybrids which manage, despite their confused ancestry, to achieve just this transcendence. Each deserves a place in any collection.

Saxifraga 'Alpenglow' seems to have originated at the Alpenglow Gardens in Surrey, British Columbia. With small clumps of rosettes, tall stems (if anything slightly too tall) with beautifully poised large pale pink-buff flowers, this cultivar exhibits a shy poise which marks it out. It came to Horný from Lincoln Foster in the late 1970s and it was Horný, Soják & Webr who named it. It says much about the quality of 'Alpenglow' that among all these plants with obscure heritages it was the parent of one of my other choices: Lincoln Foster's 'Peach Blossom', which has almost stemless flowers. Not at all like its tall parent, *Saxifraga* 'Peach Blossom' has soft very pale warm pink flowers which are darker at the heart and have overlapping petals.

The search for a truly orange *Porophyllum* hybrid has been a long one. Before World War Two a plant called 'Tangerine' from Geoffrey Gould was said to be the best orange, but this seems to have been lost. A more recent cultivar, 'Magion', a deep orange but rather intractable plant from Frantisek Holenka in the mid-1970s, seemed to show how difficult the search was. Nevertheless the attempts continued. *Saxifraga* 'Bohemia' from Miroslav Kraus survives well on the rock garden. It has robust foliage with stems of strong orange flowers. Unfortunately, the colour derives from an overlay of red pigment over yellow, and the red fades rapidly to a straw colour. Not the most select of hybrids but one that holds its place as the most robust of all the orange *Porophyllum* hybrids, *Saxifraga* 'Má Vlast' is a sibling.

Winton Harding produced a number of wonderful hybrids including 'Red Poll', 'Nancye' and 'Winton', but there are three more of his seedlings which deserve attention: 'Lilac Time', 'Goring White' and 'Citronella'. *Saxifraga* 'Lilac Time' is a rather difficult plant with large lilac-pink flowers on tall stems, almost certainly with *S. marginata* 'Sorrento' as one parent. *Saxifraga* 'Goring White' seems to have one of the white-flowered Himalayan species such as *S. stolitzkae* or *S. andersonii* as one parent but the other is very obscure. Its pairs of white flowers have a typical Himalayan flower shape with a cupped centre but without stamens. To save the best for last, however: *Saxifraga* 'Citronella' has extremely well-formed, large, light yellow flowers, each petal beautifully rounded with a slightly recurved surface. There are up to about six flowers on each strong stem. The foliage is firm and the rosettes are nicely in proportion with the flowers. This is said to have been a seedling of 'Edgar Irmscher', and it seems likely that the other parent was *S. marginata* 'Sorrento'. *Saxifraga* 'Edgar Irmscher' is another plant with considerable charm but whose parentage is obscure. It originated with Sündermann's nursery and its tall flower stems over strong dark foliage carry up to about a dozen pale orange-yellow flowers with darker red-purple calyces.

Saxifraga 'Naarden' and 'Vecerní Hvězda' (translated as "Evening Star") are sister seedlings from Karel Lang. In this case we know their parentage. One parent is again *S. marginata* and the other is the small and difficult orange 'Magion'. This was a seedling of 'Winifred' but its other parent is obscure. This is a rather more deliberate production than most of the others here. Both the plants are first-class with tall multi-flowered stems over strong foliage, 'Vecerní Hvězda' with clear pale yellow flowers, 'Naarden' with the yellow flowers flushed with orange-pink.

Saxifraga 'Peach Melba', the final plant I would mention here, shows just how such seedlings may come about. It comes from David Victor and appeared in a batch of pots in which there had been no germination and which had been put aside for discarding. After removing the labels he noticed a seedling in one pot before emptying it, but it was impossible to determine which label had come from the pot. *Saxifraga* 'Peach Melba' is very similar in general appearance to 'Bohemia', which may be its parent, but the orange-red flowers are turned subtly to the colour of the blush on the skin as a peach and the name is a good one.

Although there are many dozens of other cultivars of obscure parentage, a few should be recorded here. With multiple yellow flowers are 'Vlasta', probably a Czech hybrid and a bit slow, 'Vltava' from Frantisek Holenka, which will cope on the rock garden, and 'Ken McGregor' from Winton Harding with robust foliage, one of the very earliest to flower and easy on the open rock garden. Others include 'Nugget' and 'Petra' with yellow flowers, and white-flowered 'Lidice', which is clearly linked to *S. marginata*.

Saxifraga 'Bohemia' in David Victor's alpine house. Photograph John Howes.

Saxifraga 'Naarden'.

Keeping Up

It's never possible to be completely up-to-date in a field where things are moving rapidly. *Porophyllum* hybrids have never appeared at a faster rate. This is partly the result of the changes in commercial horticulture. Most of the hybrids that appeared before 1939 were plants which made their way from commercial nurseries of which those of Russell Vincent Prichard and Franz Sündermann were the most important for *Porophyllum* hybrids. Sündermann's nursery still functions today and, to demonstrate their continuing place in saxifrage history, lists two new cultivars: 'Alpengarten Sündermann' and 'Rosemarie Paulmichl' (not to be confused with the much older and nice, little, but rather difficult cultivars 'Rosemarie' and 'Rosemarie Alba'). Meanwhile catalogues from Jakob Eschmann in Switzerland regularly list new cultivars that are rarely found elsewhere. More generally, however, since 1945 there has been a continual winnowing of the large nurseries interested in such plants. Increasingly, they have become the preserve of the small specialist nursery, often one-person operations. A handful of hybridizers produce nearly all of today's new plants. Taking over from Miroslav Kraus and Frantisek Holenka in the Czech Republic, Karel Lang is obviously the outstanding figure, with Jan Bürgel and Oldrich Maixner and others including Zdenek Dite adding smaller numbers of new crosses. Twenty years ago the most important British producers of new hybrids were Winton Harding, Sergio Bacci and Brian Burrow; more recently the most prolific producer of crosses has been Ray Fairbairn, and some of the crosses of John Mullaney and Ian Spencer are worth a place in any list.

Saxifraga 'Peach Melba'. Photograph Paul Kennett.

Growing *Porophyllum* Cultivars

The *Porophyllum* saxifrage hybrid cultivars include some of the most beautiful of all cushion plants. Some are only suitable for the alpine house, frame or trough but most are very hardy and very suitable for the open rock garden. The major requirement for all such plants is that drainage should be good and that there should be an adequate supply of water. The ideal is that of the mountain homes of the parental species with cool nights, strong winds, high light levels and plentiful rain. Least good are damp wet soils. Large-scale producers' practice of using peat-based composts allows rapid growth of a plant to fill a pot but renders it almost impossible to wean the plant out of its compost and on into any non-peaty or mix. Any plant grown in peat-based compost in a pot should be avoided unless it is going to be turned into cuttings.

One common question is why an apparently healthy *Porophyllum* cushion in the rock garden should develop dead brown patches. These dead patches are usually the result of over-exposure to strong summer sun, allied to insufficient moisture, and it is noticeable that these brown patches are usually on the side of the cushion facing south or southwest. In the mountains the bright sun heats the thinner air up less and there is therefore much more rapid cooling at night. One approach to the problem is to shade *Porophyllum* cushions in the summer, ideally by siting plants on the northeast side of the rockwork, getting shade at least part of the day. Another is to ensure that there is a regular supply of moisture. It is also important to recognize that different crosses have very different abilities to withstand full sun. In general terms the hybrids with smaller brighter yellow flowers stand up to the sun much better than those with smaller bright pink flowers. The small yellow crosses generally have either *Saxifraga sancta* or *S. ferdinandi-coburgi* in their parentage and these are species which themselves come from southern Europe. Crosses involving Himalayan species such as *S. poluniniana* or *S. georgei* (which are involved in most of the new small, rich pink or red hybrids) will need much more shade and moisture. Crosses with *S. lowndesii* need particularly shaded or cool positions.

All *Porophyllum* hybrid cultivars are clonal cultivars and are therefore only kept true by vegetative propagation through cuttings.

Flowering Times

The hybrid cultivars flower over a long period from midwinter to midspring. For me the earliest come into flower in January, or in an exceptional year in very late December. With my late-flowering hybrids and species only coming into flower in April, it is possible to have almost four months of flowering out of this group. For others, this chronology may be advanced or retarded by a week or two, or compressed in areas with particularly long deep winters which hold back the start of the flowering season.

Midwinter. The very first cultivars to flower are 'Maria Luisa' and 'Krasava' with 'Iris Prichard' and 'Karel Čapek' also usually coming into flower before the end of the month.

Late winter. February and March are the months in which most cultivars and species flower so the calendar gets very crowded. In the first half of February 'Galaxie', 'Nottingham Gold' and 'Winifred' are reliable and a number of the *S.* ×*poluanglica* cultivars are usually well into flower. The second half of February will have such cultivars as 'Cranbourne' and 'Riverslea', and by the end of the month the season is coming to its peak with 'Walter Irving' and 'Bridget', and many of the species especially, *S. burseriana*, coming into flower.

Porophyllum saxifrages in pots in the alpine house.

Early spring. At the beginning of March plants are coming into flower every day with such cultivars as 'Faldonside', 'Gregor Mendel', 'Alba' and 'Gold Dust', followed by 'Nancye' and 'Parcevalis'. By the middle of March *S. ferdinandi-coburgi* and many forms of *S. marginata* are flowering as well as hybrids such as 'Hocker Edge'. At the very end of the month *S. stolitzkae* is likely to be in flower.

Midspring. Early April will see such cultivars as 'Golden Prague' and *S.* ×*stuartii* 'Lutea' and species such as *S. corymbosa* still coming into flower. In the second half of April a handful of plants come into flower, with *S. spruneri* usually one of the last.

Section *Porphyrion* subsection *Porophyllum* Hybrids

Wild Hybrids

These are discussed in greater detail in Chapter 6.

Saxifraga ×*akinfievii* Galushko & Kudriashova (1967). (*S. dinnikii* × *S. juniperifolia*). Hybrid from the central Caucasus.

Saxifraga ×*biasolettoi* Sündermann (1915). (*S. federici-augusti* × *S. sempervivum*). Produced as an artificial hybrid by Sündermann. More recently discovered by J. Bürgel in the wild.

Saxifraga ×*columpoda* Holubec (2001). (*S. columnaris* × *S. scleropoda*). Hybrid from the Caucasus first collected in 1996.

Saxifraga ×*dinninaris* Holubec (2001). (*S. columnaris* × *S. dinnikii*). Hybrid from the Caucasus first collected in 1996.

Saxifraga ×*luteo-purpurea* Lapeyrouse (1801). (*S. aretioides* × *S. media*). Very variable. A number of nothomorphs have been described but collections in the 1990s showed that the hybrids in the wild cross the whole spectrum of combinations from one parent to the other, often not matching the described nothomorphs. Various forms are found in cultivation. There is an older plant under the name 'Aurantiaca' and collections by A. Young in 1990: AA7, AA12 and SA17.

Saxifraga ×*tukuchensis* J. Bürgel (1998). (*S. andersonii* × *S. hypostoma*). Common in central Nepal where the parental species grow in close proximity. Most plants in cultivation as *S. hypostoma* are *S.* ×*tukuchensis*.

Saxifraga ×*wehrhahnii* Horný, Soják & Webr (1974). (*S. marginata* × *S. scardica*). Produced as an artificial hybrid by Sündermann. More recently discovered by J. Bürgel in the wild.

Other wild hybrids which have been described are:

Saxifraga ×*degeniana* Handel-Mazetti & Wagner (1935). (*S. glabella* × *S. spruneri*). If correct this is a very interesting hybrid between species putatively in sections *Porphyrion* and *Saxifraga*.

Saxifraga ×*gyoerffiana* Wagner (1935). (*S. sempervivum* × *S. scardica*). There is some doubt over the status of this hybrid.

Saxifraga ×*karacardica* J. Bürgel (1995). (*S. karadzicensis* × *S. scardica*). In cultivation.

Saxifraga ×*paxii* Engler & Irmscher (1919). (*S. corymbosa* × *S. paniculata*). If correct this is an intersectional hybrid between species from sections *Porphyrion* and *Ligulatae*.

Saxifraga ×*saleixiana* Gaussen & LeBrun (1962). (*S. aretioides* × *S. caesia*). An interesting hybrid from the Pyrenees which is the only one between a *Kabschia* and a *Squarrosae* species.

A hybrid of *S. poluniniana* and *S. cinerea* has also been recorded and collected in Nepal by Jan Bürgel and Tim Roberts.

Artificial Crosses

Each section of the list below groups cultivars according to when the cross was first made. Details of date and raiser are given for the original cultivar distributed and published in each group. Cultivars which are believed to be extinct have been omitted here and included in the Appendix of Lost Cultivars.

Kabschia–Kabschia crosses before 1915

Saxifraga ×*apiculata* (*S. marginata* × *S. sancta*). Strong multi-flowered stems with pale to mid-yellow flowers over mats of strong green foliage. Great rockery plants. Cultivars: 'Alba', 'Albert Einstein', 'Gregor Mendel' (ca.1894: F. Sündermann), 'Primrose Bee', 'Pseudo-pungens', 'Pungens', 'Spartakus'.

Saxifraga ×*bilekii* (*S. ferdinandi-coburgi* × *S. tombeanensis*). Small, slow, dense foliage. 3–5 pale yellow flowers. Cultivars: 'Castor' (1913: F. Sündermann), 'Favorit'.

Saxifraga ×*borisii* (*S. ferdinandi-coburgi* × *S. marginata*). Generally strong. Cushions of green foliage with multi-flowered stems of mid-yellow flowers. Varied with many excellent rock-garden plants. Cultivars: 'Aemula', 'Aladdin', 'Aldebaran', 'Becky Foster', 'Blanka', 'Claudia', 'Eve Young', 'Faust', 'Josef Mánes', 'Karlštejn', 'Katrin', 'Kyrilli', 'Margarete', 'Marianna', 'Marie Stivínová', 'Mona Lisa', 'Pseudo-borisii', 'Pseudo-kyrilli', 'Rachael Young', 'Rusalka', 'Sofia' (pre-1906: J. Kellerer), 'Vesna', 'Vincent Van Gogh', 'Wheatley Lion', 'Zlatava'.

Saxifraga ×*boydii* (*S. aretioides* × *S. burseriana*). Solitary yellow flowers, usually quite large on thin red stems, over tight rather pointed grey-green foliage. Many excellent crosses often best in a pot or trough. Cultivars: 'Aretiastrum', 'Cherrytrees',

'Cleo', 'Corona', 'Faldonside', 'Friar Tuck', 'Hindhead Seedling', 'Kelso', 'Klondike', 'Luteola', 'Mondschein-Sonate', 'Nottingham Gold', 'Old Britain' (1890: J. B. Boyd), 'Oriole', 'Pilatus', 'Pollux', 'Sulphurea', 'White Cap', 'William Boyd'.

Saxifraga ×*bursiculata* (*S. burseriana* × *S.* ×*apiculata*). Only cultivar 'King Lear' (pre-1911: E. H. Jenkins) is tall with multiple white flowers.

Saxifraga ×*elisabethae* (*S. burseriana* × *S. sancta*). Robust weather-resistant mats of green foliage with multi-flowered stems of medium-sized yellow flowers. Good plants for open rockery, generally poor in pots. Cultivars: 'Boston Spa', 'Brno', 'Carmen' (1898: F. Sündermann), 'Cream Seedling', 'Elizabeth Sinclair', 'Foster's Gold', 'Galahad', 'Icicle', 'Jason', 'Leo Gordon Godseff', 'Lorelei', 'Mars', 'Midas', 'Millstream Cream', 'Minehaha', 'Mrs Leng', 'Ochroleuca', 'Primrose Dame', 'Sylva', 'Tully'.

Saxifraga ×*eudoxiana* (*S. ferdinandi-coburgi* × *S. sancta*). Mats of green, pointed foliage, multi-flowered stems of small bright yellow flowers. Fast and easy-going. Cultivars: 'Eudoxia' (pre-1906: J. Kellerer), 'Gold Dust', 'Haagii'.

Saxifraga ×*fontanae* (*S. diapensioides* × *S. ferdinandi-coburgi*). Tight, slow, few-flowered, yellow. Cultivar: 'Amalie' (pre-1915: F. Sündermann), 'Anna'.

Saxifraga ×*geuderi* (*S. ferdinandi-coburgi* × *S.* ×*boydii*). Only cultivar 'Eulenspiegel' (pre-1915: E. Heinrich) is probably not the plant grown under this name today, which appears to have different parentage.

Saxifraga ×*grata* (*S. aretioides* × *S. ferdinandi-coburgi*). Small, slow, green foliage, stems with 3–4 medium-sized bright yellow flowers. Cultivars: 'Annemarie' (1915: F. Sündermann), 'Gratoides'.

Saxifraga ×*irvingii* (*S. burseriana* × *S. lilacina*). The first cross using a Himalayan species, the first pink-flowered *Porphyrion* cross. Small cushions of spiny grey-green foliage, solitary pale pink flowers on red stems. Cultivars: 'Dobruska', 'Eliot Ford', 'Gem', 'Harry Marshall', 'His Majesty', 'Jenkinsiae', 'Lusanna', 'Mother of Pearl', 'Mother Queen', 'Pearly Gates', 'Rubella', 'Russell V. Prichard', 'Timmy Foster', 'Walter Irving' (1909: W. Irving).

Saxifraga ×*leyboldii* (*S. marginata* × *S. vandellii*). Tight cushions, slow, tall strong flower stems of multiple white flowers. Cultivars: 'August Hayek' (1915: F. Sündermann), 'Zlin'.

Saxifraga ×*malbyana* (*S. aretioides* × *S. diapensioides*). Small cushions, dense foliage, slow, 3–6 pale yellow flowers. Cultivars: 'Hedwig', 'Primulina' (ca.1894: J.

Atkins), 'Wilhelm Tell'.

Saxifraga ×*paulinae* (*S. burseriana* × *S. ferdinandi-coburgi*). Greyish to green cushions with tallish stems of quite large yellow flowers. Good in pots or troughs. Cultivars: 'Bettina', 'Franzii', 'Kolbiana', 'Paula' (1906: F. Sündermann), 'Pseudo-franzii', 'Pseudo-paulinae', 'Winton'.

Saxifraga ×*petraschii* (*S. burseriana* × *S. tombeanensis*). Grey-green cushions with flower stems, usually red, with 1 or 2 white flowers. Good rock-garden plants. Cultivars: 'Ada', 'Affinis', 'Assimilis', 'Demeter', 'Dulcimer', 'Flush', 'Funkii', 'Grosser Prinz', 'Hansii', 'Kaspar Maria Sternberg' (1900: F. Sündermann), 'Prospero', 'Saskia', 'Schelleri', 'White Star'.

Saxifraga ×*pseudo-kotschyi* (*S. marginata* × *S. kotschyi*). Only cultivar 'Denisa' (1906: F. Sündermann) has cushions of green foliage with stems of 3–7 yellow flowers.

Saxifraga ×*salmonica* (*S. burseriana* × *S. marginata*). Usually easy-going rock-garden plants typically with 3–4 white flowers often early-flowering. Cultivars: 'Friesei', 'Jenkinsii', 'Kestoniensis', 'Maria Luisa', 'Melrose' (pre-1890: J. B. Boyd), 'Mrs Helen Terry', 'Obristii', 'Pichleri', 'Pseudo-salomonii', 'Rosaleen', 'Salomonii', 'Schreineri'.

Saxifraga ×*steinii* (*S. aretioides* × *S. tombeanensis*). Only cultivar 'Agnes' (1915: F. Sündermann) has small, dense foliage, creamy-white flowers. Very scarce.

Saxifraga ×*wehrhahnii* (*S. marginata* × *S. scardica*). Tall stems with up to a dozen small white flowers. Rarely grown. Cultivars: 'Hannelore', 'Pseudo-scardica' (pre-1900: F. Sündermann). This cross has now been recorded in the wild by J. Bürgel.

Kabschia–Engleria **crosses before 1915**

Saxifraga ×*boeckeleri* (*S. ferdinandi-coburgi* × *S. stribrnyi*). Only cultivar 'Armida' (ca.1913: F. Sündermann) has tight pointed foliage, tall flower stems with multiple small orange-yellow flowers with dark sepals.

Saxifraga ×*clarkei* (*S. media* × *S. vandellii*). Only cultivar 'Sidonia' (ca.1908: F. Sündermann) has spiny foliage, tall stems with many small pale pink flowers.

Saxifraga ×*edithae* (*S. marginata* × *S. stribrnyi*). Small to medium rosettes of flattened grey-green leaves, stems with middle-sized pale pink flowers. Good in pots and troughs. Cultivars: 'Arabella', 'Bridget', 'Edith' (pre-1905: F. Sündermann), 'Karel Stivín', 'Milada', 'Pseudo-edithae'.

Saxifraga ×*heinrichii* (*S. aretioides* × *S. stribrnyi*). Only cultivar 'Ernst Heinrich' (ca.1915: F. Sündermann) has cushions of rosettes of flattened leaves with stems of about 10 small yellow-orange flowers. Not difficult in the open.

Saxifraga ×*hoerhammeri* (*S. federici-augusti* × *S. marginata*). Only cultivar 'Lohengrin' (ca. 1915: Dr Hörhammer) has small cushions of quite large rosettes of flattened leaves, stems with multiple small pink flowers.

Saxifraga ×*hofmannii* (*S. burseriana* × *S. sempervivum*). Cushions of small dark green foliage, stems of very small violet-pink flowers. Cultivars: 'Bodensee' (pre-1915: F. Sündermann), 'Ferdinand'.

Saxifraga ×*kellereri* (*S. burseriana* × *S. stribrnyi*). Cushions of quite large grey-green rosettes with tall multi-flowered stems with middle-sized pale pink flowers, calyx often dark red. Cultivars: 'Johann Kellerer' (1906: J. Kellerer), 'Kewensis', 'Pseudo-suendermannii', 'Suendermannii', 'Suendermannii Major', 'Suendermannii Purpurea'.

Saxifraga ×*mariae-theresiae* (*S. burseriana* × *S. federici-augusti*). Slow, spiny foliage, multi-flowered stems with small pink flowers, dark red sepals. Cultivars: 'Gaertneri', 'Theresia' (pre-1915: F. Sündermann).

Saxifraga ×*stuartii* (*S.* ×*luteo-purpurea* × *S. stribrnyi*). Small cushions of rosettes with flattened leaves. Tallish stems with small yellow or pink flowers. Cultivars: 'Lutea', 'Rosea' (both 1913: F. Sündermann).

Saxifraga ×*thomasiana* (*S. stribrnyi* × *S. tombeanensis*). Only cultivar 'Magdalena' (1915: F. Sündermann) is extremely rare. Slow, small cushions, stems with up to 10 small pale pink flowers.

Engleria–Engleria crosses before 1915

Saxifraga ×*bertolonii* (*S. sempervivum* × *S. stribrnyi*). Large rosettes of flattened leaves, tall arched red stems with very small dark red flowers. Cultivars: 'Amabilis', 'Andrea', 'Antonio' (1906: F. Sündermann), 'Berenika', 'Ludmila Šubrová', 'Remus', 'Samo', 'Turandot'.

Saxifraga ×*biasolettoi* (*S. federici-augusti* × *S. semper-vivum*). Medium to large rosettes of flattened narrow leaves, tall arched stems with very dense head of very small dark red flowers and calyces. Suitable for rock garden. Cultivars: 'Crystalie', 'Desdemona', 'Feuerkopf', 'Jorg', 'Lohmuelleri', 'Phoenix' (1912: F. Sündermann). This cross has now been recorded in the wild by J. Bürgel.

Saxifraga ×*doerfleri* (*S. federici-augusti* × *S. stribrnyi*). Medium to very large rosettes of flattened leaves. Tall dark stems of many small dark red flowers. Dense to loose inflorescence. Can be very impressive. Cultivars: 'Dalibor', 'Ignaz Dörfler' (pre-1915: F. Sündermann), 'Josef Janouš', 'Tycho Brahe'.

Saxifraga ×*fleischeri* (*S. federici-augusti* × *S. corymbosa*). Large rosettes, tall stems with very small yellow to red flowers densely clustered at top. Cultivars: 'Buchholzii', 'Fantomas', 'Mephisto' (pre-1915: F. Sündermann).

Saxifraga ×*gusmusii* (*S. corymbosa* × *S. sempervivum*). Rosettes of grey-green flattened leaves with medium-tall stems with many very small, dull orange-yellow flowers. Cultivars: 'Perluteiviridis' and 'Subluteiviridis' (both pre-1912: F. Sündermann), 'Thorpei', 'Václav Hollar'.

Saxifraga ×*schottii* (*S. corymbosa* × *S. stribrnyi*). Small groups of medium-large flat-leaved rosettes, Arched stems, branched, with small orange-yellow to orange-red flowers. Cultivars: 'Deborah Bacci', 'Per-stribrnyi' and 'Sub-stribrnyi' (both pre-1913: F. Sündermann), 'Sedlečko', 'Tábor'.

New crosses between the Wars

Saxifraga ×*anglica* (*S. aretioides* × *S. media* × *S. lilacina*). Usually resulting from crossing *S.* ×*luteo-purpurea* and *S. lilacina*, these form small cushions with deep pink flowers. Some are very attractive, many desirable. Best suited to pots. Cultivars (some very rare indeed): 'Amberglow', 'Amberine', 'Arthur', 'Beatrix Stanley', 'Beryl', 'Christine', 'Clare', 'Cranbourne', 'Delight', 'Felicity', 'Flamenco', 'Grace Farwell', 'Harlow Car', 'Jan Amos Komenský', 'Jan Hus', 'Myra' (1918: R. Farrer), 'Myra Cambria', 'Pearl Rose', 'Peggy Eastwood', 'Quarry Wood', 'Seville', 'Sunrise', 'Sunset', 'Winifred'.

Saxifraga ×*anormalis* (*S. pseudolaevis* × *S. stribrnyi*). Only cultivar is 'Gustav Hegi' (1920s: F. Sündermann) with medium-sized rosettes and stems with very small orange flowers, suitable for pots or a trough.

Saxifraga ×*arco-valleyi* (*S. lilacina* × *S. marginata*). Small cushions with quite large pale pink flowers on short stems. Pots or troughs. Cultivars: 'Allendale Andante', 'Antonin Dvorak', 'Arco' (1917 or 1919: F. Sündermann), 'Dainty Dame', 'Hocker Edge', 'Labe', 'Ophelia', 'Sara Sinclair', 'Silver Edge' (variegated).

Saxifraga ×*gloriana* (*S. lilacina* × *S. obtusa*). Small cushions with medium-sized pale pink flowers on short stems. Pots or troughs. Cultivars: 'Amitie' (1925: R. V. Prichard), 'Chez Nous' (variegated), 'Godiva' (1925: R. V. Prichard).

Saxifraga ×*hardingii* (*S. aretioides* × *S. media* × *S. burseriana*). Small cushions of grey-green foliage, buff-pink-orange petals, red nectary ring. Cultivars: 'Benvenuto Cellini', 'Buster', 'C. M. Prichard' (1925: R. V. Prichard), 'Iris Prichard', 'Lorenzo Ghiberti'.

Saxifraga ×*hornibrookii* (*S. lilacina* × *S. stribrnyi*). Small dark green cushions with stems having 1 or 2 dark purple flowers. Suitable for pots and troughs. Not always easy to maintain long-term. Cultivars: 'Ariel', 'Bellisant' (may be extinct), 'Celeste Aurora', 'Coningsby Queen', 'Delia' (1925: R. V. Prichard), 'Ellie Brinckerhoff', 'Laurent Ward' (1925: R. V. Prichard), 'Lydia', 'Riverslea' (1925: R. V. Prichard), 'Romeo', 'Rubin'.

Saxifraga ×*ingwersenii* (*S. lilacina* × *S. tombeanensis*). Small slow, pale pink flowers. Almost or wholly extinct. Cultivar: 'Simplicity' (1925: R. V. Prichard).

Saxifraga ×*kayei* (*S. aretioides* × *S. burseriana* × *S. ferdinandi-coburgi* × *S. sancta*). Dark green cushions with strong yellow flowers. The only cultivar is 'Buttercup' (early 1930s: R. V. Prichard).

Saxifraga ×*laeviformis* (*S. marginata* × *S. pseudolaevis*). The only cultivar is 'Egmont' (1920: F. Sündermann) with small cushions and quite short stems of small yellow flowers.

Saxifraga ×*landaueri* (*S. burseriana* × *S. stribrnyi* × *S. marginata*). Quite large rosettes, tall stems with medium-large pale pink flowers. Good in troughs. Cultivars: 'Elias', 'Leonore' (1920: F. Sündermann), 'Schleicheri'.

Saxifraga ×*megaseaeflora* (*S. aretioides* × *S. burseriana* × *S. lilacina* × *S. media*). This cross can be achieved in a variety of ways. All tend to make fairly robust cushions and have pastel-coloured flowers in a spectrum from orange-buff through buff-yellow, white to pale pinks and salmons. Generally easy and pretty but usually flowers last better with protection. There are five groups:

Prichard's Monument Group (*S.* ×*anglica* × *S. burseriana*). Soft pinks, white: 'Dana', 'Edward Elgar', 'Karel Čapek', 'Krákatit', 'Krasava', 'Mrs Gertie Prichard', 'Mrs Harry Lindsay', 'Pluto', 'Robin Hood' (1931: R. V. Prichard), 'Saturn'.

Holenka's Miracle Group (from *S.* ×*anglica* × *S.* ×*boydii*). Warm buff to orange-yellow: 'Bertramka', 'Bohdalec', 'Chodov', 'Galaxie', 'Hradčany', 'Josef Čapek', 'Jupiter', 'Kampa', 'Liboc', 'Loreta', 'Manekyn', 'Nusle', 'Olsany', 'Opotov', 'Prosek', 'Pruhonice', 'Radlice', 'Roztyly', 'Semafor', 'Troja', 'Vladana', 'Zbraslav'.

S. 'Jupiter' × *S. lilacina*. Pale pinks to pale buff-yellows: 'Letna', 'Macocha', 'Norman', 'Podoli', 'Poseidon', 'Rokoko', 'Ruzyn˘e', 'Strahov', 'Zeus'.

S. 'Jupiter' × *S.* ×*boydii* ('Hindhead Seedling' or 'Luteola'). Pale yellows, buff and orange: 'Grebovka', 'Humoreska', 'Karlin', 'Michle', 'Smíchov', 'Symfonie', 'Vinohrad(n)y', 'Vítkov', 'Vyšehrad'.

Miscellaneous others. Various colours: 'Artemis', 'Jan Neruda', 'Radka', and possibly 'Karel Hasler', 'Marcela', 'Violeta'.

Saxifraga ×*prossenii* (*S. sancta* × *S. stribrnyi*). Cushions of dark green foliage with stems of very small orange flowers. Cultivars: 'Prometheus', 'Regina' (both pre-1920: F. Sündermann).

Saxifraga ×*rosinae* (*S. diapensioides* × *S. marginata*). Only cultivar is 'Rosina Sündermann' (1936: F. Sündermann) with small mat of foliage, quite short multi-flowered stems of off-white flowers. Unusual.

Saxifraga ×*semmleri* (*S. ferdinandi-coburgi* × *S. pseudolaevis* × *S. sancta*). Only cultivar is 'Martha' (pre-1920: F. Sündermann) with dark green rather loose foliage and short stems of small bright yellow flowers.

Saxifraga ×*smithii* (*S. marginata* × *S. tombeanensis*). Only cultivar is 'Vahlii' (pre-1920: F. Sündermann) with small cushions, small foliage, quite tall stems with around 4–6 large white flowers. Pretty but rather difficult.

Saxifraga ×*stormonthii* (*S. desoulavyi* × *S. sancta*). Only cultivar is 'Stella' (1920: F. Sündermann) with dark green spiky foliage and stems of small bright yellow flowers.

Saxifraga ×*urumoffii* (*S. ferdinandi-coburgi* × *S. corymbosa*). Only cultivar is 'Ivan Urumov' (1920: F. Sündermann) with small cushions, quite large rosettes and tall stems with dense cluster of small yellow flowers. Plants in cultivation in UK do not match description in Horný et al.

Saxifraga ×*webrii* (*S. sancta* × *S. scardica*). Strong cushions of dark green foliage with bright yellow flowers. Good on the rock garden. Cultivars: 'Monika', 'Pygmalion' (1930s: UK).

New crosses 1945–1970

Saxifraga ×*boydilacina* (*S. aretioides* × *S. burseriana* × *S. lilacina*). Small cushions, usually grey-green, large pastel yellow, pink or buff flowers. Very pretty, easy-going. Cultivars: 'Alan Martin', 'Cereus', 'Discovery', 'Moon Beam' (1970s: H. L. Foster),

'Olympus', 'Penelope' (1970s: R. Dunford), 'Perikles', 'Pink Star'.

Saxifraga ×byam-groundsii (*S. aretioides* × *S. burseriana* × *S. marginata*). Only cultivar 'Lenka' (1975: Horný) makes dark green cushions, single large yellow flowers. Good for rock garden.

Saxifraga ×fallsvillagensis (*S. burseriana* × *S. marginata* × *S. tombeanensis*). Cushions with multiple large white flowers on tall stems. Cultivars: 'Banshee' (1967: H. L. Foster), 'Fanfare', 'Laura Sinclair', 'Mir', 'Sabrina', 'Swan'.

Saxifraga ×finnisiae (*S. aizoides* × *S. aretioides* × *S. lilacina* × *S. media*). Only cultivar 'Parcevalis' (1950s: UK). Small mid-green foliage, flowers small orange. Suitable for a trough.

Saxifraga ×lincolni-fosteri (*S. aretioides* × *S. burseriana* × *S. diapensioides*). Small cushions, very tight foliage, slow, stems with 1 or 2 pale yellow flowers. Cultivars: 'Diana' (1969: H. L. Foster), 'Oradour', 'Salome'.

Saxifraga ×margoxiana (*S. ferdinandi-coburgi* × *S. marginata* × *S. sancta*). Only cultivar 'Parsee' (1969: H. L. Foster) has cushions, tall multi-flowered stems with large yellow flowers.

Saxifraga ×millstreamiana (*S. burseriana* × *S. ferdinandi-coburgi* × *S. tombeanensis*). Slow, green cushions, short stems with few pale yellow flowers. Does well on rockeries. Cultivars: 'Eliot Hodgkin' (1974: H. L. Foster), 'Luna'.

Saxifraga ×pragensis (*S. ferdinandi-coburgi* × *S. marginata* × *S. stribrnyi*). Only cultivar: 'Zlatá Praha' (translated as "Golden Prague") (1961: F. Holenka) has dark green foliage, stems with small orange-yellow flowers, red sepals.

Saxifraga ×wendelacina (*S. lilacina* × *S. wendelboi*). Small cushions, pretty pale pink flowers with recurved petals. Pot or trough. Cultivars: 'Allendale Joy', 'Wendrush' and 'Wendy' (1974: H. L. Foster).

New crosses since 1975

Saxifraga ×abingdonensis (*S. burseriana* × *S. poluniniana*). Small cushions of spiny grey-green foliage. Red stems with prolific white flowers. Trough. Cultivars: 'Judith Shackleton' (1992: Jason Shackleton), 'Wellesbourne'.

Saxifraga ×baccii (*S. ×anglica* × *S. stolitzkae*). Hard foliage, tall stems, deep pink flowers. Trough or pot. Cultivars: 'Dora Ross', 'Irene Bacci' (1993: S. Bacci).

Saxifraga **Beat Group** (*S. lowndesii* × *S. ×anglica*). Small cushions with more or less stemless purple flowers. Cultivars: 'Beatles' (1999: J. Bürgel), 'Vysoké Mýto' (1999: J. Bürgel & O. Maixner).

Saxifraga **Blues Group** (*S. lowndesii* × *S. ×poluanglica*). Various crosses used. Small cushions with intensely coloured pink to dark purple-red flowers. Pot culture. Cultivars: 'Elvis Presley', 'Gina Lollobrigida', 'Louis Armstrong', 'Satchmo', 'William Shakespeare' (all 1999: J. Bürgel & O. Maixner).

Saxifraga ×caroli-langii (*S. dinnikii* × *S. marginata*). Desirable. Hard slow-growing cushion. Very large palest pink flowers. Petals longitudinally corrugated like *S. dinnikii*. Cultivar: 'Verona' (2004: K. Lang).

Saxifraga ×caroliquarti (*S. alberti* × *S. lowndesii*). Slow, very pale pink flowers. Cultivar: 'Ivana' (1991: K. Lang).

Saxifraga ×cimgani (*S. alberti* × *S. lilacina*). Neat cushion with attractive warm pink flowers. Cultivar: 'Harry Smith' (1996: K. Lang).

Saxifraga **Concinna Group** (*S. cinerea* × *S. dinnikii*). Cultivars vary with cushions from small and hard to larger and softer ('Beinn Alligin'), flowers from pale pink to strong cerise ('Ben Loyal'). Cultivars: 'Beinn Alligin', 'Beinn Eighe', 'Beinn Na Callich', 'Beinn Resipole', 'Ben Loyal' (2000: John Mullaney).

Saxifraga **Conspecta Group** (*S. kotschyi* × *S. ×cullinanii*). The original cultivar 'Pablo Picasso' (2004: K. Lang) has large orange-red flowers, buds bright red. Can be difficult, needs protection. Two newer cultivars are 'Rembrandt van Rijn' and 'Paul Gaugin'.

Saxifraga ×cullinanii (*S. subverticillata* × *S. lilacina*). One cultivar 'Radvan Horný' (1996: K. Lang) with soft cushions liable to aphid attack if grown under cover. Pretty with rich pink flowers.

Saxifraga **Decora Group** (*S. kotschyi* × *S. ×polulacina*). Original cultivar 'Marc Chagall' (2004: K. Lang) has flowers starting strong vermilion fading to straw-coloured. The other, much newer cultivar is 'Auguste Renoir'.

Saxifraga **Exclusive Group** (*S. lowndesii* × *S. lilacina*). Cultivars: 'Allendale Elegance', 'Allendale Elite' (both 2000: R. Fairbairn), 'Excellence', 'Exhibit'.

Saxifraga **Firenze Group** (*S. ×malbyana* × *S. stolitzkae*). Small tight cushions with white or yellow flowers. Cultivars: 'Andrea della Robbia', 'Luca della Robbia' (both 1997: S. Bacci).

Saxifraga ×goringana (*S. cinerea* × *S. ×anglica*). Tall stems over dark green rosettes with pink ('Anne Beddall') to cerise ('Nancye'). Unusual. Pot or trough. Cultivars: 'Anne Beddall', 'Nancye' (both 1987: W. Harding).

Saxifraga **Harmonia Group** (*S. cinerea* × *S. aretioides*).

Yellow flowers on tallish stems. Attractive but not as easy as might be expected. Cultivars: 'Allendale Beauty' (1997: R. Fairbairn), 'Mirko Webr'.

Saxifraga **Honor Group** (*S. dinnikii* × *S. stribrnyi*). Relatively large rosettes. Flowers mauve-pink, nodding, 3–4 per stem. Cultivar: 'John Byam-Grounds' (2004: K. Lang).

Saxifraga **Impressio Group** (*S. kotschyi* × *S. lilacina*). Two cultivars (both 2004: K. Lang) with pale orange flowers ('Edouard Manet') or vermilion fading to orange ('Claude Monet').

Saxifraga ×*izari* (*S. aretioides* × *S. sempervivum*). Small cushions. Arched stems, very small dull orange-yellow flowers. Cultivars: 'Allendale Boon', 'Eva Hanzliková' (1996: K. Lang).

Saxifraga ×*kepleri* (*S. cinerea* × *S. ferdinandi-coburgi*). Large yellow flowers on tall thin stems. Pot or trough. Not as easy as might be expected. Cultivars: 'Allendale Angel' (1996: R. Fairbairn), 'Orion'.

Saxifraga ×*krausii* (*S. ferdinandi-coburgi* × *S. ×anglica*). Small cushions with small orange flowers. Suitable for trough or pot. Cultivars: 'Jan Palach' (1993: J. Bürgel), 'New Europe'.

Saxifraga **Lasciva Group** (*S. lowndesii* × *S. ×cimgani*). Cultivar: 'Albrecht Dürer' (2003: K. Lang).

Saxifraga ×*lismorensis* (*S. aretioides* × *S. georgei* × *S. lilacina* × *S. media*). Usually resulting from crossing *S. ×anglica* with *S. georgei* these make small cushions or mats with prolific small deep pink, red or violet-purple flowers. Suitable for pots or troughs. Avoid strong sun. Cultivars: 'Allendale Acclaim', 'Allendale Bamby', 'Allendale Beau', 'Allendale Betty', 'Allendale Blossom', 'Allendale Bravo', 'Allendale Brilliant', 'Lismore Carmine' (1992: B. Burrow), 'Lismore Gem', 'Lismore Pink' (1992: B. Burrow).

Saxifraga **Magnus Group** (*S. cinerea* × *S. ×luteo-purpurea*). Cultivar: 'Brian Arundel' (2004: K. Lang).

Saxifraga **Milford Group** (*S. aretioides* × *S. marginata*). Hard cushions, tall stems of yellow flowers, usually nodding when they first open. Cultivars: 'Aldo Bacci' (1993: S. Bacci), 'Alice', 'Marsilio Ficino'.

Saxifraga ×*novacastelensis* (*S. hypostoma* × *S. poluniniana*). Small cushions, white stemless flowers. Pots only. Cultivar: 'Allendale Pearl' (1994: R. Fairbairn) and 'Allendale Celt', although it may be that the first parent was *S. ×tukuchensis* rather than *S. hypostoma*.

Saxifraga **Pardubice Group** (*S. federici-augusti* × *S. poluniniana*). Scarce cultivar with small pink flowers.

Cultivar: 'Karel Pěch' (1999: J. Bürgel & O. Maixner).

Saxifraga ×*poluanglica* (*S. ×anglica* × *S. poluniniana*). Free-flowering pale to dark pink cultivars best in a pot or trough with some shade. Cultivars: 'Barford', 'Brailes', 'Brendan', 'Charlecote', 'Combrook', 'Edgehill', 'Frank Sinatra', 'Goldeneye', 'Honington', 'Hunscote', 'Idlicote', 'Kineton', 'Loxley', 'Maria Callas', 'Miluj Mne', 'Peter Burrow', 'Radway', 'Red Poll' (1988: W. Harding), 'Tvoje Píseň', 'Tvoje Radost', 'Tvůj Polibek', 'Tvůj Přítel', 'Tvůj Sen', 'Tvůj Úsměv', 'Tvůj Úspěch', 'Walton', 'Wasperton'.

Saxifraga ×*polulacina* (*S. lilacina* × *S. poluniniana*). Easy going pink cultivars which need some shade. Cultivars: 'Cathy Read', 'Kathleen', 'River Thame', 'Tvoje Víra', 'Tvůj Den' (1991: J. Bürgel).

Saxifraga ×*pololuteo-purpurea* (*S. poluniniana* × *S. ×luteo-purpurea*). Cultivars are fairly easy-going: 'Lužníce' with white flowers, 'Sázava' with pink. (Both 1992: J. Bürgel).

Saxifraga ×*proximae* (*S. quadrifaria* × *S. ×anglica*). Very small cushions with stemless pink flowers. Pots. Cultivars: 'Květy Coventry', 'Slzy Coventry' (also as trade designations 'Květy Coventry' COVENTRY FLOWERS and 'Slzy Coventry' COVENTRY TEARS) (both 1998: K. Lang).

Saxifraga ×*pulvilacina* (*S. lilacina* × *S. pulvinaria*). The only cultivar 'Niobe' (1992: O. Maixner) has a very small cushion and very small lilac flowers. Pretty—for a pot or trough. Needs protection from sun.

Saxifraga ×*quagrata* (*S. ×grata* × *S. quadrifaria*). Small, slow, difficult, with bright but cool yellow flowers. Cultivars: 'Sirius Alfa', 'Sirius Beta' (both 1992: K. Lang).

Saxifraga ×*rayei* (*S. burseriana* × *S. wendelboi*). The only cultivar, 'Allendale Snow' (1994: R. Fairbairn), is slow, with spiny grey-green leaves. White flowers on tall stems.

Saxifraga **Renaissance Group** (*S. ×borisii* × *S. stolitzkae*). Hard cushions, multiple white or yellow flowers on medium stems. Cultivars: 'Andrea Cesalpino', 'Francesco Redi' (1994: S. Bacci), 'Galileo Galilei' (1994: S. Bacci), 'Pierantonio Micheli'.

Saxifraga **Safran Group** (*S. poluniniana* × *S. meeboldii*). Small cushions with 1 or more yellow flowers with orange anthers. Very slightly scented. Only cross of *S. meeboldii*. Only named cultivar is 'Honeybunch' (2007: M. McGregor).

Saxifraga ×*siluris* (*S. vandellii* × *S. ×anglica*). Small cushions. Pink flowers. Pot or trough. Cultivar:

'Joachim Barrande' (1998: K. Lang).

Saxifraga **Swing Group** (*S. poluniniana* × *S. wendelboi*). Charming, easy-going free-flowering cushions. White flowers flushed pink. Cultivars: 'Allendale Charm', 'Mary Golds' (1995: T. Golds), 'Teide', 'Tenerife'.

Saxifraga **Toscana Group** (*S.* ×*elisabethae* × *S.* ×*anglica*). This group arose from crossing of 'Galahad' and 'Winifred'. Small cushions with single quite large pink or buff-yellow flowers. Red nectary ring. Similar in shape and size to *S.* ×*irvingii*. Cultivars: 'Amedeo Modigliani' (1991: S. Bacci), 'Giacomo Puccini', 'Ottone Rosai'.

Saxifraga **Vanessa Group** (*S. poluninana* × *S. lowndesii*). Small rather lax cushions. Pale pretty pink flowers. Pots or troughs, keep moist. Easy to root cuttings in damp sand. Cultivars: 'Bryn Llwyd', 'Cio-Cio-San' (1997: M. McGregor), 'Marilyn Monroe'.

Saxifraga ×*youngiana* (*S. lilacina* × *S. marginata* × *S. stribrnyi*). Only cultivar is 'Lilac Time' (1990: W. Harding) which makes a small cushion of robust rosettes. Tall stems with large pale pink flowers. Not as easy as it looks. Scarce. Pot or trough.

Saxifraga ×*zenittensis* (*S. vandellii* × *S. lilacina*). Only cultivar, 'Mikuláš Koperník' (2000: K. Lang) has slow-growing cushions, large pink flowers on short stems.

There are other as yet unnamed groups of crosses of which two must stand out:

Saxifraga cinerea × *S. poluniniana*. Pretty, white ('Mollie Broom', 'Claire Felstead') to rich pink ('Meg'), and not difficult. Cultivars: 'Amy', 'Claire Felstead', 'Meg', 'Mollie Broom', 'Sarah Felstead' (all 1996: J. Mullaney). Jan Bürgel and Tim Roberts report this cross in the wild in Nepal.

Saxifraga diapensioides × *S.* ×*luteo-purpurea*. Small attractive cultivar with buff-pink flowers. Only cultivar is 'Moai' (ca.2000: K. Lang).

The Best of the Bastards

There are at least a hundred other cultivars of variously obscure or unknown parentage in cultivation, some old, some very new. Many are little more than smudged versions of other cultivars, but there are some that stand out:

'Alpenglow'. Tall cultivar from Lincoln Foster (late 1960s) with small cushions. Stems are slightly too tall but flowers are buff-pink, well-proportioned and open, with a red nectary ring. One of the classic cultivars.

'Barleycorn'. Compact cultivar from Ian Spencer (1999) from a cross of 'Wilhelm Tell' and 'Riverslea' with small yellow flowers with an orange flush at the centre.

'Bohemia'. A robust cultivar with bright orange to orange-red flowers which tend to fade badly but are deeper in colour if grown in the open. Miroslav Kraus (1987).

'Citronella'. Tall beautifully proportioned cultivar from Winton Harding (1994). Flowers are clear yellow, petals almost circular and slightly convex.

'Edgar Irmscher'. A cultivar from Sündermann (ca.1960) with tall flower stems with quite small flowers with pale orange petals and dark purple calyx.

'Goring White'. Small cultivar from Winton Harding (1994) with white flowers in pairs.

'Naarden'. Tall multi-flowered cultivar from Karel Lang (1999). Flowers are yellow with an orange-pink flush. Sister seedling to 'Večerní Hvĕzda'.

'Peach Blossom'. Small cushion with flowers on short stems. Flowers are pale buff-pink with a slightly darker, pinched centre. Lincoln Foster (1972).

'Peach Melba'. A strong cultivar, from David Victor (2001), with tall multi-flowered stems with the flowers a rich peach blush.

'Večerní Hvĕzda'. Tall, multi-flowered, with clear pale yellow flowers . A first-class cultivar from Karel Lang (1999). Sister seedling to 'Naarden'.

'Winton's Dream'. Tall with small clear pink flowers. From Winton Harding.

8 · Dwarf Cushion Saxifrage Relatives

Section *Porphyrion 3 – Florulentae, Xanthizoon, Squarrosae* and *Oppositifoliae*

In any group of plants, some species are likely to be thought of as rather odd, in various ways not fitting well with what have been considered their closest relatives. Saxifrages are no exception and it has become increasingly obvious that a small number of species, some from quite different sections of the genus, are much better seen as closely associated with the *Porphyrion* saxifrages of subsection *Porophyllum* (*Kabschia*, *Engleria* and *Tetrameridium*). The work of Douglas Soltis, Elena Conti and others has clarified relationships that have previously puzzled both botanists and gardeners. Breeding incompatibility between groups which look very similar has been demonstrated as reflecting underlying evolutionary separation. Although this work has made these new relationships clear, the formal taxonomic descriptions of these new relationships has lagged behind and the various groupings here need formal description as new botanical combinations. The current taxonomic status of each grouping is given in the listing at the end of the chapter.

Saxifraga florulenta on cliffs near St Martin-Vésubie in the Maritime Alps. Photograph John Howes.

Florulentae

For many years *Saxifraga florulenta* has been treated as a silver saxifrage belonging to section *Ligulatae*. But it was always anomalous with the rosette, leaves, marginal hairs and flower shape all falling some way outside the range otherwise seen in that section. It is a plant of the hard granites and gneiss of the Maritime Alps where the rosettes—large, single and monocarpic—can be found on the sheer cliffs or the side of large boulders which have tumbled down to lower slopes. It has been a plant which has fascinated botanists and horticulturalists, the latter because it has resisted all efforts to domesticate it. Attempts to grow it usually end in total frustration: seed is difficult to germinate, plants are difficult to keep from year to year, and death pre-empts flowering. It is a Red Data Book plant, so any attempt to collect it is illegal, and it might even be thought of as the Giant Panda of the saxifrage world—certainly not any evidence for intelligent design. Even in the Maritime Alps it is restricted, with the Mercantour east of St Martin-Vésubie being a good base for finding it. Its whole range is about 50 kilometres along the mountains of the French–Italian border ending just to the west of Isola—where a wolf loped across the road as we descended from Isola down into Italy.

The reasons why *Saxifraga florulenta* was placed in section *Ligulatae* are gross morphological ones: large leafy rosette, hydathodes on the leaves, and terminal many-flowered panicle. But each of these characteristics raises questions. It has a single large rosette of leaves with hydathodes along the edge of the leaf. In section *Ligulatae* these secrete lime (even in *S. cotyledon* which is found growing on granite) but in *S. florulenta* no lime is secreted from the hydathodes.

The leaves of *Saxifraga florulenta* are mid- to dark green, springy rather than stiff. Plants take a number of years to come to flowering size, individual leaves die after a couple of years but they are persistent, remaining on the plant till flowering. Leaves are up to about 6 cm long and about 0.5 cm wide, rather narrower towards the base. The apex of the leaf is acuminate with a sharply pointed tip. The margin is thin, translucent and cartilaginous, and there are stiff translucent hairs along the margin toward the base. In fact, apart from the presence of the hydathodes, the leaves are much more like those of some species from section *Ciliatae* subsection *Rosulares* than those of section *Ligulatae*.

Cesati named this section *Tristylis* because the flowers usually have 3 styles and a tripartite ovary rather than 2 styles and bipartite ovary typical in the genus (although the terminal flower is usually 5-parted rather than 3-parted, with 8 or 9 sepals and petals, 5 styles and 15 stamens).

Flowering takes place only after many years and only in years when conditions are particularly favourable, so that in some years many plants flower, in others none—a synchrony similar to that of many other long-lived monocarpic species. The flower stem is quite stiff but hollow and glandular-hairy; the inflorescence cylindrical or narrowly pyramidal up to about 25 cm tall but it may be less than half this. The pedicels, normally single-flowered, are carried all the way up the stem. Bland records one 18 cm stem as having 118 flowers on 102 "branches" with single flowers, and only 8 with two flowers. The flowers are rather pinched, not opening wide; the petals are typically pale pink and are dramatically set off by the russet-red stems and calyx, but in a minority of plants the stems are dark purple-green and the flowers very pale.

Research by Conti and Rutschmann suggests that the evolution of *Saxifraga florulenta* occurred prior to the Pleistocene glaciations. It does not hybridize with any other species and varies very little, and it is likely that it has a narrow genetic constitution due to repeated near-extinctions.

Saxifraga florulenta.

Xanthizoon (and *Mutatae*)

If seen out of flower the two species grouped here appear quite dissimilar. *Saxi-fraga aizoides*, till now the sole member of its section, makes extensive mats of leafy stems, with its leaves being more or less cylindrical, while *S. mutata* makes one or a few rosettes of broadly oblong leaves. However, phytogenetic analysis has now made clear that it is genetically very close to *S. aizoides* and similarities can be found. The inflorescence of *S. mutata* is tall and well-branched but the orange-yellow pigmentation of the flowers is clearly similar to that of *S. aizoides*. Similarly, although the leaves of *S. mutata* are broadly ovate, flattened and in a rosette, the thickened texture of the leaves is much closer to that of *S. aizoides* than it is to the section *Ligulatae* species. Lime encrustation in both species is present but limited, and the cartilaginous margin of *S. mutata* leaves is unlike those in section *Ligulatae*. Hybridization is not uncommon between the two species with the hybrid *S. ×hausmannii* having acquired various other epithets in the past: *S. ×regelii*, *S. ×girtanneri* and *S. ×inclinata*.

Saxifraga florulenta in flower. This historic photograph shows a pale-flowered plant, but more commonly the flowers are a warmer pink. Photograph Sturt Piggin (Saxifrage Society Slide Library).

Saxifraga aizoides above Gavarnie in the French Pyrenees.

Saxifraga aizoides. The typical yellow form.

Saxifraga aizoides var. atrorubens.

Saxifraga aizoides is a distinctive plant which makes extensive mats in the right conditions. Its foliage is bright green with small deposits of lime on the rather thickened, almost fleshy, linear leaves and in the typical form found in western Europe it has yellow flowers. It is a widespread alpine-arctic species, in Europe from the Pyrenees to Finland and northwestern Russia. In northern North America it reaches, but barely crosses, the US–Canadian border in both the Appalachians and the Rocky Mountains. It is a plant which requires a ready supply of moisture and is typically found in or at the edge of streams or in sites where moisture seeps out from the underlying rocks. Although it can be found high up in the mountains it can be found down to sea-level in more northerly latitudes.

Saxifraga aizoides. A pale orange form with spotted petals. Slovenia.

From the eastern Alps eastward and southward plants can be found with red-pigmented petals, in some cases producing flowers that have bronze or orange petals. A variety with mahogany-red petals (var. *atrorubens*) has been described from the Apuan Alps where it apparently grows in crevices of "dry-looking" rocks.

Saxifraga aizoides does not do well in cultivation unless its demand for a fairly constant supply of moisture can be met. If this is available then it can thrive. In the drier conditions of eastern England, var. *atrorubens* with its rich red flowers seems to require less attention which makes sense given the comments about the southern European home of this variety. It is not difficult to propagate all forms of the species as cuttings in damp sand, where they root readily. *Saxifraga aizoides* is a fecund parent, producing wild hybrids with *S. caesia* and *S. squarrosa* (both from section *Porphyrion* series *Squarrosae*), *S. oppositifolia* (section *Porphyrion* subsection *Oppositifoliae*), *S. paniculata* (section *Ligulatae*), *S. umbrosa* (section *Gymnopera*) and *S. mutata*.

Saxifraga mutata is at home in the Alps from France through to Austria and Slovenia and there are isolated populations in the Carpathians. It can be found on open slopes or on rock faces and needs a situation with fairly constant moisture. It has a rosette, rarely with side rosettes, with its broad leaves having a finely toothed, translucent, cartilaginous margin with lime pores (often not actually secreting lime) very near the edge of the leaf. In general it is a monocarpic species since side rosettes rarely develop to become self-sufficient. Two subspecies have been described depending on the branching of the inflorescence: subsp. *mutata* throughout most of the range except the Carpathians with the inflorescence having side branches developing from about half-way up the stem, and subsp. *demissa* in the Carpathians, with the inflorescence having side branches from the base. In theory this is fine—except that many plants in the Alps also branch from low down.

The flowers of *Saxifraga mutata* have long, very narrow, pointed orange petals widely separated, with the broad triangular sepals clearly visible between. There may be up to about 8 flowers per branch and up to 200 or more flowers in the inflorescence but in plants typical of subsp. *mutata* flowering may be much more sparse, with fewer flowers on fewer branches.

Seed of *Saxifraga mutata* is regularly available and is easy to germinate. It takes two to four years to grow it on to flowering but seedlings and larger plants are easily lost if they are allowed to get dry.

Saxifraga mutata growing near Mount Tombea, Italy.

Squarrosae

Saxifraga caesia is a charming plant, at home in the mountains of southern Europe from the Pyrenees to the Balkans. The cushions of heavily encrusted silver-grey foliage carry lots of thin, delicate flower stems each with around half a dozen small circular white flowers. It is quite distinctive and it seems so prolific, on rocky slopes or bare earth banks, that it seems to be an obvious target for the gardener. Yet it is one of the less tractable species in the rock garden, rather fugitive; it is not hard to root cuttings or difficult to raise young seedlings, but it remains stubbornly hard to grow successfully in the open rock garden or in pots. Plants can, however, be established successfully in tufa. *Saxifraga squarrosa* is rather less widespread, being confined to the Eastern Alps and somewhat less vigorous in the wild, but it too can grow and flower in tufa.

Both *Saxifraga caesia* and *S. squarrosa* seem poised between the dwarf cushion *Kabschia* and the small *Ligulatae* species and there has been disagreement in the past as to their proper position. It now seems clear that they belong with section *Porphyrion* but that they do not belong to the *Kabschia–Engleria–Tetrameridium* group but to an *Oppositifoliae–Xanthizoon–Squarrosae* group. This makes some sense of the breeding compatibility with *S. aizoides* and their incompatibilty with the *Kabschia–Engleria–Tetrameridium* and *Ligulatae* saxifrages.

Among the handful of hybrids that *Saxifraga caesia* and *S. squarrosa* form, *S. ×patens* (a hybrid between *S. caesia* and *S. aizoides*) is particularly nice, very much like a pale yellow *S. caesia*, very pretty and rather easier to keep than *S. caesia* itself. Another hybrid, *S. ×tirolensis* (between *S. caesia* and *S. squarrosa*) is not rare in the wild, but all the other hybrids listed are very rare or disputed.

Saxifraga squarrosa.
Vršič Pass, Slovenia.

Oppositifoliae

The four species here have one key characteristic in common—they have opposite leaves. They share this with the *Tetrameridium* species which make small cushions and have white flowers, but the *Oppositifoliae* species have rather looser stems, and usually have purple or orange flowers (although there are white-flowered forms of both *Saxifraga biflora* and *S. oppositifolia* and the latter can look very like *S. alpigena*). Gornall's grouping of the two sections (*Tetrameridium* and *Oppositifoliae*) together as series in subsection *Oppositifoliae* was based on morphological similarities and it now seems clear that the phytogenetic evidence suggests they are in fact rather less close than was supposed by Gornall. The Sino-Himalayan species with opposite leaves belong in the *Kabschia–Engleria–Tetrameridium* group and the species allied to *S. oppositifolia* in the *Oppositifoliae–Xanthizoon–Squarrosae* group. A morphological difference between the two groups of opposite-leaved species is that the margins of the pairs of opposite leaves are confluent in the *Tetrameridium* whereas the pairs meet at an acute angle in the *Oppositifoliae* species.

Saxifraga oppositifolia
'Theoden'.

Saxifraga oppositifolia
subsp. *rudolphiana*.
Ankögel, Austria.

Saxifraga oppositifolia, the purple saxifrage, is a very common and widespread circumboreal species found widely in Europe (from Spain, Italy and Greece northwards), in Asia (including the Himalaya) and in North America (south to Colorado). It is very varied with eight or nine subspecies described (and some supported as species by narrow-species botanists): in Europe there are five subspecies; in North America three.

In general *Saxifraga oppositifolia* is an arctic-alpine species found at high altitudes in more southerly locations but down to sea-level further north. Apart from

An example of *Saxifraga ×kochii* from the *S. biflora* end of the range, with leaves very like those of *S. biflora*, the yellow nectary disc of that species, but with rather paler petals than in typical *S. biflora*. Grossglockner, Austria.

the various subspecies (and varieties) which have been identified, it is striking how varied plants can be. Variations in size and vigour are accompanied by a great spectrum of colour from pale pink through to deep violet-purple. White-flowered plants can also be found and are grown, but the range of colours in the wild is not fully mirrored among the cultivated varieties. One of the most striking of all alpine plants is *S. oppositifolia* subsp. *rudolphiana*, which is largely confined to the Austrian Alps. With tiny foliage and full-sized deep, rich purple flowers, this would grace any collection—but it is intractable. Although seed will germinate readily enough to encourage the enthusiast, it seems to defeat even the most dedicated, expiring in the hot days of summer. However, with this exception, *S. oppositifolia* is a very rewarding species for the gardener and can produce beautiful displays of flower. It is easy to grow from seed, and cuttings strike well. Plants can be grown very successfully in pots or troughs, although it does less well in tufa than might be expected, and in a site where it will not dry out it can be very pretty on the rock garden. If you have a source of water constantly keeping your rock garden from getting too dry—regular rain, underground water, or artificial irrigation all count—then this is no problem. If not, then a shaded site or more moisture-retentive compost would be helpful.

Most of the plants in cultivation come from the typical subspecies, subsp. *oppositifolia*, or from subsp. *blepharophylla*. Many of the cultivars are named after locations where the plants were originally collected, with recent collections such as 'Borg d'Oisins' being very attractive. Among the most successful older cultivars are 'W. A. Clark', 'Latina', 'Ruth Draper' and 'Splendens', which is one of my favourites. Above all, however, is *S. oppositifolia* 'Theoden' which came from a col-

Saxifraga subsp. *augustana*. This spectacular display is rarely achieved in cultivation. Madone de Fenestre, Maritime Alps, France. Photograph Paul Kennett.

lection in the Pennines with neat foliage and slightly more pointed petals and very noticeable orange anthers.

The other three species in the subsection are much more restricted in the wild and only *Saxifraga retusa* is regularly cultivated. *Saxifraga biflora* is almost totally restricted to the Alps, with just one small population in Greece. It is even more demanding of high, cool, damp locations such as snow-fed moraine than is *S. oppositifolia*, but in such locations the two species can often be found together, with hybridization quite common, and very common in some places. The flowers of *S. biflora* are typically a more reddish purple than in *S. oppositifolia* and have a yellow nectary disc; the hybrids, *S. ×kochii*, can vary a lot but inherit this in part and are much easier to grow than is *S. biflora*.

Saxifraga retusa is found in scattered locations in the European mountains from the Pyrenees to the Carpathians and Tatras with two subspecies, subsp. *retusa* usually found on granites, gneiss and schists and subsp. *augustana* on base-rich rocks. *Saxifraga retusa* can make a pretty display of small heads of small mauve or pink flowers with pointed petals, but it is too small to make any impact except in a trough or pot. It is not generally a difficult species to keep going in a trough, and will survive sun better than the preceding species.

The remaining species is *Saxifraga nathorstii* from Greenland, which appears to have originated as a hybrid between *S. oppositifolia* and *S. aizoides* and, with chromosome doubling, has become a fertile polyploid species. Although variable, it usually resembles an orange-flowered *S. oppositifolia*. Cuttings root fairly readily, but unsurprisingly, given its place of origin, it requires very cool and moist conditions.

Section *Porphyrion* Tausch

Florulentae

(Section *Ligulatae* subsection *Florulentae* (Engler &
Irmscher) Gornall)

Saxifraga florulenta Moretti (1823). Long-lived
monocarpic species with rosettes to 15 cm retaining
many layers of dead foliage. Leaves mid- to dark green,
3–6 × 0.4–0.7 cm, smooth, oblong, slightly expanded
toward tip, acuminate-pointed. Hydathodes but no
lime encrustation, margin translucent, ciliate margin
toward base. Stems to 25 cm densely hairy, branched
from base, up to about 100 flowers, pale or warm pink,
not opening wide. Tripartite ovary, 3 styles (terminal
5-parted). 2500–3500m, France and Italy (Maritime
Alps), always on granite or gneiss.

Xanthizoon

(Section *Xanthizoon* (Grisebach) and section *Ligulatae*
subsection *Mutatae* (Engler & Irmscher) Gornall)

Saxifraga aizoides Linnaeus (1753). Mats of leafy
stems. Leaves more or less cylindrical to 22 × 4 mm
with lime pore near tip (sometimes up to 5 pores),
little encrustation. Flowers 1–15, petals elliptic,
broadly spaced, yellow to red, often spotted orange
or red, to 7 × 3 mm. Europe Pyrenees, Apennines
and Balkans northwards to Britain, Scandinavia and
northwest Russia. Arctic. North America southwards
in Appalachians and Rocky Mountains to US border.
A variety with red flowers, **var.** *atrorubens*, has been
described from the Apuan Alps in northern Italy.

Saxifraga mutata Linnaeus (1762). Single monocarpic
rosette to 15 cm, sometimes small group of rosettes.
Broad oblong leaves, to 7.0 × 1.5 cm thickened or
fleshy, margin cartilaginous, finely toothed, lime glands
near edge, little or no encrustation. Flower stems to
10–50 cm, broad ovate stems leaves in lower part.
Inflorescence glandular-hairy, branched with up to 8
or more flowers per branch and 200 or more flowers in
all. Petals very narrow, pointed, orange-yellow shading
to red at base to 8 × 1.5 mm, widely separated, broad
triangular sepals clearly visible between petals. Alps
and Carpathians.

    subsp. *mutata*. Inflorescence branched from half-
way. Alps.

    subsp. *demissa*. Inflorescence branched from base.
Carpathians.

Note: Many plants do not conform well morphologically
or geographically to this division into two subspecies.

Hybrids of *Xanthizoon* species
S. ×*forsteri* (*S. mutata* × *S. caesia*).
S. ×*hausmannii* (*S. aizoides* × *S. mutata*).
S. ×*larsenii* (*S. aizoides* × *S. paniculata*). Artificial
hybrid.
S. ×*patens* (*S. aizoides* × *S. caesia*).
S. ×*primulaize* (*S. aizoides* × *S. paniculata*). Artificial
hybrid.
S. ×*sotchensis* (*S. aizoides* × *S. squarrosa*).

Squarrosae

(Section *Porphyrion* series *Squarrosae* (Engler &
Irmscher) Gornall)

Saxifraga caesia Linnaeus (1753). Mats or cushions
of rosettes. Flower stems to 12 cm, 2–8 flowers.
Leaves oblong-spathulate, recurved to 4 × 1.5 mm,
usually 7 lime pores near leaf edge. Petals white,
obovate to 6 mm. Widespread in Pyrenees, Alps,
northern Apennines, Tatras, Capathians and southern
ex-Yugoslavia.

Saxifraga squarrosa Sieber (1821). Similar to *S. caesia*
but foliage less encrusted and green rather than grey,
usually rather smaller, leaves half the width (4 × 0.75
mm) less recurved, or only at tip, usually 3 lime pores.
Flower stems usually shorter with fewer and smaller
flowers. Southeastern Alps: Italy, Austria, Slovenia.

Hybrids of *Squarrosae* species:
S. ×*forsteri* (*S. caesia* × *S. mutata*). Doubtful.
S. ×*patens* (*S. caesia* × *S. aizoides*).
S. ×*saleixiana* (*S. caesia* × *S. aretioides*). Doubtful.
S. ×*sotchensis* (*S. squarrosa* × *S. aizoides*). Recorded
once.
S. ×*tirolensis* (*S. caesia* × *S. squarrosa*).

Oppositifoliae

(Section *Porphyrion* subsection *Oppositifoliae* Hayek)

Saxifraga biflora Allioni (1773). Small mats, 2–3 or
more flowers per stem. Leaves opposite, slightly
fleshy, obovate-circular to 9 × 6 mm, usually 1 lime

pore. Flowers purple to pink (or white), yellow nectary disc, petals to 10 × 6 mm. Hybrids (*S. ×kochii*) with *S. oppositifolia* common.

subsp. *biflora*. Leaves with single pore. Usually 2 or more flowers, pedicels short. Alps.

subsp. *epirotica*. Leaves with 3–5 lime pores. Single flowers, pedicels longer. Greece: Papigno, Ioannina province.

Saxifraga oppositifolia Linnaeus (1753) [incl. *S. czekanowskii* Siplivinsky (1972), *S. vulcanica* Siplivinsky (1972), *S. duthei* Gandoger (1899)]. Very variable. Mats of stems with opposite leaves paired or columnar, flower stems to 2 cm, solitary flowers. Leaves variable in shape, typically to 5 × 2 mm with 3 lime pores, some encrustation, marginal hairs near base. Flowers purple to pink (occasionally white). Widespread: Europe, Asia, North America.

subsp. *oppositifolia*. Leaves opposite, oblong-obovate, usually 1 lime pore. Petals 7–12 mm. Throughout range.

subsp. *asiatica*. Marginal hairs grade to marginal teeth. Not widely accepted.

subsp. *blepharophylla*. Flower stems to 0.5 cm. Compact foliage, leaves to 5 mm. Petals 5–8 mm, sepals long. Austrian Alps.

subsp. *glandulisepala*. Foliage not as small as in subsp. *smalliana*, sepals hairy on backs. Alaska, Yukon, British Columbia.

subsp. *paradoxa*. Leaves alternate, often 3 pores. Pyrenees.

subsp. *rudolphiana*. Flower stems very short. Foliage tight, leaves very small to 2 × 1.3 mm, petals 5–7 mm. Austrian Alps, very restricted in Italy.

subsp. *smalliana*. Foliage small, dense, sepals hairless on back. Alaska and Yukon.

subsp. *speciosa*. Flower stems short. Leaves broad or circular to 5 mm. Petals 8–12 mm. Apennines.

Various cultivars have been introduced, most recent ones being named after collection sites. Beyond these there are a few individual cultivars that deserve notice. Among the most popular are 'Theoden', 'Ruth Draper', 'Latina', 'Splendens', 'Vaccariana', and 'W. A. Clark', as well as many collected forms. 'Corrie Fie' (sometimes as 'Corrie Fiadh') is a good white-flowered form. There are three crosses between 'Ruth Draper' and 'Splendens': 'Greenslacks Claire', 'Greenslacks Heather' and 'Greenslacks Valerie'.

Saxifraga retusa Gouan (1773). Small mats or cushions of tight leafy branches, 1–5 flowers. Leaves to 4 × 2 mm, tip recurved sharply. Flowers open, in tight head, mauve-purple, petals pointed to 5 × 2.5 mm. Scattered in Pyrenees, Alps, Carpathians, Tatras.

subsp. *retusa*. Calyx hairless. 1–3 flowers. Silicaceous rocks. Throughout range.

subsp. *augustana*. Calyx hairy, 3–5 flowers. Limestone. Alps in France and Italy.

Saxifraga nathorstii (Dusen) Hayek (1905). Variable, usually similar to *S. oppositifolia* with orange flowers. Polyploid hybrid species of *S. oppositifolia* × *S. aizoides*. Eastern Greenland.

Hybrids of *Oppositifoliae* species:

S. ×kochii Hornung (*S. oppositifolia* × *S. biflora*). This hybrid can be common where the two parental species are in close proximity and individuals vary widely. Precedence is not fully clear with regard to the name of this cross. Various other names have been ascribed. *S. ×zermattensis* Hayek may have precedence. One named cultivar: 'Firebrand'.

9 · London Pride Saxifrages
Section *Gymnopera*

London pride is ubiquitous—yet most people who have it in their gardens don't even know it is a saxifrage. It has become so much part of the English garden because of its ability to cope with long neglect in dark urban settings as well as more obviously amenable rural ones, where it holds a place at the front of cottage borders. English cities in the 19th and early 20th centuries had much higher levels of pollution from the burning of coal than any western city today. Where they could be found at all, hunched between blocks of flats and terraces of houses, private gardens in many parts of the inner cities would be small and dark and have poor soils. Plants which could thrive in such conditions would always be prized. London pride, derived from woodland plants accustomed to shade and shelter, making mats of tough evergreen foliage, fitted the bill exactly and the airy froth of delicate flowers was a bonus.

Saxifraga 'Walter Ingwersen'.

Noel Coward used its resilient nature as a metaphor for the spirit of the Blitz in his patriotic song of the Second World War, and its name has been adopted for a well-known beer from the Chiswick brewer Fuller's. But it had a whole slew of other common names giving voice to the charming clouds of pretty little white or pink flowers. Among these are Prattling Parnell, Prince's Feather (or sometimes King's Feather), None-so-pretty, Look-up-and-kiss-me, and Pretty Nancy or Nancy-pretty. The fact that a garden plant has acquired so many common names means that it must be one that the "common people" could get and grow.

The Origins of London Pride

Many of the names for London pride are surprisingly old. The first for which I can find a recorded date is prattling Parnell. This is not, as I had initially assumed, connected with the 19th-century Irish nationalist Parnell but is much older, being used specifically in this context by Gerard in 1597 when a parnell was a flighty girl or harlot and our saxifrage is "Our London Dames pratling Parnell". Another old usage was "The Prince's Feather", which is recorded by Parkinson in his *Paradisus* in 1629. The name "pretty Nancy" is the title of a sea-shanty, sometimes as Pretty

London pride's wonderful cloud of flowers, with *Saxifraga* 'Dentata' in the foreground (left). Photograph John Howes.

London pride.

Nancy of Yarmouth, but it is more likely, in the reverse form "Nancy-pretty", to be a dialect form of "none-so-pretty", which is recorded as a horticultural name from Miller's *Gardeners Dictionary* of 1731. In normal usage "none-so-pretty" was used for an item of millinery, and other names such as "whimsey" and "St Anne's needlework" have similar origins.

It is clear, then, that the plant has a long history in cultivation. The name "London pride" seems to appear first in Molyneux's *Philosophical Transactions* in 1697 referring to "*Cotyledon, sive Sedum serratum Latifolium Montanum guttato flore … vulgarly call'd by the Gardners London Pride : I suppose because of its pretty elegant Flower*". Not all these different names were being used for exactly the same plants, although they were not distinguished as separate species until Brotero in 1805. Parkinson appears to have been referring to *Saxifraga umbrosa*, while Molyneaux, although quoting the Latin of Parkinson, was referring to *S. spathularis* which he had seen in Ireland. London pride as we know it today is a hybrid of these two species, obviously a horticultural hybrid since they do not occur together in the wild. It is usually supposed, and often stated, that the name "London pride" refers to George London and the Brompton Nursery of London & Wise rather than to the city of London, and although Molyneaux does not make this comment, the date of his usage does not preclude it, since the nursery had come to George London in 1689.

London & Wise

The Brompton Park Nursery, as it was originally, was set up by Roger Looker in 1681 when the Stuart king Charles II was still on the throne. First crowned in Scotland on New Year's Day 1651, within a year he had to flee the parliamentary forces and only returned to London in 1660. The Restoration was a period of theatrical license and artistic liberty, and also of economic growth. New money fostered a new interest in gardening. A few small nurseries were set up, but the Brompton Park Nursery was a much more significant enterprise. This was the first large-scale nursery in England, extending to at least 50 acres in rural Brompton, part of Kensington. It was very much the fashionable place to be, about five miles from the centre of London. When William III came to the throne in 1689 he bought Nottingham House, renamed it Kensington Palace and lived there rather than in London to help alleviate his asthma. The Brompton Park Nursery was a little less than a mile from Kensington Palace—the right place at the right time.

Roger Looker was not alone in the nursery venture; his partners were Moses Cook, who corresponded with the writer John Evelyn about the use of yew trees in the garden, John Field and George London; but Roger Looker was the Queen's gardener and this was a business on an appropriate scale. Estimates are that at its peak the nursery may have had over one million seedling trees on site. But it was not Looker, Cook and Field who would profit. Looker died in 1685, Field in 1687, and perhaps unsurprisingly Cook retired in 1689. This left George London, who took on as a partner Henry Wise, previously an apprentice at the nursery. They would run London & Wise as partners till George London died in 1713; Henry Wise then continued till his death in 1738. These were men who knew about advertising their role; they wrote *The Retir'd Gardn'r* (based on French gardening texts) and had published La Quintinye's *The complete gard'ner: or, directions for cultivating and right ordering of fruit-gardens and kitchen garden*—"Now compendiously abridg'd, and made of more use, with very considerable improvements"—in a translation that probably owed something to John Evelyn. Fruit trees were a major part of the work of the Brompton Park Nursery from its inception, but the nursery was also responsible for most of the new plant introductions into Britain at this time. Brompton stocks were one of their introductions; London pride seems to have been another.

After London's death the influence of the nursery was maintained and at least two further apprentices are of interest: Stephen Switzer, author of *The Practical Fruit Gardener*, published in 1724; and Charles Bridgeman, who worked on the gardens of Blenheim with Vanbrugh who was famous as a playwright as well as an architect, and was responsible for the phrase "much of a muchness" in his play *The Provok'd Husband*. Bridgeman went on to design the gardens at Stowe among others, and maintained the tradition of the nursery's founder Roger Looker by becoming the royal gardener, this time to George II. Eventually the grounds of the nursery became part of the new exhibition quarter where the Victoria & Albert Museum was built. London pride now grows everywhere, but its origins in the nursery trade are far from humble.

The *Gymnopera* Species

There are four species in section *Gymnopera*, all European, three of which hybridize readily with one another in cultivation as well as in the wild. Their general form is akin to that of many of the North American *Micranthes* although they are not particularly closely related to them. There is a basal tuft or rosette of leaves, more or less evergreen, thickened, with a flattened blade and a petiole usually at least as long and in some cases up to three times as long. Horizontal stems at or just below ground level produce new rosettes at their tips so that very extensive mats can develop. The flower stems are quite tall, have no stem leaves and may have up to 50 flowers in the inflorescence. The flowers are small, white or pale pink, usually with one or two larger yellow spots at the base of the petals and a scattering of smaller pink or red ones above those, and have fully superior ovaries.

Saxifraga spathularis, one of the parents of London pride, is found throughout western Ireland and in the mountains of northwestern Spain and northern Portugal. It has tough, dark green leathery leaves with a strongly and sharply toothed margin and is found in woodland and on shady banks. *Saxifraga hirsuta* is found in extreme southwestern Ireland and in Spain, from the northwestern mountains through to the Pyrenees just west of Andorra, and has soft, crenate, hairy leaf blades with long thin petioles. In subsp. *hirsuta*, a plant of the shaded woodland floor, the blade is circular, while in subsp. *paucicrenata* the rather smaller blade is rather more elongated and the plant is found on exposed limestone. *Saxifraga spathularis* and *S. hirsuta* overlap throughout the range of *S. hirsuta* in Ireland and just overlap in Spain, but occupy rather different niches. Hybrids are found in both countries, more commonly in Ireland where they can form hybrid swarms of plants grading from one parental species to the other. This hybrid is *S. ×polita*, but the historical treatment by botanists of this and the other hybrids is often confused.

Saxifraga umbrosa, the other parent of London pride, is found throughout the central Pyrenees and in the western part of this range it is sympatric with *S. hirsuta* with which it also forms hybrid swarms. This hybrid is *S. ×geum*, but again this name has a very chequered history, having also been used for *S. hirsuta* itself. *Saxifraga umbrosa* has oblong slightly crenate leaves with petioles about the same length as the blade. The petioles are not really seen in the flat rosettes, while in other species the petioles are longer and clearly visible. Although *S. umbrosa* is usually found in damp shady habitats, it can be found growing at the open edge of woodland and even in more open habitats if there is a little shade at the base of small shrubs.

The final species in the section is *Saxifraga cuneifolia*, which just overlaps with *S. umbrosa* at the eastern end of the range of that species, but it spreads across all the way through the Alps and is found again in the Carpathians. Given the ease with which the other species hybridize with one another, and indeed in some cases with species from other sections, it is interesting that *S. cuneifolia* does not hybrid-

Saxifraga spathularis growing on rocks (middle left). Killarney, Co. Kerry, Ireland.

Saxifraga spathularis.

ize with *S. umbrosa* where they are found together in the wild. Attempts to create artificial hybrids have also failed. *Saxifraga cuneifolia* has smooth spathulate leaves, smaller than in the other species. In subsp. *robusta* they are larger with a somewhat toothed margin, but in subsp. *cuneifolia* they are entire.

Saxifraga hirsuta carpeting the woodland floor, Co. Kerry.

The species are typically found in sheltered shady conditions and make very large mats of rosettes in the right conditions. *Saxifraga umbrosa* can be found in more open situations, often at the base of vegetation at the edge of woodland, or even at higher altitudes at the base of rhododendron bushes in the open. In Ireland *S. spathularis* can be found on open rocky slopes, but is much more at home in shady woodland, growing over boulders, or even on the damp walls toward the mouth of a cave. The typical subspecies of *S. hirsuta* is a plant of the woodland floor where it can grow in great profusion in deep shade, along with wood violets and oxalis, although subsp. *paucicrenata* is typically found on exposed limestone. *Saxifraga cuneifolia* is fairly flexible in its requirements; it can grow on very lightly shaded and often quite dry but sheltered banks, but it can also be found in much more shaded situations growing on rocks and boulders in woodland.

Saxifraga cuneifolia.
Maritime Alps.
Photograph John Howes.

The Hybrids

Apart from the artificial hybrid London pride, *S. ×urbium* (*S. spathularis × S. umbrosa*), there are two wild hybrids, *S. ×polita* (*S. hirsuta × S. spathularis*) and *S. ×geum* (*S. hirsuta × S. umbrosa*), but both names have been blurred in their use and historical references are often confusing. Both of the hybrids are quite common in the wild, *S. ×geum* in the western Pyrenees and *S. ×polita* in southwestern Ireland, and the latter is also found although less commonly in northwestern Spain. Unlike some hybrids, both these are fertile and further inter-hybrid crossing and back-crossing lead to hybrid swarms where plants can be found across a cline from one parental species to the other.

Although the two wild hybrids can only be met in Ireland and Spain, there are a number of self-sustaining colonies of *Gymnopera* saxifrages in England and Scotland derived from cultivated stock. These are variously derived from London pride, the species and other old garden forms.

Gymnopera Saxifrages in the Garden

While London pride is the best known of the hybrids, quite a few other *Gymnopera* saxifrages are available to the gardener and none requires special treatment. Most of the plants in the section seem to thrive in heavy soils, deal with hard frosts and cope well with deep shade and long dry periods. Propagation is extremely easy: a rosette can be broken off and the short broken stem pressed directly into the open garden soil. Best of all positions for the *Gymnopera* saxifrages are places in the garden where dappled sunlight catches the flowers.

The species are not difficult to grow but the parents of London pride, *Saxifraga umbrosa* and *S. spathularis*, are not so often met with in gardens partly at least because garden stocks of these and *S. hirsuta* so readily cross, back-cross and sometimes re-cross with the offspring, gradually smudging the identities of their ancestors. The fourth species, *S. cuneifolia*, is usually met by the gardener in the smaller of the subspecies, subsp. *cuneifolia*, and is usually treated as a plant for the rock garden or trough where its small glabrous spathulate leaves form small mats. The other subspecies, subsp. *robusta*, seems an equally good plant for the gardener but is much more rarely found in nurseries. In the garden *S. cuneifolia* is often found in a variegated form and there is a nice plant called 'Fanzetta', which appears to be a selection of *S. cuneifolia* with particularly neat, broadly spathulate foliage.

London Pride Group cultivars

Many of the cultivars have been listed as belonging to particular species and hybrids with little justification. The use of
the cultivar-group concept is particularly appropriate in such
a case and it is used here to describe all those cultivars of the
section apart from those of *Saxifraga cuneifolia*. All require
similar treatment and many, although not all, have obscure
heritage. Although some of the London Pride Group cultivars have become extinct, there are still about eight distinct
and reasonably available plants that are worth growing. Most
are smaller plants, but two which are of very similar size to
London pride, with flower stems about 30–40 cm tall, are 'Miss Chambers', with
much deeper pink flowers and dark scalloped foliage with petioles often stained purple, and 'Dentata', which appears to be a selection of *S.* ×*polita* with white flowers; its
mature foliage has circular saw-toothed leaf blades and long petioles.

Flowers of various
Gymnopera saxifrages
(left to right): *Saxifraga
hirsuta*, *S.* 'Miss
Chambers', London
pride.

There were a number of other old cultivars which were selected for their foliage. One that is still available is *Saxifraga* 'Crispa', a small form with foliage like
London pride itself, with scalloped oblong leaves on petioles of more or less equal
length. Other forms such as 'Crinkle', 'Aegilops' with more scalloped edges, and
'Serratifolia' with serrate edges to the leaves, may still be in circulation.

Saxifraga 'Dentata'
(with saw-toothed
leaves) and 'Miss
Chambers' (extreme
right, with darker pink
flowers) in a border.

Among the smaller cultivars are charming plants. *Saxifraga* 'Walter Ingwersen'
(and 'Clarence Elliott', which seems to be the same plant today even if they were
different originally) is said to be a form of *S. umbrosa* which is no more than half
the normal size and has clouds of pink, rather than white,
flowers. This form has sometimes been called var. *primuloides*. This has never been formally described and hence is
better treated as the cultivar 'Primuloides' if a further name
is needed. Apparently there is a small white form under the
German name 'Weisse Elliott', although whether it actually
derives from 'Clarence Elliott' is unclear.

A number of cultivars have variegated foliage, the largest of which can lighten the darker shade of a winter corner. There are a range of names for the variegated forms
of *S.* ×*urbium* ('Aureopunctata', 'Variegata', 'Variegata
Aurea') which all seem to refer to the same plant. It has
leaves splashed with yellow in an irregular way and is quite
robust. There are also variegated forms of *S. spathularis*
and cultivar names are often used interchangeably so only
sight of a plant will confirm whether it is derived from
S. spathularis or *S.* ×*urbium*. There is also a variegated
form of *S. cuneifolia* which can be quite charming.

Saxifraga 'Dentata'.

Saxifraga 'Crispa'.

The other major selections have been of varieties with richer coloured flowers. As well as the full-sized 'Miss Chambers', the darkest, there are the smaller 'Letchworth Gem' and 'Hartside Pink'. Two other forms which I have not seen but which may still exist are 'Chelsea Pink' and 'London Cerise'.

Intersectional Hybrids

The species in section *Gymnopera* are promiscuous, each of them forming intersectional hybrids with species from section *Ligulatae*. Although in some cases the parentage is obscure, it is probable that they each hybridize with *S. paniculata*, and in some cases with other *Ligulatae* as well. Two of the hybrids with *S. paniculata* are quite readily available and distinctive. *Saxifraga ×andrewsii* is the hybrid involving *S. spathularis*, with strap-shaped leaves with lime beads along the margins. The foliage makes this a distinctive plant. *Saxifraga* 'Winifred Bevington' is a charming hybrid, probably of *S. umbrosa* and *S. paniculata*, with the rosettes of rounded, lime-beaded foliage. The flowers are small but pretty pink

Saxifraga cuneifolia 'Variegata'. Photograph Paul Kennett.

with deeper pink anthers, clearly having a strong *Gymnopera* influence but with the overall effect being more like a silver saxifrage. A hybrid has also been reported of *S. hirsuta* and *S. paniculata* (*S. ×wildiana*).

While *S. cuneifolia* does not hybridize with any of the other *Gymnopera* species, it does hybridize with both *S. paniculata* (to give *S. ×zimmeteri*) and with *S. crustata*. This has been called *S. ×pseudo-forsteri*, but this name has not been validly published. Both of these are small plants with white flowers but do not generally excite as much attention as the other intersectional hybrids here. A hybrid of *S. cuneifolia* with *S. callosa* has also been collected and the leaves clearly shows the characteristics of both.

The cross between *Saxifraga umbrosa* 'Primuloides' and *S. aizoides* produced *S.* 'Primulaize', which probably originated in the nursery of Maurice Prichard. The oldest record appears to be in his 1929 catalogue, when four colour forms were listed: pale pink, salmon, crimson and rose. The normal form today is 'Primulaize Salmon', although the pale pink form may also still exist.

Although all of these intersectional hybrids are attractive plants, they tend to need more attention than do the pure *Gymnopera* species and cultivars.

Flower of *Saxifraga* ×*zimmeteri*. Photograph Paul Kennett.

Rosettes of *Saxifraga* ×*zimmeteri*.

Saxifraga 'Primulaize Salmon'.

The recently discovered hybrid between *Saxifraga cuneifolia* and *S. crustata*.

Section *Gymnopera* D. Don

Species

Saxifraga cuneifolia Linnaeus (1759). Smallest species in the section forming mats of evergreen leafy rosettes. Leaves are smooth, hairless, circular or roundly spathulate, sometimes with toothed margin, varying widely in size up to 2.5 × 2.2 cm with a petiole about as long again. Flower stems to 25 cm with numerous white flowers, petals sometimes having yellow basal and a few tiny red spots. Anthers pale pink, ovaries green. Southern Europe from eastern Pyrenees across France and the Alps to the Carpathians.

  subsp. *cuneifolia*. Smaller leaves with almost untoothed margin. Usually fewer than 10 flowers. Maritime Alps and northern Apennines.

  subsp. *robusta* D. A. Webb. Larger leaves with distinctly although not deeply toothed margin. Usually more than 10 flowers. Throughout range of species.

  Cultivars: 'Fanzetta', 'Variegata'.

Saxifraga hirsuta Linnaeus (1759). Loose mats of leafy tufts. Hairy, circular or broadly elliptic, roundly scalloped, soft leaves up to 4.0 × 5.0 cm, on narrow hairy petioles often up to 10 cm. Flower stems typically 20–30 cm with numerous small flowers with white petals usually with a yellow basal spot and sometimes tiny pink ones. Pale pink anthers, ovaries pale. Southwestern Ireland, northern Spain.

  subsp. *hirsuta*. Leaf-blade reniform to circular. Deep shade, woodland floor. Throughout range of species. Down to sea-level in Ireland. Up to 2000m in Spain.

  subsp. *paucicrenata* (Leresche ex Gillot) D. A. Webb. Leaf blade circular to oblong. Plants smaller. Picos de Europa and western Pyrenees on rocky limestone exposures in mountains up to 2000m.

Saxifraga spathularis Brotero (1805). Mats of evergreen leafy rosettes. Broadly oblong, sharply to gently toothed, leathery, shiny dark green leaves to 5.0 × 3.0 cm with a cuneate base with a flattened petiole of much the same length. Flower stem to 50 cm with numerous small flowers with white petals with yellow basal spots and smaller deep pink ones. Bright pink anthers, ovaries pink. Damp, shady places in woodland, often on boulders. Western Ireland, northwestern Spain and Portugal.

Saxifraga umbrosa Linnaeus (1762). Central Pyrenees. Dense mats of evergreen leafy rosettes. Oblong, scalloped, smooth but not shiny, leathery blade, typically 2.0 × 3.0 cm with cuneate base and short petiole, usually no more than half length of blade. Flower stem to 35 cm with numerous flowers with white petals with yellow basal spots and tiny pink spots. Anthers bright pink, ovaries bright pink. Shady and damp places. Central Pyrenees.

Hybrids

S. ×*geum* Linnaeus (1753) (*S. umbrosa* × *S. hirsuta*). Very confused historically with name often used for *S. hirsuta*. The wild hybrid is found in hybrid swarms where parents are sympatric with plants variously intermediate between both ancestral species. Typically leaf blade shorter and more rounded than *S. umbrosa* but sparsely hairy. Not rare in central Pyrenees. In cultivation in European gardens more commonly than British ones.

S. ×*polita* (Haworth) Link (1821) (*S. hirsuta* × *S. spathularis*). Fertile wild hybrid often in hybrid swarms with plants variously intermediate between both parental species. Typically with circular blade of *S. hirsuta* but with sharply toothed margin, sparsely hairy, and with long petiole. Not rare in southwestern Ireland where parental species are sympatric. Less common in northern Spain. Not difficult to cultivate.

S. ×*urbium* D. A. Webb (1963) (*S. umbrosa* × *S. spathularis*). London pride. This hybrid is an artificial one. Leaf blades are typically shorter, with longer petioles, than in *S. umbrosa* and often slightly darker green. Common in British gardens. Very tough and easy in wide variety of conditions.

London Pride Group

Many of these cultivars have been listed as belonging to particular species and hybrids with little justification. The use of the cultivar-group concept is particularly appropriate in such a case.

'Aureopunctata'. Variegated form of London pride.

'Chamber's Pink Pride' see 'Miss Chambers'.

'Clarence Elliott'. See 'Walter Ingwersen'.

'Dentata'. Distinctive cultivar. Same size as London pride but with sharply toothed, more or less hairless round blade on long petiole.

'Gracilis'. Like London pride but rather smaller although not as small as 'Walter Ingwersen'.

'Hartside Pink'. Small with pink flowers.

'Letchworth Gem'. Small with pink flowers.

London pride. See *S.* ×*urbium*.

'Miss Chambers' (also as 'Chamber's Pink Pride'). Similar leaf and size to London pride but with darker pink flowers and purple-stained stems.

'Primuloides' (sometimes invalidly as *S.* ×*urbium* var. *primuloides*). This may be the same as 'Walter Ingwersen' and 'Clarence Elliott'.

'Variegata'. Variegated form of London pride.

'Variegata Aurea'. Variegated form of London pride.

'Walter Ingwersen'. Small (about half the size of London pride) with pink flowers. Does not appear to be distinct from 'Clarence Elliott'.

'Weisse Elliott'. A German cultivar, presumably with white flowers.

Other cultivars in this group which may still be in cultivation are: 'Aegilops', 'Chelsea Pink', 'Colvillei', 'Crinkle', 'Dixter Form', 'London Cerise', 'Morrisonii', 'Rubrum' and 'Serratifolia'.

Intersectional Hybrids

S. ×*andrewsii* (probably *S. spathularis* × *S. paniculata*). Narrow linear, toothed leaves, encrusted along margin. Flower stems to about 25 cm. Flowers like London pride, but fewer and larger.

S. ×*jaeggiana*. Synonym of *S.* ×*zimmeteri*.

S. ×*zimmeteri* (*S. cuneifolia* × *S. paniculata*). Foliage similar to *S. paniculata*. Flowers white.

'Primulaize Salmon' (*S.* 'Primuloides' × *S. aizoides*). Slightly toothed oblong leaves. Flower stems to 15 cm with very distinct pink-orange flowers with narrow oblong petals. Can be short-lived.

'Tazetta' (*S. cuneifolia* × *S. taygetea*). Small plant with leaves having broadly expanded spathulate tip without any toothing. White flowers. Occasionally in cultivation but often little more than form of *S. cuneifolia*.

'Winifred Bevington' (*S. paniculata* × *S. umbrosa*). Rounded, rather incurved dark green leaves with clear lime-encusted margins. Stems to 20 cm with small, pretty pale pink flowers with pink anthers.

Other hybrids include:

S. ×*pseudo-forsteri* (*S. crustata* × *S. cuneifolia*).

S. ×*wildiana* (*S. hirsuta* × *S. paniculata*).

S. ×*wisleyensis* (invalid) (*S. paniculata* × *S. umbrosa*).

and plants have been collected of **S. callosa × S. cuneifolia** but have not yet been described.

10 · Arctic-Alpine Bulbiliferous Saxifrages
Section *Mesogyne*

The *Mesogyne* saxifrages are some of the more reclusive species and, although some can be found on rock faces, open scree or tundra, they are just as likely to be found sheltering under the overhang of rocks. There are around a dozen species found up to very high altitudes in the mountains of Asia, Europe and North America and up into the high Arctic. Most of them are small plants, some very small, forming a tuft of palmate-lobed leaves rather like those of a very small ivy-leaved pelargonium. The flowers are almost always white with ovaries at least two-thirds superior and are either solitary or on stems which have no more than about four flowers. They are adapted to survive the long harsh winters by producing axillary bulbils usually in the axils of the basal leaves but in *Saxifraga cernua* also on the flower stem. Only when the snow melts will growth commence with the bulbils sprouting leaves or tiny runners.

The larger species such as *Saxifraga sibirica* and *S. cernua* have vase-shaped flowers with the white petals curving slightly outwards towards the tip. It is not difficult to see why Engler felt that their proper home was with the bulbiferous species of section *Saxifraga*, with their flowers looking very similar, although the bulbils in those species grouped around *S. granulata* allow them to survive hot dry summers rather than long cold winters. The most obvious differences between the two sections is that the *Mesogyne* species have more or less superior rather than inferior ovaries, now seen as a much more significant characteristic; and the palmate leaves with their lobed blades have narrow petioles which can be quite long. They also have non-lime-secreting hydathodes on their leaves, similar to those in section *Gymnopera*. The flowers of *S. rivularis*, *S. hyperborea* and *S. bracteata* have much smaller petals, even in relative terms, and relatively thicker flower stems, but again are superficially similar to the smaller species from section *Saxifraga* such as *S. tridactylites*.

Saxifraga cernua on Pike's Peak in the Rocky Mountains in Colorado.

Saxifraga sibirica on the Rhotang Pass, northwest India. In this very damp and shaded position, the stolons are clearly visible.

Saxifraga radiata, Wooley Road, Seward Peninsula, Alaska. Photograph Ian Bainbridge.

The *Mesogyne* Species

Saxifraga sibirica and *S. radiata*

There are three very widespread species, *Saxifraga cernua*, *S. sibirica* and *S. rivularis*. The largest species in the section, and the most obviously attractive, is *S. sibirica*, which is found all the way from the eastern shore of the Pacific westward through Russia and the Himalaya as far as Bulgaria. It grows in damp or rocky spots forming tufts of growth and may have short runners so it can make small mats of typically ivy-shaped leaves, in this case with 5–7 lobes. The degree of dormancy in *S. sibirica* may depend on the geographic and ecological location of a particular specimen. Plants in Europe, where it is said to be found down to 500 metres probably retain foliage for much longer periods and in some cases remain evergreen. In the Himalaya it is certainly found up to 5100 metres. In far northerly latitudes, from the Yukon to the Taimyr, *S. sibirica* seems to be replaced by *S. radiata* with smaller basal leaves and shorter stems. A rather obscure taxon is *S. exilis* which, as originally described by Stephan, is now included in *S. radiata*.

Saxifraga cernua, S. granulifera and S. carpatica

The other widespread species with a reasonably large flower is *Saxifraga cernua* with a solitary flower stem (although occasionally it may make a small tuft with more than one flower stem) which carries, at most, a single terminal flower and numerous small dark red bulbils up the stem in the axils of the stem leaves. The cluster of basal leaves are broadly kidney-shaped and typically about half the size of those of *S. sibirica* with 3–7 broad lobes. The flower stem may be up to about 15 cm tall and the terminal flower, if it has one, is rather pretty, like that of *S. sibirica* slightly vase-shaped and pure white. In many populations no viable seed seems to be set—it may be self-incompatible—and reproduction is achieved through the bulbils which means that all the individuals in a local population will be genetically identical. *Saxifraga cernua* is circumboreal, being distributed around the Arctic and subArctic. In North America it is found down the mountains of the west as far as Colorado and down as far as the Great Lakes in Canada; in eastern Asia it is found down to Sakhalin and then in disjunct populations in Japan and China. There are also disjunct populations in the higher reaches of the Alps and Carpathians, and it has also been recorded from the Himalayas.

Saxifraga granulifera is also found in the Himalaya, from Nepal and Bhutan, and then spreads through to Tibet and Sichuan. It is clearly related to *S. cernua*, having tiny axillary bulbils, sometimes in clusters; but they are very much smaller, each no more than 1 mm in diameter. It is also much more spindly, up to about 25 cm tall with up to 5 flowers, but they are only half the size of those of *S. cernua*.

Saxifraga carpatica occupies scattered locations in the Carpathians, and the Rila and Pirin Mountains, from Poland southwards to Bulgaria as an allopatric species between the ranges of *S. cernua* to the north and west and *S. sibirica* to the south and east. In general terms it is like a scaled-down version of *S. sibirica* with flowers intermediate between those of *S. sibirica* and *S. rivularis*, and is distinguishable from *S. cernua* because it does not have bulbils on the flower stem.

Saxifraga rivularis and S. hyperborea

Saxifraga rivularis is much smaller all round than *S. sibirica*, forming tufts or small mats in damp or shady spots. The flowers are much smaller, with the white petals no more than about 5 mm long. Flower stems can be up to 15 cm tall with a single terminal flower, and there may be up to another 3 or 4 single flowers on spreading

branches, but it usually has solitary flowers and is very often much smaller than this. The basal bulbils develop small runners enabling it to form small mats. This helps distinguish it from *S. hyperborea*, which has no such runners and hence remains as a small tuft. *Saxifraga hyperborea* is a diploid species (*S. rivularis* is tetraploid) which is generally even smaller, with rather smaller red rather than white petals; most of its leaves have 3 rather than 5 lobes and have a cuneate rather than a cordate base. *Saxifraga rivularis* is a circumpolar species extending southwards in the Rocky Mountains and in eastern Canada, and in Europe it is found as far south as Scotland, while *S. hyperborea* is also found in the arctic part of this range. Very small plants from the arctic tundra along the coasts of far-eastern Russia and from Alaska have been classified as *S. rivularis* subsp. *arctolitoralis*. *Saxifraga rivularis*, along with *S. cernua*, is one of the species from this section found in Britain, in the Scottish mountains.

Saxifraga rivularis subsp. *arctolitoralis*. This tiny plant was photographed near Council, Seward Peninsula, Alaska.

Saxifraga rivularis (or *S. debilis*) on Pike's Peak, Colorado.

Saxifraga svalbardensis and *S. opdalensis*

There are two other European taxa which are thought to be of comparatively recent hybrid origin. Genetic analysis has suggested that *Saxifraga svalbardensis* from the Svalbard Peninsula in Spitzbergen originated as a hybrid between *S. rivularis* and *S. cernua*, with the former being the seed parent and the latter supplying the pollen. It also seems probable that *S. opdalensis* from southern Norway and Sweden, clearly distinct from *S. svalbardensis*, is also derived from hybridization of *S. cernua* and *S. rivularis*.

Saxifraga flexuosa, *S. debilis* and *S. yoshimurae*

Saxifraga flexuosa, which is found from Kamchatka and Alaska and may extend down to Colorado, is maintained by some taxonomists as a separate species. If it has more than a single flower, the inflorescence is a narrow one with white flowers, narrower hypanthium, shorter sepals, less hairy stems and clawed petals. Like *S. hyperborea* it is diploid, and it seems likely that it will generally become accepted that it is best dealt with under that species. Even less supported as a species is *S. debilis*, which in general is used to refer to small glabrous plants from the Rocky Mountains. The general dimensions of these tiny plants are in line with those of *S. hyperborea* rather than *S. rivularis*, but they have white flowers and their leaves almost always have 5 lobes and are cordate at the base rather than cuneate. *Saxifraga debilis* is sometimes treated as a subspecies of one or other of these and Gornall treats it under *S. flexuosa*. It is probable that the Rocky Mountains plants should be seen as specimens of *S. rivularis*.

Saxifraga yoshimurae, which was described from Sakhalin by two Japanese botanists, is not now recognized by Russian botanists—possibly for nationalistic reasons—and is probably being treated by them under *S. rivularis* rather than *S. hyperborea* since specimens show its basal leaves to have 5 rather than 3 lobes.

Saxifraga bracteata

Outside of Europe, *Saxifraga bracteata* is undisputed as to its status and is one of the more intriguing of the species in this section. It is not very restricted in geographical range—being found from coastal regions from northern British Columbia to Okhotsk and Japan—but it is restricted ecologically and is usually confined to sea cliffs, usually in very inaccessible places. On the Seward Peninsula, for example, its recorded localities are at least ten miles from the nearest road across the tundra. More robust than *S. rivularis*, although not necessarily taller, it has the flowers clustered at the top of the flower stem surrounded by a ruff of leaves.

Saxifraga bracteata. St
Paul, Pribiloff Islands.
Photograph Verna Pratt.

Growing *Mesogyne* Saxifrages

Although most of the species are far too small for anyone to worry much, *Saxifraga sibirica* is a pretty plant. With its vase-shaped white flowers and rather attractive ivy-shaped foliage this would make a nice addition to a stone wall. Unfortunately, although seed is very occasionally available and can sometimes be germinated, it seems impossible to maintain plants through the summer. *Saxifraga cernua* also seems like a plant that a specialist would be interested in, but although plants are occasionally raised from seed, or more probably bulbils, they never seem to last for any length of time and certainly do not seem to enable further propagation to take place easily. My guess is that the shady side of a piece of tufa might offer the best chance for success, and certainly a cool moist climate and a sheltered site offer the best hope. Obviously these are not plants to look for in nurseries: the only sources are likely to be the seed exchanges of the major rock-gardening societies or the expeditions of seed collectors.

Section *Mesogyne* Sternberg

Saxifraga bracteata D. Don (1822). Tufts of palmately lobed foliage generally like *S. sibirica* but with 3–6 lobes, and inflorescence congested with cauline leaves forming an involucral ruff around the flowers. Coastal situations, particularly cliffs, from British Columbia through Alaska and Kamchatka to northern Japan. Never common.

Saxifraga carpatica Sternberg (1831). Flower stem to 20 cm, 1–4 flowers. Small tufts of foliage with 5–9 lobed leaves, up to 1.2 × 1.6 cm, with petiole up to 4 cm. Flowers off-white to pink, petals up to 7 mm. Damp shady rocks and screes. 1400–1700m, Carpathians and Bulgaria: Rila and Pirin.

Saxifraga cernua Linnaeus (1753). Solitary stems with basal leaves typically with 3–7-palmate-lobed blade 1.0 × 1.5 cm on stems 2–3 times longer. Flower stems 3–30 cm with at most a single white terminal flower with petals up to 12 × 5 mm, and with numerous small dark red bulbils up the stem in axils of stem leaves. Damp or shaded places or tundra. Circumpolar (from sea-level in Arctic), south to Colorado (3300m) in Rocky Mountains, Great Lakes, UK (where no seed is ever set), Alps and Carpathians.

Saxifraga flexuosa Sternberg (1831) Close to *S. rivularis*, but with stems 3–12 cm with a very straight, erect inflorescence of 1–4 flowers on upright pedicels. Leaves smaller and more deeply and acutely lobed. Flowers noticeably smaller. Northeast Siberia, Kamchatka, Alaska, Pacific North America to, possibly, Colorado. It seems possible that this may be subsumed within *S. rivularis*.

Note: *S. debilis* Engelmann (1863). This has now been incorporated in *S. flexuosa* or in some people's eyes in *S. hyperborea* subsp. *debilis*, under which name small *Mesogyne* specimens in Colorado are often identified. It is not supported as a separate species by many botanists.

Saxifraga granulifera Harry Smith (1960). Related to *S. cernua* but with much thinner stems and smaller leaves. Stems are 10–25 cm tall with 1–5 or more flowers. Stems only 0.4–1.2 mm (sic) thick, with just 6–8 roundly palmate-lobed leaves, 1.0 × 1.3 cm, with tiny (to 0.7 mm) bulbils in the leaf axils and no basal bulbils. Flowers white or (possibly) pale yellow with oblong-linear petals 7 × 2.5 mm. 2700–4300m, Nepal, Bhutan, eastern Tibet.

Saxifraga hyperborea R. Brown (1823). Only definitely accepted as a species in its own right rather than as a variety of *S. rivularis* in recent years. Distinguished from *S. rivularis* most obviously by smaller size, usually 3- (rather than 5-) lobed leaf blade with cuneate base, red flowers, and being diploid. Circumpolar and possibly Rocky Mountains. (See note under *S. debilis* in entry for *S. flexuosa*.)

Saxifraga opdalensis Blytt (1892). Hybrid origin (probably *S. cernua* × *S. rivularis*). Very local in Norway and Sweden.

Saxifraga radiata J. K. Small (1905) [incl. *S. exilis* Stephan (1822)]. Close to *S. sibirica*, which it replaces in northerly latitudes, but with small basal leaves on shorter stems and short sepals. Yukon, Alaska, arctic Russia from Taimyr to Chukotka and down to Okhotsk.

Saxifraga rivularis Linnaeus (1753) [incl. *S. arctolitoralis* Jurtsev & V. V. Petrovsky (1981)]. Flower stem 3–15 cm with single terminal flower or possibly 2–5 on long lower branches. Palmate 5-lobed leaf blade, typically to 1.2 × 1.7 cm, cordate base, on petiole 2–6 times length of blade. Tetraploid. Circumpolar (to sea-level in Arctic), south in Rocky Mountains to Colorado (3500m or more), in eastern Canada to US border, in Asia to Sakhalin, in Europe to UK.

subsp. *arctolitoralis* (Jurtsev & V. V. Petrovsky) Jørgensen & Elven (*S. arctolitoralis*). Very similar to *S. hyperborea*, from which it is distinguished, if at all, by even smaller size, 2–3 cm tall, details of the relationship between calyx tube and sepals, and the fact that it is tetraploid rather than diploid. Russia: far-eastern arctic coastal tundra, and in Alaska.

Saxifraga sibirica Linnaeus (1762). Tufted. Flower stem 5–18 cm with 2–7 flowers. Petiolate leaves with 5–7 palmate-lobed blade 0.5–2.0 × 0.8–3.0 cm. Pure white petals up to 15 × 6 mm. Cool places, usually damp rocks. 500–5100m, Russia (Urals to Khabarovsk), Aegean, Bulgaria, Caucasus, Iran to west Himalaya, China.

Saxifraga svalbardensis Øvstedal (1983). Hybrid origin (probably *S. cernua* × *S. rivularis*) from Spitzbergen (Svalbard).

Saxifraga yoshimurae Miyabe & Tatewaki (1938). Flower stem 8–15 cm tall with 1–5 flowers. Differs from *S. hyperborea* by reniform leaves having 5 acute lobes and being more or less glabrous, pubescent pedicels and narrower petals. Petals white, linear, 4 mm long. Sakhalin. It is probably best seen as a subtaxon of *S. rivularis*.

11 · Yellow Summer Saxifrages
Section *Ciliatae*

The *Ciliatae* saxifrages are the most numerous group of saxifrages in the genus. From northwest India along the Himalaya to Bhutan and northern Burma, up into Tibet and to Qinghai, across into Sichuan and Yunnan, there are over two hundred species with hardly any straying outside these Asian heartlands. For me these plants carry their wild heritage with them like rare antelope or endangered birds echoing their remote origins. Few of them make it to the garden, and then usually only with fey impermanence, but it certainly makes them no less intriguing.

Saxifraga hirculus.

There is a great variation in the form of these species. There are tiny cushion plants from the high mountains, tall plants from the rich alpine meadows, species with rosettes of leaves, species which form tufts, species which spread like strawberries. Some are spectacularly hairy with long, curly, brown hairs cloaking much of the plant; some form tiny globular rosettes with fringes of fine hairs. These are truly fascinating plants which are generally intransigent as far as the gardener is concerned, although some species are grown by specialists and there are others that hold out promise.

Most of the section *Ciliatae* species have yellow flowers and fit into the Himalayan flora alongside the yellow-flowered species from other families with flowers often indistinguishable in colour from the geums, potentillas, composites and buttercups among which they grow. Obviously these narrow-spectrum floral displays are evidence of competition for a narrow range of pollinators. In some areas up to seventy percent of the species in the high meadows have yellow flowers. Although the vast majority of the saxifrage species are yellow-flowered, there are ones with deep red, pink, pale yellow or white flowers, and some of the yellow-flowered species have dramatically spotted or blotched petals. Many of the species have small raised calloses toward the base of the petals. The ovaries are usually superior but may be semi-inferior and in a very few cases wholly so, and they vary quite substantially in shape from narrowly conical to flattened spherical. The flower stems are leafy and these leaves are often more significant than the basal leaves, which in some species wither away well before flowering. In general the leaves are entire, although in a very small minority of species the margin is toothed.

The Subsections

With the great diversity of form that the species display the section has been subdivided into four big subsections (*Hirculoideae*, *Gemmiparae*, *Rosulares* and *Flagellares*) and three very much smaller ones (*Hemisphaericae*, *Serpyllifoliae* and *Cinerascentes*).

Subsection *Hirculoideae* Engler & Irmscher. About 110 species, of which only one is found outside Asia. They are variable in form but the basic pattern is of a basal tuft of leaves from which there are erect leafy flowering stems with at least the lower nodes and petiole bases with characteristic brown curly (crispate) hairs. Some species form small tufts; others form mats and in these the flower stems may be very short.

Subsection *Gemmiparae* Engler & Irmscher. 14 Asian species which have flower stems with leathery or shiny leaves and leafy buds in axils of stem leaves or rhizome scales.

Subsection *Cinerascentes* Engler & Irmscher. One Asian species with leafy buds in axils of stem leaves, distinguished from subsection *Gemmiparae* by having grey leaves.

Subsection *Serpyllifoliae* Gornall. Three North American and Siberian species which make mats of small rosettes of thickened and flattened leaves.

Subsection *Rosulares* Gornall. Over 50 Asian species of mat- or rosette-forming species with thickened or fleshy, non-shiny leaves.

Subsection *Hemisphaericae* (Engler & Irmscher) Gornall. Two Asian and one North American species making mats of small globular rosettes with hairy leaf margins. Very similar to some species in subsection *Rosulares*.

Subsection *Flagellares* Gornall. 17 Asian and one circumboreal species which have fine runners arising from axils of basal leaves with leafy buds or embryo plants at the tips.

To these Harry Smith added the grex *Cinctae* to accommodate the Nepalese *Saxifraga excellens*, a rather anomalous species which Gornall has treated as belonging in subsection *Hirculoideae*.

Saxifraga hirculus near Nome, Alaska. Usually this only forms a small tuft, but in perfect conditions it can form impressive clumps.

Subsection *Hirculoideae*

The *Hirculoideae* are numerous and variable but since they are almost wholly absent from Europe and North America this variety is largely unappreciated. There are over 100 species in China and the broad Himalayan region, but only *Saxifraga hirculus*, which is found widely in northern Europe and in North America from the arctic to Colorado, extends beyond these heartlands.

The basic morphology of the *Hirculoideae* is of a simple leafy stem rising from a tuft of basal leaves (rather than a rosette), with the leaves being entire. Flowering is typically during or after the height of the summer rains and the basal leaves may persist until flowering and seed production or may be caducous, withering away before seed production. Characteristic of this subsection are the brown, crimped hairs found at the nodes and base of the petioles. These hairs may be very long and leaves and pedicels may also be covered in these brown crispate hairs.

In some cases the tufts and stems may be solitary; in other cases mats of foliage are formed and the flowers are then often solitary and more or less sessile. The largest species are up to 75 cm tall with stems of up to 30 flowers. These larger species often have broad basal leaves, sometimes broadly arrow-shaped, and tend to grow among other plants in taller meadows, while the smaller ones tend to have narrow oblong or lanceolate leaves, and be plants of higher altitudes or sparser habitats.

Almost all of the species have yellow flowers with the only exceptions being *Saxifraga pardanthina* and *S. bergenioides* which have deep red or purple petals. Most species have unspotted petals but about 20 species have spotted petals, sometimes extremely heavily marked. Petals may be narrowed at the base to form a short claw.

With so many species in this subsection it is not surprising that seven series have been described which provide basic patterns of growth in these species although there are some species which are difficult to allocate in such a classification. There is a fundamental split between those in which the basal leaves are caducous, withering away before fruiting, and those in which the basal leaves are persistent to fruiting.

Series in subsection *Hirculoideae* in which basal leaves are caducous
Various characteristics are important when distinguishing the species. Size and
number of flowers are obvious variables, but there is a clear division between species in which the lower leaves have petioles and those where they are sessile. In
those with sessile lower leaves, the nature of hairs on the pedicels is used as a
distinguishing characteristic; in some species they have only long brown crispate
hairs, in some only short glandular hairs, in some a mixture of both. Another characteristic which can be important, particularly among those with sessile leaves, is
whether the petals have raised calloses toward their base.

Series *Densifoliatae*. Basal leaves caducous, stem leaves much the same size
up the stem, oblanceolate or obelliptic, up to 1.5 cm long. While at least a couple
of species that Engler & Irmscher identified in this series are now seen as better
placed in section *Rosulares*, the remainder are split almost equally between species in which the middle and lower leaves are sessile and those which are petiolate.
Examples of species in this series are *Saxifraga peplidifolia* and *S. kintschingingae*.

Series *Turfosae*. Basal leaves caducous, stem leaves much the same size up the
stem, oblanceolate or obelliptic, about 3–4 cm long. Most of these species have
sessile middle and lower leaves; in only a few are they petiolate. Examples are *Saxifraga kingiana*, *S. moorcroftiana* and *S. subamplexicaulis*.

Series *Stellariifoliae*. Basal leaves caducous, stem leaves much the same size
up the stem, cordate-ovate. All the species have petiolate lower and middle leaves.
Examples are *Saxifraga giraldiana*, *S. eglandulosa* and *S. cardiophylla*.

Series *Cinctae*. Large cauline leaves, no basal leaves, stems red-brown crispate
pilose. Flowers in axillary and apical inflorescences. Distinguished from all other
Saxifraga species by having filaments fused at the base. There is only one species,
S. excellens, which has petiolate lower and middle leaves.

Series in subsection *Hirculoideae* in which basal leaves are persistent
A key characteristic among these species, again apart from size and flower number,
is whether the basal leaves have a hairy or glabrous upper surface. Beyond this,
such characteristics as the leaf shape and particularly the shape of the leaf base, and
the type of hairs on the pedicels, are valuable in identification.

Series *Hirculoideae*. Basal leaves persistent to flowering, leaves getting smaller
from base upwards, petals ovate or obovate, less than three times as long as broad.
Some of the species have glabrous upper surfaces to the basal leaves, others have
hairy surfaces. Examples of species in this series are *Saxifraga hirculus*, *S. caveana*
and *S. diversifolia*.

Series *Lychnitidae*. Basal leaves persistent to flowering, leaves getting smaller from base upwards, petals oblong-linear, three times or more as long as broad. About six species, all with the upper surfaces of the basal leaves being hairy. Examples are *Saxifraga lychnitis*, *S. viscidula* and *S. pseudohirculus*.

Series *Nutantes*. Petioles of basal leaves sparsely red-brown pilose, flowers nodding. Two similar species, *Saxifraga nigroglandulifera* and *S. bergenioides*. The latter has hairy basal leaf surfaces and purple petals.

Since most of these species are Chinese the key text is *The Flora of China* (Pan Jintang et al), and my brief descriptions of the Chinese species derive from that. Subsequent to that have been the species described by H. Chuang in 2001. The descriptions of non-Chinese species are derived from the original papers or, for species described earlier, from those in Engler & Irmscher. Although the schema laid out may seem clear enough, it can be extremely difficult—as in section *Rosulares*—to ascribe specific names to individual plants.

Saxifraga nigroglandulifera in the Everest region of Nepal. This species shows the nodding flowers which are common in other genera that flower during the monsoon— and the closeness of *Saxifraga* and *Bergenia*. Photograph George Smith (Saxifrage Society Slide Library).

Subsection *Gemmiparae* and subsection *Cinerascentes*

Subsection *Gemmiparae* is defined by the leafy buds, or gemmae, which are found in the axils of the leaves. In most of the 17 species these leafy buds may be found in almost all the leaf axils up the stems, but in *Saxifraga gouldii* and *S. wardii* they are found only in the axils of the leaf scales on the rhizome. In some species, by flowering time, the buds may develop into non-flowering shoots, and in other cases species are described as branched, or multi-branched. The general form of the plants however is of a single stem with shiny or leathery but not thickened leaves up the stem, often clustered some distance up the stem almost to form a rosette, with the largest leaves usually being found about halfway up the stem. Although a few species have much shorter stems, most are from 15–30 cm tall and are very often found at slightly lower altitudes than the subsection *Rosulares* species. All the species have yellow flowers except *S. strigosa* and *S. gemmipara*, which have white flowers with coloured spots.

Saxifraga bergenioides.
Potrang La, Tibet.
Photograph Pam Eveleigh.

Saxifraga brachypoda
in Bhutan. Photograph
Anne Chambers.

This plant from subsection *Gemmiparae*, photographed in
Sikkim, seems to be *Saxifraga macrostigmatoides*, although
this would be outside the range in which it has previously
been recorded. *Saxifraga wardii* is very similar but with
hairy petal margins. Photograph Vojtěch Holubec.

Saxifraga cinerascens is the only species in subsection *Cinerascentes* and is distinguished by having silvery leaves rather than the green leaves of the subsection
Gemmiparae species, and the leafy buds often develop into sterile branches by
flowering time.

Subsection *Serpyllifoliae*

The three North American and Siberian species, *Saxifraga aleutica*, *S. serpyllifolia* and *S. chrysantha*, which make up this subsection are all characterized by
forming mats of small rosettes of thickened and flattened leaves and they all have
yellow flowers. In the Rocky Mountains, in high screes often fed by melting snow,
S. chrysantha can be fairly common and is a glorious plant with its golden-yellow
flowers. *Saxifraga serpyllifolia* from Alaska is similar but rather smaller, and even
more reduced is *S. aleutica*, which is confined to the tops of mountains in the
Aleutian Islands.

Saxifraga chrysantha.
Summit Lake, Mount
Evans, Colorado.

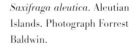

Saxifraga aleutica. Aleutian
Islands. Photograph Forrest
Baldwin.

Saxifraga aurantiaca, one of the mat-
forming species in subsection *Rosulares*,
with sepals already reflexing, glandular-
hairy pedicels and spotted petals.
Sichuan. Photograph Dieter Zschummel.

Subsection *Rosulares* and subsection *Hemisphaericae*

There are over 50 species in subsection *Rosulares*, forming mats or rosettes, and only three in subsection *Hemisphaericae*. The foliage is not shiny but is usually thickened or fleshy. Plants may be glabrous or densely glandular-hairy.

The species of subsection *Rosulares* can be divided between those which form mats of small leaves, such as *Saxifraga jacquemontiana*, and those, such as *S. umbellulata* or *S. candelabrum*, which make only one (or very few) larger rosettes. The mat-forming species usually have solitary flowers, either sessile or on stems no more than a couple of centimetres tall; the rosette-forming species have stems with more flowers, up to 30 in some species.

The three species from subsection *Hemisphaericae* are *Saxifraga eschscholtzii*, *S. hemisphaerica* and *S. zhidoensis*, and these make mats or cushions of very small globular rosettes with hairy leaf margins. The flowers, which are more or less sessile, have no nectary disc and the sepals have ciliate margins. *Saxifraga eschscholtzii*

*Saxifraga jacquemont-
iana* makes mats of
small glandular-hairy
rosettes and has
almost sessile flowers.
Baralacha Pass at
around 5100 metres,
India.

Subsection *Rosulares*
is a large and complex
group of very closely
related species. This
is probably *Saxifraga
unguiculata*. Da
Xue Shan, Yunnan.
Photograph Vojtěch
Holubec.

Saxifraga umbellulata
photographed in the Tsangpo
Gorges, southeast Tibet.

Saxifraga eschscholtzii.
Photograph Verna Pratt.

Saxifraga punctulata with almost
white petals with coloured spots.
Nepal. Photograph George Smith
(Saxifrage Society Slide Library).

Saxifraga lhasana is
very closely related to
S. umbellulata and is
unusual in subsection
Rosulares in having
pure white flowers.
Photograph Jozef
Lemmens.

crosses the Bering Straits from Asia into Alaska and is the only species from either subsection found outside Asia.

The majority of *Rosulares* species have yellow flowers, but there are a few significant exceptions among both the mat-forming and the rosette-forming species. Among those forming mats or cushions there are three with white flowers, *Saxifraga williamsii*, *S. brevicaulis* and *S. sessiliflora*, which are extremely closely related to one another. These were described by Harry Smith and he placed them as anomalous species in section *Porphyrion*. Cytotaxonomic work has confirmed suspicions about their misplacement by Harry Smith and they now seem to fit more comfortably in section *Rosulares*. It also helps explain why they have never been successfully introduced to cultivation despite their obvious attractions. There are also some of the rosette-forming species that have white or palest yellow flowers, most notably *S. punctulatoides*, *S. punctulata* var. *punctulata* and *S. lhasana*. From subsection *Hemisphaericae*, *S. eschscholtzii* can also have pink or white instead of the more usual yellow flowers.

In trying to identify species the most important characteristic is whether the plant forms mats or there is only a single rosette (or at most a very small group of rosettes). In the species which form rosettes the plant may have many flowers, but this is not true of all the rosette-forming species. The leaves may be glabrous or hairy, and in some cases they are thickened and pustulate. Other characteristics which may be important are whether the leaf margin is hairy, and whether the sepal margins are hairy or glabrous. All these characteristics can mean that it is very difficult to identify individual species if they are not examined in the field or in a herbarium. Photographs regularly fail to show all the characteristics needed for

Saxifraga flagellaris on
the tundra. Wooley, north
of Nome, Alaska.

Saxifraga consanguinea is a very variable subsection
Flagellares species. This specimen has solitary
orange-yellow flowers. Mi La, north of Rutok, 150 km
west of Lhasa, Tibet. Photograph Dieter Zschummel.

full identification. Nevertheless—or perhaps because of this
elusiveness—I find these species intriguing.

Subsection *Flagellares*

Of all the *Ciliatae* saxifrages it is those from subsection
Flagellares that are best known to the gardener. There are
eighteen species, five with pink or red-purple flowers, the
rest with yellow. Only one species is found outside Asia:
Saxifraga flagellaris is distributed circumboreally, with only
S. hirculus matching it in being so widely distributed. Like the
strawberry, *Flagellares* saxifrages have aerial stolons or runners with leafy buds (or the potential to develop them) at their
tips by which they can spread themselves, making loose mats
across the rocky or damp ground in which they are found in
the wild. In some cases plants may form extensive groups of
rosettes and runners, in others no more than a few rosettes
around the parental rosette.

Cultivation of *Ciliatae* Saxifrages

Few of the subsections contribute more than a couple of species to even the specialist collection. The only subsection of
which species are in regularly cultivation is subsection *Flagellares*, although occasionally specialist nurseries list species, often with collection numbers rather than
species names, from other subsections. The best sources remain occasional dona-
tions to the specialist seed exchanges.

The species from subsection *Hirculoideae* are not easy. These are plants for the
specialist but seed is occasionally available and plants can be brought to flower. The

Saxifraga consanguinea.
A specimen with
larger rich red petals
with taller stems and
multiple flowers. Tibet.
Photograph Dieter
Zschummel.

Saxifraga haplo-phylloides. It is possible to grow *Hirculoideae* species from seed. This specimen was grown by Jane Jopling.

Saxifraga candelabrum is a *Rosulares* species which appears in cultivation intermittently. This specimen is in circulation as "*Saxifraga* sp. coll. Napa Hai".

winter seems to be the most difficult period, with even well-established plants requiring very careful and limited watering if they are to reappear the following spring.

From subsection *Serpyllifoliae*, *Saxifraga chrysantha* is occasionally grown by specialists and has been shown in flower, but although seed is often collected it remains the preserve of the truly dedicated enthusiast.

The *Gemmiparae* are difficult plants to maintain in cultivation even if they can be obtained. They never seem to appear in the lists of even the most specialist nursery, but seed is occasionally collected by Himalayan seed collectors. If plants could be obtained propagation would have to be from seed or by rooting the leafy axillary buds. *Saxifraga strigosa* was grown by one or two specialists in Scotland for a number of years but it now seems to have died out.

Many of the subsection *Rosulares* species are highly desirable and the general failure to bring them into cultivation successfully is a great disappointment. Of the cushion- and mat-forming species, *Saxifraga caveana* and others would be extremely attractive but I have never seen plants in cultivation. *Saxifraga jacquemontiana* is grown by Henry and Margaret Taylor in Invergowrie in eastern Scotland but few others succeed; Ger van den Beuken in Holland reports that although seed is not difficult to germinate he has been unable to bring plants on from there. But if the mat-forming species have proved intractable, there has been more success with the rosette-forming species. *Saxifraga signata* is seen occasionally and *S. candelabrum* seems to have a toehold in cultivation from a collection at Napa Hai near Zhongdian in Yunnan. This is a rather fascinating species, one of the largest in the subsection, with a splendid stem of yellow tiger-striped flowers with dark globular ovaries and red anthers. The rosette is itself interesting, with glandular pubescent leaves up to some 5 cm, with the broadened tip having a notched apex. This seems to take a few years to get to flowering size and the plant appears to be wholly monocarpic. Seed collected after the late summer flowering has germinated readily and with care it is a species that might become well-established. Other species from wild-collected seed have been grown but identification has been tentative.

A number of species from subsection *Flagellares* are in cultivation but although there are five species with red or pink flowers, only ones with yellow flowers have made it into cultivation so far. Of these *Saxifraga flagellaris* is the most common although not the most decorative. *Saxifraga brunonis* has the most numerous runners, thin, red and shiny, sometimes form-

Saxifraga candelabrum. Close-up of the colourful flowers. The soft yellow petals are dramatically marked by dark red spots and lines, heightened by the large dark orange-brown anthers. The petals have pairs of raised calloses at the base and these can be seen as a ring of small yellow spots.

ing a great mass of threads below which the leaves may be relatively insignificant. In extreme cases the plant has the air of a somewhat distracted red spun-sugar candy confection—delicious and decorative. *Saxifraga neopropagulifera* is another species with a mass of red runners, but this is not generally in cultivation. In general the species in cultivation enjoy being well-watered in summer and are reasonably hardy but dislike winter wet: they may be happiest in the alpine house in the sand of the plunge rather than in a pot. Outside they may need overhead protection in winter.

Saxifraga sp. CLD990 is clearly another of the *Rosulares* species, possibly *S. sediformis.* It is intriguing because the flowers are zygomorphic (bilaterally symmetrical) rather than rotationally symmetrical. Photograph Beryl Bland.

Section *Ciliatae* Haworth

Subsection *Hirculoideae* Engler & Irmscher

Unless otherwise specified, petals are yellow, clawed and without calloses.

At least petioles or leaf bases and stem nodes have long red-brown crispate marginal hairs. Groups A1 and A2 contain the species from series *Densifoliatae*, *Turfosae*, *Stellariifoliae* and *Cinctae*; groups B1 and B2 contain those from series *Hirculoideae*, *Lychnitidae* and *Nutantes*.

A small number of species are variable with regards to some key characteristics. Rather than arbitrarily assigning these to a particular group, with a qualifying note, entries for these four species appear in two locations: *S. moorcroftiana* appears in groups A1 and B2; *S. nigroglandulifera*, *S. sphaeredana* and *S. sinomontana* in B1 and B2.

Subsection *Hirculoideae*—group A1

1. Basal leaves absent or shrivelled by flowering/fruiting time.
2. Lower and median cauline leaves sessile.

Saxifraga auriculata Engler & Irmscher (1912). Stems 26–35 cm, 3–11 flowers, pedicels with crispate and short glandular hairs. Leaves ovate-lanceolate to 1.7 × 0.9 cm. Petals 6 × 1.8 mm, 2-callose. 3200–4700m, Tibet, Sichuan.

Saxifraga bijiangensis H. Chuang (2001). Stems 10–12 cm, solitary flowers, pedicels crispate-hairy. Leaves lanceolate, mucronate, margin sparsely hairy to 1.0 × 0.25 cm. Petals 9 × 4.5 mm. 4350m, Yunnan.

Saxifraga brachyphylla Franchet (1890). Cespitose. Stems 10–50 cm, 2–14 flowers, pedicels with crispate and short glandular hairs. Oblong-ovate leaves to 0.8 × 0.35 cm. Petals 4.5 × 2 mm, 4-callose. 2500–3700m, Yunnan.

Saxifraga bulleyana Engler & Irmscher (1912). Stems 9–30 cm, 1–5 flowers, pedicels with crispate and short glandular hairs. Densely brown-crispate. Leaves to 1.5 × 0.85 cm. Petals 6.5 × 4 mm, 2–4-callose. 3000–4600m, Yunnan.

Saxifraga congestiflora Engler & Irmscher (1914). Stems 16–28 cm, 6–10 flowers, pedicels crispate-hairy. Oblanceolate leaves to 2.8 × 0.3 cm. Petals 5.5 × 1.6 mm, callosed. 3700–4300m, Sichuan.

Saxifraga hypericoides Franchet (1896) [incl. *S. trinervia* Franchet (1886)]. Densely cespitose. Stems 11–19 cm, 1–8 flowers, pedicels with crispate and short glandular hairs. Cauline leaves oblong 1.0 × 0.3 cm. Petals yellow or orange, 4.6 × 1.8 mm, (2)-callose. 2700–4600m, Sichuan, Yunnan.

Saxifraga kingdonii Marquand (1929). Stems 5–30 cm, 1 or 2 flowers, pedicels glandular-hairy not crispate. Leaves ovate-orbicular to 3.0 × 1.3 cm, both surfaces hairy. Petals 10 × 8 mm, 5–7-callose. 4000–4800m, Tibet, Burma.

Saxifraga kingiana Engler & Irmscher (1912). Stems 70–75 cm, about 14 flowers, pedicels glandular-hairy not crispate. Leaves softly hairy, ovate-cordate to 5.1 × 2.4 cm. Petals 7 × 6 mm, lilac-spotted. 3700–3900m, Nepal to Bhutan, Tibet.

Saxifraga latiflora J. D. Hooker & Thomson (1857). Stems 10–15 cm, 1–3 flowers, pedicels glandular-hairy not crispate. Leaves oblong-elliptic to 3 × 1 cm. Petals 10.5 × 5 mm. 4000–4600m, Sikkim.

Saxifraga moorcroftiana Wallich ex Sternberg (1828). Stems 18–52 cm, 2–12 flowers, pedicels glandular-hairy not crispate. Leaves glabrous, cordate to 6.0 × 2.0 cm. Stem leaves narrowed in middle. Petals 8.2 × 4.2 mm, not clawed. 3500–4400m, Kashmir to Bhutan, Tibet, Yunnan, Sichuan. Note that occasionally basal leaves are retained to anthesis.

Saxifraga nangqenica J. T. Pan (1990). Stems 3–5 cm, solitary flowers, pedicels crispate-hairy. Leaves narrowly oblong 0.8 × 0.25 cm. Petals 6.5 × 4 mm, not clawed. 5200m, Qinghai.

Saxifraga subamplexicaulis Engler & Irmscher (1912). Stems to 29 cm, 3–10 flowers, pedicels glandular-hairy not crispate. Leaves ovate 3 × 1.9 cm, hairy margins and backs. Petals to 7.2 × 4 mm. 2900–3900m, Yunnan.

Subsection *Hirculoideae*—group A2

1. Basal leaves absent or shrivelled by flowering/fruiting time.
2. Lower and median cauline leaves petiolate.

Saxifraga cardiophylla Franchet (1886). Stems 16–36 cm, 4–13 flowers. Lower leaves cordate to 4.5 × 3.2 cm, petiole 0.7–6 cm, upper ovate-lanceolate to 3.2 × 1.65 cm. Leaves long-hairy, especially lower surface. Petals to 7.5 × 3.6 mm. 6-callose. 2500–4300m, Sichuan, Yunnan.

Saxifraga dongchuanensis H. Chuang (2001). Stems 10–15 cm, solitary flowers. Leaves glabrous, ovate-rhombic to 0.6 × 0.4 mm, narrowing at tip, petiole to 0.5 cm. Petals not callose, to 7 × 4 mm. 3500m, Yunnan.

Saxifraga eglandulosa Engler (1912). Cespitose. Stems 8–15 cm, 1–3 flowers. Leaves brown hairy, ovate 1.8 × 1 cm plus petiole to 1.2 cm, cordate. Petals uncallosed, 7 × 6.5 mm, not always clawed. Pedicels brown crispate-hairy. 3600–4500m, Tibet, Yunnan.

Saxifraga egregioides J. T. Pan (1990). Stems 8–14 cm, 1 or 2 flowers. Cauline leaves, surfaces glabrous, to 1.0 × 0.85 cm plus petiole to 0.75 cm. Petals to 5.3 × 3.8 mm, 4-callose. 3400m, Tibet.

Saxifraga excellens Harry Smith (1960). Stems 25–35 cm. 3–8 leaves obovate-elliptic to 9.5 × 5.3 cm, petiole to 7 cm. Flowers in terminal and axillary clusters, petals red, to 9 × 6 mm, not callose. This species is very unusual in the *Saxifraga* with filaments united at the base but otherwise conforming to subsection *Hirculoideae*. 3600–4200m, Nepal.

Saxifraga giraldiana Engler (1901). Cespitose. Stems 8–22 cm, 1–6 flowers. Leaf surfaces glabrous, leaves to 1.3 × 1.1 cm plus petiole to 1.2 cm. Petals to 7.8 × 3.8 mm, brown-spotted, 4–6 callose. 1000–4000m, Sichuan, Yunnan, Hubei, Shaanxi.

Saxifraga habaensis C. Y. Wu ex H. Chuang (2001). Stems 5–7 cm, solitary flowers. Leaves long-hairy, ovate to 0.7 × 0.55 cm, petiole 0.2–1.2 cm. Petals to 7 × 3 mm, not apparently callose. Yunnan.

Saxifraga haplophylloides Franchet (1890) [incl. *S. turfosa* Engler & Irmscher (1912)]. Stems 12–45 cm, 3–13 flowers. Ovate cauline leaves very sparsely hairy to 4.4 × 1.9 cm, petiole to 1.0 cm. Petals to 7.6 × 5.3 mm, 6-callose. 3600–3700m, Yunnan.

Saxifraga harry-smithii Wadwha (1986). Cespitose. Stems 15–30 cm, normally solitary flower. Leaves to 2 × 1.2 cm, lower cuneate based, petiole to 3.2 cm, upper subcordate. Petals to 9.2 × 7.5 mm, not callose, some orange spots. Sepal backs glabrous. 3900–4600m, Bhutan.

Saxifraga implicans Harry Smith (1960). Stems 11–50 cm, 3–12 flowers. Leaves, brown hairy, ovate-cordate to 4 × 2.7 cm, petiole to 4 cm. Petals to 8 × 4 mm, small orange spots, 6–8-callose. 3500–4200m, Tibet, Sichuan, Yunnan.

Saxifraga insolens Irmscher (1935). Stems 47–49 cm, 14–16 flowers. Cauline leaves glabrous, ovate to 4 × 2.1 cm plus petiole, cordate. Petals not callose, 5.5 × 2.5 mm. 3800–4000m, Yunnan.

Saxifraga kintschingingae Engler (1912). Stems 7–10 cm, 1 or 2 flowers. Leaves lanceolate, obtuse 0.7 × 0.3

cm, petiole to 1.2 cm. Petals usually uncallosed, to 5.5 × 3 mm. Sikkim.

Saxifraga lamninamensis H. Ohba (1984). Stems 10–25 cm, 4–5 flowers. Leaves to 2 × 1 cm, petiole to 2 cm. Petals not callosed, to 7.5 × 4 mm, unclawed. 3200–4200m, Nepal, Bhutan. This might be more appropriately incorporated in *S. hookeri* (according to Grierson & Long).

Saxifraga lushuiensis H. Chuang (2001). Stems 20–35 cm, 15 or more flowers. Leaves triangular-ovate, base truncate. Petals to 6 × 3 mm, short claw, not apparently callose. 2700m, Yunnan.

Saxifraga megacordia C. Y. Wu ex H. Chuang (2001). Stems 40–60 cm, multi-flowered (up to about 20). Leaves ovate narrowing towards tip, cordate, to 4.5 × 2.5 cm, lower with petiole to 4.5 cm, upper sessile. Petals to 6 × 3 mm, uncallosed, short-clawed. 3800–4000m, Yunnan.

Saxifraga namdoensis Harry Smith (1960). Stems to 25 cm, 3–7 flowers. Lower leaves to 2.2 × 0.9 cm, with petiole to 1 cm, sessile leaves to 2.8 × 0.9 cm. Petals not callose, to 11 × 7 mm, not clawed. 4500m, Nepal.

Saxifraga nayarii Wadwha (1984). Cespitose. Stems 20–28 cm, solitary flowers. Leaves elliptic to 2.9 × 1.3 cm, lower smaller and petiolate. Petals not callose, to 10 × 8.5 mm, orange-spotted, not clawed. 3900–4600m, Tibet (according to Wadwha) but not considered in *Flora of China* so doubtful.

Saxifraga omphalodifolia Handel-Mazzetti (1929) [incl. *S. valleculosa* H. Chuang (2001)]. Stems 22–34 cm, usually zigzag, 9–11 flowers. Cauline leaves to 3.7 × 3.4 cm, cordate, glandular-hairy, petiole to 3.5 cm. Petals to 7.2 × 3.4 mm, (4–8)-callose. 3800–4200m, Tibet, Sichuan, Yunnan. There are two varieties sometimes minutely distinguished (var. *retusopetala* and var. *callosa*). Chuang accords var. *callosa* specific status as *S. valleculosa* (3000–4100m, Yunnan, Sichuan) but does not describe or illustrate it as having a zigzag stem.

Saxifraga peplidifolia Franchet (1890) [incl. *S. petrophila* Franchet (1890)]. Densely cespitose. Stems 2–14 cm, 1–3 flowers. Cauline leaves, surfaces short glandular-hairy, elliptic-oblong 0.6 × 0.2 cm plus petiole to 0.35 cm. Petals 5 × 3 mm, 2-callose. Pedicels with short and long hairs. 2700–4600m, Sichuan, Yunnan.

Saxifraga sikkimensis Engler (1912). Densely cespitose. Stems 13–20 cm, 3–9 flowers. Leaves lanceolate 1.3 × 0.4 cm, plus shorter petiole. Petals uncallosed, to 6 × 3.5 mm. 4000–5000m, Nepal, Sikkim. Note that plants in cultivation under this name are usually the

Flagellares species *S. mucronulatoides* (*S. flagellaris* subsp. *sikkimensis*).

Saxifraga smithiana Irmscher (1935). Stems 26–34 cm, 1–7 flowers. Leaf surfaces glabrous, ovate to 2.7 × 1.7 cm, petiole to 2.5 cm, (sub)cordate. Petals to 6.5 × 4.8 mm, orange-spotted, 6-callose. 3700–4000m, Yunnan.

Saxifraga stellariifolia Franchet (1886). Cespitose. Stems 7–35 cm, 1–6 flowers. Cauline leaves, sparsely long-hairy, to 1.2 × 0.7 cm plus petiole. Petals to 8 × 3.6 mm, 4–6-callose. 3000–4300m, Sichuan, Yunnan.

Saxifraga subaequifoliata Irmscher (1935). Stems 18–37 cm, 6–30 flowers. Leaves glandular-hairy, ovate to 3.5 × 0.7–2.5 cm, possibly cordate, petiole to 3.3 cm. Petals to 6.8 × 3.6 mm, purple-spotted, (4–8)-callose. 3000–4200m, Tibet, Sichuan, Yunnan.

Saxifraga yezhiensis C. Y. Wu (1990). Stems 6–11 cm, 1–3 flowers. Cauline leaves oblong to 9 × 2.8 cm plus petiole. Petals 5 × 2.2 mm, 2-callose. Pedicels with short glandular and very long crispate hairs. 3600m, Yunnan.

Subsection *Hirculoideae*—group B1

1. Basal leaves persistent to flowering.
2. Upper surface of basal leaves glabrous.

Saxifraga aristulata J. D. Hooker & Thomson (1857) [incl. *S. macrostigma* Franchet (1890)]. Cespitose. Stems 2–10 cm, 1 or 2 flowers, pedicels with glandular and crispate hairs. Leaves ovate-linear to 0.8 × 0.13 cm, petiole to 0.67 cm. Petals to 6 × 2 mm, 2-callose. 3000–5000m, India and Nepal to Tibet, Sichuan, Yunnan.

Saxifraga caveana W. W. Smith (1911). Cespitose. Stems 2–4 cm, solitary flowers, pedicels with glandular and crispate hairs. Leaves oblong-ovate to 1.0 × 0.5 cm, petiole to 1 cm. Petals to 10 × 6 mm. 4500–4800m, Nepal, Sikkim, Bhutan, Tibet.

Saxifraga chadwellii Wadwha (1986). Densely cespitose. Stems 7–12 cm, solitary flowers, pedicels with only crispate hairs. Leaves lanceolate to 1.6 × 0.8 cm, petiole to 1.7 cm. Petals 6.0 × 2.5 mm. 4100m, Ladakh. Status doubtful.

Saxifraga champutungensis H. Chuang (2001). Stems 8–10 cm, 1–3 flowers, pedicels with short glandular hairs. Leaves oblanceolate to 1.0 × 0.25 cm, aristate, basal with long petiole. Petals deep yellow to 7 × 4.5 mm. 3700–4000m, Yunnan.

Saxifraga ciliatopetala (Engler & Irmscher) J. T. Pan (1985). Cespitose. Stems 7–30 cm, 2–5 flowers, pedicels with only crispate hairs. Cauline leaves oblong-linear to 2 × 0.6 cm, lower with petiole to 0.8 cm. Petals to 9.6 × 6.3 mm, brown-crispate hairy

margins, 2-callose. 3900–5100m, Nepal, Tibet, Sichuan, Yunnan.

Saxifraga culcitosa Mattfeld (1931). Cespitose. Stems 1 cm, solitary flowers, pedicels with only crispate hairs. Leaves (ob)lanceolate 0.3 × 0.08 cm, apex aristate, petiole to 0.3 cm. Petals to 2.3 × 0.6 mm, orange, 2-callose. 4000–5100m, Sichuan.

Saxifraga dahaiensis H. Chuang (2001). Stems 3–6 cm, solitary flowers, pedicels with glandular and crispate hairs. Leaves to lanceolate-ovate 0.7 × 0.25 cm, basal smaller, petiolate. Petals to 5.5 × 3.5 mm. 3700m, Yunnan.

Saxifraga diapensia Harry Smith (1924). Cespitose. Stems 1–8 cm, solitary flowers, pedicels with glandular and crispate hairs. Leaves ovate-lanceolate, to 1.2 × 0.5 cm, petiole to 0.8 cm. Petals to 11 × 7 mm, sometimes spotted, 2-callose. 3500–5300m, Tibet, Sichuan, Yunnan.

Saxifraga elliptica Engler & Irmscher (1912). Cespitose. Stems 3–7 cm, solitary flowers, pedicels with only crispate hairs. Leaves ovate-lanceolate to 0.9 × 0.4 cm, petiole to 0.75 cm. Petals to 8.6 × 5.3 mm, 2-callose. 4000–4800m, Nepal, Sikkim, Tibet.

Saxifraga erectisepala J. T. Pan (1990). Stems 15–30 cm, 3–15 flowers, pedicels with short glandular hairs. Basal leaves cordate to 4.8 × 3.8 cm, petiole to 9.7 cm. Petals to 13.7 × 7.1 mm, (2–3)-callose. 3300–4200m, Tibet.

Saxifraga gonggashanensis J. T. Pan (1990). Stems 3–17 cm, 1 or 2 flowers, pedicels with glandular and crispate hairs. Basal leaves suboblong 0.6 × 0.15 cm, petiole to 1 cm. Petals 5.6 × 3.5 mm, orange, 2-callose. 4600m, Sichuan.

Saxifraga heleonastes Harry Smith (1924). Stems 4–29 cm, 1–5 flowers, pedicels with only crispate hairs. Leaves oblong-lanceolate to 3.7 × 0.9 cm, petiole to 4 cm. Petals to 12 × 7 mm, 2-callose. 3600–4800m, Shaanxi, Sichuan, Yunnan, Tibet.

Saxifraga heteroclada Harry Smith (1960). Cespitose. Stems 2–19 cm, 1–3 flowers, pedicels with glandular and crispate hairs. Cauline leaves to 1.4 × 0.2 cm, basal leaves smaller. Petals to 8.2 × 5 mm, 4–6-callose. 3500–4200m, Tibet, Burma.

Saxifraga heterocladoides J. T. Pan (1985). Cespitose. Stems 6–19 cm, 1–3 flowers, pedicels with glandular and crispate hairs. Cauline leaves 1.2 × 0.2 cm, basal leaves smaller. Petals to 9.9 × 5.1 mm, 6–7-callose. 4000m, Tibet.

Saxifraga hirculus Linnaeus (1753). Stems 6–21 cm, 1–4 flowers, pedicels with only crispate hairs. Basal leaves elliptic-lanceolate to 2.2 × 1.0 cm, petiole to 2.2 cm. Petals 10.3 × 6.8 mm, 2-callose. Sea-level to 5100m, North America, Europe, Asia.

Saxifraga lepida Harry Smith (1960). Cespitose. Stems 5–8 cm, solitary flowers, pedicels with glandular and crispate hairs Leaves lanceolate-linear to 1.5 × 0.2 mm. Petals to 6 × 4 mm, spotted, clawed. 3100–3800m, Nepal, Bhutan. Note that *S. lepidostolonosa* may be conspecific.

Saxifraga lepidostolonosa Harry Smith (1960). Cespitose. Stems 4–5 cm, solitary flowers, pedicels with glandular and crispate hairs. Leaves oblanceolate 1.0 × 0.12 cm, petiole to 0.8 cm. Petals to 4.5 × 2.8 mm, brown-yellow. 4700m, Tibet. Note that *S. lepida* may be conspecific.

Saxifraga matta-viridis Harry Smith (1960). Densely cespitose, stems less than 1 cm, solitary flowers. Whole plant hairless. Leaves subcylindric, weak and fleshy, to 0.7 × 0.05 mm, plus petiole. Petals to 4.2 × 1.6 mm, not callose. 3900–4500m, Sikkim, Bhutan.

Saxifraga montanella Harry Smith (1960). Cespitose. Stems 3–8 cm, solitary flowers, pedicels with only crispate hairs. Leaves ovate-oblong-lanceolate to 1.1 × 0.6 cm, basal with petiole to 0.7 cm. Petals to 12.5 × 8.2 mm, 2-callose. 3300–5200m, Nepal to Bhutan, Tibet, Qinghai, Sichuan.

Saxifraga nakaoi Kitamura (1955). Densely cespitose. Stems 3–5 cm, solitary flowers, occasionally possibly to 3, pedicels with short glandular hairs. Basal leaves ovate or ovate-lanceolate to 0.6 × 0.2 cm, petioles to 1.5 cm, stem leaves without petioles 0.6–0.8 cm. Petals to 5.5 × 4.5 mm, many very small calloses. 3500–5000m, northwest India to Bhutan.

Saxifraga nakaoides J. T. Pan (1985). Stems 6–7 cm, 2–3 flowers, pedicels with glandular and crispate hairs. Basal leaves elliptic to 0.7 × 0.35 cm, petiole 0.65 cm. Petals to 9.7 × 4.5 mm, 6-callose. 4200m, Tibet.

Saxifraga nigroglandulifera Balakrishnan (1970) [*S. nutans* J. D. Hooker & Thomson (1857)]. Stems 5–36 cm, 2–14 nodding flowers, pedicels with glandular and crispate hairs. Basal leaves elliptic to 4 × 1.6 cm, petiole to 6 cm. Petals to 9.6 × 3 mm, not clawed. 2700–5000m, Nepal to Bhutan, Tibet, Sichuan, Yunnan.

Saxifraga parva Hemsley (1895). Cespitose. Stems to 4.5 cm, solitary flowers, pedicels with only crispate hairs. Leaves ovate-oblong to 0.7 × 0.2 cm, lower with petiole to 0.9 cm. Petals to 6.4 × 4.7 mm, 2-callose. 4200–4900m, Nepal, Bhutan, Tibet, Qinghai, Xinjiang.

Saxifraga przewalskii Engler (1883). Cespitose. Stems 4–12 cm, 2–6 flowers, pedicels with only crispate hairs. Basal leaves ovate-oblong to 2.5 × 0.8 cm, petiole to 3 cm. Petals purple beneath, red-spotted, to 5.2 × 2.1 mm, 2-callose. 3700–5000m, Gansu, Qinghai, Sichuan, Tibet.

Saxifraga saginoides J. D. Hooker & Thomson (1857). Cespitose to 1–1.5 cm, solitary flowers, pedicels with only crispate hairs. Leaves linear to 0.68 × 0.1 cm. Petals to 4.4 × 1.9 mm, sometimes 2-callose. 4300–5500m, northwest India to Bhutan, Tibet, Sichuan.

Saxifraga sinomontana J. T. Pan & Gornall (2000) [*S. montana* Harry Smith (1924)]. Cespitose, stems 4–35 cm, 2–8 flowers, pedicels with only crispate hairs. Leaves elliptic-oblong to 3.4 × 0.5 cm, petiole to 4.5 cm. Petals to 12.5 × 6.9 mm, 2-callose. 2700–5300m, Kashmir to Bhutan, Tibet, Gansu, Qinghai, Shaanxi, Sichuan, Yunnan, Xinjiang. Note that this description applies to var. *sinomontana* (var. *amabilis* has upper surface brown crispate-hairy).

Saxifraga sphaeredana Harry Smith (1960). Cespitose, stems 10–17 cm, 1–5 flowers, pedicels with short glandular hairs. Basal leaves cordate-ovate to 3.1 × 1.9 cm, petiole to 5.3 cm. Petals to 10 × 7 mm, spotted orange, (4)-callose. 3300–4100m, Nepal, Tibet. Note that this description relates to subsp. *sphaeredana* (subsp. *dhwojii* has both surfaces variously pilose).

Saxifraga sublinearifolia J. T. Pan (1990). Stems 2–4 cm, solitary flowers, pedicels with glandular and crispate hairs. Leaves suboblong to 0.4 × 0.1 cm, petiole to 0.4 cm. Petals to 3.2 × 1.6 mm, orange, 2-callose. Sichuan.

Saxifraga subspathulata Engler & Irmscher (1912). Cespitose. Stems 4–7 cm, solitary flowers, pedicels with glandular and crispate hairs. Leaves subspathulate-lanceolate 0.3 × 0.15 cm, petiole to 1.3 cm. Petals 3.5 × 2 mm, base tapered. 3500m, India, Sikkim, Bhutan, Tibet.

Saxifraga tangutica Engler (1883). Cespitose. Stems 3–31 cm, normally 8–24 flowers, pedicels with only crispate hairs. Basal leaves ovate-oblong to 3.3 × 0.8 cm, petiole to 2.5 cm. Petals possibly purple beneath, to 4.5 × 2.5 mm, 2-callose. 2900–5600, Kashmir to Bhutan, Tibet, Gansu, Qinghai.

Saxifraga tibetica Losinskaja (1926). Cespitose. Stems 2–16 cm, solitary flowers, pedicels with only crispate hairs. Leaves lanceolate-oblong to 1.4 × 0.6 cm, petiole to 1.3 cm. Petals purple beneath to 0.5 × 0.2 mm, 2-callose. 4300–5600m, Qinghai, Xinjiang, Tibet.

Saxifraga triaristulata Handel-Mazzetti (1923). Cespitose. Stems 1–2 cm, solitary flowers, pedicels with only crispate hairs. Leaves oblong-spathulate apex 1–3-aristate. Petals 5 × 2 mm. 4700m, Sichuan.

Subsection *Hirculoideae*—group B2
1. Basal leaves persistent to flowering.
2. Upper surface of basal leaves variously hairy as specified.

Saxifraga bergenioides C. Marquand (1929) [incl. *S. haematochroa* Harry Smith (1960)]. Cespitose. Stems 13–20 cm, 1–4 nodding purple flowers. Leaves oblong-elliptic to 2.3 × 0.9 cm, petioles to 4.3 cm, upper surface of basal leaves crispate hairy. Purple petals to 14.5 × 4 mm, not callose. 4200–5000m, Tibet.

Saxifraga cacuminum Harry Smith (1924). Cespitose. Stems 2–6 cm, solitary flowers. Leaves, basal rosetted, oblong-lanceolate to 1.0 × 0.25 cm, upper surface of basal leaves with short glandular hairs, petiole to 0.5 cm. Petals to 8 × 3 mm, 2-callose. 4700–5200m, Sichuan.

Saxifraga calopetala Harry Smith (1960). Stems to 36 cm, 9–14 flowers. Leaves, basal petiolate, lowest cauline to 8 × 3 cm, cuneate base, upper surface of basal leaves with long non-glandular hairs. Petals orange, dark-spotted, to 8 × 4 mm, 2-callose, sepals glandular-hairy below. Whole plant covered in long cottony hairs. 3000–3300m, Burma.

Saxifraga chumbiensis Engler & Irmscher (1912). Cespitose, stems 6–11 cm, solitary flowers. Leaves elliptic-oblong, subcuneate, to 1.2 × 0.45 cm, upper surface of basal with long non-glandular hairs. Petals to 7.5 × 4.2 mm, not callose, sepals glabrous below. 4600–5800m, Sikkim, Bhutan, Tibet.

Saxifraga cordigera J. D. Hooker & Thomson (1857). Cespitose, stems 4–6 cm, solitary flowers. Leaves ovate to 0.6 × 0.5 cm, basal with ciliate petiole, upper surface with long non-glandular hairs, cauline cordate. Petals obovate to 1.1 cm, not callose, sepals glabrous below. 4000–5000m, Nepal, Sikkim, Tibet.

Saxifraga deminuta Harry Smith (1960). Cespitose. Stems to 1–2 cm, solitary flowers. Leaves to 1.0 × 0.25 cm, lanceolate, upper surface of basal with long non-glandular hairs. Petals to 4.5 × 3 mm, not callose, unspotted, sepals glabrous below. 4300m, Bhutan.

Saxifraga dianxibeiensis J. T. Pan in C. Y. Wu (1990). Cespitose, stems 12–19 cm, 1–3 flowers. Basal leaves ovate-cordate to 2 × 1.6 cm, upper surface with short glandular hairs, petiole to 2.6 cm. Petals to 6.4 × 5 mm, 8–9-callose. 3800–4500m, Yunnan.

Saxifraga diffusicallosa C. Y. Wu in J. T. Pan (1985). Stems 17–26 cm, 1–4 flowers. Leaves ovate to 1.4 × 0.5

cm, lower with petiole to 3 cm, upper surface of basal leaves with long non-glandular hairs. Petals to 8.1 × 4.5 mm, 6–7-callose, sepals glandular-hairy below. 3200–4000m, Tibet.

Saxifraga diversifolia Engler & Irmscher (1828). Stems 16–43 cm, 5–17 flowers. Basal leaves ovate-cordate to 5 × 2.6 cm, upper surface with short glandular hairs, petiole to 9.2 cm. Petals to 8 × 5.1 mm, usually not callose. 2800–4300m, Kashmir to Bhutan, Burma, Tibet, Sichuan, Yunnan.

Saxifraga egregia Engler (1883). Stems 9–32 cm, 3–9 flowers. Basal leaves cordate-ovate to 3.25 × 2 cm, upper surface with short glandular hairs, petiole to 5 cm. Petals to 8 × 3.5 mm, 4–6-callose but may vary more. 2800–4500m, Tibet, Gansu, Qinghai, Sichuan, Yunnan.

Saxifraga forrestii Engler & Irmscher (1912). Cespitose. Stems 5–13 cm, 1–4 flowers. Leaves ovate-elliptic to 0.8 × 0.4 cm, lower with petiole to 1.3 cm, upper surface with long non-glandular hairs. Petals to 7 × 3.1 mm, 4-callose, sepals glabrous below. 2700–3900m, Yunnan.

Saxifraga gedangensis J. T. Pan (1990). Stems 23–25 cm, up to 9 flowers. Basal leaves ovate to 4.4 × 2.6 cm, upper surface with short glandular hairs, petiole to 5 cm. Petals to 7.3 × 3.5 mm, 8 (or more)-callose, not clawed. 3400m, Tibet.

Saxifraga glabricaulis Harry Smith (1960). Cespitose, stems 2–4 cm, solitary flowers. Leaves ovate-lanceolate to 0.8 × 0.3 cm, upper surface of basal leaves with short glandular hairs, short petiole. Petals to 8 × 5.5 mm. To 4800m, Nepal to Bhutan, Tibet.

Saxifraga glaucophylla Franchet (1890). Stems 19–42 cm, 5–30 flowers. Basal leaves ovate-oblong to 7 × 2.5 cm, upper surface with short glandular hairs, petiole to 4 cm. Petals to 6.5 × 2.9 mm, 4–6-callose. 2600–3900m, Sichuan, Yunnan.

Saxifraga gongshanensis T. C. Ku (1989) [incl. *S. setulosa* C. Y. Wu (1990)]. Stems 5–6 cm, solitary flowers. Leaves oblong to 0.5 × 0.16 cm, petiole to 1 cm, upper surface of basal leaves crispate hairy. Petals to 5 × 3.6 mm, 4-callose. 3900m, Yunnan.

Saxifraga hengduanensis H. Chuang (2001). Stems 5–15 cm, 1 or 2 flowers. Leaves to 2.0 × 0.6 cm, cauline narrower, petiole to 6 cm, lessening up stem, upper surface of basal leaves with long non-glandular hairs. Petals 7.5 × 4.5 mm, sepals glandular-hairy below. 3000–4300m, Yunnan.

Saxifraga hirculoides Decaisne (1844). Stems to 15 cm, solitary flowers. Leaves ovate-oblong to 0.9 × 0.36 cm, petiole to 1.6 cm, upper surface of basal leaves crispate hairy. Petals to 6 × 3.3 mm, not callose. 4000–5600m, Kashmir to Nepal, Tibet, Qinghai, Mongolia.

Saxifraga hookeri Engler & Irmscher (1912). Stems 9–24 cm, 3–6 flowers. Basal leaves ovate-cordate to 2.1 × 1.3 cm, upper surface with short glandular hairs, petiole to 4.3 cm. Petals to 8.1 × 5.7 mm, 4-callose. 3300–4200m, Tibet.

Saxifraga isophylla Harry Smith (1960). Cespitose. Stems 4–24 cm, 2–9 flowers. Leaves lanceolate-elliptic to 1.3 × 0.5 cm, petiole to 1.2 cm, upper surface of basal leaves crispate-hairy. Petals to 9.8 × 4.2 mm, 4–8-callose. 3700–4700m, Tibet.

Saxifraga linearifolia Engler & Irmscher (1912). Cespitose, stems 3–5 cm, solitary flowers. Leaves oblong-lanceolate to 0.5 × 0.15 cm, upper surface of basal leaves with short glandular hairs, petiole to 0.5 cm. Petals to 5 × 3.5 mm, not callose. 3900–4200m, Sichuan, Yunnan.

Saxifraga litangensis Engler (1922). Cespitose, stems 3–8 cm, 1–3 flowers. Leaves oblong to 1.35 × 0.3 cm, upper surface of basal leaves with short glandular hairs, lower petioles to 0.75 cm. Petals to 7 × 3.3 mm, 2-callose. 4000–5400m, Sichuan, Tibet.

Saxifraga lychnitis J. D. Hooker & Thomson (1857). Cespitose. Stems 3–15 cm, 1 or 2 flowers. Leaves, basal rosetted, spathulate, to 1.5 × 0.45 cm, upper surface of basal leaves with short glandular hairs. Flowers nodding especially in bud, petals to 9 × 2.7 mm, not callose. 4300–5500m, Kashmir to Bhutan, Tibet, Sichuan, Qinghai.

Saxifraga maxionggouensis J. T. Pan in C. Y. Wu & J. T. Pan (1990). Stems about 26 cm, about 10 flowers. Basal leaves ovate-cordate to 3.3 × 2.8 cm, upper surface with short glandular hairs, petiole to 3 cm. Petals to 4 × 4.2 mm, 4-callose. 3700–3800m, Sichuan.

Saxifraga moorcroftiana Wallich ex Sternberg (1828). Stems 18–52 cm, 2–12 flowers. Leaves cordate to 6.0 × 2.0 cm, upper surface with short glandular hairs. Stem leaves narrowed in middle. Petals 8.2 × 4.2 mm, not clawed. 3500–4400m, Kashmir to Bhutan, Tibet, Yunnan, Sichuan. Note: usually loses basal leaves by flowering.

Saxifraga nigroglandulifera Balakrishnan (1970) [*S. nutans* J. D. Hooker & Thomson (1857)]. Stems 5–36 cm, 2–14 nodding flowers. Basal leaves elliptic to oblong 4 × 1.6 cm, upper surface with short glandular hairs, petiole to 6 cm, usually glabrous. Petals to 9.6 × 3 mm, not callose. 2700–5000m, Nepal to Bhutan, Tibet, Sichuan, Yunnan.

Saxifraga nigroglandulosa Engler & Irmscher (1912).

Cespitose. Stems 5–10 cm, usually solitary flowers. Leaves ovate to 2 × 0.6 cm, petiole to 1.8 cm, upper surface of basal leaves with long non-glandular hairs. Petals to 13 × 9 mm, 2–11-callose, sepals glandular-hairy below. 3300–4800m, Tibet, Burma, Yunnan, Sichuan.

Saxifraga oresbia J. Anthony (1933). Cespitose. Stems 6–15 cm, 1–3 flowers. Leaves, basal rosetted, obovate-spathulate to 0.9 × 0.45 cm, upper surface of basal leaves with short glandular hairs. Petals 12.5 × 4.2 mm, not callose. 4200–4500m, Sichuan.

Saxifraga palpebrata J. D. Hooker & Thomson (1857). Cespitose. Stems 3–5 cm, solitary flowers. Leaves to 0.5 × 0.25 cm, upper surface of basal with long non-glandular hairs. Petiole to 0.5 cm. Petals to 6 × 4 mm, sepals glabrous below. 4000–5000m, Sikkim.

Saxifraga pardanthina Handel-Mazzetti (1929). Stems 20–50 cm, 4–11 purple flowers. Lower leaves oblong-lanceolate to 7 × 2.8 cm, upper surface with short glandular hairs. Purple petals to 6 × 4 mm, black-spotted, not callose or clawed. 3000–3900m, Sichuan, Yunnan.

Saxifraga parnassifolia D. Don (1821). Stems 11–24 cm, 6–11 flowers. Leaves cordate-ovate to 4 × 3 cm, upper surface with short glandular hairs, petiole to 2.7 cm. Petals to 7.9 × 4 mm, 2–3-callose. 2700–4000m, India to Bhutan, Tibet.

Saxifraga peraristulata Mattfeld (1931). Cespitose, stems 2–6 cm, solitary flowers. Leaves 1.0 × 0.15 cm, lower with petiole to 0.8 cm, upper surface of basal leaves with short glandular hairs. Petals to 5.5 × 2.5 mm, 2-callose. 4100–4700m, Sichuan, Yunnan.

Saxifraga pratensis Engler & Irmscher (1914). Stems 12–20 cm, 2–7 flowers. Basal leaves ovate to 2.4 × 1.5 cm, upper surface with short glandular hairs, petiole to 3 cm. Petals to 8.4 × 4 mm, 4–6-callose. 3800–4800m, Tibet, Sichuan, Yunnan.

Saxifraga pseudohirculus Engler (1901). Cespitose. Stems 4–17 cm, 1–12 flowers. Cauline leaves 3.5 × 0.35 cm, petiole to 1.2 cm. Upper surface of basal leaves with short glandular hairs. Petals to 11 × 3 mm, 2-callose. 3100–5000m, Tibet, Gansu, Qinghai, Shaanxi, Sichuan.

Saxifraga rizhaoshanensis J. T. Pan (1990). Cespitose, stems 6–8 cm, 2 flowers. Leaves to 0.6 × 0.1 cm, lower with petiole to 0.25 cm, upper surface of basal leaves with long non-glandular hairs. Petals to 4.2 × 1.7 mm, 2-callose, sepals glandular-hairy below. 4300–4500m, Sichuan.

Saxifraga rolwalingensis H. Ohba (1984). Stems

14–25 cm, 3–5 flowers. Leaves 6 × 0.9 cm, petiole to 2 cm, basal sometimes lost by flowering, upper surface with short glandular hairs. Petals to 8.5 × 6.2 mm, unclawed. 4200–4300m, Nepal.

Saxifraga sheqilaensis J. T. Pan (1990). Stems 29–45 cm, 7–13 flowers. Basal leaves subelliptic to 2.9 × 1.4 cm, upper surface with short glandular hairs, petiole to 2.3 cm. Petals to 6.2 × 4 mm, 6–7-callose. 4100m, Tibet.

Saxifraga sinomontana J. T. Pan & Gornall (2000) [*S. montana* Harry Smith (1924)]. Cespitose. Stems 4–35 cm, 2–8 flowers. Leaves elliptic-oblong to 3.4 × 0.5 cm, petiole to 4.5 cm, upper surface of basal leaves crispate-hairy. Petals to 12.5 × 6.9 mm, 2-callose. 2700–5300m, Sichuan. Note that this description applies to var. *amabilis* (var. *sinomontana* has glabrous upper surfaces of basal leaves and is far more widespread).

Saxifraga sphaeredana Harry Smith (1960). Cespitose, stems 10–17 cm, 1–5 flowers. Basal leaves cordate-ovate to 3.1 × 1.9 cm, upper surface with short glandular hairs, petiole to 5.3 cm, brown-hairy below, lowest leaves also brown-hairy above. Petals to 10 × 7 mm, spotted orange, (4)-callose. 3300–4100m, Nepal, Tibet. Note that this description relates to subsp. *dhwojii* (subsp. *sphaeredana* has both surfaces glabrous).

Saxifraga subomphalodifolia J. T. Pan in C. Y. Wu & J. T. Pan (1990). Stems to 30 cm, up to 18 flowers. Basal leaves cordate 1.7 × 1.4 cm, upper surface with short glandular hairs, petiole 3.2 cm. Petals orange to 8 × 4.3 mm, 6-callose. 4200m, Sichuan.

Saxifraga subtsangchanensis J. T. Pan (1990). Cespitose, stems 4–5 cm, solitary flowers. Leaves to 1.0 × 0.35 cm, lower with petiole to 1.1 cm, upper surface with long non-glandular hairs. Petals to 8 × 4 mm, not clawed, sepals glandular-hairy below. 4100–4300m, Tibet.

Saxifraga tigrina Harry Smith (1960). Cespitose, stems to 45 cm, 5–20 flowers. Basal leaves ovate-elliptic 4 × 3 cm, cordate, upper surface with short glandular hairs, with petiole. Petals purple-spotted, to 7 × 4.9 mm, 8-callose. 3000–3600m, Tibet. Note: leaf base sometimes cuneate.

Saxifraga tsangchanensis Franchet (1889). Cespitose. Stems 3–15 cm, 1–3 flowers. Leaves to 1.2 × 0.5 cm, lower with petiole to 3.2 cm, upper surface with long non-glandular hairs. Petals to 8 × 3.7 mm, orange-spotted, 2–11-callose, sepals glandular-hairy below. 3000–4600m, Tibet, Yunnan.

Saxifraga virgularis Harry Smith (1960). Densely cespitose. Stems 7–20 cm, 1–2 flowers. Leaves to 1.4 × 0.1 cm, including petiole, upper surface of basal with long non-glandular hairs. Petals orange, not spotted, to 8 × 4.7 mm, not callose, sepals glabrous below. 3900m, Burma.

Saxifraga viscidula J. D. Hooker & Thomson (1857). Cespitose. Stems 5–7 cm, 1 or 2 flowers. Leaves oblong 0.6 × 0.25 cm, upper surface of basal leaves with short glandular hairs. Petals to 11 × 3 mm. 3200–4700m, Sikkim.

Saxifraga yaluzangbuensis J. T. Pan (1978). Cespitose, stems 3–12 cm, 1–3 flowers. Leaves oblong 0.85 × 0.27 cm, upper surface of basal leaves with short glandular hairs, petioles to 0.9 cm. Petals to 13 × 3 mm, not callose, glandular-hairy. 4300–4800m, Tibet.

Position unclear in subsection *Hirculoideae*

Saxifraga amabilis H. Ohba & Wakabayashi (1987). Cespitose. Stems 30–50 cm, solitary flowers. Leaves sessile, wavy hairs, oblanceolate-ovate to 0.5 × 0.2 cm. Basal leaves probably persistent. Petals to 6.5 × 4 mm, 2–4-spotted. Sepals illustrated hairy beneath. 4000–4600m, Nepal.

Saxifraga burmensis Harry Smith ex Wadwha (1983). Stems to 25 cm, to 7 red flowers. Leaves ovate-triangular cordate to 2.5 × 2 cm, petiole to 1 cm. Petals to 4.1 × 2.9 mm. Base of stem missing in type specimen. Burma. Status doubtful.

Saxifraga harai H. Ohba & Wakabayashi (1987). Densely cespitose. Stems to 4–5 cm, solitary flowers. Leaves linear 0.8 × 0.15 cm, with petiole of same length. Basal leaves probably persistent. Petals to 8 × 5 mm. Suggested to be polyploid derivative of *S. aristulata*, but hair types on pedicel not clear. 4400–4700m, Nepal.

Saxifraga mallae H. Ohba & Wakabayashi (1987). Cespitose. Stems 3–8 cm, solitary flowers. Leaves linear-lanceolate to 2.5 × 0.2 cm. Basal leaves probably persistent. Petals to 9 × 5 mm, usually spotted. Associated with *S. lepida*, but petals not clawed. 3900–5000m, Nepal.

Saxifraga parnassioides Regel & Schmalhausen (1882). Stems 8–12 cm, 2 flowers. Leaves glabrous, basal cordate, cauline ovate to 1.5 × 1 cm. Petals to 5 mm. Close to *S. pratensis*, but basal leaves may not be persistent. 3000–4300m, Central Asia (Turkestan).

Saxifraga zimmermannii Baehni (1956). Stems 6–10 cm, usually 1 but very rarely to 3 flowers. Basal leaves lanceolate to 1.0 × 0.6 cm, petiole to 2 cm. Petals yellow. 4100m, Nepal.

Subsection *Gemmiparae* Engler & Irmscher and subsection *Cinerascentes* Engler & Irmscher

Gemmae (leafy buds) in all or some leaf axils. All species have unbranched stems except in species where gemmae develop into branches. All have yellow flowers except *S. strigosa* and *S. gemmipara*, which have white flowers. The only species in subsection *Cinerascentes* is *S. cinerascens* and this is indicated in the list.

Saxifraga balfourii Engler & Irmscher (1912). Stems may be branched, 6–18 cm, 1–5 flowers. Median leaves elliptic to 2.9 × 1.3 cm, entire margin, densely strigose. Petals to 7.7 × 4.2 mm. 2350–4600m, Yunnan.

Saxifraga brachypoda D. Don (1821). Stems 5–19 cm, 1–3 flowers. Cauline leaves entire, crowded to 1.2 × 0.3 cm, upper surface glabrous, margin more or less hairless. Petals to 9 × 5.2 mm, uncalloused. 3000–5000m, northwest India to Bhutan, Burma, Tibet, Sichuan, Yunnan.

Saxifraga brachypodoidea J. T. Pan (1990). Stems 5–8 cm, solitary flowers. Cauline leaves crowded to 0.7 × 0.2 cm, entire, upper surface glabrous, margin ciliate. Petals to 5.2 × 1.8 mm, uncalloused. 4200–4300m, Tibet.

Saxifraga cinerascens Engler & Irmscher (1912). Stems 5–9 cm, 1–4 flowers. Gemmae often developing into sterile shoots by flowering. Leaves grey. Lower leaves gathered to rosette, to 1.2 × 0.2 cm. Leaves entire, upper surface glabrous. Petals to 6 × 4 mm. 2800–4400m, Yunnan. Note that this species belongs to subsection *Cinerascentes*, of which it is the only member.

Saxifraga erinacea Harry Smith (1960). Stems 1.5–2.5 cm, solitary flowers. Gemmae often developing into sterile shoots by flowering. Cauline leaves crowded, to 0.65 × 0.15 cm, margin sharply ciliate. Leaves entire, upper surface glabrous. Petals to 7.5 × 3 mm, cordate base with claw, uncalloused. 4000–4600m, Tibet, Bhutan.

Saxifraga filicaulis Wallich (1828). Stems multi-branched, 9–24 cm, 1–3 flowers. Gemmae often developing into sterile shoots by flowering. Stem leaves to 1.2 × 0.2 cm, entire, upper surface glabrous, margins more or less hairless. Petals to 8 × 3.1 mm. 2100–4800m, Kashmir to Bhutan, Tibet, Shaanxi, Sichuan, Yunnan.

Saxifraga gemmipara Franchet (1896). Stems multi-branched, 9–24 cm, 2–12 white flowers. Median leaves tend to rosette, to 2.9 × 0.9 cm, entire margin, upper surface strigose, lower sometimes. Petals white, spotted yellow or purple, to 5.5 × 3.5 mm. 1700–4900m, Sichuan, Yunnan, Thailand.

Saxifraga gouldii C. E. C. Fischer (1939). Stems 7–25 cm, 2 or 3 flowers. Gemmae only in rhizome scale axils. Cauline leaves to 1.1 × 0.2 cm. Leaves entire, upper surface glabrous. Petals to 11 × 6 mm, apical margin glandular ciliate (var. *gouldii*) or laciniate (var. *eglandulosa*), uncalloused. 4000–4200m, Tibet and possibly Bhutan.

Saxifraga hispidula D. Don (1821). Stems usually branched 4–23 cm, 1–4 flowers, usually 1. Median leaves subelliptic-ovate to 2 × 1 cm, with 3–5 acute apical lobes, upper surface hairy. Petals to 7.3 × 5 mm. 2300–5600m, northwest India to Bhutan, Burma, Tibet, Sichuan, Yunnan.

Saxifraga macrostigmatoides Engler (1922). Stems 1.3–15 cm, solitary flowers. Gemmae developing into sterile shoots by flowering. Cauline leaves to 0.74 × 0.22 cm, upper surface glabrous, margins entire and glandular-ciliate. Petals to 8 × 4 mm. 3900–5000m, Tibet, Sichuan, Yunnan.

Saxifraga oreophila Franchet (1896). Stems multi-branched, 7–12 cm, 1–4 flowers. Median leaves to 1.5 × 0.15 cm, upper surface glabrous, apex aristate, margin recurved, entire, may be glandular-hairy. Petals to 5 × 2.7 mm. 2600–3200m, Yunnan.

Saxifraga serrula Harry Smith (1960). Stems branched, 4–16 cm, solitary flowers. Cauline leaves to 1.0 × 0.15 cm, entire, upper surface glabrous. Petals 7.5 × 4 mm, uncalloused. 3000m, Bhutan.

Saxifraga strigosa Wallich (1828). Stems may be branched, 5–28 cm, 1–10 white flowers. Median leaves tend to rosette, ovate-oblong to 2.7 × 1.3 cm, strigose, margin dentate. Petals white, red-brown spots, to 5.5 × 2.6 mm. 1800–4200m, northwest India to Bhutan, Burma, Tibet, Sichuan, Yunnan.

Saxifraga substrigosa J. T. Pan (1985). Stems not usually branched, 5–30 cm, 1–10 flowers. Gemmae sometimes developing by flowering. Median leaves strigose to 4.3 × 1.3 cm, margin serrate/dentate. Petals to 7 × 4.3 mm. 2700–4200m, Nepal, Tibet, Yunnan.

Saxifraga wallichiana Sternberg (1831). Stems 10–30 cm, 1–4 flowers. Cauline leaves crowded, to 1.8 × 0.8 cm, entire, upper surface glabrous, margin glandular-hairy. Petals 6.6 × 3.1 mm, 2-callose. 2000–5000m, northwest India to Bhutan, Burma, Tibet, Sichuan, Yunnan.

Saxifraga wardii W. W. Smith (1913). Stems 2.5–10 cm, solitary flowers. Gemmae only in rhizome scale axils. Cauline leaves to 1.1 × 0.6 cm, entire, upper surface glabrous. Petals to 11 × 9.1 mm, margin may be glandular-ciliate (var. *wardii*) or non-glandular ciliate (var. *glabripedicellata*), uncallosed. 1200m (var. *glabripedicellata*), 3500–4800m (var. *wardii*), Tibet, Yunnan, Bhutan.

Saxifraga wenchuanensis T. C. Ku (1989). Stems 7–9 cm, solitary flowers. Cauline leaves to 0.8 × 0.15 cm. Petals to 5.8 × 3 mm, uncallosed. 4300m, Sichuan.

Saxifraga zayuensis T. C. Ku [incl. *S. yunlingensis* C. Y. Wu (1990)]. Stems 3–7 cm, 1 or 2 flowers. Cauline leaves crowded, to 1.1 × 0.2 cm, entire, upper surface glabrous. Petals to 7 × 3.5 mm, margin may be sparsely glandular-hairy near base. 3800–4400m, Yunnan.

Subsection *Serpyllifoliae* Gornall

Saxifraga aleutica Hultén (1936). Stems to 2.5 cm, solitary flowers. Leaves hairless to 5 mm. Petals greenish-yellow to 3.5 mm. Aleutian Islands.

Saxifraga chrysantha A. Gray (1877). Stems 2–8 cm, solitary flowers. Leaves hairless or nearly so, to 0.7 × 0.2 cm. Petals golden-yellow to 7 mm long. Sepals reflexed. Sometimes treated as subspecies of *S. serpyllifolia*. Rocky Mountains from Wyoming to New Mexico.

Saxifraga serpyllifolia Pursh (1814). Stems 2–8 cm, solitary flowers. Leaves slightly hairy, to 0.7 × 0.2 cm. Petals yellow, occasionally purple, to 7 mm long. Sepals ascending. Japan to Alaska, Yukon and British Columbia.

Subsection *Rosulares* Gornall and subsection *Hemisphaericae* (Engler & Irmscher) Gornall

The three species in subsection *Hemisphaericae* (*S. zhidoensis*, *S. hemisphaerica* and *S. eschscholtzii*) are all in Group A.

Subsection *Rosulares*—group A and subsection *Hemisphaericae*

Mats or cushions, or non-rosetted branched shoots, flowers usually solitary (or 2–5). All species have yellow flowers except *S. sessiliflora*, *S. williamsii* and *S. brevicaulis* which have white or pink flowers, *S. eschscholtzii* which may have pink or white flowers, and *S. engleriana* which may have deep red-orange petals instead of the more normal yellow. Subsection

Hemisphaericae species (*S. zhidoensis*, *S. hemisphaerica* and *S. eschscholtzii*) may also be seen to have nectary rings, as may *S. contraria* and *S. engleriana*.

Saxifraga anisophylla Harry Smith (1960). Stems 6–16 cm, 1–3 flowers. Leaves 0.7 × 0.14 cm, basal leaf margins ciliate. Petals 6.5 × 3.2 mm, spotted orange. 3900m, Burma.

Saxifraga atuntsiensis W. W. Smith (1913). Stems 0.5–2.0 cm, solitary flowers. Leaves 0.4 × 0.2 cm. Basal leaf margin glabrous. Petals 6 × 4 mm. 4300–5200m, Sichuan, Yunnan.

Saxifraga aurantiaca Franchet (1890) [incl. *S. confertifolia* Engler & Irmscher (1914)]. Stems 4–10.5 cm, up to 12 flowers. Leaves 0.6 × 0.16 cm, margins sparsely short-ciliate. Petals orange- or purple-spotted, 5.9 × 2.6 mm. Sepals reflexed by fruiting. 3000–4200m, Sichuan, Yunnan, Shaanxi.

Saxifraga baimashanensis C. Y. Wu (1990). Stems 3.5–4.5 cm, solitary flowers. Leaves 0.37 × 0.12 cm, margin toothed/ciliate. Petals orange-spotted, 4.6 × 2.3 mm. Sepal margins glabrous. 4600–4700m, Yunnan.

Saxifraga brevicaulis Harry Smith (1958). Stems 2–4 cm, solitary flowers. Leaves 0.4 × 0.15 cm, margins ciliate. Petals white with pink base, 8 × 4 mm, persistent in fruit. Sepal margin pubescent/ciliate. 4400–4700m, Tibet. See note under *S. williamsii*.

Saxifraga carnosula Mattfeld (1931). Stems 7–12 cm, 1 or 2 flowers. Leaves 0.55 × 0.15 cm, basal leaf margins glabrous. Petals 6 × 2.2 mm. 3000–4900m, Sichuan, Yunnan.

Saxifraga chrysanthoides Engler & Irmscher (1912). Stems 1–3 cm, solitary flowers. Leaves 0.6 × 0.15 cm, outer margin sparsely ciliate. Petals 6 × 3 mm. Sepal tip margin ciliate. 2700–5300m, Yunnan.

Saxifraga contraria Harry Smith (1960). Stems 1–5 cm, solitary flowers. Leaves 0.2 × 0.1 cm. Petals 3.5 × 1.3 mm. Conspicuous nectary disc. 4200–4800m, Nepal to Bhutan, Tibet.

Saxifraga densifoliata Engler & Irmscher (1912). Stems 4.5–10 cm, up to 7 flowers. Leaves 0.44 × 0.15 cm, margins ciliate. Petals slightly orange-spotted, 6.5 × 2 mm. Sepals reflexed by fruiting. 4000–4500m, Tibet, Sichuan, Yunnan.

Saxifraga dongwanensis H. Chuang (2001). Densely cespitose, stems to 6 cm, solitary flowers. Leaves to 0.5 × 0.2 cm. Basal leaf margin glabrous. Petals to 7 × 2 mm. Yunnan.

Saxifraga drabiformis Franchet (1890). Cespitose, stems 6–10 cm, solitary flowers. Leaves 0.6 × 0.15 cm. Basal leaf margin glabrous. Petals 8 × 6 mm. 3300–

4900m, Yunnan.

Saxifraga draboides C. Y. Wu (1990). Stems 2.5–5 cm, solitary flowers. Leaves 0.5 × 0.14 cm, margin pubescent/ciliate. Petals 8 × 5 mm. Sepal margin glandular-hairy. 3800–4700m, Sichuan, Yunnan.

Saxifraga dshagalensis Engler (1922). Stems 4.5–7.5 cm, 1 or 2 flowers. Leaves 0.5 × 0.17 cm, margin sparsely short-ciliate. Petals orange-spotted 6.9 × 2.9 mm. 5000–5600m, Tibet, Sichuan.

Saxifraga engleriana Harry Smith (1924). Stems 1.5–3.5 cm, solitary flowers. Leaves 0.5 × 0.2 cm. Petals yellow, or very rarely red-orange, 4.1 × 2.5 mm. Conspicuous nectary disc. 4100–4700m, Tibet.

Saxifraga eschscholtzii Sternberg (1822). Stems to 1 cm, solitary flowers. Leaves to 0.3 cm long, margin fimbriate, in tiny globular rosettes. Petals yellow, pink or white. Sepal margin fimbriate. May be seen to have nectary disc. 300–1500m, Yukon, Alaska, Siberia. Note: subsection *Hemisphaericae*.

Saxifraga exigua Harry Smith (1924). Densely cespitose. Stems 1–3 cm, solitary flowers. Leaves and margins glabrous to 0.34 × 0.17 cm. Petals, as sepals, to 1.7 × 1 mm. 5000–5600m, Sikkim. May be conspecific with *S. inconspicua*.

Saxifraga filifolia J. Anthony (1933). Stems 3–7 cm, solitary flowers. Leaves 0.5 × 0.1 cm, margin ciliate. Petals yellow or orange, 7 × 2.5 mm. Sepal margins glabrous. 3000–4300m, Tibet, Yunnan, Burma.

Saxifraga finitima W. W. Smith (1913). Stems 2.5–5 cm, solitary flowers. Leaves 0.55 × 0.22 cm, margins glandular-hairy. Petals with red/brown spots, 7 × 4 mm. Sepal margin glandular-hairy. 3500–4900m, Tibet, Sichuan, Yunnan.

Saxifraga flexilis W. W. Smith (1913). Stems 4.0–8.5 cm, 1 or 2 flowers. Leaves 0.55 × 0.15 cm, margins sparsely ciliate or glabrous. Petals orange-spotted, 6 × 2.2 mm. 4100–4700m, Sichuan, Yunnan.

Saxifraga gemmigera Engler (1901) [incl. *S. gemmuligera* Engler (1912)]. Stems 4.5–17 cm, solitary flowers, leafy axillary buds up the stem. Leaves 0.5 × 0.2 cm, margin sparsely ciliate. Petals 4.6 × 3 mm. Sepal margin glabrous. 3100–4700m, Gansu, Shaanxi, Sichuan, Yunnan.

Saxifraga glacialis Harry Smith (1924). Stems 2.5–7.0 cm, 1–6 flowers. Leaves 1.0 × 0.25 cm, margins hairy or glabrous. Pedicel glabrous. Petals may have purple backs, but upper surface is unspotted, 5 × 2.5 mm. Ovary dark purple. 4100–5000m, Qinghai, Sichuan, Yunnan.

Saxifraga hemisphaerica J. D. Hooker & Thomson

(1857). Stems 2–5 cm, solitary flowers. Leaves 0.56 × 0.18 cm, margin ciliate/laciniate. Petals 3.5 × 1.0 mm. Sepal margin ciliate/laciniate. Obvious nectary disc. 4500–5000m, northwest India to Bhutan, Tibet, Qinghai. Note: subsection *Hemisphaericae*.

Saxifraga inconspicua W. W. Smith (1911). Flowers solitary and sessile. Leaves 0.3 × 0.05 cm. Basal leaf margin glabrous. Petals to 2 mm long. 4600–5300m, Sikkim.

Saxifraga jacquemontiana Decaisne (1844). Stems to 2 cm, solitary flowers. Leaves 0.5 × 0.17 cm, margin long glandular-hairy. Petals 5.1 × 3 mm. Sepal margin glandular-hairy. 4000–5300m, Kashmir to Bhutan, Tibet.

Saxifraga jainzhuglaensis J. T. Pan (1991). Stems to 2 cm, solitary flowers. Leaves ovate 0.7 × 0.25 cm, margins long glandular-hairy. Petals 2.7 × 2 mm. Sepal margin glandular-hairy. 3900–4200m, Tibet.

Saxifraga jaljalensis H. Ohba & S. Akiyama (1992). Stems to 2 cm, solitary flowers. Leaves to 1.0 cm. Petals orange-spotted, 5 × 4 mm. 4300m, eastern Nepal. Details of leaf margin not specified in original description but basal leaves sparsely hairy above and glabrous below, sepal margins also not specified.

Saxifraga llonakhensis W. W. Smith (1911). Stems 4–9 cm, solitary flowers. Leaves 0.8 × 0.1 cm, margin shortly ciliate. Petals obscurely spotted, 9.2 × 3.1 mm. Sepal margin with short glandular hairs. Note: rarely up to 3 flowers. 3700–4600m, Nepal, Sikkim, Tibet, Yunnan, Burma.

Saxifraga medogensis J. T. Pan (1990). Stems to 4.5 cm, solitary flowers. Leaves 0.3 × 0.1 cm, margin sparsely ciliate. Petals 4.4 × 2.6 mm. Sepal margins glabrous. 3700m, Tibet.

Saxifraga microviridis H. Hara (1975) [*S. microphylla* Royle ex J. D. Hooker & Thomson (1857)]. Cespitose, stems to 1 cm, solitary flowers. Leaves and margins glabrous to 0.5 × 0.2 cm. Petals green-yellow 3 × 1 mm, less than sepals or absent. 3900–5600m, Kashmir to Bhutan.

Saxifraga minutifoliosa C. Y. Wu ex H. Chuang (2001). Stems 3–5 cm, solitary flowers. Leaves 0.25 × 0.1 cm, margin ciliate. Petals 5.5 × 2 mm. Sepal margins glabrous. 3000–3400m, Yunnan.

Saxifraga miralana Harry Smith (1960). Stems 4–4.5 cm, solitary flowers. Leaves 0.6 × 0.15 cm, margin ciliate. Petals orange-spotted 5.1 × 2 mm. Sepal margins glabrous. 4100–5100m, Tibet.

Saxifraga nanella Engler & Irmscher (1914). Stems 1–4 cm, 1–5 flowers. Leaves 0.8 × 0.3 cm, margin glandular-ciliate. Petals orange-spotted, 5 × 2.2 mm. 3000–5800m, Nepal, Tibet, Qinghai, Xinjiang, Yunnan.

Saxifraga nanelloides C. Y. Wu (1990). Stems 2.5–3 cm, solitary flowers. Leaves 0.63 × 0.1 cm, margin sparsely ciliate. Petals 5.6 × 3.1 mm. Sepal margins glabrous. 4000m, Yunnan.

Saxifraga paiquensis J. T. Pan (1990). Stems 1–1.5 cm, solitary flowers. Leaves broadly oblong-elliptic 0.4 × 0.2 cm, surface and margin short glandular-hairy. Petals 5 × 3.2 mm. Sepals with short glandular hairs. 4400–4800m, Tibet.

Saxifraga perpusilla J. D. Hooker & Thomson (1857). Stems 1–2 cm, solitary flowers. Leaves 0.36 × 0.1 cm, margin deeply laciniate. Petals 3.5 × 1.8 mm, orange-spotted. 3700–5800m, Nepal to Bhutan, Tibet, Yunnan. Note: sepal margins may be glabrous or laciniate.

Saxifraga prattii Engler & Irmscher (1914). Stems 2.5–6 cm, 1 or 2 flowers. Leaves 0.5 × 0.17 cm, margins sparsely short-ciliate. Petals 7 × 4 mm. 2500–5300m, Tibet, Sichuan, Yunnan. Note: var. *prattii* has hairy sepal margins; var. *obtusata* has glabrous sepal margins.

Saxifraga sessiliflora Harry Smith (1958). Stems 2–3 cm, solitary flowers. Leaves 0.6 × 0.25 cm, margin toothed/ciliate. Petals are white possibly with pink bases 3.5 × 1.0 mm, persistent in fruit. Sepal margin toothed/ciliate. 4200–5000m, Tibet. See note under *S. williamsii*.

Saxifraga stella-aurea J. D. Hooker & Thomson (1857). Stems 1–8 cm, solitary flowers. Leaves 0.5 × 0.2 cm, margins shortly glandular-ciliate. Petals orange-spotted, 7 × 3.4 mm. Sepal margin glandular ciliate. 3000–5800m, northwest India to Bhutan, Tibet, Qinghai, Sichuan, Yunnan.

Saxifraga tatsienluensis Engler (1922). Stems 5–9 cm, 1–4 flowers. Leaves 0.44 × 0.15 cm, basal leaf margin sparsely ciliate. Petals 6.5 × 2 mm. 3800–4000m, Sichuan.

Saxifraga uninervia J. Anthony (1933). Stems 3–4 cm, 1–4 flowers. Leaves 0.8 × 0.2 cm, basal leaf margin glabrous. Petals 5 × 2.5 mm. 5000m, Yunnan.

Saxifraga versicallosa C. Y. Wu ex H. Chuang (2001). Stems 2.5–6 cm, solitary flowers. Leaves lanceolate to 0.8 × 0.2 cm. Petals to 6.5 × 4 mm, callose. Sepal margin pubescent/ciliate. 3500–4200m, Yunnan, Sichuan. Note: basal leaves are only sparsely glandular-hairy but margin may not be.

Saxifraga williamsii Harry Smith (1958). Stems to 1 cm, solitary flowers. Leaves 0.5 × 0.17 cm. Petals

white 6 × 4 mm, persistent in fruit. Sepal margin pubescent/ciliate. 4000–4800m, Nepal. Closely related to *S. brevicaulis* and *S. sessiliflora* which may all be conspecific. Originally described as somewhat anomalous members of section *Porphyrion*.

Saxifraga zhidoensis J. T. Pan (1978). Stems 1–2 cm, solitary flowers. Leaves 0.36 × 0.1 cm, margin ciliate/laciniate. Petals 2.4 × 1.3 mm. Sepal margin ciliate. May be seen to have nectary disc. 4900–5000m, Qinghai. Note: subsection *Hemisphaericae*.

See also *S. unguiculata*, *S. taraktophylla* and *S. gyalana*, which are listed in group B but could equally be listed above.

Subsection *Rosulares*—group B

Well-defined rosette (although sometimes may be cespitose), usually multi-flowered. Leaves carnose, not shiny, often rough. All species with yellow flowers except *S. punctulatoides*, *S. punctulata* var. *punctulata* and *S. lhasana* which have pale yellow or white flowers; *S. sanguinea* which has pale yellow flowers, and *S. gyalana* which may have orange petals. Many have dramatically spotted petals. All these species are found in Tibet, Sichuan or Qinghai.

Saxifraga brunneopunctata Harry Smith (1960). Stem 2–6 cm, 1–11 flowers. Leaves 0.7 × 0.25 cm, upper surface glabrous. Petals 5 × 1.6 mm, yellow, brown-spotted. 4000–4900m, Tibet.

Saxifraga candelabrum Franchet (1890) [incl. *S. bonatiana* Engler & Irmscher (1912)]. Stem 5–38 cm, up to 30 flowers. Leaves 6 × 1.4 cm, with broadly toothed apical margin. Upper surface of basal leaves pubescent. Petals 6.1 × 3.1 mm, yellow with orange or purple spots or blotches. 2000–4200m, Sichuan, Yunnan.

Saxifraga daochengensis J. T. Pan (1990). Stem 17–18 cm, 19–28 flowers. Leaves 2.3 × 0.8 cm. Upper surface of basal leaves pubescent. Petals 5 × 4 mm, yellow with purple back and possibly base. 3600m, Sichuan.

Saxifraga dielsiana Engler & Irmscher (1912). Stem 12–15 cm, to 30 or more flowers. Leaves 2.2 × 0.85 cm. Upper surface of basal leaves pubescent. Petals 7 × 2.5 mm, yellow. 2100–2600m, Sichuan, Yunnan.

Saxifraga elatinoides Handel-Mazzetti (1923). Stem 2–6 cm, solitary flower. Leaves 0.3 × 0.1 cm, upper surface glabrous. Petals 5 × 3 mm, yellow. 3000–4700m, Sichuan, Yunnan.

Saxifraga gyalana Marquand & Airy-Shaw (1929). Cespitose, stem 5–9 cm, 1–6 flowers. Leaves 0.86 × 0.17 cm, upper surface pubescent. Petals

6.8 × 2.4 mm, yellow, orange or orange-spotted. 2300–4100m, Tibet.

Saxifraga heterotricha Marquand & Airy-Shaw (1929) [incl. *S. anadena* Harry Smith (1960)]. Stem 6–12 cm, 1–6 flowers. Leaves 0.52 × 0.21 cm, upper surface glabrous. Petals 6.2 × 2.5 mm, yellow, orange-spotted. 3000–4200m, Tibet.

Saxifraga lhasana Harry Smith (1960). Stem 5–10 cm, 2–23 flowers. Leaves 1.35 × 0.3 cm, upper surface glabrous, margin ciliate. Petals 9 × 3.2 mm, white, pink or pale yellow. 3000–4700m, Tibet. Note: J. T. Pan treats this as a variety of *S. umbellulata*.

Saxifraga lixianensis T. C. Ku (1989) [incl. *S. subsediformis* J. T. Pan (1990)]. Stem 4.5–6.5 cm, 13–15 flowers. Leaves 0.95 × 0.35 cm, upper surface pubescent. Petals 4.9 × 2.9 mm, yellow, orange-mottled at base. Sichuan.

Saxifraga pasumensis Marquand & Airy-Shaw (1929) [incl. *S. muricola* Marquand & Airy-Shaw (1929)]. Stem 5–10 cm, 2–23 flowers. Leaves 1.35 × 0.3 cm, upper surface glabrous, margin ciliate. Petals 9 × 3.2 mm, yellow. 3000–4100m, Tibet. Note: J. T. Pan treats this as a variety of *S. umbellulata*.

Saxifraga pellucida C. Y. Wu (1990). Stem 9–20 cm, 2–7 flowers. Leaves 0.5 × 0.15 cm, upper surface glabrous. Petals 6 × 2.5 mm, yellow, orange spots. 2700–3400m, Tibet, Yunnan.

Saxifraga punctulata Engler (1912). Cespitose, stems 1.5–6 cm, 1–3 flowers. Leaves 0.5 × 0.14 cm, pustulate towards tip.

var. *punctulata*. White or pale yellow flowers with petals to 9 × 5.5 mm. 4600–5400m, Nepal, Sikkim, Tibet.

var. *minuta*. Yellow flowers with petals to 3.5 × 2 mm, spotted yellow, orange and dark red. 4800–5800m, Tibet.

Saxifraga punctulatoides J. T. Pan (1985). Stem 3–6 cm, 3–10 flowers. Leaves 0.4 × 0.14 cm, pustulate towards tip. Petals 7 × 3.5 mm, white, spotted purple. 4800–5100m, Tibet.

Saxifraga sanguinea Franchet (1894). Stem 5–15 cm, 3–23 flowers. Leaves 1.3 × 0.3 cm, upper surface glabrous. Petals 7.3 × 2.3 mm, normally yellow but may be red. Purple-spotted, red backs. 3300–4500m, Tibet, Qinghai, Sichuan, Yunnan.

Saxifraga sediformis Engler & Irmscher (1912). Stem 7–20 cm, 5–33 flowers. Leaves 2.0 × 0.55 cm, upper surface pubescent. Petals 7.5 × 3 mm, yellow. 2700–4600m, Tibet, Sichuan, Yunnan.

Saxifraga signata Engler & Irmscher (1912). Stem

10–20 cm, 4–24 flowers. Leaves 1.6 × 0.3 cm, upper surface glabrous. Petals 8.7 × 4 mm, yellow, purple-spotted. 2800–4600m, Tibet, Qinghai, Sichuan, Yunnan.

Saxifraga signatella Marquand and Airy-Shaw (1929). Stem 2.5–7.5 cm, 1–12 flowers. Leaves 0.92 × 0.28 cm, upper surface glabrous. Petals 7 × 2.2 mm, yellow, purple-spotted. 3900–5400m, Tibet.

Saxifraga taraktophylla Marquand & Airy-Shaw (1929). Cespitose, stems 12–15 cm, 1–7 flowers. Leaves 0.97 × 0.1 cm, upper surface glabrous. Petals 6.1 × 2.2 mm, yellow. 3500–3900m, Tibet.

Saxifraga umbellulata J. D. Hooker & Thomson (1857). Stem 5–10 cm, 2–23 flowers. Leaves 1.35 × 0.3 cm, margin glabrous, pustulate towards tip. Petals 9 × 3.2 mm, yellow. 3100–4400m, Tibet.

Saxifraga unguiculata Engler (1883) [incl. *S. limprichtii* Engler & Irmscher (1913), *S. vilmoriniana* Engler & Irmscher (1912)]. Cespitose, stems 2.5–14 cm, 1–8 flowers. Leaves 0.8 × 0.15 cm, upper surface glabrous. Petals 7.5 × 2.9 mm, yellow, orange spots. 1800–5600m, Tibet, Qinghai, Sichuan, Yunnan, Gansu, Hebei, Ningxia, Shaanxi.

Saxifraga yushuensis J. T. Pan (1978). Stem 4.5–6 cm, 2–10 flowers. Leaves 0.85 × 0.3 cm, pustulate towards tip. Petals 7.6 × 4.5 mm, yellow, purple-spotted. 4300–4400m, Qinghai.

Subsection *Flagellares* Gornall

All species with runners (aerial stolons) with leafy buds at tips. Runners (stolons) are from axils of basal leaves except in *S. tentaculata* and *S. flaccida*, glandular-hairy, often sparsely, except in *S. tentaculata* in which they are glabrous. Stems glandular-hairy except as specified. Petals clawed and callosed unless specified. Ovary superior to inferior.

Saxifraga angustata Harry Smith (1924). Glandular-pilose. Stems 8–12 cm, 5–6 flowers, pedicels to 1.0 cm. Rosette leaves 1.5 × 0.15 cm. Petals red or pink, to 3.5 × 2 mm, similar length to sepals. Ovary inferior. 4200–4300m, Sichuan.

Saxifraga brunonis Wallich ex Seringe (1830) [*S. brunoniana* Wallich ex Seringe (1828)]. Stems more or less glabrous 6–16 cm, 3–9 flowers, branches to 6.6 cm, with pedicels to 2.4 cm. Stolons 4–24 cm. Rosette leaves fleshy, shiny, 1.3 × 0.25 cm. Petals yellow, to 8 × 4 mm, much longer than sepals. Ovary subsuperior. 2800–4000m, Kashmir to Bhutan, Burma, Tibet, Sichuan, Yunnan.

Saxifraga consanguinea W. W. Smith (1913). Stems glandular-hairy 0.5–8.5 cm, 1–10 flowers, pedicels to 0.6 cm. Stolons to 12 cm. Rosette leaves to 0.9 × 0.3 cm, upper surface glabrous. Petals red, pink or yellow, to 2.6 × 2 mm, similar length or shorter than sepals. Ovary semi-inferior. 3000–5400m, Nepal, Tibet, Qinghai, Sichuan. May be conspecific with *S. pilifera*.

Saxifraga deqenensis C. Y. Wu (1990). Glandular-pilose. Stems 3–6 cm, 3–5 flowers, pedicels to 0.3 cm. Rosette leaves to 1.6 × 0.4 cm. Yellow petals 3.8 × 2.4 mm, similar length to sepals. Ovary subinferior. 4500–4600m, Yunnan.

Saxifraga flaccida J. T. Pan (1985). Sparsely hairy. Stems 2–4 cm, 1–3 flowers, pedicels to 1.4 cm. Stolons from axils of median cauline leaves. Rosette leaves to 1.0 × 0.32 cm, leathery, glabrous, margin glandular. Petals yellow, to 4.6 × 1.5 mm, much longer than sepals. Ovary subsuperior. 5000m, Tibet.

Saxifraga flagellaris Willldenow ex Sternberg (1810) [incl. *S. macrocalyx* Tolmatchev (1956)]. Stems to 15 cm, 1–7 flowers, pedicels to 1 cm. Runners to 15 cm. Rosette leaves to 1.6 × 0.5 cm. Petals yellow, to 10 × 6 mm, much longer than sepals. Ovary position varies between subspecies from superior to subsuperior (one-third inferior). Europe, North America, Asia. For most purposes best treated as a polymorphic species. Various subspecies have been described, some of which have been given specific status by various botanists, and a number of the other species in the list have at times been treated as subspecies:

subsp. *flagellaris*. Superior ovary. Caucasus.

subsp. *crandallii* (Gandoger) Hultén. Ovary partly inferior. Narrow petals and hypanthium. Rocky Mountains: Montana to New Mexico.

subsp. *platysepala* (Trautvetter) Porsild. Ovary partly inferior. Circumpolar.

subsp. *setigera* (Pursh) Tolmatchev (*S. macrocalyx* Tolmatchev, *S. flagellaris* subsp. *stenosepala* Trautvetter). Ovary superior. Hypanthium broad. China, Russia, Alaska, Yukon, British Columbia. *S. macrocalyx* is described from Altai and Tien Shan. Other subspecies which have been described include subsp. *crassiflagellata*, subsp. *komarovi* (probably now included in *S. stenophylla* as subsp.), subsp. *sikkimensis* (now *S. mucronulatoides*) and subsp. *megistantha* (now included in *S. mucronulata*).

Saxifraga josephii Engler (1900). Stems sparsely pubescent 1–13 cm, 3–5 flowers, pedicels to 2 cm. Rosette leaves leathery, shiny 1.4 × 0.2 cm, surface glabrous, margin ciliate. Petals yellow, to 6 × 2 mm,

much longer than sepals. Ovary superior. 1300–2100m, Henan, Shaanxi. May be conspecific with *S. brunonis*.

Saxifraga loripes J. Anthony (1933). Pubescent. Stems 4–11 cm, 1–4 flowers, pedicels 0.1 cm. Rosette leaves to 1.0 cm, surfaces glabrous, margins glandular-ciliate. Petals yellow, to 7 × 5 mm, much longer than sepals. Ovary subsuperior. 3700–4000m, Sichuan.

Saxifraga microgyna Engler & Irmscher (1912). Glandular-pilose. Stems 3.5–20 cm, 3–15 flowers, pedicels to 0.35 cm. Stolons to 15 cm. Rosette leaves to 0.73 × 0.32 cm. Petals yellow to pink, not always clawed, to 3.2 × 1.4 mm, similar length or shorter than sepals. Ovary inferior. 3000–4900m, Tibet, Qinghai, Sichuan, Yunnan.

Saxifraga mucronulata Royle (1839). Densely glandular-pubescent. Stems 2–4 cm, 1–5 flowers, pedicels to 0.3 cm. Stolons. Rosette leaves fleshy to 0.95 × 0.2 cm, margins ciliate not glandular. Petals yellow, not callose, to 4.4 × 2.2 mm, much longer than sepals. Ovary semi-inferior. 2800–5400m, Kashmir to Sikkim, Tibet, Sichuan, Yunnan.

Saxifraga mucronulatoides J. T. Pan (1991) (*S. flagellaris* subsp. *sikkimensis*). Stems densely pubescent to 21 cm, up to 12 flowers, in dense head. Stolons. Rosette leaves to 1.1 × 0.3 cm. Petals yellow, to 6 × 3.5 mm, much longer than sepals. Ovary semi-inferior. 3400–5200m, Nepal to Bhutan, Tibet.

Saxifraga nangxianensis J. T. Pan (1978). Glandular-pubescent. Stems 2.5–10 cm, 4–9 flowers, pedicels to 0.6 cm. Stolons to 12 cm. Rosette leaves to 0.83 × 0.3 cm. Petals yellow to purple, to 3.8 × 2.5 mm, similar length to sepals. Ovary subinferior. 4500–5500m, Tibet.

Saxifraga neopropagulifera Hara (1976). Stems 1–12 cm, 1–5 flowers, pedicels to 0.6 cm. Stolons from basal axils. Rosette leaves to 0.8 × 0.3 cm, oblong-spathulate. Petals yellow to 3.5 × 1.5 mm, similar length to sepals. 4500–5800m, Nepal.

Saxifraga parkaensis J. T. Pan (1979). Stems 1.5–4 cm, 1–3 flowers, pedicels to 0.75 cm. Stolons to 10 cm. Rosette leaves slightly fleshy to 0.8 × 0.26 cm, apex mucronate. Petals yellow, to 8 × 4 mm, much longer than sepals. Ovary semi-inferior. 5100–5300m, Tibet.

Saxifraga pilifera J. D. Hooker & Thomson (1857). Pubescent. Stems up to 3 cm, up to 3 or more flowers, short pedicels. Stolons 10 cm or more. Leaves 0.65 × 0.2 cm. Petals pink or orange-red, to 2.5 × 1.5 mm, similar length or shorter than sepals. Ovary inferior. Nepal to Bhutan. 4200–5000m. May be conspecific with *S. consanguinea.*

Saxifraga stenophylla Royle (1939). Stems densely hairy 5–18 cm, 1–3 flowers, pedicels to 1.4 cm. Stolons 4–12 cm. Rosette leaves leathery to 1.3 × 0.45 cm, margins glandular-ciliate. Petals yellow, not callosed or clawed, to 12 × 7.5 mm, much longer than sepals. Ovary subsuperior. 3700–5000m, Pakistan, Tadjikhistan, Kashmir to Sikkim, Tibet, Sichuan, Yunnan.

Saxifraga tentaculata C. E. C. Fischer (1941). Glabrous. Stems 2.5–6 cm, 1 or 2 flowers, pedicels to 0.8 cm. Stolons to 22 cm, from axils of median cauline leaves. Leaves to 1.2 × 0.4 cm. Petals yellow 3.2 × 2.6 mm, similar length to sepals. Ovary subinferior. 4000–4600m, Nepal to Bhutan, Tibet.

12 · Rough-Leaved Saxifrages
Section *Trachyphyllum*

Most of the *Trachyphyllum* saxifrages live in the Arctic and subArctic, although various species are found as far south as Japan, the Cascades and the Alps, and many are delightful although sometimes challenging plants for the rock garden. They are characterized by having stiff hairs on the margin and tip of their evergreen leaves. Some form mats or cushions but some are smaller, forming little more than extended tufts. The flowers are white or very pale yellow and are usually spotted with yellow or red spots, or both, with the yellow spots towards the base and the red spots towards the tip.

For the gardener then there are obvious attractions—species with spotted flowers that can make a nice cushion sound ideal for the rock garden—but few of the species are grown. The major difficulty for many gardeners lies in their geographic origins: as arctic or arctic-alpine plants they really want cool conditions. Nevertheless it is quite possible to grow them in a cool spot on a rock garden or in a large plastic pot.

The general appearance of a plant and its pattern of growth are functions of its environment. In the far north, where the *Trachyphyllum* saxifrages are most numerous, plants have to survive long cold dark winters and then exploit a short summer during which there is continuous sunlight. Like those animals that do not migrate, they have to hunker down during the winter months, energy expenditure kept to a minimum, and then be active non-stop during the summer, maximizing energy capture.

The *Trachyphyllum* saxifrages are not alone in *Saxifraga* in having their centre of diversity on the tundra and in the mountains of the Arctic and subArctic: section *Mesogyne* has a very similar distribution pattern. But these two sections deal with the yearly cycle in very different ways. The *Mesogyne* species survive the winter as resting bulbils and then form tufts of flat-bladed palmate leaves that maximize their energy-capturing surfaces through the summer. The *Trachyphyllum* saxifrages, on the other hand, are evergreen, with small, tough, pointed leaves in rosettes which close up rather tighter in winter. The leaves have stiff marginal hairs adding to the insulating layers and they often form dense mats of vegetation

Saxifraga bronchialis subsp. *austromontana*. Obstruction Point, Olympic Mountains, Washington.

with the stems entangled with one another. With such small leaves the plant has minimal energy needs in winter, but when summer comes these leaves are supplemented by the numerous leaves on the flower stems which are usually twice the size of the evergreen ones and which add enormously to the plant's productive capacity.

Although there are two species found in the European mountains, the section is seen more appropriately as having a trans-Pacific distribution, across the Bering Straits, with the European species being seen as extensions from pan-Arctic proto-species. In Asia, they spread down through far-eastern Russia to Japan, Korea, and far-eastern China; in North America they spread down from Alaska through northern Canada to the Cascades and Rocky Mountains.

The species boundaries of *Trachyphyllum* saxifrages are an area of great potential confusion. In no other group within the genus have the different approaches of botanists brought up in Russian and non-Russian traditions been more obvious. The narrow species approach to the *Trachyphyllum* has been developed through major papers by Siplivinsky (1971), Khokryakov (1979) and Zhmylev (1988, 1992), who have between them listed around 20 species in Asia which might for the most conservative non-Russian botanist be no more than two or three species.

The *Trachyphyllum* Species

Flowers of *Saxifraga cherlerioides* showing the typical pattern of yellow and red spots. Photograph John Howes.

The basic form is a small mat of rosettes from which leafy shoots develop each year; these shoots may root at points along their length. The leaves are typically needle-shaped or lanceolate with the apex being pointed. In a minority of species the leaves may be much broader, and may have a rounded or toothed apex. Along the leaf margin of most species there are stiff bristly hairs, sometimes very thick, which are characteristic of the section. The marginal hairs are usually straight and evenly spaced, sticking out at right angles to the longitudinal axis of the leaf, although in a few species they are strongly curved. The flowers may be solitary but may be in clusters, typically cymose, of up to twelve. The petals are either white or creamy-white, or pale yellow to yellowish-green, and they are usually spotted with yellow or red spots or both. Petals are usually lanceolate, although they may be somewhat oblong, and may have a fairly blunt apex, and they may be clawed or unclawed. The ovary is strongly superior. The most important features by which species are distinguished are the shape and size of the foliage, the length of the marginal hairs, and the shape and colour of the petals.

European Species

Only two *Trachyphyllum* species, *Saxifraga aspera* and
S. bryoides, are found in Europe. Both are found in similar situations, growing over or among silicaceous rocks in the mountains. Both species can be found in the Pyrenees and Alps and
S. aspera is also found in the northern Apennines, and *S. bryoides* in the Carpathians and the mountains of Bulgaria.

Saxifraga aspera is typically found between 1000 and 2200
metres on rather bare rocky ground, although it is tolerant of
a range of conditions. A useful clue perhaps for the gardener
is that it can be found prospering in the same conditions as
S. paniculata and the two species can be found growing
together just above the road to the east of St Martin-Vésubie
in the Maritime Alps. It usually forms just a few clusters of
rosettes from which there are just a few flower stems. Prostrate
shoots may root and form larger mats, but they tend not to be
the dense mats typical of *S. bryoides*. The flowers are quite
large, up to 2 cm but more typically 1.5 cm diameter, with
pale creamy-white petals which usually have a large yellow
blotch toward the base and smaller spots of yellow, orange or red above that.

Saxifraga aspera.
St Martin-Vésubie,
Maritime Alps.

The other European species, *Saxifraga bryoides*, grows in many of the same
areas although often at rather higher altitudes, from 1800 metres upwards to
well over 3000 metres in more specifically alpine conditions. While the shoots of
S. aspera clearly stem from central rosettes, those of *S. bryoides* form such a dense
mat that it is not always easy to determine their starting point. It has much smaller
leaves, about half the length of those of *S. aspera*, both on the horizontal shoots

Saxifraga bryoides. The
flowers are very similar
in size to those of *S.
aspera*, but the foliage
is very different. Above
Belvedere, Maritime
Alps.

where they reach 5 mm in length, and on the flowering stems, where they reach 8 mm. The flowers may be as large as those of *S. aspera*, which is larger than would be expected from the size of the foliage, and the flower colour and the marks on the petals are like those of *S. aspera*.

Asian and American Species with Pointed Leaves

The view of Webb & Gornall to these Asian and American species is of a broadly defined *Saxifraga bronchialis* with a number of subspecies: including subsp. *austromontana* from North America; subsp. *funstonii* from the region on either side of the Bering Sea (Beringia); subsp. *spinulosa* from northern Russia, and the type subsp. *bronchialis* from eastern Russia to northeastern China. Reidar Elven, working on the Panarctic Flora Project, would probably accept at least two broad species, although perhaps not with the same boundaries as Webb & Gornall.

From a Russian point of view, exemplified most recently in the work of Zhmylev, there is a split between those species (or subtaxa) which should be associated with *Saxifraga bronchialis* and those which should be associated with *S. spinulosa*. While there are some other species which seem not to fit well within this framework, particularly *S. derbekii* (and these are discussed later), it seems possible to maintain two such groups even if many of the species recognized by the Russian botanists would not be given the same status by European botanists.

Bronchialis aggregate. Entire, awl-shaped or linear leaves, bright white petals, spheric-ovoid capsules. Possible species: *S. bronchialis* (including *S. austromontana*), *S. stelleriana* (*S. algisii*, *S. balandinii*), *S. caulescens*, *S. omolojensis* (*S. multiflora*, *S. ledeboriana*) and *S. anadyrensis* (perhaps as a high-altitude ecotype or variety of *S. omolojensis*).

Spinulosa aggregate. Lanceolate (and broader) leaves, pale yellow petals, elongated cone-shaped capsules. Possible species: *S. spinulosa* (including *S. firma*, *S. submonantha*), *S. funstonii* (possibly including *S. codyana*), *S. cherlerioides* (including *S. rebunshirensis*, *S. kruhsiana*).

Bronchialis aggregate

From the narrow species point of view, *Saxifraga bronchialis* has linear or subulate leaves typically up to 9 mm long and no more than 2 mm wide, with stiff hairs along the margins. The flowers have white, unclawed petals (which have yellow spots toward the base and red spots towards the tip), and it has round rather than conical capsules. The typical subsp. *bronchialis* ranges widely across northern Russia eastwards to the Russian Far East (not including the far northeast) while in North America subsp. *austromontana* is found in the Cascades and Rocky Mountains.

The other taxa included in the Bronchialis aggregate have narrower distributions in Russia. *Saxifraga caulescens*, which has leaves up to 20 mm long, may be a hybrid between a narrow *S. bronchialis* and *S. spinulosa* or may be no more than a local form in the Baikal and Trans-Baikal regions. *Saxifraga stelleriana*, which is found slightly inland, is smaller and may not even deserve status as a taxon. *Saxifraga omolojensis* has narrow, pubescent leaves with only very short marginal hairs, and small, narrow petals, and comes from the Russian Far East from Chukotka down to Okhotsk. *Saxifraga anadyrensis* from mountain areas of Magadan has smaller needle-like leaves with hairless margins and may be a subtaxon of *S. omolojensis*. *Saxifraga kolymensis* is an obscure taxon, probably fitting in the Bronchialis aggregate, with needle-like leaves and white, spotted flowers, and is from Magadan and Yakutsk.

Saxifraga funstonii is unique among the *Trachyphyllum* saxifrages in having only yellow spots on the petals. North of Nome, Alaska.

Spinulosa aggregate

The Spinulosa aggregate has *Saxifraga spinulosa*, or *S. bronchialis* subsp. *spinulosa*, at its heart. This is distinguished by having lanceolate to oblong leaves up to 15 mm long and 2 mm wide, shorter hairs on the leaf margins, and it has yellowish petals with yellow and red spots. The leaves are also described as having a curved rather than keeled lower-profile in cross-section. Its range is from northwest Russia to Kamchatka being sympatric with *S. bronchialis* subsp. *bronchialis* in much of this range. From northern Russia across to Alaska *S. funstonii* (*S. bronchialis* subsp. *funstonii*) with typically oblong leaves with quite short hairs on the margins is easily recognized by having only yellow spots on its pale yellow petals which are distinctly although broadly clawed. In the northeast of Alaska and on into the Yukon *S. codyana* (*S. bronchialis* subsp. *codyana*) is distinguished from *S. funstonii* by having hairless leaves with only glandular margins. In the Ussuri coastal region of Russia there is also an obscure taxon, *S. ascoldica*, which may also belong in the Spinulosa aggregate.

Saxifraga funstonii (*S. bronchialis* subsp. *funstonii*) north of Nome on the Seward Peninsula, Alaska.

The remaining taxa in the Spinulosa aggregate cluster around *Saxifraga cherlerioides*. Most taxonomists, although not all, accept this as a good species with a geographic range including Kamchatka, Sakhalin and the Kuril Islands and Rebun. It has oblong to spathulate leaves and unclawed petals, which are variously described as white, cream or greenish-yellow, having yellow and red spots. *Saxifraga kruhsiana* seems to be a small alpine form of *S. cherlerioides* from Kamchatka and Okhotsk. Two other taxa now seem to be generally accepted as varieties of *S. cherlerioides*, with var. *rebunshirensis* generally rather larger than typical, and var. *microglobularis* a dwarf form.

Saxifraga derbekii

The most obvious species with pointed leaves which does not fit into the Bronchialis–Spinulosa aggregate analysis adequately is *Saxifraga derbekii*, with the combination of leaf shape and flower colour leaving it outside the definition of either group. It makes a small mat of rosettes of small lanceolate leaves which have a ciliate margin. The flowers have pure white oblong-ovate petals with tiny pinkish-red spots and are instantly recognizable, flower colour, spotting and petal shape all being distinctive.

Saxifraga derbekii in the Botanic Garden in Anchorage, Alaska.

Asian and American Species with Broad or Tridentate Leaves

While most of the *Trachyphyllum* species have pointed leaves, a few deviate from this. *Saxifraga tricuspidata* is found from Greenland to Alaska. It is generally found on or among rocks, and has the general air of a robust form of *S. bronchialis* or *S. cherlerioides* but with the apex of the leaves being split into three sharp teeth, the outer two often being angled outwards. Among the people of the Arctic it has the Inuit names *tiinnguat*, *kaillarnaqutit* and *a'asaat*, the first referring to its use as a tea, the second to its prickly leaves, and the last perhaps an onomatopoeic exclamation at being pricked. The foliage is said to have been used as bedding for young husky puppies—the dried and prickly leaves helping to toughen the tender pads on their feet.

The flowers of *Saxifraga tricuspidata* are typical in having white flowers with yellow and red spots. In parts of Canada identification can be difficult as there is at least one form (f. *subintegrifolia*) which may have untoothed leaves.

In western North America there are two other species, *Saxifraga vespertina* and *S. taylorii*, with leaves which may be toothed at the apex. It is argued that these represent glacial-survival populations of *Trachyphyllum* saxifrages which, cut off from their ancestral connections, adapted as conditions improved, and they have leaves which are relatively broader than those of *S. tricuspidata*. Both these species have a limited range and each has at least part of their range along the Pacific coast, where conditions during glaciation would be less severe. The more widespread of the North American species is *S. vespertina*, which is found in the Olympic Mountains and Cascades of Oregon and Washington. Typically it is found in mats on damp cliffs. This has broad leaves, shorter than in *S. tricuspidata*, with stiff marginal hairs. Although the leaves are usually entire, they may well have a small tooth on either side of a larger, broad apical one.

The other North American species is *Saxifraga taylorii*. This has three clear teeth at the end of the broadened leaf, but is distinctive because it has wide open, unspotted white flowers with a well-developed nectary disk. This makes it sound a

Saxifraga tricuspidata growing
on rocks near Turnagain Arm
south of Anchorage, Alaska.

Saxifraga tricuspidata in front
of the Greenland ice-cap.
Kangerlussuaq, Greenland.
Photograph Ian Bainbridge.

rather attractive and certainly interesting plant, but it is very restricted in the wild
being found only in a small part of the Queen Charlotte Islands (Haida Gwaii) and
very rarely on the adjacent British Columbian mainland. Most of the locations for
S. taylorii are some 20 miles west or southwest of Sandspit on the southern half of
the Queen Charlotte Islands along narrow logging roads which are regularly used
by monster logging trucks, and up through forest rich in grizzly bears to appealing
places such as Mosquito Lake. Despite the obvious attractions of finding such an
obscure plant in the wild, it was too out of the way during my trip to photograph
saxifrages in the west of North America. It really needed five days to get there and
back and give myself a fair chance of finding the plant, so it was a real pleasure to
find that Rick Lupp had the plant at his nursery in Washington State. A plant he
sent me has survived well but with as yet no flowers.

   Across the other side of the Pacific, on the Kuril Islands and in northern Japan,
there is another group with tridentate leaves. Two species have been described but
it seems likely that both of these—*Saxifraga nishidae* described from rocky places
in the Yuubari Mountains of Hokkaido where it is rare, and *S. arinae*, much more
recently described from the southernmost of the Kuril Islands—are examples of
a single species. The leaves of *S. nishidae* are described as 4–10 mm long and 2–3
mm wide, and it has stems carrying one to three flowers which have white, obovate,
6–7 mm long, petals spotted with yellow and red. By comparison *S. arinae* is distinguished only by having more shortly ciliate leaf margins, up to six flowers on a
stem, and smaller petals. It seems pretty certain that this should be included with

S. nishidae, possibly as a variety, and that its separation as a species may reflect the nationalistic disputes over the Kuril Islands.

Growing *Trachyphyllum* Saxifrages

Whatever the problems for the taxonomist, the situation is far simpler for the gardener. Although in general these plants have been ignored by all but the specialist grower, a number of them seem to be quite easy to grow in a pot or on a rockery. They are straightforward from seed, if it will germinate. This can be a problem with some wild-collected seed from the Arctic, but generally not with seed of *Saxifraga aspera*, *S. bryoides* and *S. derbekii*. Cuttings root fairly readily in damp sand; longer shoots can be broken into short segments and pegged down horizontally rather than inserted vertically.

The two European species, *Saxifraga bryoides* and *S. aspera*, are fairly regularly available from the seed exchanges of the major rock-gardening societies and *S. aspera* is quite easy from seed. It has creamy-white petals with rich deep cadmium-yellow blotches at the base, and is worth trying. I have it filling a couple of 9-inch pots sitting outside and after a run of heavy rains in June (not that usual for us) it flowered quite well. *Saxifraga bryoides* is certainly available from nurseries and as one of the few European species might be expected to be straightforward, but I find it, like the American *S. vespertina*, difficult to maintain for any length of time. The major difficulty I find with both of these species is that the foliage of what looks like a perfectly healthy plant suddenly comes away from the roots. This is probably associated with damp compost, particularly in autumn when growth has stopped, and it would seem that a more open gritty mix is needed. Whatever the reason it means that an eye has to be kept on these species in particular and if this happens I use the now detached material for cuttings.

Much more robust in general terms is *Saxifraga cherlerioides*, usually found in a robust form which may well be var. *rebunshirensis*, which produces vigorous growth, good foliage and pretty although rather scattered white, yellow and red-spotted flowers. Growing in a heavy soil in a rather shady spot at the base of a rockery, *S. bronchialis* 'Nana' has survived happily for around ten years but unfortunately it has rarely flowered and the flowers were small and had small and narrow petals.

In general, the long list of Russian taxa remains the preserve of the botanist. The Russian botanist Dr Alexandra Berkutenko, based in Magadan, has an on-line seedlist which lists a number of *Trachyphyllum* saxifrages most years as well as a handful of other *Saxifraga* and *Micranthes*, but of these only *Saxifraga derbekii* seems to have even a toe-hold in cultivation. I have now had plants of this for about five years and one has flowered twice. It was very distinctive, with blunt recurved pure white petals with a small sprinkling of tiny dark red pinprick spots at their base. It was exciting for me to see this flowering quite well in a trough in Anchorage Botanic Garden and it was clear that we were growing the same species, possibly from the same collection. Others from her collections which have germinated successfully and are now one-year-old seedlings are *S. omolojensis* and *S. kruhsiana*.

Among the American taxa there are a few that are fairly readily available. *Saxifraga vespertina* is regularly listed by nurseries (often as *S. bronchialis* subsp. *vespertina*), and *S. tricuspidata* is occasionally available. I have found *S. vespertina* to be impermanent in a pot and *S. tricuspidata*, which has very vigorous growth in spring and early summer, can also suffer similar problems. This is a handsome plant which would be worth going to some effort to get and establish. Very well worth searching for on seedlists would be *S. funstonii* (*S. bronchialis* subsp. *funstonii*), which would make a very distinctive and attractive rock-garden subject, and I have half a dozen small seedlings from last year's NARGS seed exchange. Although this is a species centred on the lands either side of the Bering Straits, and the seed I had was collected in Alaska, my experience of it on the Seward Peninsula was that it was a plant of fairly dry rocky ground and I hope that this will give it a chance in my dry but often much warmer conditions.

Section *Trachyphyllum* (Gaudin) W. D. J. Koch

Saxifraga aspera Linnaeus (1753). Mats of rosettes and prostrate shoots. Leaves to 17 × 1.5 mm on flower stems, half as long on prostrate shoots, margins with stiff right-angled hairs. Flowers up to 20 mm, creamy-white petals usually with large yellow blotch toward the base and smaller spots of yellow above. Silicaceous rocky ground 1000–2200m, European Mountains: Pyrenees, Alps, Apennines.

Saxifraga bronchialis Linnaeus (1753). Flower stems 5–20 cm. Leaves are typically 5–15 × 1–3 mm, pointed with a spiny tip, linear or subulate, with a margin with stiff patent hairs. Flowers are white to very pale creamy-yellow, petals 3–6 × 1.5–3 mm, with red and yellow spots. (In a narrow view, key characteristics are narrow linear leaves, white rather creamy-yellow petals, and ovoid-spherical capsules.)

    subsp. *bronchialis*. Leaves linear-lanceolate. Petals unclawed 5–6 × 2–2.5 mm white with red spots. Widespread: northern Russia across to the Pacific coast but not in the far (Beringian) northeast.

    subsp. *austromontana* (Wiegand) Piper. Linear-lanceolate leaves, short marginal hairs. Flowers with unclawed white petals with red and yellow spots.

    North America: Cascades and Rocky Mountains. In a broad view (such as that of Gornall) other subtaxa would be subsp. *funstonii* (Small) Hultén (very pale yellow petals with only yellow spots), subsp. *spinulosa* (Adams) Hultén (oblong to lanceolate leaves) with *S. cherlerioides* recognized as a species (for narrow-species view see below). Some taxa would simply be unrecognized (*S. caulescens*, *S. stelleriana*, *S. ascoldica* and *S. kolymensis*). There may also be a case for *S. omolojensis* (including *S. anadyrensis*) at species level. For a narrow-species approach see supplementary list below main species list here which discusses the species in the Bronchialis and Spinulosa aggregates.

Saxifraga bryoides Linnaeus (1753). Dense mats of shoots with flower stems to 5 cm, occasionally to 8 cm. Leaves about 5 mm on shoots and 8 mm on flower stems. Flowers up to about 18 mm with creamy-white petals spotted yellow and red. Silicaceous rocks, 1800–3000m or higher, Pyrenees, Alps, Carpathians, Bulgaria.

Saxifraga cherlerioides D. Don (1822). Leaves oblong

to spathulate, sometimes with mucronate tip, typically 6–8 × 1.5 mm. Petals cream with yellow and perhaps red spots. Not clawed. Russia: Sakhalin, Kuril Islands, Kamchatka, Okhotsk. *S. kruhsiana* Fischer ex Seringe is probably a small northerly alpine form of this species with globular foliage and yellow-green flowers from the mountains of Kamchatka and Okhotsk. Generally treated as a separate species rather than a subspecies of *S. bronchialis* although not by all.

var. *rebunshirensis* (Engler & Irmscher) Hara. Rather larger than the typical form of the species, leaves lanceolate 6–15 × 1.5–3 mm. Red-spotted petals. Japan (Rebun), Sakhalin.

var. *microglobularis* (A. P. Khokhryakov) Zhmylev. Flower stems 5–6 cm. Dwarf with leaves broadly lanceolate, very small, 2–2.5 × 1 mm with cartilaginous ciliate margin. Tiny globose axillary buds and tips. Flowers with narrowly elliptic petals to 3 × 1.3 mm, white or greenish-yellow. Russian Far East.

Saxifraga derbekii Siplivinsky (1971). Flower stems 8–10 cm with lax foliage 5–9 flowers. Loose cushions of leafy stems, 2–4 cm long, with leaves 4–7 × 1–2 mm, linear-lanceolate, ciliate with aristate apex. Petals oblong-ovate, 7 × 3 mm, white, with small pinkish-red spots near the base. Russian Far East: lowland rocky areas near the Sea of Okhotsk.

Saxifraga nishidae Miyabe & Kudo (1917) [incl. *S. arinae* Zhmylev (1988)]. Short, slender branched stems forming loose tufts or mats. Flower stems 3–7 cm with 1–3 flowers. Leaves 4–10 × 2–3 mm with the tip deeply cut into three narrow aristate lobes. Flowers with narrowly oblong petals, 6–7 mm long, white with darker spots. Japan (Hokkaido: Yuubari Mountains), rare in rocky places. Very similar plants from Kuril Islands have been described as *S. arinae* Zhmylev with leaves rather shorter and broader 4–6 × 2–4 mm. Up to 6 flowers per stem, white obovate petals 4 × 2.5 mm.

Saxifraga taylorii Calder & Savile (1959). Flower stem 3–12 cm with up to 5 wide-open flowers. Leaves cuneate-spathulate, 4.5–10 × 2.5–5.5 mm, with 3 apical mucronate lobes. Hairs quite long (according to Zhmylev). Petals up to 7 × 4 mm with short claws, white, unspotted. Disk strongly developed. Loose rocky slopes. British Columbia: Queen Charlotte Islands.

Saxifraga tricuspidata Rottboll (1770). Leaves (narrowly) cuneate, 6–15 × 1.5–5 mm, with 3 mucronate teeth at apical margin but sometimes with no teeth. Petals not clawed, white-cream with yellow,

orange and red spots. Alaska, Canada, Greenland.

Saxifraga vespertina (J. K. Small) Fedde (1906). Leaves broadly ovate to spathulate, 4–10 × 1.6–3.2 mm, with stiff marginal hairs, usually entire but sometimes with a small tooth on either side of a central broad tooth. Petals 4–6 mm, not clawed. This has a very limited distribution in North America, confined to the Olympic Mountains and Southern Cascades and the Columbia River Gorge.

Narrow species allied to *Saxifraga bronchialis*

Bronchialis aggregate

Apart from *S. bronchialis* with its subspecies (subsp. *bronchialis* and subsp. *austromontana*) the following would be recognized:

Saxifraga anadyrensis Losinskaja (1939). Bronchialis aggregate. Small needle-like linear leaves with smooth hairless margin. White petals, spotted with red and yellow. Probably a high alpine form of *S. omolojensis*. Russia: Magadan (Khrebet Kolymski and Cherskogo and mountains near mouth of River Lena).

Saxifraga caulescens Siplivinsky (1971). Bronchialis aggregate. Probably no more than a local form of *S. bronchialis* but possibly separate species, possibly of hybrid origin between *S. bronchialis* and *S. spinulosa*. Linear-lanceolate leaves, 13–20 × 1.5–2.5 mm, with short marginal hairs. Flowers with white, spotted, petals 5–6.5 mm long. Has been recorded as a Siberian species among rocks in larch and pine woods. Current Russian practice seems to confine this species to Mongolia where *Flora of China* identification would define it as *S. bronchialis* subsp. *bronchialis*.

Saxifraga omolojensis A. P. Khokhryakov (1979) [*S. ledeboriana* Holub (1984), *S. multiflora* Ledebour (1812)]. Bronchialis aggregate. Flower stems 8–10 cm. Rigid needle-like leaves 8–12 × 2 mm, pubescent with dense white hairs, very shortly glandular-ciliate margins. Flowers with narrowly elliptic white petals 4–5 × 2 mm with many dark red and yellow spots. Russia: Chukotka to Okhotsk.

Saxifraga stelleriana Merk ex Seringe (1830) [incl. *S. algisii* T. V. Egorova & Siplivinsky (1970), *S. balandinii* Zhmylev (1999)]. Bronchialis aggregate. Primarily distinguished by its smaller size. Linear-lanceolate ciliate leaves up to 5.5 × 1.3 mm with mucronate apex. Flowers white and possibly unspotted. Russia: Angara to Okhotsk and Zea and Lake Baikal.

Spinulosa aggregate

Apart from *S. cherlerioides* the following would be recognized at species level:

Saxifraga funstonii Small (1905). Spinulosa aggregate. Leaves are rather broader and more oblong that those of *S. bronchialis*. Petals palest yellow with yellow spots, broadly clawed. Hairs are quite short. Dry scree and rocky places. Russia (Taimyr and Amgun to Chukotka), Alaska, Yukon and northern British Columbia. If *S. codyana* Zhmylev is maintained as a taxon it would be as a subspecies or variety of *S. funstonii* in Spinulosa aggregate and hence of *S. bronchialis* in a broader approach. Leaves are hairless but with glandular margins. Petals have only yellow spots and are 5 × 2 mm (smaller than *S. funstonii*). Yukon, Alaska. Treated as a subspecies of *S. bronchialis* by most western authors.

Saxifraga spinulosa Adams (1817) [incl. *S. firma* Litvinov ex Losinskaja (1939), *S. submonantha* Khokhryakov & Kuvaev (1994)]. Spinulosa aggregate. Oblong to lanceolate (rather than needle-like) leaves about 15 × 2 mm. Cross-section showing a curved rather than keeled lower surface, and shorter hairs on the leaves. Smaller (than *S. bronchialis*) unclawed yellowish-white petals with yellow and red spots. Tundra. Russia from northwest (Urals) to Kamchatka and Chukotka. Note: *S. firma* is included here by Zhmylev, although earlier, Calder & Savile had seen it as synonymous with *S. funstonii*. If treated separately, *S. submonantha* refers to smaller plants and is limited to the Taimyr peninsula.

There are also two obscure taxa:

Saxifraga ascoldica Siplivinsky (1971). Probably in Spinulosa aggregate. Flower stems 4–10 cm with 2–5 flowers. Dense cushion of leafy stems up to 3 cm long, leaves up to 8 × 1.5 mm wide, lanceolate to linear-lanceolate, ciliate. Flowers with oblong white, purple-spotted, petals about 5 × 1.5 mm wide. Very limited in Russia: Ussuri.

Saxifraga kolymensis A. P. Khokhryakov (1970). Probably in Bronchialis aggregate. Flower stem 10–15 cm. Leaves stiff linear, needle-like, 5–10 × 1.5 mm with shortly ciliate margin. Flowers with elliptic petals, 5–6 × 2 mm, white with yellow and dark red spots. Siberia, Magadan.

13 · Mossy Saxifrage Species
Section *Saxifraga* 1

The mossy saxifrage hybrids are well known to gardeners, and it is easy to assume that the species are merely rather poor shadows of these garden hybrids. Nothing could be further from the truth. Stone walls in picturesque Cotswold villages, parched roadsides in southern Andalucia and the rocky heights of the Alps are all among the habitats for these highly adapted species, which can be found from the Mediterranean to the Arctic. Outlying members are found in the Caucasus, the mountains of northern Africa in Morocco and Algeria, across northern North America to the Rocky Mountains and then on down into South America along the Andes. This section has more African species than any other and the only South American species in the genus. But it is in Europe, and southern Spain and northern Italy in particular, that their rich diversity is displayed. There are about 80 species in the section and this diversity means that these species can serve gardeners in a much wider range of climates than has generally been recognized.

Saxifraga bourgaeana on damp cliffs by the side of the road above Grazalema in Andalucia, Spain.

Taxonomy of Section *Saxifraga*

Given so many species with often quite different habits and morphology, it is not surprising that the section has been subdivided. The species now included in this section are sufficiently different for them to have inhabited different sections in Engler's earlier classification, with species split between section *Dactyloides* (now subsection *Triplinervium*), section *Tridactylites* (now subsection *Tridactylites*), and section *Nephrophyllum* (now subsection *Saxifraga* plus *S. irrigua* and *S. latepetiolata*) which also included what are now the *Mesogyne* species. The major revision to Engler's approach was undertaken by Gornall (1987), and there have been modifications of this by Vargas so that we now have:

Section *Saxifraga*
    Subsection *Saxifraga*
        Series *Saxifraga*
        Series *Biternatae* (Engler & Irmscher) Gornall
    Subsection *Triplinervium* (Gaudin) Gornall
        Series *Gemmiferae* (Willkomm) Pawłowska
        Series *Cespitosae* (H. G. L. Reichenbach) Pawłowska
        Series *Axilliflorae* (Willkomm) Pawłowska
        Series *Ceratophyllae* (Haworth) Pawłowska
        Series *Pentadactyles* (Lázaro Ibiza) P. Vargas
        Series *Aquaticae* (Engler) Pawłowska
        Series *Arachnoideae* (Engler & Irmscher) Gornall
    Subsection *Holophyllae* (Engler) Engler & Irmscher
        Series *Androsaceae* (Engler & Irmscher) Pawłowska
        Series *Muscoideae* (Engler & Irmscher) Pawłowska
        Series *Sedoides* (Gaudin) Pawłowska
        Series *Tenellae* (Engler & Irmscher) Pawłowska
        Series *Glabellae* (Engler & Irmscher) Pawłowska
    Subsection *Tridactylites* (Haworth) Gornall

This follows Gornall's classification except in the adoption of series *Pentadactyles* following Vargas's splitting of series *Pentadactyles* (with terminal flower stems) from series *Ceratophyllae* (with axillary flower stems). Vargas went on to split the species of series *Cespitosae* between series *Pentadactyles* and subsection *Holophyllae*, but I have not followed Vargas in this, nor in his reallocation of series *Gemmiferae* from subsection *Triplinervium* to subsection *Saxifraga*.

As far as the gardener is concerned, most of the species which are grown are found in subsection *Triplinervium*. Some species from subsection *Saxifraga* can be grown, but the species of the latter two subsections (*Holophyllae* and *Tridactylites*) are generally rather difficult and many are not particularly dramatic. The garden hybrids, which are dealt with in the next chapter, are primarily a product of crosses of species within subsection *Triplinervium*, although it has been argued that *Saxifraga granulata* was also involved.

Taxonomic ambiguities in section *Saxifraga*

My general approach in this chapter has been to follow the morphological analyses of Webb & Gornall (1987) and Vargas (1997). However, phylogenetic work, notably that of Vargas, Morton & Jury (1999) as well as earlier work by Soltis et al (1996), has made it clear that, although further such work is needed, it will lead to a radical revision of the section. Various points can be made about their studies and about such a revision:

1. The two subsection *Triplinervium* series *Cespitosae* and *Ceratophyllae* are quite clearly separated from one another, and the implications of Vargas (1997) that would have eliminated the *Cespitosae* are unwarranted. They are, however (Soltis et al), part of a clade (complete and exclusive evolutionary branch) quite separate from series *Arachnoideae*, which is also at present in the *Triplinervium*.

2. Series *Ceratophyllae* needs to be expanded to include a number of species currently allocated to other sections. *Saxifraga continentalis* and *S. hypnoides* from series *Gemmiferae* belong here; and at least *S. camposii* from series *Pentadactyles*.

3. Series *Pentadactyles* (also in subsection *Triplinervium*) is not monophyletic (consisting of an exclusive group of taxa derived from a single ancestor) and its status or list of constituents needs to be reconsidered. Vargas et al (1999) analysed just two species from this series. *Saxifraga camposii* clearly belongs in the *Ceratophyllae*, while *S. pentadactylis* was closer to *S. exarata* (the only *Cespitosae* species analysed) than it was to any other species considered. To this may be added the finding of Soltis et al that *S. latepetiolata* (from *Pentadactyles*) is close to *S. cuneata* (in *Ceratophyllae*). It may be that series *Pentadactyles* should be maintained, but further research is required.

4. Series *Arachnoideae* may be remote from subsection *Triplinervium* rather than belonging to it as had previously been considered. *Saxifraga arachnoidea* was on a single branch remote from all the other species considered by Vargas et al. Previously, among the species Soltis et al had analysed, *S. arachnoidea* was quite clearly separated from a clade containing species from series *Cespitosae* and *Ceratophyllae*. It was most closely related to *S. tenella* with *S. paradoxa* the next closest, the three forming another clade. It seems therefore that series *Arachnoideae* is not a monophyletic group and will need to be reconsidered.

5. Series *Gemmiferae* (also in subsection *Triplinervium*) was considered in detail by Vargas et al but not by Soltis et al. It is clearly not monophyletic but at its core is a group of species (centred on *Saxifraga globulifera*) which should be regarded as a new narrower series *Gemmiferae*. Outside of this *Gemmiferae* sensu stricto, *S. hypnoides* and *S. continentalis* (*S. fragosoi*) belong in the *Ceratophyllae*, and *S. conifera* probably belongs in a separate new series.

6. Our observations of living material *in situ* suggest that the North African species previously allocated to series *Gemmiferae* do not all belong there. Of these one (*Saxifraga embergeri*) is properly placed in series *Gemmiferae*; one (*S. maweana*) may belong in series *Gemmiferae* but is more likely to be a member of the *Pentadactyles* or *Ceratophyllae* allied to species such as *S. maderensis*; and one

(*S. werneri*) is clearly not a member of the *Gemmiferae* and has some resemblances to members of series *Cespitosae*.

7. Series *Saxifraga* was represented in the analysis of Vargas et al by *Saxifraga granulata*, which was shown to be closely allied to the broad *Ceratophyllae* clade rather than to the *Gemmiferae*, the *Cespitosae*, *S. conifera* or *S. arachnoidea*. This may have implications for the split of subsections *Saxifraga* and *Triplinervium*.

8. Subsection *Tridactylites* was clearly monophyletic in the study of Vargas et al, but no species from subsection *Holophyllae* were analysed by them and only *Saxifraga tenella* was analysed by Soltis et al. It is probable that the *Holophyllae* is not a single closely related unit and that a number of the series represent more widely separated groups.

While it has not been possible to come to firm conclusions about the precise outcome of further work (except that substantial changes to the taxonomy of this section are inevitable), those areas where fairly unambiguous results have been obtained are noted within the body of the chapter and in particular in the treatment of series *Gemmiferae*.

Subsection *Saxifraga*

The ten species of this subsection are distinguished by being predominantly summer-dormant and by having small bulbs, usually called bulbils, in the axils of the basal leaves. The bulbs or bulbils may be less than 2.5 mm in diameter in *Saxifraga granulata*, but may be up to about 8 mm in *S. carpetana*. However small, these are quite different from the bulbils of *S. cernua* from section *Mesogyne*, and of *S. mertensiana* from section *Heterisia*, which are carried on the inflorescence.

Following the dry summer months, growth recommences in the autumn with each bulb giving rise to a tuft of more or less complex leaves and usually a single flower stem. Larger mats or cushions may arise from growth of a cluster of the previous year's bulbs. The centre of diversity for the subsection is clearly Spain: the three series *Biternatae* species are all confined to small areas in Andalucia, while of the seven species in series *Saxifraga*, only *S. bulbifera* is not found in the Iberian peninsula.

Series *Saxifraga*

The seven species in this series form a tuft of basal leaves with single flower stems. The leaves have a broad blade, either lobed or with a crenate margin, sometimes with a long stalk, and the flower stem is quite tall and usually only narrowly branched. *Saxifraga granulata* is the most widespread species, but in various parts of Europe it is replaced by *S. carpetana*, *S. bulbifera* and *S. corsica*, each of which has a very similar form. In some places, particularly in southern Italy, species may overlap, but these species are generally fully allopatric.

Saxifraga granulata in a Derbyshire meadow.

The meadow saxifrage, *Saxifraga granulata*, with its tall stems of vase-shaped white flowers and crenate, rounded leaves with longish petiole, is found from Finland and north-western Ukraine all down through western Europe to the Atlas Mountains in Morocco. It is not a rare plant, often being found in large numbers. Typically in Britain it is a plant of grassy meadows where it flowers in May, but further south it can flower much earlier, for example in February among the grass below the Puerto Nuevo in Ronda under the blossoming almond, while at higher altitudes it will again be flowering in May. It extends as far as the Anti-Atlas Mountains some way south of Marrakesh, where again it can be found flowering in February and March on grassy banks under small trees. After flowering the plant dies down to pass the summer and autumn as dormant bulbils, formed in the axils of the basal leaves, from which the new shoots will grow for the following year.

In Spain there are two subspecies. *Saxifraga granulata* subsp. *graniticola* makes small plants no more than 10 cm tall, while subsp. *granulata* has two varieties: var. *granulata*, which is the norm, and var. *glaucescens*, which can have flower stems to 45 cm and has very hairy leaf blades.

Saxifraga granulata subsp. *granulata* var. *glaucescens* has tall, more widely branched stems and very hairy leaves. Grazalema, Andalucia.

Saxifraga carpetana is usually very similar to *S. granulata*, although slightly smaller than the typical variety, but the generally hairy basal leaves are stalkless and the inflorescence rather more capitate. Effectively a Mediterranean evolution from *S. granulata*, which it replaces throughout most of its range, *S. carpetana* is found through the dry heart of Spain, in Mediterranean north Africa (subsp. *carpetana*), and in Sicily, extreme southern Italy, Albania and Greece through to the coast of western Turkey (subsp. *graeca*). The petals are noticeably hairy in many specimens.

Flowers of *Saxifraga carpetana* showing glandular-hairy petal surface. Los Cabanos, Cazorla, Andalucia.

Saxifraga carpetana growing on a well-drained rock garden.

Saxifraga dichotoma is pretty much co-extensive with *S. carpetana* in Spain and is also found in north Africa. It is distinguished by more deeply lobed, more or less hairless leaves with the lobes in outline like splayed fingers, a rather more diffuse inflorescence, and often less hairy petals, which are often suffused pink. It also flowers from March to May, rather earlier than *S. carpetana*, which flowers from May to June. In some parts of Spain plants with intermediate characters between *S. carpetana* and *S. dichotoma* can be found.

Saxifraga corsica, again very similar to smaller forms of *S. granulata*, is confined to Corsica, Sardinia, the Balearics and a small area of the coast of eastern Spain. *Saxifraga bulbifera* is found from Corsica and Sardinia, throughout Italy and then eastwards through former Yugoslavia, Albania, northern Greece, Romania, Bulgaria, Hungary, Slovakia and into eastern Austria. Again it is very similar to the other species under consideration, but it is easily distinguished at flowering time by axillary bulbils which form up the flowering stems as well as in the axils of basal leaves. *Saxifraga cintrana*, from a small area around Lisbon, has shorter stems (up to about 15–18 cm rather than the 25–30 cm of the foregoing species) but the flowers are very similar in shape and size to those of *S. granulata*.

The remaining species in this series is *Saxifraga haensleri*, which is again found in southern Spain, but is much smaller than the other species, with both leaves and flowers much smaller. Its inflorescence is branched, but otherwise it looks like a large *S. tridactylites* but with flowers about twice the size, and it may be that these two species are more closely related than the current taxonomy tends to suggest.

The species in this series hybridize very little. *Saxifraga granulata* crosses with *S. rosacea* in the wild in Germany (*S. ×freibergii*), and is reported to cross with *S. cespitosa* in Sweden. These crosses are of interest as representing the sort of cross that is said by Engler to have been involved in Arends's production of early garden hybrids. There may be crosses between *S. bulbifera* and *S. carpetana* in southern Italy and Sicily.

Series *Biternatae*

The three species in this series are closely related to those of series *Saxifraga* but they look quite dissimilar. Rather than having a tuft of basal leaves and a single fairly simple flower stem, these species give the appearance of a small cushion, with the leaves more intricately divided and the flower stems being both shorter and often much more complex. Each species is narrowly endemic in Andalucia and confined within those areas to specific niches.

Saxifraga bourgaeana is very easy to find on the most shady bits of the damp cliff immediately above Grazalema on the main road, up to the top town car park, and it is abundant in the general area of the Sierra de Grazalema where conditions are right. There is also an isolated and rather impoverished population of *S. bourgaeana* (not *S. gemmulosa*, as is sometimes suggested) high up on the limestone cliffs of Los Esparteros, about 60 kilometres away near Moron de La Frontera. The leaves of *S. bourgaeana* are bright green, with three separated leaflets each deeply lobed. The reddish flower stems are also quite complex, branched widely and in a fairly angular way from quite low down, with the nodes being quite swollen, almost like a knee. The flowers are wide open with each petal having three quite clearly defined yellow-green veins, and the yellow ovary surface (the ovaries are fully inferior) is very noticeable. In most locations *S. bourgaeana* is found alongside *S. globulifera*, which takes the slightly less shady and slightly less damp situations. These two species hybridize occasionally to produce *S. ×camboana*, which has foliage with tight globular buds rather like that of *S. globulifera*, but which has a much more complex inflorescence like that of *S. bourgaeana*.

East of the Sierra de Grazalema, between Ronda and the coast, *Saxifraga gemmulosa* can be found in the ultra-basic "red earth" of the Sierra Bermeja, 20 kilometres or so south of Ronda. *Saxifraga gemmulosa* is a delightful species. It makes a small cushion with finely divided leaves with the three separate lobes each deeply divided, and has a delicate branched inflorescence. The dark blue-green colour of the leaves complements the dark red branches of the inflorescence, which in turn set off the white flowers very effectively. The petals have three

Saxifraga bourgaeana. Grazalema, Andalucia. Photograph Paul Kennett.

Saxifraga gemmulosa.
Sierra Bermeja,
Andalucia.

Saxifraga biternata.
El Torcal, Andalucia.

Saxifraga pubescens
subsp. *iratiana* with
petals showing the three
nerves after which
subsection *Triplinervium*
is named.

obvious veins but they are not so strongly coloured as those of *S. bourgaeana*. It is by far the smallest of the three species in series *Biternatae*, with the cushions often being no more than 10 cm in diameter. We found it in a roadside gulley growing in sods or among rather than on the rocks and this seems quite typical.

The most spectacular of the species here is *Saxifraga biternata*, which is found north of *S. bourgaeana* in an area centred on El Torcal, a spectacularly eroded lime-stone massif inland from Malaga. *Saxifraga biternata* gets its name from its biter-nate leaves, with each leaflet so divided that each lobe is stalked, with the terminal of the three main leaflets itself so divided that there appear to be five full leaflets, each complexly lobed. Like those of *S. bourgaeana*, its leaves are bright green, but it is the large flowers that make it so spectacular. The flowers are each up to about 2.5 cm in diameter and shaped like the vase of an epergne—an upward-facing conical funnel with a splayed mouth.

Subsection *Triplinervium*

This is the largest subsection, with something over 50 species in it, and it contributes some wonderful plants to the garden flora. A couple of species are biennial (*Saxifraga latepetiolata* and *S. petraea*), but the vast majority are evergreen perennials forming mats or cushions of foliage. The species do not form bulbils or bulbs, but they may be drought-adapted in that the foliage may fold in on itself to form resting summer-dormant leafy buds or gem-mae. The name for the subsection derives from the three nerves on the petals, which are easily seen in most species.

The species within the subsection have been subdivided into seven series:

Series *Gemmiferae*—about 5 species—drought-adapted summer-dormant axillary buds—another 6 or 7 species here need to be reassessed

Series *Cespitosae*—about 16 species—densely cushion-forming, terminal inflorescence

Series *Axilliflorae*—2 species—loose mats, axillary inflorescence

Series *Ceratophyllae*—6 species—leafy mats, axillary inflorescence

Series *Pentadactyles*—13 species—leafy mats or cushions, terminal inflorescence

Series *Aquaticae*—1 species—stoloniferous, leafy terminal inflorescence

Series *Arachnoideae*—4 species—loose inflorescence

As with much of the taxonomy of this section, this subsection and the placement of series seem likely to undergo further revision.

Series *Gemmiferae*

The species from this series are primarily Spanish and north African (one species has been recorded from the Caucasus, *Saxifraga trautvetteri*, but it seems likely that it is misplaced in this series). The core of the series is a group centred on *S. globulifera*. Their most obvious characteristic is the way in which they are drought-adapted to minimize summer moisture loss. After flowering, as summer looms, their leaves fold in on themselves to develop conical, ovoid or globular leafy buds, or "gemmae", minimizing the exposed leaf area. In many cases the leaves have long fine hairs to help minimize moisture loss.

Saxifraga globulifera is quite variable, with the north African populations exhibiting the greater variety: some populations are much more robust than others, and other variations include leaf form and hairiness. Typically it forms attractive hemispherical cushions, which can colour dramatically as the leaves form spherical buds for summer. The white flowers are not large but are held on delicate stems. In Andalucia there are two other allopatric species. One is the small mat-forming *S. erioblasta*, which has cobwebby gemmae in summer; its white flowers turn pink once they have been successfully pollinated. The second is *S. reuteriana*, which has foliage very like that of a robust *S. globulifera*, with similar gemmae in summer, but with much larger creamy greenish-yellow flowers. The petals turn under at the edges to form a strangely pointed, concave pentagonal outline in some specimens, while in others the petals are rather less tightly folded and have an edge like a gently frilled petticoat. It appears that *S. reuteriana* is a relatively recent evolution from Spanish populations of *S. globulifera*, to which it has more in common genetically than do Spanish and north African populations of *S. globulifera* itself. Another species which is found in both Spain and north Africa is *S. rigoi*, and again this has foliage which turns a deep carmine—particularly striking when set against the cool white flowers. The north African *S. tricrenata* is now generally regarded as a form of *S. rigoi*.

Saxifraga globulifera.
Grazalema, Andalucia.
Photograph John
Howes.

Saxifraga erioblasta.
Sierra Nevada, Spain.

As a plant *Saxifraga embergeri* is much less dramatic, although its setting, at the bottom of the gorge of the Oued Agenour in the Monts des Zaian, is rather spectacular. This is certainly the smallest of the species in this series, with tiny foliage and flowers. It is clearly related to *S. globulifera* and *S. rigoi* but is extremely drought-adapted, with most plants already being well into their summer dormancy, their foliage dry and crisp, when we found them in mid- to late May. This has very numerous summer-dormant gemmae which are rather flattened-globular and no more than 2 mm diameter, with the flowers similar in size to those of *S. tridactylites*.

It is now becoming obvious that the remaining species which have been included in series *Gemmiferae* are more appropriately seen to belong elsewhere. Of the European species *Saxifraga hypnoides* and *S. continentalis* seem to belong among the species of series *Ceratophyllae*, and *S. conifera* may well be best seen in a series

Saxifraga erioblasta.

Flowers of *Saxifraga erioblasta*
showing colour change.

Saxifraga reuteriana.
Sierra del Valle, above
Estacion de Gobantes,
Andalucia.

Saxifraga embergeri on rocks
(foreground) with dwarf fan
palm, Chamaerops humilis
(background). Gorge of Oued
Agenour, Oulmès des Thermes,
Monts des Zaian, Morocco.

on its own. *Saxifraga continentalis*, which is widespread from Spain and Portugal into France, and the allopatric *S. hypnoides*, which replaces it in northern Europe, both have finely divided leaves. *Saxifraga hypnoides* makes green leafy cushions or mats, but *S. continentalis* is marked by its habit in summer of folding its leaves together to form narrow linear or conical resting gemmae, with the long hairs making the backs appear quite silvery. *Saxifraga conifera*, from northern Spain, has undivided leaves, but can otherwise look very similar to small forms of *S. continentalis*, with shorter flower stems and smaller flowers.

Saxifraga maweana.
Beni Hosmar, near
Tetouan, western Rif,
Morocco.

While the European species are reasonably well known, the north African members of this series are much less so: *Saxifraga numidica* from Algeria is only known from the type collection, and there are also *S. embergeri* (belonging with *S. globulifera*) and *S. maweana* and *S. werneri*. During our 2007 expedition these three species were all found and photographed. This was particularly important in the case of *S. werneri*, which had previously, like *S. numidica*, only been known from the type collection from the 1920s. A further species from this series, from the Rif mountains of Morocco, *Saxifraga maweana*, restricted to limestone in the mountains of the northwestern Rif, is rather larger than most of the species in this series and most resembles *S. maderensis* and *S. pickeringii* from series *Ceratophyllae* in general leaf shape—although in this case the flower stems are terminal rather than axillary as in those species. *Saxifraga maweana* has prominent and numerous elongated gemmae. It is also clear that this has no connection with the old giant mossy hybrid 'Wallacei', which confirms Farrer's view.

One of the most beautiful of all saxifrage species, and one

Saxifraga werneri. The structure of the inflorescence and the deepening colour are very clear in this picture. This is the first time that this species, discovered in the 1920s but not investigated since in the wild, has ever been photographed. Jbel Kraa, near Chefchaouen, western Rif, Morocco.

Saxifraga werneri. The foliage of most plants turns deep red as the plant flowers and sets seed. In a minority the stems, leaves and sepals remain a cheerful green, although many of the flowers that have been pollinated are already showing strongly pink.

Saxifraga werneri. At its best the effect can be very beautiful.

of the most intriguing of the Moroccan species, is *Saxifraga werneri*, which is confined to Jbel Kraa near Chefchaouen in the western Rif. It had been placed in series *Gemmiferae* on the strength of the type collection but had not been photographed before our find in 2007, and our observations pose a number of questions about its placement. It had been described as forming loose cushions ("modérément et ± lâchement cespiteuse" in Maire's words), having drought-adapted gemmae ("portant une ou plusieurs gemmes hivernantes") and from 10 to 25 flowers (Valdes et al) in a much-branched inflorescence. In major respects the plants we found differed from this: no plants were found that formed cushions, no drought-adapted gemmae were observed, and many plants had many more flowers than indicated, in some cases far more.

The general appearance of the plants of *Saxifraga werneri* that we found was of single small rosettes but with sometimes spectacular heads of flowers. The rosettes resembled the individual rosettes of such series *Cespitosae* species as *Saxifraga exarata*, *S. cebennensis* or *S. pubescens*. In an area of 5 square metres ($5m^2$) we counted 45 flowering plants. Only one of these definitely had more than one rosette, and one other might have done so (although this was possibly two plants growing together). There were about 150 non-flowering plants, about 25 percent being more or less full-sized rosettes, 1–1.5 cm, and 75 percent being noticeably smaller, 0.3–0.4 cm. Without much more study it is impossible to be certain, but it seems much more likely that *S. werneri* is generally biennial or shortly monocarpic rather than truly perennial. There was little sign of gemmae, although a few plants had 4 or 5 axillary buds. If gemmae are formed (and we saw none) they may detach to form the new small plants, but they do not seem to develop as cushions. The other variation from the descriptions was in the number of flowers per stem. In some cases there were only a small number of flowers, in one instance only 2, but there were plants with far more than the 10–25 indicated. We found many plants had over 30 flowers. In general larger plants had about 35–40 flowers, but there were occasional plants with many more and we counted one plant with 78 flowers in one inflorescence of 11 main branches. The branches of these inflorescences come from so low down that you have to follow them back to confirm that they are all branches rather than separate stems.

The discrepancies between our observations and the descriptions derived from the original collection call into question the place of this species in series *Gemmiferae* and make it seem more appropriate, pending further study, to consider it as allied to series *Cespitosae*. The many-flowered inflorescence allied to the small single rosette of foliage suggests that plants may generally be monocarpic, probably usually biennial. Further study of this species will be of great interest.

Series *Cespitosae*

This group of species makes dense cushions of small evergreen leafy rosettes. In some cases the cushions may become mats, but more often the only root system is associated with the central stem. The leaves are usually divided at the tip into oblong or lanceolate divisions, which may diverge or lie parallel; the leaves are usually hairy and in many cases have sticky glandular hairs, and there may be longitudinal grooves in the surface. The flowers are terminal and flower stems typically have 2–9 flowers in a fairly compact flat cyme. They do not have the drought-adapted gemmae of series *Gemmiferae*.

This series is extremely widespread, with some species having spread well beyond the European heartland of the series. In Europe *Saxifraga exarata* is common in the Alps, while *S. rosacea* and *S. cespitosa* are more common in the mountains of northern Europe; *S. cespitosa* then extends far beyond Europe into arctic North America and then down the Rocky Mountains as far as Colorado.

While some of the species have spread out of the mountain ranges of southern Europe, it is there that most of the species in this series are found. *Saxifraga exarata* is found in all the mountain groups from the Pyrenees to the Caucasus and is split into a number of subspecies; these include subsp. *moschata*, which is one of the taxa involved in the production of the mossy saxifrage hybrids. For Engler this was a separate species (*S. moschata*), a position Vargas revives (enhanced by moving it to subsection *Holophyllae*)—but Webb & Gornall make a good case for its status as a subspecies of *S. exarata*. This has small, widely separated petals, usually dull yellow and sometimes dull red, but in the other subspecies of *S. exarata* the petals are broader and usually white. Most of the other species here are much more limited in distribution: *S. nevadensis* in the Sierra Nevada; *S. hariotii* in the

Left: *Saxifraga cespitosa* in the Olympic Mountains, Washington State.

Saxifraga exarata subsp. *exarata*. St Martin-Vésubie, Maritime Alps.

Saxifraga exarata subsp. *moschata*. St Anton, Lechtaler Alpen, Austria.

western, and *S. pubescens* in the central and eastern Pyrenees, and *S. cebennensis* in the Cevennes.

The handful of South American saxifrages are all closely related to *Saxifraga cespitosa*. The most common is *S. magellanica* from the far south up as far as Ecuador. This is a very variable species in overall size, leaf length and width, flower size and so on, but is clearly related to *S. cespitosa*, with hairy foliage and off-white flowers.

Three other South American taxa have been distinguished: *Saxifraga adenodes*, which is densely hairy and comes from higher altitudes in Chile; *S. boussingaultii* from very high altitudes in Ecuador, which is very dwarf with tiny petals; and *S. pavonii* from Chile and Argentina, which is most clearly distinguished by having unguiculate (clawed) petals. This analysis has stood since Engler & Irmscher's monograph, and further study might lead to a revision. Only *S. magellanica* is in cultivation and that is tenuous, as the species tends to succumb to high summer temperatures.

Saxifraga magellanica. Bariloche, Argentina. Photograph Ian Bainbridge.

In the past various other taxa have been distinguished: *Saxifraga verticillata* and *S. pontica* from the Caucasus are both now normally included in *S. exarata*; *S. lactea* from Siberia probably belongs in *S. cespitosa*; and the more recently described *S. kittredgei* from Oregon also seems properly to be included in *S. cespitosa*.

Many of the species in this series can be grown successfully. The hybrid cultivars, which are discussed in detail in the next chapter, are largely derived from hybridization of *Saxifraga exarata* subsp. *moschata* and *S. rosacea*, both from this section.

Series *Axilliflorae*

The two species in this series form a mat of loose, straggly stems with thin, soft leaves divided into three to five narrow lobes. There are from one to three white flowers on more or less leafless axillary flower stems. *Saxifraga praetermissa* is found in damp conditions in the Pyrenees, usually by streams, while *S. wahlenbergii* grows in the Carpathians along the Slovakia–Polish border, usually among damp rocks, and both are found from 1000 metres up to around 2500 metres. There is, however, a case that *S. wahlenbergii*—which has rather odd worm-like hairs more or less flat on the surface of the leaves and inflorescence—should be grouped with the newly described *S. styriaca*. This has similar hairs and it has been suggested that the two species should be placed in a series *Perdurantes* Pawłovska within subsection *Holophyllae*.

Saxifraga praetermissa. Ordesa, Spanish Pyrenees. Photograph Paul Kennett.

Series *Ceratophyllae*

These species make evergreen mats or cushions and some are very vigorous. *Saxifraga trifurcata* is a good example of the species in this series, although the plant usually grown under this name with large mats of dark green toughened and finely divided leaves is either what was known as *S. trifurcatoides* (now usually regarded as merely a variant of *S. trifurcata*) or *S. ×schraderi*, the hybrid of *S. trifurcata* with *S. continentalis*.

Many of the species have thickened or leathery leaves and most have broadened flat blades. The flower stems are axillary, and this distinguishes them from the species of series *Pentadactyles*, where they are terminal. Three of the species are found in Spain and the remainder are the sole members of the genus in Madeira.

The three European species are all found in northern Spain. *Saxifraga cuneata*, with a broadened blade, is found in the mountains of Cantabria east of the Picos as far as the western Pyrenees. In the far northwest of Spain, *S. babiana* is found in a small area of Cantabria, but east of this *S. trifurcata* is found in the Picos de Europa and the mountains of Cantabria. *Saxifraga babiana* has foliage rather like that of a small *S. trifurcata* except that the leaves are hairy, with long dense hairs, and are apparently crimson-tinged at the base.

The remaining species are found in Madeira: *Saxifraga maderensis, S. pickeringii* (which is often treated as a subspecies of *S. maderensis*) and *S. portosanctana*. An interesting characteristic of these is that the anthers are pinkish orange rather than yellow, as they are in almost all other species in the section.

Of the mainland European species, *Saxifraga trifurcata* is widespread in gardens and *S. cuneata* is straightforward. The three Madeiran species are all occasionally found in cultivation; the first has rather softer leaves than the other two, which have leathery leaves.

Series *Pentadactyles*

There are thirteen species in this series, only two of them not found in Spain. They are very varied in their general form and habit: some make small evergreen cushions of finely divided leaves; some quite large mats of divided but toughened leaves, and some have larger, broad but more divided leaves. Most are evergreen perennials, some forming evergreen mats, but others are much shorter-lived, with *Saxifraga latepetiolata* being biennial and *S. genesiana* often lasting for only a year or two longer. None has bulbils or summer-dormant gemmae. Vargas separates series *Pentadactyles* from series *Ceratophyllae* on the basis of the terminal rather than axillary flower stems and this seems a useful recognition, but phylogenetic research indicates that further revision will be necessary. Some species are allied with (if they do not actually belong to) the *Cespitosae*, while others are allied to the *Ceratophyllae*.

Saxifraga pickeringii. The flower stem can clearly be seen to be axillary.

Saxifraga pede-
montana subsp.
pedemontana
above Madone
de Fenestre,
Maritime Alps.

Saxifraga
latepetiolata is a
beautiful biennial
species.

Saxifraga pedemontana is one of only two species in this series (the other is *S. irrigua*) not to be found in Spain. It is a well-known species among specialist gardeners and forms small cushions of rosettes with soft leaves. It is the most widespread species of the series, always found growing among acid rocks such as granites and gneiss. It has disjunct populations at various altitudes in different mountain groups: the Maritime Alps (subsp. *pedemontana*), the Middle and High Atlas (subsp. *demnatensis*), the Cevennes (subsp. *prostii*), Corsica and Sardinia (subsp. *cervicornis*), and from the Ukraine–Bulgaria border down into northeastern Greece (subsp. *cymosa*). These subspecies vary considerably, with subsp. *pedemontana*, the largest, having flower stems up to about 20 cm with up to twelve large white flowers. Various subspecies are cultivated. At its southeastern limit it is geographically closest to the other non-Spanish species, *S. irrigua*, but in appearance this is more like the group of species centred on *S. geranioides* and *S. genesiana*.

The eastern and central Pyrenees are home to a number of species from this series: *Saxifraga geranioides*, which is associated with other species in northeastern Spain; *S. intricata*, which also has a small population in northwestern Spain; and *S. pentadactylis*, which has other major populations in the mountains of northern and central Spain.

Saxifraga geranioides forms a cushion of relatively few but large rosettes with stiff, sharply cut leaves. The recently separated *S. genesiana* from Montseny near Barcelona has rather softer lobed, but less sharply cut, leaves. Both have quite

Saxifraga latepetiolata
(left) and S. genesiana.

Saxifraga camposii.
Los Pontones, Cazorla,
Andalucia.

tall stems of white flowers, *S. geranioides* typically having 10–15 flowers but occasionally up to 30 flowers, and *S.
genesiana* typically having much the same number of flowers but occasionally having up to 50. Many plants in cultivation under the name *S. geranioides* belong to *S. genesiana*.
This seems to be quite short-lived, many individual plants
being little more than biennial but readily self-seeding. *Saxifraga latepetiolata* is from slightly further southwest in Spain
and is fully biennial. It carries up to 100 flowers, with the
lower branches long and broadly spread to help form a very
broad pyramidal inflorescence. The Crimean *S. irrigua* is very
similar to *S. geranioides*, with sharply cut leaves. The obscure
S. luizetiana from the Middle Atlas in Morocco may be closely
allied to this group.

Saxifraga pentadactylis* and *S. vayredana* form small cushions of rather stiff brittle stems with finely divided leaves, with
the foliage of *S. vayredana* having a very distinctive spicy, predominantly cinnamon, scent. More robust, but clearly similar,
is *S. canaliculata*, in which the stiff green leaves have a narrow
groove along the centre of the narrow, parallel leaf segments.
The foliage is noticeably sticky in the spring, as is that of many of the other species
here, but in *S. canaliculata* it is particularly so. *Saxifraga moncayensis* is another
species close to these, with spicy-scented leaves and cushions not unlike those of
S. pentadactylis.

In southeastern Spain *Saxifraga camposii* is found in the provinces of Granada
and Almeria and makes cushions of bright green foliage, very much the image of
a typical mossy saxifrage. From here to the eastern Pyrenees and on into southeastern France, this is replaced by the often very similar *S. fragilis*.

Saxifraga aquatica with black-veined white (*Aporia crataegi*). Above the Col de Tourmalet, French Pyrenees.

Saxifraga petraea. Tombea massif, Italy.

Series *Aquaticae*

Distinguished most obviously by the tall leafy flower stems and narrow inflorescence, *Saxifraga aquatica* is at home in the sphagnum bogs of the central Pyrenees where icy water irrigates the roots. It is an evergreen perennial and can be abundant in the right conditions, forming small but quite dense mats from stoloniferous stems. The individual leafy flower stems are terminal and stand singly rather than as clustered groups. The strong upright stems are typically about 30 cm tall with upward-facing white flowers held close to the top of the stem.

Webb & Gornall placed *Saxifraga irrigua* and *S. latepetiolata* in this series, but following the treatment of Vargas these two species are here placed in series *Ceratophyllae*.

Series *Arachnoideae*

There are four species in this series having flat broad-bladed leaves with a rounded outline which is obtusely toothed or crenate, but it seems likely that this is not a monophyletic taxonomic unit and there may need to be a split between *Saxifraga arachnoidea* and the remainder. The four species all prefer shaded habitats, in some cases deeply shaded. Three of the species are found in Italy. *Saxifraga petraea* is the most widespread in the Italian Alps, while *S. arachnoidea* is restricted to the Tombea massif, west of Lake Garda, and *S. berica* to the lowland Berici hills just south of Vicenza. The fourth species, *S. paradoxa*, which for many years was separated as *Zahlbrucknera paradoxa*, is found in south-eastern Austria.

The Berici hills rise from the northern Italian plains just south of the Venice–Milan autostrada south of Vicenza, and in July seem an unlikely home for a saxifrage. Although they are little more than 125 metres high, the hills loom over the landscape of the sultry Venetian plain. Temperatures even in early July regularly reach 35 degrees Celsius (95 degrees Fahrenheit) and thunderstorms are a regular occurrence. The steep slopes are covered with scrubby woodland and in here, growing in holes in the soft limestone, deep under overhangs in the very shaded and dense woodland on the northern slopes, *Saxifraga berica* has little further to retreat. By July the flowers are well past and the new foliage is well into growth, the neat fresh leaves contrasting with the older, dust-covered foliage of the previous year.

Isolated now in these hills from any other suitable habitat, *Saxifraga berica* illustrates the problem that island species throughout the world face, particularly at a time of climate change. Probably only dramatic intervention in the form of an attempt to establish a population further north in the main body of the pre-Alps provides any long-term prospect for survival. Like all the species in this series, *S. berica* has palmate leaves, although the lobes are more rounded than in the other species. As in *S. petraea*, the flowers are white and the notched petals are clearly of different sizes, not in the same way as in the section *Irregulares* species, where one or two petals are dramatically extended, but with the five petals clearly graduating from smaller to larger. Compared with the much larger range of *S. petraea*, the small isolated population of *S. berica* makes a good example of peripatric speciation.

The most widespread of the four species is *Saxifraga petraea*, which grows readily on shady banks or in the mouths of caves. Each of the others is even more highly specialized or restricted in habitat terms, growing only under the overhang of rocks or cliffs, usually in quite deep shade in places where there is little if any competition. In July 2006 we found a typical colony of *S. paradoxa* in southern Austria, in the extremely deep shade under an enormous boulder, showing no sign of having flowered. It seems likely that such a colony might go some years without flowering.

Saxifraga berica.

If *Saxifraga berica* is an unusual species in a precarious predicament, *S. arachnoidea* is even more highly adapted—albeit not quite so threatened, since its home is in the middle altitudes, 600–1850 metres, on the Tombea massif. Again it is found in deep shade, this time in the dusty limestone rubble at the eroded base of rock faces. Here *S. arachnoidea* can form a continuous intertwined hairy mass—the spider's web after which the plant is named—with the individual plants impossible to

Saxifraga arachnoidea.
Monte Tombea, Italy.

Right: *Saxifraga depressa*. Pordoi, Dolomites.

separate from one another. The whole of the plant is covered with very fine, long, sticky hairs. Again, summer temperatures can be very high, but the higher altitude means lower night temperatures and much colder winters. The leaves, well buried in the hairy mass, are palmate like the other species in the series. Unlike them, however, *S. arachnoidea* has much more regular flowers, 5–8 mm in diameter, with fairly rounded petals of a pale creamy-yellow that seem to float towards the surface of the mass. This is an intriguing species which can only be appreciated in the wild since, as Richard Gornall notes, herbarium specimens can resemble nothing so much as "loosely woven cotton wool … Under any but the most careful handling this tangled mass of hairs mats together into a felt or strings, so that most herbarium specimens give a very poor idea of the habit and general appearance of the plant."

Subsection *Holophyllae*

The species in this subsection are very diverse, but the essential characteristic from which they get their name is that they have entire leaves, although in a couple of species these may be lobed. Engler & Irmscher divided the twelve species into six grexes, the equivalent of today's series, and five of these have been maintained by Gornall with the sixth, series *Aphyllae*, being incorporated into series *Sedoides*. This might seem like an over-elaborate subdivision, but the variation within the subsection is such that it seems useful. The proposed series *Perdurantes* is discussed later. It may be that some of the series here will find a new position in a future revision.

Series *Androsaceae*—5 species—leafy flower stems, flowers white to dull yellow
Series *Muscoideae*—2 or 3 species—entire glandular-hairy leaves, flowers white to orange-red
Series *Sedoides*—2 or 3 species—flowers greenish-yellow
Series *Tenellae*—1 species—flowers white, very narrow pointed leaves
Series *Glabellae*—1 species—flowers white, leaves entire

The species in series *Androsaceae* make a nicely coherent group. *Saxifraga androsacea* is very widespread in the mountains of southern Europe, being found in the Pyrenees, Auvergne, Alps, Carpathians, Rila and Pirin. As in all the species, the leafy terminal flower stems come from near the base of last year's stems and the plant makes a small mat. The leaves have a flattened, usually entire blade and there are long hairs around the margin. The flowers are pure white with oblong petals and the centre of the flower is quite constricted. *Saxifraga depressa*, which is confined to the western Dolomites, is a much more robust plant, with rather broader leaves, lobed at the tip, and more flowers per stem (up to seven rather than just one or two) but it is clearly closely related to *S. androsacea*, with extremely similar white flowers. It is hairy, but the hairs are short glandular ones, and there are none of the long hairs of *S. androsacea*. *Saxifraga italica*, from the Apennines, is rather like a smaller version of *S. depressa*, and *S. seguieri*, which is found widely

Saxifraga androsacea.
Ankögel, Hohe Tauern,
Austria.

Saxifraga androsacea
flowers.

in the Alps, has smaller dull yellow flowers. There is one species from Sikkim, *S. coarctata*, which seems to fit best in this series.

Saxifraga muscoides and *S. facchinii* from series *Muscoideae* can be characterized as making small, compact cushions of small, entire, glandular-hairy leaves which at least partly turn silvery grey when they die before turning brown later. The flowers, creamy-white in *S. muscoides* and yellow-red in *S. facchinii*, have notched petals and are on short, compact stems. *Saxifraga muscoides* is widespread in the Alps, while *S. facchinii* is confined to higher altitudes in the western Dolomites.

Saxifraga sedoides and *S. aphylla* from series *Sedoides* make rather loose mats with entire or slightly three-lobed leaves, blunt in *S. aphylla*, apiculate in *S. sedoides*. Unlike the *Muscoideae* species, the dead leaves turn brown. *Saxifraga aphylla* is widespread in the Alps from central Switzerland eastwards; *S. sedoides* is found in the east and south of this range, in the Apennines, and also in much of former Yugoslavia. They both have dull or greenish-yellow petals. *Saxifraga presolanensis* has off-white flowers often stained greenish-yellow and is found in a very small area to the north of Lake Iseo in northern Italy. Although otherwise fitting well here, it has newly dead leaves that show the silvery-grey characteristic of the *Muscoideae*.

Saxifraga glabella is a rather peculiar species, placed in its own series *Glabellae*, which appears to have small lime glands around the edge of the upper surface of the leaf—which may mean that it has been misplaced in section *Saxifraga*. It might be more appropriately grouped with *S. spruneri*, which is itself a somewhat anomalous species in section *Porphyrion*. A hybrid between the two, *S. ×degeniana*, has been reported and, although Gornall records that it is not wholly convincing, such a hybrid would support the view that at least one of these species is misplaced and

Saxifraga facchinii.
Pale del San Martino,
Dolomites, Italy.
Photograph Paul
Kennett.

further investigation would be valuable. *Saxifraga glabella* has a compact head of small white flowers with broad petals, which has at least a superficial resemblance to that of *S. spruneri*.

The final species in the subsection is *Saxifraga tenella*, which is alone in series *Tenellae*. This has extremely narrow leaves, about a centimetre long, ten times as long as broad, with a fine point, quite unlike any of the other species in the subsection.

A case has also been made that a series *Perdurantes* Pawłovska should be added to include the newly described *Saxifraga styriaca* and *S. wahlenbergii*, both of which have some characteristic appressed vermiform hairs on their leaves. It is worth noting that hybrids of both species with *S. androsacea* are reported and that *S.* ×*melzeri* (*S. androsacea* × *S. styriaca*) is said to be quite common in the area where *S. styriaca* is found.

Saxifraga sedoides subsp. *hohenwartii.*
Hoch Obir, Kärnten, Austria.

Saxifraga sedoides subsp.
hohenwartii flowers.

Saxifraga tridactylites.
Stow-on-the-Wold,
Gloucestershire, England.

Saxifraga tridactylites.
Grazalema, Andalucia.
Photograph John Howes.

Subsection *Tridactylites*

The four species in this subsection are either annual or biennial. The annuals are winter annuals, flowering early in the year as an adaptation to summer drought. The most widespread is the often tiny annual *Saxifraga tridactylites*, which is found throughout Europe (except Iceland) and then on well into the Middle East. The other widespread species is the biennial *S. adscendens*, a rather taller plant found in North America as well as in much of Europe from Scandinavia as far as the Caucasus. In the Balkans *S. blavii* can be found alongside *S. tridactylites*, although no hybrids are formed. *Saxifraga osloensis* is found in southern Sweden and seems to have arisen as a stabilized polyploid hybrid of *S. adscendens* and *S. tridactylites*.

Growing Wild Mossy Saxifrages

The great range of form among the section *Saxifraga* species represents the ways in which these have found their homes in very different ecological and climatic niches. As far as the gardener is concerned *Saxifraga granulata* is the most available of the bulbous species in series *Saxifraga*. It is a shame that it is so rarely grown, because although it is quite difficult to maintain in a pot, it survives very successfully where I have introduced it into grass. This is done by growing plants from seed and then planting them into the lawn when they are dormant at the end of the

Dovedale moss,
Saxifraga hypnoides.

Fair Maids of France,
Saxifraga granulata
'Flore Pleno'.

second year. Since the plant dies down completely after flowering the lawn can be mowed right through the summer and into autumn. In late autumn the leaves start to appear and then in spring the new flower stem emerges. A very attractive double form, 'Flore Plena' or Fair Maids of France, is sometimes available and this also grows well in grass. Although my experience of growing *S. carpetana* is shorter, it seems to be established successfully on a very well-drained rock garden.

The most common species in gardens is *Saxifraga hypnoides*, Dovedale moss, which forms mats of foliage and is clearly similar to the mossy saxifrage hybrids. This is very easy in ordinary soil. Its small, mid-green, very finely divided leaves can redden very prettily in winter, but it does not usually flower prolifically. *Saxifraga trifurcata* (possibly as *S.* ×*schraderi*) is the other wild taxon common in the garden. It forms large dark green mats of divided foliage with white flowers held on strong, thin stems typically about 25 cm tall, and happily grows in ordinary garden soil—no need here for the well-drained soils of the rock garden.

The serious enthusiast may find both *Saxifraga hypnoides* and *S. trifurcata* rather too easy and perhaps too vigorous for the average rock garden today, which is much smaller than that of years ago, but there are plenty of rather more refined alternatives. *Saxifraga canaliculata* is a good choice for a rock garden in place of *S. trifurcata*, with rather more finely divided, stiff dark green leaves, and with more compact heads of upward-facing more numerous (but smaller) white flowers. Similarly the lighter green stiff- and broad-leaved *S. cuneata* can make a cushion up to

The garden form of *Saxifraga trifurcata* is a wonderful plant but is not typical of the species in the wild. Photograph John Howes.

40 cm across. The Madeiran species (*S. maderensis*, *S. pickeringii* and *S. portosanctana*) might hold a place on the rock garden, but seem better in pots.

The other species which I am very fond of and which can manage perfectly well on the rock garden or in a pot is *Saxifraga continentalis*. It readily seeds itself and appears on drier parts of my rock garden. The flowers are very similar to those of *S. hypnoides*—perhaps slightly smaller, and certainly much more frequent—but in the summer, during hot dry weather, the foliage folds in to the distinctive, narrow, pointed gemmae and can wait for the autumn and winter rains before opening out again to make a green cushion. Other species to try growing on the rock garden include *Saxifraga rosacea*, an important part of the ancestry of the mossy saxifrage hybrids. This is a species of cooler, more moist habitats and it certainly needs this in cultivation, where it is usually more successful in a shady trough than in the open rock garden. *Saxifraga cespitosa* is a more clearly arctic-alpine species and is regularly available, but is generally difficult and can prove short-lived.

Cushion-forming species which are suitable for troughs include *Saxifraga pedemontana* with quite large pure white flowers, and *S. exarata*. Among the smaller plants which are particularly successful in troughs are *S. exarata* subsp. *moschata*, with its small cushions and small pale yellow flowers, and *S. vayredana* with foliage smelling of spices.

Suitable for pots in the alpine house or frame is a group of nice species with tight cushions of variously soft, sticky rosettes: *Saxifraga pubescens* (either as the slightly larger 'Snowcap' or the more petite subsp. *iratiana*), *S. cebennensis* and *S. nevadensis*. The last of these is uncommon, but the former are in the nursery trade and can make beautiful domed, almost hemispherical, cushions, with experts growing plants up to 30 cm across. While such large plants can be produced given sufficient attention, these plants are particularly charming when they are only about 10 cm in diameter. *Saxifraga magellanica* is occasionally available, but is very susceptible to summer heat (as well as molluscs).

The series *Gemmiferae* species *Saxifraga globulifera* is not too difficult in a pot and might be successful on the rock garden, and *S. reuteriana* is fast-growing but short-lived in a pot and presents a long-term challenge to the grower. *Saxifraga erioblasta* is charming in a pot but is very difficult to maintain in the long term, and *S. rigoi* can be grown in a pot if it can be obtained.

The species of series *Biternatae* are pretty plants. *Saxifraga gemmulosa* is extremely difficult, but *S. bourgaeana* can be grown in a pot under cover. Its foliage dies away completely in summer and then in the autumn the complex bright green

Saxifraga vayredana
in a trough.

leaves start to appear as watering is increased. It seems best to treat this as a summer-dormant plant, kept dry in summer and only watered gently through its growing period. *Saxifraga biternata* is said not to be too difficult, but I have no personal
experience of growing it. Of the other species, two obviously stand out: *Saxifraga
latepetiolata* and *S. genesiana*. The former is biennial and has a spectacular pyramidal inflorescence in its second year with up to a hundred pure white, upward-facing, vase-shaped flowers. The flower stem and the foliage can turn deep red and the
whole is dramatic. Seed is usually produced in great quantity and it is easy—too
easy, some would say—to establish a population in the plunge beds of an alpine
house. *Saxifraga genesiana*, often grown under the name *S. geranioides*, is not dissimilar. Although it is not biennial it often behaves like one, growing rapidly from a
seedling to flower in its second year, with a large inflorescence of pure white flowers over a large green leafy rosette. Plants will grow on, producing more rosettes,
but they age quickly and become well past their best two years later. This also self-
seeds in the alpine house, seeming particularly fond of pots of dwarf bulbs. This
unfortunate tendency is certainly one which is compensated for by the dramatic
flowering stems, sometimes even overtopping those of *S. latepetiolata*—although
lacking the ultimate refinement of that species.

Saxifraga genesiana
grown in a pot in the
alpine house.

Section *Saxifraga*

Subsection *Saxifraga*

Bulbils in the axils of basal leaves. White flowers unless otherwise specified.

Series *Saxifraga*

Tuft of leaves with single fairly tall flower stem. Flowers usually vase-shaped, petals not opening flat.

Saxifraga bulbifera Linnaeus (1753). Kidney-shaped, crenate, basal leaves, blade to 1.8 × 2.4 cm, petiole to 5 cm. Flower stems 15–50 cm, usually no more than 8 flowers, 10–15 stem leaves, axillary bulbils up the stem as well as at the base. Inflorescence compact. Petals 10 × 4.5 mm. Similar to *S. granulata* and *S. carpetana*. Distinguished by having axillary bulbils forming up the flowering stem as well as at the base. Europe from Bosporus to Czech Republic and Switzerland, and through Balkans to Sicily and western Italy.

Saxifraga carpetana Boissier & Reuter (1842). Leaves crenate rather than deeply lobed (as in *S. dichotoma*), broadly ovate to kidney-shaped blade to 1.7 × 1.2 cm. Stems 10–25 cm, 4–12 flowers in narrow compact inflorescence, petals with glandular-hairy upper surface. Bulbs slightly larger than in *S. granulata*. Drier stony habitats. Flowers more concentrated in upper part of inflorescence, petals often hairy. Spain, north Africa, southern Italy, Sicily, Balkans.

   subsp. *carpetana*. Basal leaf blade ovate. Spain, Mediterranean north Africa.

   subsp. *graeca*. Basal leaf blade circular to kidney-shaped. Italy to Greece.

Saxifraga cintrana Willkomm (1889). Leaves with kidney-shaped, 5–11-crenate blade 1.5 × 2.0 cm, petiole to 5 cm. Flower stems to 18 cm, up to 5 stem leaves. Very variable inflorescence usually widely branched, 4–25 flowers. Petals glandular-hairy to 11 × 7 mm. Central Portugal centred on Lisbon.

Saxifraga corsica (Seringe) Grenier & Godron (1849). Leaves with kidney-shaped blade to 1 × 1 cm, petiole to 3 cm. Quite similar to *S. granulata*, which does not occur in the same areas, but leaves more tri-lobed and flower stem branched from lower part and pedicels thinner. Petals to 15 mm. Shady rocks and walls, sometimes screes. Corsica, Sardinia, Balearics, and Spain near Valencia and Alicante border.

   subsp. *corsica*. Delicate. Spain.

   subsp. *cossoniana*. Robust, leaves deeply lobed. Corsica and Sardinia.

Saxifraga dichotoma Willdenow (1810). Deeply divided basal leaves, blade 0.7 × 1.0 cm, with 3–15 diverging finger-like lobes. Stems 6–25 cm, 2–7 flowers in compact inflorescence. Petals often tinged pink, glandular-hairy margin and upper surface. Flowers earlier than sympatric *S. carpetana*. Central Spain, Morocco, Algeria.

   subsp. *dichotoma*. Robust to 25 cm, inflorescence less compact, petals 7–10 mm.

   subsp. *albarracinensis*. Delicate, to 15 cm, inflorescence compact, petals 5–8 mm.

Saxifraga granulata Linnaeus (1753). Basal leaves with kidney-shaped, 5–13-lobed or crenate blade typically to 2 × 3 cm, cordate at base, petiole to 5 cm. Flower stems to 30 cm, 4–30 flowers. Very widespread throughout Europe (Finland and Ukraine to southwestern Europe) to Morocco. In some parts of southern Europe it is replaced by other species.

   subsp. *granulata*. Larger subspecies.

      var. *granulata*. Green leaves, may be hairy, stems typically to 30 cm. Throughout range including Spain and Portugal.

      var. *glaucescens*. More glaucous, usually very hairy leaves, stems to 45 cm. Spain, Portugal, French Pyrenees.

   subsp. *graniticola*. Smaller, stems typically no more than 10 cm. Spain and Portugal.

Saxifraga haenseleri Boissier & Reuter (1842). Smallest of series; small, cuneate leaves, 3–7 rounded divisions at tip, blade to 0.7 × 0.6 cm, petiole to 2 cm. Widely branched inflorescence 8–15 cm with 6 to many small flowers, petals to 6 × 2.5 mm. Not unlike a larger *S. tridactylites* but with noticeably larger flowers, and more open branching inflorescence. Often found in same locations as *S. granulata* and *S. carpetana*. Southern Spain.

Series *Biternatae* (Engler & Irmscher) Gornall

Leaves more divided, making cushions rather than tufts, not leathery. Flowers open flat or vase-shaped (*S. biternata*).

Saxifraga biternata Boissier (1840). Leaves to 8 × 4 cm long, divided into 3 separated lobes, central lobe subdivided into 3 lobes, all stalked, deeply subdivided usually to 3 clear broad lobes. Flower stems to 10 cm with very large, vase-shaped flowers with softly reflexing petals to 15 × 6 mm (or more), largest of any *Saxifraga* species. Cliffs and fissured rocks. Spain: Andalucia centred on El Torcal.

Saxifraga bourgaeana Boissier & Reuter (1856). Leaves bright green, blade to 1.5 × 2.5 cm, divided into 3 broadly cuneate lobes each part stalked, each lobe subdivided, on narrow petiole to 5 cm. Loosely branched inflorescence, stems to 20 cm. Petals to 8 × 5 mm. Described as an evergreen perennial, in cultivation it is usually summer-dormant. Wet cliffs. Spain: Andalucia centred on Ronda and Grazalema.

Saxifraga gemmulosa Boissier (1838). Intricate dark blue-green foliage. Leaves to 4.0 × 1.5 cm, with 3 widely divergent apical divisions (sometimes subdivided), narrower than in *S. bourgaeana*. Stems 5–18 cm. Pure white flowers, petals to 7 × 4 mm. Very difficult in cultivation–summer-dormant, susceptible to botrytis. Very limited distribution on ultra-basic rocks. Spain: Andalucia (Sierra Bermeja).

Subsection *Triplinervium* (Gaudin) Gornall

Perennial or biennial, not bulbous (or bulbiliferous). White flowers unless otherwise specified.

Series *Gemmiferae* (Willkomm) Pawłowska

Perennials. The species in this series are primarily species of southern Europe and northern Africa and most of them are highly adapted to dry summer conditions, being distinguished from others in the subsection by the leafy summer-dormant axillary gemmae (leafy buds). The flower stems are terminal.

It has become clear that the species previously grouped here represent a group which needs to be refined, and that some species have been misplaced here. These are dealt with separately after those unambiguously at home here:

Saxifraga embergeri Maire (1931). Similar to *S. rigoi* and *S. globulifera* but smaller, and gemmae are distinctive. Cushions up to 30 cm, often smaller, but foliage is tiny and flowers are very small. Leaves with petiole to 5 mm, blade with 3 divisions, at wide angle, each typically no more than 3–4 mm long with petiole and divisions both 1 mm wide. Gemmae to 2 mm diameter, flattened globular (rather than ovoid as previously described), and very numerous, typically 8–12 tightly clustered. Stems to 6 cm, up to 7 flowers (usually far fewer), petals to 4.0 × 1.25 mm. Morocco: Monts des Zaian: gorge of the Oued Agenour at

Oulmès des Thermes. Not in cultivation.

Saxifraga erioblasta Boissier & Reuter (1856). Mats of small rosettes with summer dormant, round cobwebby gemmae. Leaves usually entire, to 0.8 × 0.2 cm, occasionally 3-lobed. Flower stems to 7 cm, 1–4 flowers, petals to 5 × 4 mm, white turning pink. In cool moist conditions in cultivation it develops 3-lobed leaves but in the wild in more arid conditions they are almost all simple. Pretty little plant with small white flowers, which turn pink after pollination. Screes and rocks. 1300–2250m, southern Spain. Difficult in cultivation.

Saxifraga globulifera Desfontaines (1798). [incl. *S. trabutiana* Engler & Irmscher (1916), *S. oranensis* Munby (1906)]. Very variable. Cushions of foliage, sometimes large, leaves with petiole typically to 1.0 cm, blade to 0.5 × 1.0 cm, with 3 widely separated deep divisions, sometimes subdivided towards tip. Thin flower stems, 5–20 cm with 2–7 white flowers, petals to 7 mm. Foliage can redden dramatically, leaves folding into ovoid or globular buds in summer. Generally easy-going plant in the alpine house although tends to be somewhat impermanent. Damp rather than dry habitats in the wild, often close to *S. bourgaeana*. Cliffs or rocks, 300–1600m, Spain (Andalucia), Morocco and Algeria.

Many subtaxa have been described of which the most widely accepted are:

var. *globulifera*. Globular buds, leaves usually 5-lobed. Throughout.

var. *gibraltarica*. Many leaves 3-lobed. Buds longer. Gibraltar.

var. *oranensis*. Leaves larger, broadly bladed, hairless, shiny. Summer-dormant gemmae are oblong. Obtuse sepals. Algeria, Morocco (Rif Mountains).

var. *spathulata*. Spathulate lower leaves. Summer-dormant gemmae are oblong. Obtuse sepals. Algeria, Morocco (Rif and Middle Atlas).

var. *trabutiana*. Smaller with stiffly hairy leaves (blade plus petiole) to 1.0 × 0.5 cm, entire or 3-divided. Acute sepals. Algeria.

Saxifraga reuteriana Boissier (1845). Large stiff cushions, commonly to 30 cm occasionally to 90 cm, flower stems to 5 cm. Leaves with blade a wide fan to 1.0 × 1.5 cm, with 3 deep divisions, subdivided at tip, bluntly pointed. Foliage may turn a dramatic deep carmine. Leaves close up to large globular buds in summer. Flowers distinctive with soft pale greenish-yellow petals to 11 × 7 mm, with the edges of the petals folded under at angle on either side of the tip so that the petals can appear to be pointed. Bare cliffs, usually north-facing. Andalucia. Can be grown in the alpine house; ages rapidly.

Saxifraga rigoi Porta (1891). Leaves 3-lobed and subdivided, stems to 13 cm, 2–5 flowers. White flowers; summer-dormant buds are stalked and oblong. Foliage turns dark red in summer. Petals narrow, 12–20 mm long. Probably growable in the alpine house if it can be obtained. Spain and Morocco.

   subsp. *rigoi*. Petals 12–20 mm. Spain, north Africa.

   subsp. *maroccana* Luizet & Maire. Petals only to 9 mm. 2300–2450m, Morocco: Rif Mountains. Only known from type specimen.

   S. tricrenata from Morocco is probably another subtaxon of *S. rigoi.*

Saxifraga tricrenata Pau & Font Quer (1929). Similar to *S. rigoi* but with ovoid buds and larger petals (to 14 mm) than sympatric examples of *S. rigoi* subsp. *maroccana.* North Africa: Morocco (Rif Mountains). Not in cultivation. Probably best treated as belonging to *S. rigoi.*

Species probably misplaced in series *Gemmmiferae*

Saxifraga conifera Cosson & Durieu (1864). Leaves entire to 1 cm with long fine marginal hairs, flower stems to 8 cm, 3–7 flowers. Drought-adapted with conical, silvery, leafy buds in the summer. Petals 3–4 mm. Occasionally available. Forms a nice little plant for the sheltered trough or more likely for the alpine house. Cliffs and screes. Northern Spain including Picos de Europa. This species is probably best regarded as the sole member of a new series.

Saxifraga continentalis (Engler & Irmscher) D. A. Webb (1950) [*S. fragosoi* Sennen (1928)]. Leaves finely 3- or 5-divided with fine pointed tips. Stems 8–25 cm, 4–11 flowers. Drought-adapted continental species very close to *S. hypnoides* with which it is allopatric (and in some populations very close to *S. conifera* but with larger flowers). Narrow conical leafy buds in summer with silvery scales on lower leaf surfaces opening out in autumn through to spring. Petals 4–8 mm. Rarely available but an excellent plant for a pot or on the rockery. Spain, Portugal, southern France. Together with *S. hypnoides* this probably belongs in series *Ceratophyllae.*

   var. *continentalis*. Very narrow recurved leaf segments. France, northern Spain.

   var. *cantabrica*. Broader leaf segments. Portugal, western Spain.

Saxifraga hypnoides Linnaeus (1753). Dovedale moss. Allopatric with *S. continentalis.* Cushions of green rosettes, leaves finely 3-divided toward tip with stiff hair at each tip, flower stems 5–20 cm, 2–7 flowers, petals to 10 mm. Extremely easy to grow in the rockery, forming dense green cushions with some white flowers. Cultivars include: 'Densa', 'Egemmulosa', 'Kingii', 'Whitlavei Compacta'. Generally colours well in winter. Northern Europe: Iceland, Britain and Ireland, western Norway, Belgium and northeastern France. Does not form summer-dormant buds. Together with *S. continentalis* this probably belongs in series *Ceratophyllae.*

Saxifraga maweana Baker (1871). Leaves with blade 2.5 × 3 cm divided into 3–5 toothed or divided lobes, petioles twice length of blade. Prominent gemmae in axils of leaves on stems to 20 cm. Large white vase-shaped flowers, about 1.5 cm diameter, petals to 14 × 7 mm. Morocco: western Rif (Beni Hosmar and Jbel Kelti). Has been grown in the past but probably not now in cultivation. Inflorescence appears to be terminal (or possibly arising immediately below the terminal bud). General resemblance to *S. maderensis* rather than other members of this series and possibly belonging in series *Ceratophyllae* or, because of its apparently terminal inflorescence, series *Pentadactyles.*

Saxifraga numidica Maire (1931). Stiff dense cushion. Leafy stems with decurrent obovate-cuneate leaves. 1–3 white or pale pink flowers on stems to 3 cm, petals to 7 × 4 mm. 1800–1900m, north Africa: Algeria (Constantine province). Only known from type specimen. Position unclear.

Saxifraga trautvetteri Mandenova (1939). Obscure. Caucasus. Not in cultivation. Position unclear.

Saxifraga werneri Font Quer & Pau (1931). Until 2007, the description of this species derived from Maire (and Webb & Gornall) from the original and only previous collection. It described plants forming loose mats with a complex inflorescence of 10–25 flowers, leaves with 3–5 lobes, short petiole, and summer-dormant globular axillary buds. Our observation of plants *in situ* in 2007 extends the view of this species considerably. Most plants (95–98% of plants observed in 2007) had single rosettes (small minority with 2 rosettes) to 1–1.5 cm, resembling series *Cespitosae* species, with little if any evidence of cushion-forming or of summer-dormant gemmae. Leaves were heavily glandular with blade divided into 3–5 finger-like oblong to slightly spathulate lobes, blade to 5 mm long, 8 mm wide, on petiole to 5 mm. Foliage often deep red. Stem 5–7 cm with flat-topped terminal inflorescence always branched from or near the base, typically with up to 25

flowers, often 35–40, exceptionally up to around 78, on up to 11 main branches. Flowers 9 mm diameter, flat, pure white turning purple-pink and furling after pollination. Petals 5 × 4 mm, broadly cuneate with truncate tip. Solid or loose bare limestone. 1700–2100m, Morocco: western Rif (Jbel Kraa).
The many-flowered inflorescence allied to the small single rosette of foliage suggests that plants may usually be monocarpic, possibly usually biennial. This species is misplaced in series *Gemmiferae*.

Series *Cespitosae* (H. G. L. Reichenbach) Pawłowska

Perennials forming cushions, no summer-dormant axillary buds. Terminal flower stems. Leaves oblong-cuneate usually with divided or lobed tip. Veins often depressed in channel or groove.

Many of the species in this series can be grown successfully. The hybrid cultivars are largely derived from hybridization of *Saxifraga exarata* subsp. *moschata* and *S. rosacea* from within this section. For Vargas (*Flora Iberica*), the species in this series have been divided between series *Pentadactyles* and subsection *Holophyllae*.

Saxifraga adenodes Poeppig (1831). A densely hairy species, obovate-cuneate leaves to 1.5 × 0.7 cm, stems 6–15 cm, 3–5 flowers, petals to 9 × 5 mm. 2500–2900m, South America: Chile. Not in cultivation.

Saxifraga boussingaultii Brongniart (1835). Very tight dwarf species, with columnar shoots, leaves glabrous to 0.5 cm, apex 3-toothed, solitary stemless flowers, petals no longer than 4 mm sepals. To 4950m. South America: Ecuador. Not in cultivation.

Saxifraga cebennensis Rouy & E. G. Camus (1901). Cushions of rosettes of soft, hairy, light green cuneate leaves to 1.2 × 0.5 cm, usually 3–5-lobed at tip, grooved. Stems to 8 cm, 2–3 flowers, petals to 8 × 6 mm. 600–1600m, southern France: Cevennes. Good plant for the alpine house with softly hairy, sticky, light green foliage and white flowers. Often available and makes a good show plant.

Saxifraga cespitosa Linnaeus (1753) [incl. *S. kittredgei* Zhmylev (1993)]. Very variable. Cushion of foliage, flower stems 2–10 cm, 1–5 flowers. Leaves to 1.5 cm, often much less, 3-lobed, not grooved, margin hairy, surface possibly so, soft and green or grey-green. Petals to 6.5 mm, off-white to cream. Circumpolar, south to Britain, Quebec, Rocky Mountains to Arizona and New Mexico. Since it has a very wide distribution it would be expected that some forms would be easy in cultivation, but generally it is an arctic-alpine plant

and suffers in the heat of lowland gardens. A number of subtaxa have been described:

subsp. *cespitosa*. Throughout.

subsp. *emarginata*. Compact. No summer-dormant buds. Rocky Mountains.

subsp. *exaratoides*. Barely hairy, small petals. Rocky Mountains.

subsp. *subgemmifera*. Loose mat. Leaves long-hairy. Summer-dormant gemmae like those of series *Gemmiferae*. North America: Oregon, Washington.

subsp. *uniflora*. Single flowers. Arctic.

Saxifraga exarata Villars (1779) [incl. *S. moschata* Wulfen (1781)]. Very variable, small cushions, flower stems to 10 cm, often less, 1–7 flowers. Leaves to 2.0 cm, usually 3-lobed.

subsp. *exarata*. Leaves grooved, lobes usually divergent. Petals white or creamy-white to 6 × 4 mm. An attractive plant but less common in cultivation than might be expected. Not very easy in the open but not too difficult under glass. Alps, Balkans, possibly to Caucasus.

subsp. *ampullacea*. Leaves less divided, smooth, not hairy, bright green, flowers white with rounded petals. Central Apennines.

subsp. *carniolica*. Borders of Slovenia and Italy near Mangart. From pictures seems to be most appropriately treated as a full subspecies.

subsp. *lamottei*. Leaves not grooved, not hairy. Petals white to 5 × 3 mm. France: Auvergne.

subsp. *moschata*. Leaves not grooved, sometimes not lobed or lobes not divergent. Petals dull yellow to reddish, narrow and separated, to 4 × 2 mm. Heavily involved in the parentage of the mossy saxifrage hybrids. There seems to be a general trend from cream to red (or reddish) petals from west to east. Easy but not showy in the open. Good in a small rockery or in a large trough. Treated by Vargas as a separate species (*S. moschata* Wulfen which he places in subsection *Holophyllae*), as it was by Engler. Pyrenees and Alps and northern Balkans. Probably replaced by subsp. *pseudoexarata* in Apennines and southern Balkans.

subsp. *pseudoexarata*. Leaves grooved, petals pale dull yellow, petals to 4.5 × 2.5 mm. Alps and Apennines eastward to Balkans and possibly Caucasus.

Note: *S. pontica* and *S. verticillata* from the Caucasus are both normally included in *S. exarata*.

Saxifraga hariotii Luizet & Soulié (1911). Leaves to 0.9 cm, 3-divided, tips apiculate, grooved. Flower stems 3–7 cm, 3–12 flowers, petals to 4 × 2 mm, pale cream-white, often with reddish veins, anthers yellow. Apparently not too difficult in a pot in the alpine house. Western Pyrenees.

Saxifraga lactea Turczaninov (1840). Soft foliage, leaves to 1.2 × 0.7 cm, 3-divided at tip. Stems to 10 cm, up to 8 flowers, petals to 5.5 × 3 mm. Siberia. This should probably be included in *S. cespitosa*.

Saxifraga magellanica Poiret (1804). Very variable. Cushion of glandular-hairy leaves 0.25–2.0 × 0.3–1.3 cm, usually 3-divided or lobed at tip, sometimes widely. Stems to 10 cm, 3–4 off-white flowers, petals 3–9 mm, 3 times as long as sepals. Not easy to maintain in summer unless it can be kept cool. To 4900m, South America: Ecuador to Chile.

Saxifraga maireana Luizet (1929). Small fragile cushions. Basal leaves to 0.8 cm, cuneate with 3-divided tip, entire and spathulate above. Thin flowering stem 2–7 cm, 1–4 pink or white flowers, petals to 5 × 3 mm. 2400–2800m, north Africa: Morocco (High Atlas). Not in cultivation.

Saxifraga nevadensis Boissier (1856). Cushion of green short-hairy rosettes, flower stems to 9 cm, 2–6 flowers. Leaves to 1.2 cm, 3–5 lobes, no grooves. Flowers are white usually with red veins. Petals to 6 × 4.5 mm. Anthers orange-red. High altitude 2500–3400m on scree and schist, Spain: Sierra Nevada. Possible in a pot in the plunge bed in an alpine house. Used to be treated as a third subspecies of *S. pubescens*.

Saxifraga pavonii D. Don (1821). Dense cushion. Leaves to 2.0 cm, 3-divided at tip. Stems with 3–5 flowers, petals 10 × 3 mm, narrowed distinctively (among South American species) at base. 1800–2500m, South America: Chile, Argentina. Not in cultivation.

Saxifraga pontica Albov (1895). Caucasus. Not in cultivation. Usually included under *S. exarata*.

Saxifraga pubescens Pourret (1788). Small cushions, flower stems 3–10 cm, 5–9 flowers. Dark green, sticky hairy leaves to 1.8 cm, 3–9 oblong lobes, surface grooved. Flowers white, inflorescence compact, petals to 6 × 5.5 mm. Soft hairy foliage means that this can only be grown in a pot under glass or with protection outside. Very attractive. My favourite is subsp. *iratiana* but the rather more robust cultivar 'Snowcap' is very popular and a successful plant on the show bench.

subsp. *pubescens*. Cushions looser and larger with more divergent lobes. Petals white, anthers yellow. Eastern Pyrenees.

subsp. *iratiana*. Small cushions and leaves with more or less parallel lobes. Petals often with warm red

veins. Anthers orange-red. Central Pyrenees.

Saxifraga rosacea Moench (1794) [*S. decipiens* Erhardt (1790), nom. nud.]. Variable. Cushion- or mat-forming, flower stems 4–25 cm, 2–6 flowers. Leaves thin, 3–11 divisions, to 2.5 × 1.7 cm, surface unchannelled, glandular- or non-glandular-hairy or not. Flowers white, petals to 10 × 7 mm. Key species used in the development of the mossy saxifrage hybrids. An attractive species with white flowers, nicely shaped but not always quite as easy to maintain in the rock garden for as long a time as you would expect. Iceland, western Ireland, north Wales, central Europe from eastern France through southern Belgium, Germany to Slovakia, Poland and Austria.

subsp. *rosacea*. Leaf segments more or less non-glandular-hairy, not apiculate. Iceland, Ireland, north Wales, Germany, France.

subsp. *hartii*. Leaf segments glandular-hairy, broad. Co. Donegal, Ireland.

subsp. *sponhemica*. Leaf segments more or less non-glandular-hairy, apiculate. Belgium, Luxembourg, Rhineland areas of France and Germany, Czech Republic, Slovakia, Austria, Poland.

Saxifraga verticillata Losinskaja (1939). Caucasus. Usually included in *S. exarata*. Not in cultivation.

Series *Axilliflorae* (Willkomm) Pawlovska

Perennials. Rather straggly mossy saxifrages distinguished by white flowers which are on axillary rather than terminal flower stems. Neither of the species here is in cultivation.

Saxifraga praetermissa D. A. Webb (1963). Mats of loose foliage, leaves narrow 3–5 divided, to 1.5 cm, barely hairy. Flower stems to 15 cm, 1–3 flowers, petals to 5 mm. Permanently damp conditions. France and Spain: Pyrenees, Picos de Europa.

Saxifraga wahlenbergii Ball (1846). Loose mat. Leaves barely hairy to 1.0 × 0.5 cm, 3 blunt lobes. Flower stems to 8 cm, single flowers, petals to 5 mm. Damp shade. Carpathians: Czech Republic and Poland. A characteristic of this species is the presence of some odd vermiform hairs on leaf surfaces and inflorescence. One view is that this species should be placed in a series *Perdurantes* Pawlovska within subsection *Holophyllae* along with *S. styriaca*.

Series *Ceratophyllae* (Haworth) Pawlowska, sensu stricto

Axillary flower stems. Perennials. White flowers usually conical or vase-shaped.

Saxifraga babiana T. E. Díaz & Fernandez Prieto (1983). Dense cushion. Flower stems 10–20 cm, 5–9 flowers. Leaves typically to 2.5 cm, densely hairy, 3 deep divisions subdivided into quite narrow pointed lobes. Petals to 8 × 3.5 mm. Northwestern Spain. Not in cultivation.

Saxifraga cuneata Willdenow (1799). Cushion, flower stems 7–30 cm, 7–15 flowers. Leaves light green to 2.5 cm, blade a very broad fan with 3–5 very shallow broad lobes, glabrous, thickened as much as leathery, sticky. Petals to 8 × 5 mm. Quite straightforward but rarely seen in cultivation. Northern Spain eastwards to western Pyrenees and just into France.

Saxifraga maderensis D. Don (1821). Broad, fairly soft blade, broadly divided. 6–13 flowers. Can be grown in an alpine house. Madeira. Note: *S. pickeringii* is often treated as a variety of *S. maderensis.*

Saxifraga pickeringii Simon (1973). Broad blade, broadly divided. Up to 6 white flowers with orange stamens which set off the flowers very prettily. Leathery somewhat sticky foliage. Easy in an alpine house, possibly outside in a mild area. Madeira. Often treated as a variety of *S. maderensis.*

Saxifraga portosanctana Boissier (1856). Thickened, glabrous, leathery blade, up to 9 lobes. White flowers, narrow petals to 11 × 4 mm. Easy under cover with leathery foliage and fairly large flowers with relatively narrow petals giving a starry effect. Madeira. Not sufficiently hardy to maintain easily outdoors.

Saxifraga trifurcata Schrader (1809) [*S. ceratophylla* Dryander (1811)]. Large cushions or mats, flower stems to 30 cm, 5–15 flowers. Leaves shiny, dark green, blade to 2 × 3 cm (plus petiole as long again) with 3 divergent lobes with sharply pointed divergent subdivisions. Petals to 11 × 5 mm. Very easy in the open forming large cushions. Foliage shiny and stiffer than in some species. Plants in the garden are not typical of wild populations. In some cases they may be *S. ×schraderi*, a hybrid with *S. continentalis.* Northern Spain (not Pyrenees).

Series *Pentadactyles* (Lázaro Ibiza) P. Vargas
Terminal flower stems. Perennials or biennials (*S. latepetiolata*). White flowers usually conical or vase-shaped. Following the approach of Vargas *S. latepetiolata* and *S. irrigua* have been placed in this series. It is probable that this series needs further revision with some species closely allied to series *Ceratophyllae* and some to series *Cespitosae.*

Saxifraga camposii Boissier & Reuter (1852) [incl. *S.*

almeriensis Willkomm ex Vargas (1996)]. Cushions of finely divided foliage, flower stems to 15 cm, 6–15 flowers. Leaves a fan, 3–5-divided sometimes more, divisions usually apiculate. Petals to 12 × 4.5 mm. Not in cultivation. Southeastern Spain.
  subsp. *camposii* with petiole to 3 mm wide gradually fanning out to blade.
  subsp. *leptophylla* (*S. almeriensis*). Petiole about 1 mm wide and much more abrubt transition to blade.

Saxifraga canaliculata Boissier & Reuter (1872). Cushion of narrowly segmented, dark green, stiff, sticky foliage. Flower stems to 15 cm, 5–12 flowers. Leaves with blade of 3 narrow divisions, widely angled, outer usually shallowly notched or subdivided. Main vein on each is channelled. Petals to 10 × 7 mm. An attractive species with narrowly segmented, dark green, shiny leaves. In the spring these are sticky. The flowers are not individually particularly large but they form a nice head. Probably the easiest of this series in the open garden after *S. trifurcata.* Northern Spain, centred on Picos de Europa.

Saxifraga fragilis Schrank (1821). Cushions of divided, glabrous, rather leathery foliage, flower stems to 22 cm, 5–20 flowers. Leaf divisions obtuse to bluntly pointed. Relatively easy in the alpine house and can be grown outside. Eastern (rather than southeastern) Spain.
  subsp. *fragilis*. Leaf blade to 1.5 × 3.0 cm with petiole to 3 cm, 5–11 divisions, petals 10–14 mm. Northern part of range.
  subsp. *valentina*. Smaller leaves, 3–7 divisions, petals 7–11 mm. Southern part of range.

Saxifraga genesiana P. Vargas (1997). Few very large rosettes, densely hairy, flower stems to 20 cm, 8–15 flowers, occasionally to 50 (and more in cultivation). Leaf blade to 1.5 × 2.0 cm, a semicircular fan, 3 deep divisions each deeply and sharply divided, petiole to 3 cm. Petals to 9 × 3 mm. Recently separated from *S. geranioides* by Spanish botanists. Spain: Sierra de Montseny near Barcelona. Can be very good in a pot under glass, self-seeding in a plunge bed in the same way as *S. latepetiolata.*

Saxifraga geranioides Linnaeus (1759). Few large rosettes, densely hairy, flower stems to 25 cm, 10–15 flowers, occasionally to 30. Leaf blade to 1.5 × 2.0 cm, a semicircular fan, 3 deep broad divisions with lobed/toothed margin, petiole to 4 cm. Can be very good in a pot under glass. Eastern Pyrenees. See also *S. genesiana.*

Saxifraga intricata Lapeyrouse (1801). Small cushions,

foliage dark green, stiff, flower stems to 10 cm, 4–15 flowers. Leaves shortly hairy, entire to 9-lobed, slightly grooved, blade to 0.7 cm, petiole to 1.0 cm. Petals to 6 × 5 mm.

Saxifraga irrigua M. Bieberstein (1808). Few rosettes, flower stems to 20 cm, 5–12 flowers. Leaf blade a fan to 3 × 4 cm, 3 divisions, acutely subdivided, petiole to 7 cm. Petals to 16 × 5.5 mm. Crimea.

Saxifraga latepetiolata Willkomm (1874). Biennial, hairy, sticky, usually single rosettes, flower stems to 40 cm, 100 or more flowers. Very numerous hairy leaves, blade typically 1.5 × 2.5 cm, a semicircular fan, 3 deep broad divisions with broadly lobed margin (lobes and divisions rounded), long-hairy petiole to 5 cm. Petals to 10 × 5 mm. Northeastern Spain. Biennial but straightforward. Apparently the red coloration in foliage is enhanced at flowering if watering is severely reduced. Easily cultivated. If grown in a greenhouse, it will often self-seed in other pots and the plunge bed.

Saxifraga luizetiana Emberger & Maire (1930). Intriguing species only known from type specimen which has a mass of long "flexuous flowering stems, whose long branches intertwine to give a curiously tangled look" (Webb & Gornall). As such it has both terminal and axillary flowering stems and its place is unclear. North Africa: Morocco (Middle Atlas), 3000m. Not in cultivation.

Saxifraga moncayensis D. A. Webb (1960). Soft shortly hairy cushions. Flower stems to 15 cm, 6–12 flowers. Leaves with blade to 1.1 × 1.5 cm, 3–5 narrowly lobed, grooved, petiole to 1.3 cm. Petals to 7 × 4 mm. Spain: Sierra de Moncayo.

Saxifraga pedemontana Allioni (1795). Cushions may be loose or quite tight, flower stems to 18 cm, 2–12 flowers. Leaves not grooved, short-hairy blade to 1.5 × 2.0 cm, 3–9-lobed, petiole to 1.8 cm. One of the most attractive of the species although the subspecies vary in size and height. Most subspecies (subsp. *cervicornis*, subsp. *cymosa*, subsp. *pedemontana* and subsp. *prostii*) are quite straightforward to grow although all, except subsp. *prostii*, are best in the alpine house.

  subsp. *pedemontana*. Robust, leaves densely hairy, thickened, lobes short and wide. Stems to 18 cm. Petals to 21 × 8 mm. Maritime Alps.

  subsp. *cervicornis*. Leaves variably hairy, lobes numerous, narrow. Stems to 15 cm. Petals to 13 × 5 mm. Corsica, Sardinia.

  subsp. *cymosa*. Leaves softer and very hairy, lobes short and wide. Stems to 8 cm. Petals to 15 × 5 mm. Carpathians.

  subsp. *demnatensis*. Shortly hairy, leathery leaves. Showy. Morocco.

  subsp. *prostii*. Leaves fairly thick, lobes not narrow. Flower stem to 18 cm. Petals to 12 × 4 mm. Cevennes.

Saxifraga pentadactylis Lapeyrouse (1801) [incl. *S. losae* Sennen (1932)]. Small cushions, foliage rather stiff. Flower stems to 17 cm, 6–15 flowers, sometimes more. Leaves to 2.5 × 1.2 cm, narrowly 3–5-divided, hairless, sticky. Pyrenees, northern and central Spain. Not difficult in a pot but rather flimsy in the open.

  subsp. *pentadactylis*. Cushions small, loose. Petals white to 5 × 3 mm. Pyrenees.

  subsp. *almanzorii*. Cushions larger. Petals pale yellow to 4 × 2 mm. Spain: Avila and Caceres.

  subsp. *losae*. Cushions small, compact. Petals white to 6 × 5 mm. Central northern Spain. Note that subsp. *losae* is treated as a species by Vargas.

  subsp. *willkommiana*. Petals white to 5 × 3 mm. West central and northern Spain.

Saxifraga vayredana Luizet (1913). Small cushions. Foliage quite stiff, rather delicate, with a strong spicy smell. Leaves to 2.4 × 1.3 cm, quite deeply 3-lobed. Flower stems to 15 cm, 3–8 flowers. Petals to 6 × 4 mm. Northeastern Spain: Sierra de Montseny. The foliage is rather delicate and has a strong spicy smell. Flowers are pure white, quite small, on quite long stems. A relatively easy-going species for a pot or trough.

Series *Aquaticae* (Engler) Pawlowska

Perennial. Flowers narrowly conical or vase-shaped. *Saxifraga irrigua* and *S. latepetiolata* were placed in this series by Webb & Gornall, but more recently Vargas has placed them in series *Pentadactyles* and this has been followed here.

Saxifraga aquatica Lapeyrouse (1801). A very attractive, matted, tall, stout-stemmed leafy species with stems to 60 cm. Basal leaves with blade to 2.5 × 3.5 cm, many-divided, petiole to 3.5 cm. Inflorescence a narrow panicle, 30–70 flowers. Petals to 10 × 4 mm. Sphagnum bogs with water running below. Very difficult to cultivate. Central Pyrenees.

Series *Arachnoideae* (Engler & Irmscher) Gornall

Perennial or biennial (*Saxifraga petraea*). Leaves with flat, palmate, lobed or crenate blades on stem at least as long. Flowers open flat, solitary or in loose inflorescence. Flowers white, green (*S. paradoxa*) or yellow (*S. arachnoidea*).

Saxifraga arachnoidea Sternberg (1810). Very hairy and diffuse mass of stems, leaves and flowers. Leaves with blade to 2 × 3 cm, broadly lobed. Flower stems to 20 cm, up to 5 flowers per stem. Cream to pale yellow flowers with rounded petals to 3.5 mm seeming to float above the mass. Growing in shade at the base of overhanging cliffs and rocks. Italy: Tombea massif west of Lake Garda.

Saxifraga berica (Béguinot) D. A. Webb (1963). Shortly-hairy foliage with leaf-blade to 2.0 × 2.3 cm, roundly 10–20-lobed. Flower stems to 20 cm, up to 20 or more flowers, each notched petal of different length and width, largest to 7 × 4 mm, smallest perhaps half this. Recent seed collection has resulted in some success growing in shade in an alpine house with no overhead watering. Hairy foliage and unusual flowers, each petal being of different length. The article in the 1996 issue of the *Saxifrage Magazine* by Paul Kennett is invaluable. Italy: Berici hills, low altitude. Short-lived perennial rather than biennial as in *S. petraea*.

Saxifraga paradoxa Sternberg (1810) [*Zahlbrucknera paradoxa* (Sternberg) Reichenbach (1832)]. Hairless foliage, thin leaf blade to 2 × 4 cm, 3–9 shallow lobes, petioles to 10 cm. Flower stems to 20 cm. Flowers with green petals to 2 mm. Grows in deep shade under overhanging large boulders in deep woodland. Southeastern Austria, northern Slovenia.

Saxifraga petraea Linnaeus (1762). Long-hairy foliage, biennial. Leaves with blade to 3.0 × 3.5 cm, 3 lobes each lobed. Flowers with unequal notched petals, largest to 11 × 6 mm (often smaller), although not as exaggerated as in *S. berica*. Hairy but not obviously more so than *S. berica* except on the flowering stems. Shaded banks. Apparently quite easy in a pot if seed is available. Most widespread of this series: northeastern Italy, Slovenia to Montenegro.

Subsection *Holophyllae* (Engler) Engler & Irmscher

Perennials. Very variable. Rather unsatisfactory taxonomic unit with some anomalous species. They are generally small plants but in some cases very attractive. Most are from the Alps and the mountains of former Yugoslavia. Flowers variously shaped. Although seed of some of these species, particularly *S. androsacea*, is sometimes available, all these species seem difficult to maintain for any length of time. None of this subsection is commonly grown.

Series *Androsaceae* (Engler & Irmscher) Pawlowska
Mats of foliage. Leaves entire or with 3-divided apex, without hyaline margin. Flower stems terminal. Flowers white or dull yellow, petals obovate.

Saxifraga androsacea Linnaeus (1753). Tuft or small mat, flower stems 2–8 cm, 1 or 2 flowers. Small with entire leaves to 3.0 × 0.6 cm, margins with long hairs (also on blade of young leaves and on flower stems). White oblong petals to 7 × 3.5 mm. European mountains from Pyrenees to Carpathians, commonest in Alps.

Saxifraga coarctata W. W. Smith (1911) [*S. humilis* Engler & Irmscher (1912)]. Leaves entire or 3-toothed, glabrous, to 1.2 × 0.35 cm. Flower stems to 4 cm, 1 or 2 white flowers, petals obovate to 5.6 × 3.4 mm, often smaller and narrower. 3800–4700m, Yunnan, Bhutan, Nepal, described from Sikkim.

Saxifraga depressa Sternberg (1810). Like larger, more robust *S. androsacea* with shortly hairy leaves to 3.0 × 0.9 cm, usually 3-toothed at tip. More flowers (3–7) per 4–8 cm stem. Western Dolomites.

Saxifraga italica D. A. Webb (1963). Very like small *S. depressa*. Leaves to 1.5 × 0.4 cm, usually 3-lobed, stems 2–4 cm, 1–3 flowers, petals white, obovate, to 6 × 2.5 mm. Italy: central Apennines.

Saxifraga seguieri Sprengel (1807). Leaves entire, 2.5 × 0.3 cm, flower stems 2–7 cm, 1–3 flowers. Flowers off-white to dull yellow, petals 2–3 mm, sepals equal and wider. Alps.

Series *Muscoideae* (Engler & Irmscher) Pawlowska
Small cushions or mats. Leaves entire and glandular-hairy, and recently dead leaves are silvery-grey. Flowers white, greenish-yellow to orange-red.

Saxifraga facchinii W. D. J. Koch (1842). Small cushion. Leaves entire to 1.0 × 0.2 cm, glandular-hairy. Flower stems to 2.5 cm, 1–4 flowers, petals to 2 mm (sepals just less), orange-yellow to bright red. Western Dolomites. Extremely pretty but tiny plant which is not in cultivation.

Saxifraga muscoides Allioni (1774). Small cushions. Entire, glandular-hairy leaves to 0.5 × 0.15 cm. Flower stems 1–5 cm, 1–2 flowers, notched petals, white to pale yellow, to 5 mm. Alps, predominantly central and western. Not in cultivation. Vast majority of references to growing this species are to *S. exarata* subsp. *moschata*—a historic legacy of confusion.

Series *Sedoides* (Gaudin) Pawłowska

Small mats. Leaves usually entire. Flowers dull or greenish-yellow.

Saxifraga aphylla Sternberg (1810). Small loose mat. Leaves obtuse, 1.2 × 0.6 cm. Flower stems 2–4 cm, single flowers, petals to 2.5 × 0.5 mm, greenish-yellow. Alps, from central Switzerland eastwards.

Saxifraga presolanensis Engler (1916). Leaves 1.0 × 0.25 cm, sometimes longer. Flower stems 6–10 cm, 2–8 flowers, notched petals to 4 × 1.25 mm, off-white with greenish-yellow veins. Italian Alps north of Lake Iseo. Note that this plant is somewhat intermediate between series *Muscoideae* (because of its foliage) and series *Sedoides* (because of its inflorescence and flowers).

Saxifraga sedoides Linnaeus (1753). Loose mat. Leaves, at least some, apiculate, to 1.2 × 0.4 cm, usually entire. Flower stems 1–7 cm, 1–6 flowers, petals to 3 mm, dull yellow, anthers orange. Alps, Apennines and Balkans.

  subsp. *sedoides*. Leaves usually entire. 1–3 flowers, petals shorter than sepals. Alps especially northwestern, Apennines.

  subsp. *hohenwartii*. Leaves usually 3-lobed. 3–6 flowers, petals at least equal to sepals. Alps especially southeast.

  subsp. *prenja*. Leaves usually 3-lobed. 1–3 flowers, petals longer than sepals. Balkans.

Series *Tenellae* (Engler & Irmscher) Pawłowska

Saxifraga tenella Wulfen (1790). Very narrow, pointed, entire leaves to 1.1 × 0.2 cm, with bristle-like tip. White flowers, petals 3 mm. Leaves make it anomalous within the subsection and the section. Eastern Alps: Slovenia, Italy and Austria.

Series *Glabellae* (Engler & Irmscher) Pawłowska

Saxifraga glabella Bertoloni (1824). Small cushion. Leaves entire to 0.8 × 0.15 cm with pores (possibly lime pores) on leaves, hairless except margins, which have few glandular hairs. Flower stems to 10 cm, 3–8 flowers in compact head, petals broad to 2.5 mm. Balkans: Montenegro to Greece. Italy: central Apennines. A hybrid (*S.* ×*degeniana*) with *S. spruneri* has been reported but may be unjustified. Nevertheless both these species have characteristics that make them somewhat anomalous in their current position and might justify further study.

Position uncertain with subsection *Holophyllae*:

Saxifraga styriaca Köckinger (2003). Small mat-forming, single flowers on 0.5 cm stems lengthening considerably when seed is set. Leaves 3(–7)-divided, to 1 cm. Petals yellow-green about 1 mm long, shorter (about two-thirds) and narrower (about a quarter to a third) than sepals. Broad nectary disc. 1800–2600m. Austria (eastern Niedere Tauern). It may be that this species should be placed in a series *Perdurantes* Pawłovska within subsection *Holophyllae* along with *S. wahlenbergii*.

Subsection *Tridactylites* (Haworth) Gornall

Very small annuals and biennials including *S. tridactylites*, a British native. Very rarely grown.

Saxifraga adscendens Linnaeus (1753). Biennial (occasionally winter annual) with rosette of leaves persistent to flowering. Leaves usually up to 2.5 cm, blade 3-lobed. Flower stems 4–25 cm, 6–15 flowers, occasionally up to 40, petals to 5 mm, white, occasionally tinged pink. European mountains from Caucasus through Balkans, Carpathians, Alps, Apennines, Pyrenees, Scandinavia. Western (not eastern) North America.

Saxifraga blavii (Engler) Beck (1887). Glandular-hairy biennial. Basal leaves to 1.5 cm, 1–3-lobed, withering by flowering. Flower stems to 20 cm, 5–15 flowers, petals 5 × 3.5 mm. Ex-Yugoslavian republics and Albania.

Saxifraga osloensis Knaben (1954). Winter annual (occasionally biennial). Basal leaves in rosette, leaves to 1.5 cm, 3–5-lobed. Petals to 3.5 × 2.5 mm. Southern Sweden and just into Norway.

Saxifraga tridactylites Linnaeus (1753). Winter annual. Flower stems to 20 cm with up to 50 flowers, often far fewer, perhaps 2 cm with single flower. Leaves typically 1.0 × 0.5 cm, 3-lobed, but may be bigger. Flowers with white petals to 3 × 2 mm. Almost the whole of Europe (only completely absent from Iceland), north Africa, Turkey, Caucasus, and on to Syria, northern Iraq, northern Iran, Turkmenistan, western Russia.

Hybrids

A large number of hybrids have been described and others are as yet unnamed. Whether they have actually occurred in nature is another matter. In general these are of no importance to the gardener.

S. ×*angelisii* (*S. aphylla* × *S. sedoides*)

S. ×*baregensis* (*S. exarata* × *S. intricata*)

S. ×*cadevallii* (*S. geranioides* × *S. vayredana*)

S. ×*camboana* (*S. bourgaeana* × *S. globulifera*)

S. ×*capitata* (*S. aquatica* × *S. praetermissa*)

S. ×*ciliaris* (*S. exarata* × *S. praetermissa*)

S. ×*costei* (*S. exarata* × *S. geranioides*)

S. ×*cuspidata* synonym of *S.* ×*schraderi*

S. ×*darieuxii* (*S. hariotii* × *S. pubescens*)

S. ×*fontqueri* (*S. canaliculata* × *S. cuneata*)

S. ×*freibergii* (*S. granulata* × *S. rosacea*)

S. ×*gentyana* (*S. androsacea* × *S. exarata*)

S. ×*hausknechtii* synonym of *S.* × *freibergii*

S. ×*jouffroyi* (*S. exarata* × *S. pubescens*)

S. ×*ladanifera* synonym of *S.* × *lecomtei*

S. ×*lecomtei* (*S. geranioides* × *S. pentadactylis*)

S. ×*melzeri* (*S. androsacea* × *S. styriaca*)

S. ×*miscellanea* (*S. exarata* × *S. geranioides* × *S. pentadactylis*)

S. ×*muretii* (*S. aphylla* × *S. muscoides*)

S. ×*obscura* (*S. geranioides* × *S. pubescens*)

S. ×*padellae* (*S. androsacea* × *S. seguieri*)

S. ×*potternensis* synonym of *S.* × *freibergii*

S. ×*reyeri* (*S. sedoides* × *S. tenella*)

S. ×*richteri* (*S. exarata* × *S. hariotii*)

S. ×*schraderi* (*S. continentalis* × *S. trifurcata*)

S. ×*somedana* (*S. babiana* × *S. continentalis*)

S. ×*thrinax* (*S. androsacea* × *S. wahlenbergii*)

S. ×*trifurcatoides* (originally described as *S. trifurcata* × *S. geranioides* and now regarded as a variant of *S. trifurcata*)

S. ×*urbionica* (probably *S. continentalis* × *S. cuneata*)

S. ×*vetteri* (*S. exarata* × *S. pedemontana*)

S. ×*vierhapperi* (*S. androsacea* × *S. depressa*)

S. ×*wettsteinii* (*S. exarata* × *S. muscoides*)

S. ×*wilczeckii* (*S. intricata* × *S. pubescens*)

S. ×*yvesii* (*S. geranioides* × *S. intricata*)

There is also a dubious hybrid with *S. spruneri* from section *Porphyrion*:

S. ×*degeniana* (*S. glabella* × *S. spruneri*)

14 · Mossy Saxifrage Hybrids
Section *Saxifraga* 2

Hybrid mossy saxifrages are a group of wonderfully easy-going and widespread plants which gardeners have used in rock gardens since the end of the 19th century. Since the first hybrids appeared around 1870, nurserymen and women in Germany and Britain have expanded the range of plants enormously, searching for brighter colours and more amenable garden plants. In the early decades of the 20th century these were highly fashionable plants and could fetch high prices, but since then they have had a more chequered history.

As long as I have been interested in saxifrages, I have enjoyed growing the hybrid mossy saxifrages, but my fascination is not just with these delightful plants but also with the changing status of the garden hybrids through their history. The sunny prosperity we recreate for the years before the First World War, the war with its famous generals, the economics of the inter-war years, the privations on the Home Front in World War Two, and finally the growing prosperity of the end of the century, are all reflected in the history of the garden hybrids. Searching old books on alpine gardening and nursery catalogues from fabled nurseries evoked a world which has long gone: M. Prichard & Sons, G. P. Porter's Alpine Nursery (which was for a couple of years run by Reginald Prichard), Stuart Boothman's Nightingale Nursery, Backhouse & Sons of York, and Bakers of Codsall—with Mr Baker, a stocky and whiskered, white-haired countryman pictured on the cover (more often than not in front of fields of Russell Lupins); the older catalogues of Messrs Clibrans, and then Reginald Farrer's most interesting catalogues from Craven Nursery. In reading all of these, it was the mossy saxifrages that came to intrigue me.

The garden hybrids were developed from species at home in the mountains and wild places of Europe. The key cross in the development of our modern hybrids was of *Saxifraga exarata* subsp. *moschata*, from the mountains of south and central Europe, with *S. rosacea* from central and northern Europe, where it may be found down to sea-level. Other species were crossed with these and the continuing crossing and back-crossing has led to the current hybrids, although the number of species involved has been remarkably limited. Given the range of species which have

Saxifraga 'Stansfieldii' is typically generous with its flowers.

Mossy saxifrages
in a border.

great charm and a surprising diversity of form and geography, it is surprising how little of this variability has been exploited.

The mossy saxifrages available before 1914 are generally quite easy to trace in various books and although some famous plants such as 'Guildford Seedling', 'Rhei' and 'Clibranii' have disappeared, a surprising number of others such as 'Red Admiral', 'Sanguinea Superba' and 'Apple Blossom' have come down to us. But then, in catalogues of the 1920s and 1930s, like some long-neglected bundle of labels found in a potting shed, there were references to names that once graced mossy saxifrages that have now been lost: 'Holgate Gem', 'Draycott Beauty', 'Feltham Queen', 'Codsall Brilliant' and 'Wenlock Best of All'; 'Miss Willmott', 'Bickham's Glory', 'Grenadier' and 'Harlequin'; 'Lady Dean', 'Mrs Donaldson Hudson' and 'Queen of the Belgians'. Over the last fifteen years I have found information on around a hundred mossy saxifrage hybrids that have been lost and among them have come to light the names of about forty which had never been listed anywhere other than in the original nursery catalogues. In some cases there are tantalizing fragments of information, like the half-forgotten, half-remembered family tales of a long-gone aunt or uncle; in other cases they are merely a name.

Before the First World War and again up until World War Two, mossy saxifrages had a high reputation and a new introduction could command a high price. In 1914, Clibrans was selling 'Wenlock Best of All' at 5 shillings a plant when the average wage for working men in England was around 30 shillings a week. Plants were given the names of aristocratic women such as Lady Eveline Maud and military men such as Sir Douglas Haig and Marshall Joffre. Nursery lists increased until the demands of the Second World War devastated them, and although some nurseries survived, many others disappeared forever. Today the nursery trade in Britain has changed irrevocably. The larger nurseries such as Backhouse & Sons, Clibrans, and G. P. Porter have gone and in their place are smaller firms, often sole-trader. The mass market is served by the mass producer, often exporting from the Netherlands, where the nursery trade was transformed some years ago. It is encouraging that so many of the hybrid mossy saxifrages are still maintained in such a mass market.

There has never been a definitive account of the hybrid mossy saxifrages, so in this chapter I have been concerned to record their history (from the earliest introductions in the 1870s, through the late 19th century and on up to today), and to reflect on the array of plants that are available to the contemporary gardener, the characteristics that distinguish them and the qualities that mark them out.

Many of the plants are easily available and inexpensive, which is a clear bonus but, partly because of the lack of a definitive study, they have fallen outside the attentions of the specialist rock gardening societies. Their very reputation as "easy" plants has militated against them among the cognoscenti. In a rather surprising and paradoxical juxtaposition, many people have told me that they just can't keep them going and have asked what they are doing wrong. (I attribute most of their failures to the current horticultural use of peat- rather than loam-based composts.)

Currently about fifty named mossy saxifrage hybrids are still listed as available at UK nurseries, but nineteen of these are only listed by a single nursery and a further seven are only listed by two nurseries. In such a situation the number of available plants could contract rapidly as it has in the past. Two or three of the old "lost" cultivars (which are detailed in the Appendix of Lost Cultivars) are probably still in cultivation although they have no longer got names attached to them. It would seem that the time is ripe for an RHS Trial of these plants and representations arising from the preparation of this chapter have led to such a trial being proposed by the RHS for 2011. This will prove invaluable in clarifying and documenting the identity of plants in cultivation, and in encouraging a renaissance of these valuable plants.

The First Mossy Saxifrage Hybrids

Saxifraga 'Elegantissima'.

The historical account of the development of the mossy saxifrage hybrids rests primarily on Engler & Irmscher in *Das Pflanzenreich*. It seems clear from this that the first mossy hybrid to appear in cultivation was a plant called *Saxifraga × elegantissima*, which appeared in the Geneva Botanic Garden before 1871. They had been growing a plant under the name of *S. porphyrantha*, which was, presumably, a purple-flowered form of *S. exarata* subsp. *moschata*. Engler obtained a specimen of *S. × elegantissima* from Herr Reuter, the Curator in Geneva, and published it in *Das Pflanzenreich*. The parents were given as forms of, in today's terms, *S. exarata* subsp. *moschata* and *S. rosacea* and it was described by Engler as "loosely tufted … with young shoots 3–4 cm long" and as having dull red-purple flowers. It is of interest that a plant called 'Elegantissima' is still in cultivation today. It is of course impossible to say if they are one and the same, but this plant has many of the characteristics one might expect of such an early hybrid. It is worth noting here that throughout this treatment of the history of the mossy saxifrage hybrids I have retained names in their original form rather than modernizing their usage.

A plant called *Saxifraga Rhei superba* was one of the next important names in the history of today's mossy saxifrage hybrids: it is mentioned in correspondence between Engler and Georg Arends. In a letter of May 1916, quoted by Engler & Irmscher, Arends wrote:

> Unter dem Namen *S. Rhei* erhielt ich s. Z. (1897) von Th. Ware in Tottenham-London eine hübsche rosablühende Form, die ich zu Kreuzungszwecken benutzte. Ich suchte die Farbe leuchtender zu bekommen durch Bestäubung mit *S. hypnoides purpurea* Hort. Unter einigen hundert Sämlingen wählte ich eine besonders schöne Form aus, die ich als Verbesserung der englischen *Rhei* dann *Rhei superba* nannte.

> [In 1897 I obtained from Th. Ware of Tottenham in London a pretty pink-flowered form under the name *S. Rhei* which I used as a hybrid parent. I was trying to get a lighter-coloured flower through pollination with *S. hypnoides purpurea* Hort. Among the several hundred seedlings I obtained was a specially nice seedling which improved on the English *S. Rhei*, which I called *S. Rhei superba*.]

According to Engler, *S. hypnoides purpurea* was a hybrid between forms of what are now *S. exarata* subsp. *moschata* and *S. rosacea*, as had been *S. × elegantissima*, although the form of *S. rosacea* used was different, as it was for the production of *S. Rhei*. There is the possibility that *S. × elegantissima* might also have been involved. It has also been suggested that *S. granulata* was involved in the parentage of *S. Rhei superba*.

Other plants were in circulation and although Engler & Irmscher were wonderfully thorough, they failed to discuss some significant plants: 'Guildford Seedling' is the most important of these. This was a small but robust rich red hybrid found by Mr Upton and Mr Selfe Leonard and published by them in the *Journal of the Royal Horticultural Society* in 1902. It was introduced by the Guildford Hardy Plant Co, Millmead, Guildford, as a cross between *S. Rhei* and *S. muscoides atropurpurea* with "Soft green leaves forked at the tips, rosy-crimson flowers with a greenish-yellow centre borne freely on slender stems six inches high" and it received an Award of Merit in 1902 by 13 votes to 1. In the same year, Farrer listed this in his Craven Nursery catalogue and its status can be judged by its price:

Rhei	6d
Rhei Improved	1s 6d
Rhei Guildford Seedling	3s 6d

In 1911 the *Gardener's Chronicle* said that 'Guildford Seedling' had been eclipsed by 'Clibranii'—as it had eclipsed the earlier plants—but it was still in a couple of nursery lists up till 1939.

Mrs Lloyd Edwards

Among British saxifrage enthusiasts Mrs Lloyd Edwards should stand at the head. Her work at the very end of the 19th and the beginning of the 20th centuries was very much parallel to that being done by Arends in Germany. Unlike Arends, however, she did not run a nursery but passed her plants to Clibrans Nursery at Llandudno. The house in which she lived during the 1920s and at which she was still resident in 1930 was Bryn Oerog, which sits high above the River Dee and the Llangollen Canal just outside the village of Trevor, on the south side of the Vale of Llangollen in north Wales, and she continued to submit plants to the RHS Floral Committees until 1930.

Saxifraga 'Clibranii' was raised by Mrs Lloyd Edwards and featured in an account published in 1913 (and reprinted by Engler & Irmscher in *Das Pflanzenreich*) of her protracted efforts to improve the mossy hybrids then in cultivation:

One spring a self-sown seedling Mossy Saxifrage appeared in my little rock garden. It was probably a cross between *S. Rhei superba* and a cream coloured hairy variety called, I think, *S. hirta*, as it had some characteristics of each; but it was a great improvement on both in every way. This I named 'Apple Blossom', and it gave me the idea of trying to produce some large flowered, bright coloured varieties by hybridising.

I used the new seedling 'Apple Blossom', *S. Rhei superba* and *S.* 'Guildford Seedling' and soon got some very beautiful large flowered Mossies of different shades of colour and rigorous growth.

About this time Messrs. Thompson and Morgan of Ipswich advertised among their novelties *S. decipiens hybrida grandiflora*. I bought a packet and crossed some of the resulting seedlings with my own, to their mutual improvement. A fine red seedling I named Ruby. This flowered twice in its first season and was purchased by Messrs. Clibran's representative. He saw it in flower in the autumn and was much struck by it. As *S. Clibranii* it has gained a considerable reputation.

I continued selecting and cross-fertilising my best seedlings and produced Red Admiral, an improvement on *Clibranii* in size and colour.

I wanted a really blood red Saxifrage, free flowering and of compact growth, and in time got *S. sanguinea superba*. It shows in its neat, finely cut foliage, that Guildford Seedling was among its ancestors, and as far as colouring is concerned, I think that no redder Saxifrage can be produced. In the process of obtaining it I got many beautiful rose coloured and shaded Saxifrages, notably *S. rosea superba*, a very fine, free flowering early variety with dark stems and red buds; and *S.* Rose Beauty with beautifully shaped flowers with small centres which flowers very late.

Saxifraga 'Apple Blossom'.

Saxifraga 'Sanguinea Superba'. Photograph Winton Harding.

There was an idea the *S. decipiens hybrida grandiflora* of Messrs. Thompson and Morgan had been partly produced from *S. granulata*, but none that I raised showed any trace of such parentage.

A number of crosses were published including *S. × Clibranii* in *Gardeners Chronicle* XLV (1909), unfortunately and confusingly to cover a range of cultivars of which the original 'Ruby' was not necessarily even one. In *Das Pflanzenreich*, Engler provided the Latin diagnosis and binomial *S. × Edwardsii* along with the names and identifying features of its then known progeny, and both *S. × elegantissima* and *S. × Arendsii* were also published.

Many of Mrs Lloyd Edwards's hybrids are famous ones and the fact that 'Apple Blossom', 'Red Admiral' and 'Sanguinea Superba' are still in circulation says much for her skill and her eye.

Georg Arends

While Mrs Lloyd Edwards was clearly at the head of the field in Britain, Georg Arends was working on the mossy saxifrages in Germany. Arends's first work had been at the end of the 19th

Saxifraga 'Red Admiral'. Both forms, one larger, one smaller, are shown here.

century with the production of *S. Rhei superba* (which Mrs Lloyd Edwards was to use as a parent of 'Apple Blossom'). He also produced 'Teppichkönigin' from a similar cross to that made by Mrs Lloyd Edwards using forms of *S. exarata* subsp. *moschata* and *S. rosacea*, this time producing a smaller plant with purplish-red flowers as opposed to the blood-red of 'Sanguinea Superba'. Translated uninspiringly as "Queen of the Carpeters", this cultivar was still being listed by Prichard in the 1930s.

Arends's most important work in the genus, however, was in the production of the hybrids which went under the name *Saxifraga × Arendsii* (he also worked extensively with *Astilbe* and produced many hybrids which again carrry his name). In producing *S. × Arendsii* by crossing two hybrids, *S. × elegantissima* and (according to Engler & Irmscher) a cross between *S. rosacea* and *S. granulata* (probably *S. ×freibergii* the wild hybrid between them found in Germany), Arends was working very directly towards creating the range of garden plants with which we are very familiar. It should be noted in passing that although the name had some possible value in earlier days, its continuing use today usually signifies no more than "Hybrid Mossy Saxifrage".

Engler & Irmscher's 1916 list of plants included under *Saxifraga × Arendsii* (some from Arends, some from Mrs Lloyd Edwards) contained a dozen names:

S. × Arendsii = (*S. exarata* subsp. *moschata* × *S. rosacea*) × (*S. rosacea* × *S. granulata*)

1. Petals pink, paler beneath (*magnifica, Blütenteppich*)
2. Petals paler, becoming pink (*rosea superba*)
3. Petals purple, paler underneath (*Juwel, Purpurmantel*)
4. Petals pale pink (*Arkwrightii*)
5. Rather robust, petals pale pink (*Lady Dean, A. Lynes*)
6. Petals purple (*P. W. Hosier*)
7. Petals dark-purple, paler beneath (*Schöne v[on] Ronsdorf, splendens*)
8. Petals deep purple-red above and below (*splendidissima*)

Of these 'Arkwrightii', 'Lady Dean', 'A. Lynes' and 'P. W. Hosier' were introduced by Messrs Bakers of Wolverhampton (presumably the Bakers of Codsall of the 1920s), probably from seedlings raised by Mrs Lloyd Edwards, and published in 1909. 'Schöne von Ronsdorf' and *splendens* were introduced in 1915, but Engler (writing in 1916) gives no dates for the others. *Splendidissima* was raised by Arends but named by Engler.

It is possible to erect even more complex family trees out of Engler's notes (although whether they fully carry such weight is debatable) but it is sufficient here to note the broad outlines of Engler's scheme, with *S. × elegantissima* progressively leading to *S. × Clibranii*, *S. × Edwardsii* and *S. × Arendsii*. That a number of examples of these old cultivar groups still exist is a tribute to their popularity and either their ease of cultivation or the skill of cultivators.

Before turning to the historic garden hybrids which were overlooked by Engler & Irmscher, it is worth noting that there were many wild-collected mossy saxifrages in circulation. Among the forms of *Saxifraga exarata* subsp. *moschata* listed by Engler & Irmscher were 'Allionii', 'Atropurpurea' and 'Citrina'. Among those in circulation which they did not list were 'Coccinea', 'Colstonii' and 'Purpurea', although they did list a form under the name 'Purpurascens'. Other plants which seem to have had a wild origin were 'Affinis' and 'Crocea'.

Other historic sources and plants

A number of other sources on the early mossy saxifrages provide valuable extra information, although none is as authoritative as *Das Pflanzenreich*. General books on rock gardening, specialist works on saxifrages and nursery catalogues all contribute to the picture. Although Engler & Irmscher had taken notice of the accounts published by Mrs Lloyd Edwards, not all British authors appear to have been noticed. Most notable among the absentees are W. A. Clark, Reginald Farrer and Irving & Malby.

In 1906, W. A. Clark had mentioned the garden hybrid 'Fergusoni' although without a description, but this was rectified by Irving & Malby in 1914. They added a number of other garden hybrid mossy saxifrages, of which 'Clibranii', 'Decipiens Grandiflora', 'Guildford Seedling', 'Lady Deane' (the spelling of which seems to vary) and 'Sanguinea Superba' are all subsequently discussed, or at least mentioned, by Engler & Irmscher; and a number which are not. About these Irving & Malby wrote:

> S. *ARKWRIGHTII* is a pure white variety, the individual blooms of which are flat, and of large size, and freely produced. It is one of the taller growing kinds.
> S. *BAKERI* is one of the smaller kinds, with vivid green tufts of foliage, compact in habit, and rich carmine flowers;
> S. *BATHONIENSIS.*—A very fine, large flowered, scarlet crimson variety, with flowers produced freely on stout branching stems. It is a rapid grower and one of the best;
> S. *DITTON CRIMSON* is very similar both in habit and flowers to ['Decipiens Grandiflora'].
> S. *FERGUSONI* is an early flowering form of Guildford Seedling:
> S. *'MISS WILLMOT'.*—A pretty free-flowering variety, the large flowers being white, with chocolate markings at the base of the petals.

To these, Farrer's accounts would add two more small cultivars: 'Craven Gem' ("brilliant dark crimson") from his own Craven Nursery at Clapham in North Yorkshire and, presumably from Stormonth's Nursery near Carlisle, 'Stormonth's Seedling' ("smaller and earlier" than 'Guildford Seedling'). With 'Webbiana', these were all listed before 1913. Farrer was keen on saxifrages, particularly the encrusted silver saxifrages. The magnificent catalogues from his nursery have soft, dark brown paper covers with, in some cases, an embossed silver roundel, and Farrer was a significant figure in the introduction of obscure species up until his death in China in 1920.

A number of other very successful hybrids should be mentioned: 'Grandiflora Alba' from Arends before 1913; 'House's Variety' from Backhouse; 'J. C. Lloyd Edwards' and 'Mrs R. T. Wickham' from Mrs Lloyd Edwards (1916), the former being listed by Clibrans in the 1920s and 1930s; 'Mrs Donaldson Hudson', a pre-1912 cultivar which was listed by M. Prichard in the 1920s and 1930s; 'Tapis Rouge', listed in 1913 by both Lissadell in Ireland and by Clibrans; and 'Wenlock Best of All', which was raised by Lady C. Milnes Gaskell and introduced by Clibrans (according to their catalogue) in 1913, when it was being sold for 5 shillings—as was *Dianthus* 'Wenlock Incomparable'. There were to be other "Wenlock" saxifrages after 1918 which would also achieve success.

Also already in circulation were two other plants which are certainly still in cultivation: 'Stansfieldii' and the extremely popular 'Wallacei'. *Saxifraga* 'Stansfieldii' is a rather insignificant mossy saxifrage—or one with a wild charm, depending upon your point of view—with flowers like those of 'Pixie' or a pink-flowered *S. rosacea*, but on a much taller, more lax plant. It was already being listed by Lissadell Nursery in 1912 and may originally have been a form of *S. rosacea*.

There has been an awful lot of conjecture about the parentage of *Saxifraga* 'Wallacei', but no disagreement as to its place among the very best of the mossy saxifrage hybrids. Engler & Irmscher discuss this plant but their suggestion that it is either a synonym of *S. camposii* or a hybrid of *S. maweana* does not seem to fit the bill. Although I used to find Farrer to my taste, I have more recently found him too often overblown. However, in the case of 'Wallacei' his style (in *The English Rock Garden*) has advantages:

> This is undoubtedly the grandest of our Mossies, whether in growth or habit, in flower or out of flower. And it is a garden hybrid, having nothing whatever to do with *S. Camposii*, of which the catalogues still obstinately persist in making it a synonym, continuing to perpetuate the original error of the *Botanical Magazine*, which figured the plant (T.6640) under the name of *S. Camposii*, Boiss. and Reut.—a species at that time not in cultivation, and even now not common. The parentage of *S. × Wallacei* remains unknown; dates make it unlikely that *S. Maweana* had any share in it, and one of the most probable parents is *S. trifurcata*. With *S. Camposii* it has no relationship at all. The hybrid was raised at Edinburgh, from seed purporting to be that of *S. Maweana*; but the attribution is unconvincing, if on no other ground than that *S. × Wallacei* is said to have been growing at Kew in 1867, whereas *S. Maweana* was not introduced till 1869. In any case *S. [×] Wallacei*

is the pride and joy of every garden in every season and situation, with its wide billowing masses of rich and comfortable-looking ample green leaves, cloven five times or more to the base of the blade; the stems and shoots all have a tendency to redden, and the flowers are pure white, of enormous size and amplitude, produced in generous branching sprays that hide the whole green wave in early summer with a crest of refulgent snow.

This is valuable in that if Farrer's dates are right, 'Wallacei' predates *S.* × *elegantissima* and pushes the record back past Engler & Irmscher's, making 'Wallacei' the first hybrid mossy saxifrage. It is useful to add Reginald Malby's comment (Irving & Malby, *Saxifrages or Rockfoils*):

The lovely hawthorn-scented, large flowered S. Wallacei is very charming, when well grown—thought it seems inclined to "go off" rather more than some other kinds. In my garden it thrives best in the more moist parts, grow-ing and flowering well in vegetable soil mixed with sand.

This at least helps calm one of my concerns about some of these early accounts which talk, as Farrer does, of "wide billowing masses of rich and comfortable look-ing green leaves" and of flowers being "produced in generous arching sprays that hide the whole green wave in early summer". Such comments makes it sound like a much easier plant than the one we have now and makes my own efforts (which accord with Malby's comments) feel wholly inadequate. My experience is that it is a difficult plant to maintain for long periods, but the effort has got to be worth it: 'Wallacei' has an extravagantly large, rich white flower, with broad petals, on relatively short stems over large rosettes. Irving comments that *S. camposii* is "a plant with much less hairy stems and leaves" than 'Wallacei' and since the plant we have now as 'Wallacei' is almost totally glabrous, this adds to my conviction that the plant we are growing is not the plant that most of the authors were familiar with at this time. Having now found both *S. camposii* and *S. maweana* in the wild I can confirm that it has very litttle in common with either.

The Role of Nurseries between the Wars

The decades around the turn of the 19th and 20th centuries might seem to be the Golden Age of the mossy saxifrages—especially the cultivars—but a more proper view would be that the greatest period was in fact during the years leading up to the Second World War.

Prior to the First World War a number of nurseries had already contributed significantly to the mossy saxifrages: Thomas S. Ware of Hale Farm Nurseries of Tottenham, Thompson & Morgan, Lissadell Nursery, Arends, the Guildford

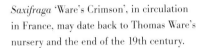
Saxifraga 'Ware's Crimson', in circulation
in France, may date back to Thomas Ware's
nursery and the end of the 19th century.

Saxifraga 'Triumph'.
Photograph John
Howes.

Nursery, Craven Nursery and Clibrans had all introduced plants to the gardening public. Most of these drop out of the story, although Arends continued to be
involved in the production of saxifrages, with 'Triumph' from the 1920s one of his
best. Arends is still operating, as is Thompson & Morgan. Of the others Clibrans
is the only one that continued to add much to the mossy saxifrages after the First
World War. But the 1920s saw a great surge of hybrids being produced by a large
number of nurseries in various parts of England: Ingwersen's in Sussex, Prichard's
in Hampshire, Bakers of Codsall (near Wolverhampton), and Backhouse & Sons of
York, supplemented by Reginald Kaye at Silverdale and Clibrans in north Wales.
All introduced mossy saxifrage hybrids, and in many cases maintained very substantial lists by the end of the decade. Some of this activity went on into the 1930s,
but there was already some decline in the lists of some nurseries, perhaps due to
falls in consumer demand during the Depression.

But the Second World War was to have a far more dramatic effect on this magnificent range of plants. With the prospect of naval blockades threatening food supplies,
the British Government introduced a propaganda campaign to "Dig For Victory".
This exhorted everyone to turn over their gardens to food production and a range of
posters and leaflets in English and Welsh appeared. One of the most famous showed
a booted foot stamping down on a spade in an image that would not have looked out
of place in Soviet Russia, to become one of Britain's wartime allies along with the
United States. Nurseries lost labour to the armed forces, and the mossy saxifrages—with their twin needs for space and regular propagation—were lost not only in
gardens but in many cases in nurseries as well. The losses were unparalleled among
other groups of saxifrages, although there were a few losses among the dwarf cushion
Porphyrion saxifrages, but there seems to have been no systematic study of losses in

other groups of ornamental plants. Combined with the decline in lists in the 1930s, something over fifty cultivars failed to reappear post-1945 and among these were some that had been particularly praised by pre-War writers. Given that there are still fewer than two hundred cultivars, the scale of the loss can be seen. At the time the loss was of nearly half the mossy saxifrage cultivars that then existed.

The Lost Cultivars

It is easy to get a sense of the cultivars lost to us by even a cursory look through old nursery catalogues and the work of writers such as Correvon. What is immediately apparent from these evocative documents is the number of mossy saxifrages stocked by many of these nurseries and the variation between the lists of the different nurseries. In the case of the mossy saxifrages these lost cultivars represent a significant part of the history. Some of the nurseries which were responsible for many of those are discussed here, but a full list of the plants is included in the Appendix of Lost Cultivars at the end of the book.

Bakers of Codsall

Bakers were responsible for some famous mossy saxifrages from the early days. Engler lists three in his discussion of *S. × Arendsii*: 'Arkwrightii', 'Lady Dean' and 'A. Lynes', which had been published in the *Gardener's Chronicle* in 1909. Two others, 'Miss Willmott' and 'P. W. Hosier' were published in the *Journal of the Royal Horticultural Society* in 1909 but, whereas Engler discusses 'P. W. Hosier', he makes no mention of 'Miss Willmott'. The 1925 catalogue lists seven mossy saxifrage hybrids: 'Apple Blossom', 'Arkwrightii', 'Codsall Gem', 'Bathoniensis', 'Lady Deane' (it was now being listed with an "e" on the end), 'Sanguinea Superba' and 'S. T. Wright', of which only 'Apple Blossom' and 'Sanguinea Superba' are now extant. In 1927 'Wenlock Sanguinea' was added; in 1931 'Rosy Gem' and 'Codsall Brilliant', and in 1938 'Codsall Maid' was listed.

Clibrans

This nursery, associated with Principality Nurseries, Llandudno Junction, had a long list in 1929 with ten mossy saxifrage hybrids listed: 'Clibrani' [sic], 'J. C. Lloyd Edwards', 'Lady Eveline Maud', 'Miss Willmott', 'Red Dwarf', 'Diana', 'Kingii', 'Queen of the Belgians', 'Rose Beauty' and 'Wenlock Best of All'. Most of these were still being listed in 1939/40 with the addition of 'Sir Douglas Haig', but of the 1929 list only 'Kingii', 'Red Dwarf' and 'Diana' seem to exist in the trade today.

Backhouse & Sons

As with many of the nurseries prominent in the inter-war years, Backhouse & Sons of Acomb, York, introduced a number of their own mossy saxifrages. Best known among their early saxifrage introductions was 'Backhousei', but 'Holgate Gem', introduced in the 1920s, was named after a local village. Although now extinct, 'Holgate Gem' was still being listed by Reginald Kaye in 1966. Other local villages were Knapton, after which the mossy saxifrage hybrids 'Knapton Pink', 'Knapton Red' and 'Knapton White' were named; and Woodthorpe which gave its name to a *Porphyrion* hybrid saxifrage. James Backhouse founded the firm in 1859, and it became very influential both as a nursery for plants and in building rock gardens, surviving until 1955. Among his important clients was Ellen Willmott, the famous gardener for whom 'Miss Willmott' was named. Clarence Elliott worked for Backhouse before setting up Six Hills Nursery, and in his turn employed a young Walter Ingwersen who left to set up a nursery at Letchworth with Gavin Jones before moving on to Ingwersen's at Birch Farm, Gravetye, near East Grinstead. W. A. Clark also worked for Backhouse before moving to Cambridge in the 1920s.

Ingwersen's

Ingwersen's Birch Farm Nursery in Sussex listed quite a number of mossy saxifrages between the wars. Their introductions were mainly the "Birch" hybrids: 'Birch Crimson' in the 1930s, and the post-war 'Birch Beauty' and 'Birch Baby'. Ingwersen's is the only British nursery of importance in the inter-war history of the mossy saxifrage hybrids that still operates and still has a good list of mossy saxifrages.

M. Prichard & Sons and G. P. Porter

Of all the nurseries active between the wars, the two nurseries in which the Prichards (Maurice and his sons Reginald M. and Russell Vincent) were involved were clearly leading lights as far as mossy saxifrages were concerned. R. M. Prichard's (later called G. P. Porter) included twenty-nine mossy saxifrages in the list they issued around 1930, and the 1932 list had nineteen. One of their last lists issued in the late 1930s still had fifteen mossy saxifrages.

Maurice Prichard's nursery issued its catalogue no. 36 in 1935 and listed twenty-one mossy saxifrages, with a very similar list in 1939. The impact of the Second World War can be seen in the 1947 list with only two mossy saxifrages, and one of their last lists in 1950 contains just seven.

The most obvious change from before the War to immediately after it is in the dramatic shortening of the lists. This would not have mattered much if between them nurseries had maintained most of the whole range then in commerce. Unfortunately it becomes clear, with a little research, that the shorter lists represented real losses, since many of the cultivars were only listed by a few nurseries. Of the twenty-nine mossy saxifrages listed by R. M. Prichard's around 1930, at least fifteen have disappeared completely, and of the twenty-one listed by Maurice Prichard's in 1935 at least twelve have been permanently lost.

Recent Introductions

In recent years some excellent newer plants have been introduced, often by small nurseries. Most have failed to become widely distributed, but some have and these include some that are first-class. Among the more obviously attractive which first appeared in the 1980s were 'Ann Parr', 'Cambria Jewel', 'Pearly Gold', 'Ruth McConnell' and 'Silver Cushion', and from the 1990s 'Beechcroft White', 'Black Beauty', 'Fleece', 'Holden Seedling', 'Ingeborg', 'Rosenzwerg' and 'Weisser Zwerg' are all plants that are worth looking for. John Tuite of West Acre Gardens in Norfolk obviously has a good eye and has been responsible for three very good introductions: 'Golden Falls' is the best known of his plants, and 'Grace' and 'Donald Mann' are two of his others. Very striking, with a rather startling combination of variegated foliage and bright red flowers, 'Gold Leaf' apparently orginated in Holland, and was introduced into the UK by Steve Furness, but it is a rather more difficult plant to grow than might be expected. Finally 'Corennie Claret', bred and named by Fred Carrie of the now defunct Tough Alpine Nursery in Aberdeenshire (and originally sold by him as 'Glowing Embers'), is a strong plant with deep red flowers which is a great addition to any collection. It is interesting to know that this was grown from a packet of Thompson & Morgan seed, in exactly the same way that Mrs Lloyd Edwards produced *Saxifraga Clibranii* all those years ago.

Selecting Plants for a Collection

One of the most difficult things in starting to build a collection of these wonderful plants is to decide just which to grow. Flower and foliage colour, size of flower, height and spread, and ease of growth, all play a part in making plants individually distinctive. Comparing older with modern cultivars reveals some very clear developments. Modern cultivars tend to have broader petals, often overlapping, and are less likely to fade than older hybrids. The green cushions can be enhanced with grey-green and white, or bright green and pale golden-yellow variegation. Differences in colour are enhanced by differences in leaf outline—some having much more rounded lobes, while others are more sharply pointed. With such variations on offer it is possible to build a collection with plants of very different sizes, flower and foliage colours and heights.

Height

Cultivars vary dramatically in terms of the length of flower stems. This is not the least surprising since, among the ancestral species, both *Saxifraga rosacea* and *S. exarata* subsp. *moschata* are plants that have quite short flower stems, while *S. granulata* was used specifically to add height and vigour to the mix.

The smallest of the hybrid mossy saxifrages may have flower stems no more than 5 cm tall. This makes them plants that are eminently suitable for the general rock garden, where many of them will last uncomplainingly for many years. The general effect of the smallest cultivars is of a cushion studded with flowers, in the vein of the dwarf cushion *Porphyrion* saxifrages, very different in scale to the taller hybrids discussed below. Among the smallest are cultivars which are tricky in the open garden such as 'Hi-Ace', which may have flower stems no more than 2–3 cm, but other very short cultivars such as 'Weisser Zwerg' are much more robust and have flowers much larger than is normal for such a low-flowering cultivar. Slightly taller than these are some small but easy-going plants which have rightly been popular for many years: 'Pixie', 'White Pixie' and 'Elf' are typical of these. 'Cloth of Gold' is another small cultivar which is very attractive but not easy to maintain. Of the older cultivars the one that should earn a place here is 'Elegantissima'.

At the other extreme are those plants which clearly have derived their robust qualities from the introduction of *Saxifraga granulata* into the hybrid mix. These may have flower stems up to 25 cm tall with flowers—which can be quite large—carried well clear of the cushion. While the cultivars with short stems have the effect of a cushion studded with flowers, the effect here is quite different: the flowers form a canopy and seem to float above the cushion. Growing such large-scale plants in a rock garden requires one that is larger than average, but these plants are versatile. In a heavy or moisture-retentive soil they perform well at the front of the border, quite able to hold their place in a way that some of the smaller cultivars would certainly fail to do.

Saxifraga 'Pixie'.

'Fleece' and 'James Bremner' are among the taller white-flowered cultivars that are fairly straightforward. Unfortunately the spectacular cultivar 'Wallacei' is too temperamental to be recommended without qualification. Among the pink cultivars 'Knapton Pink' is pretty tall and the richer pink 'Gaiety' is definitely worth looking for. The brightest red cultivars such as 'Holden Seedling' are generally rather shorter, but there are some excellent tall darker red plants. The darkest of all is 'Black Beauty' but, like many plants with very dark flowers, it needs careful companion planting to make sure it does not disappear against a shady background. Rather brighter are 'Four Winds', 'Red Admiral', 'Sir Douglas Haig' and 'Pompadour'. Many of the tallest cultivars are older crosses; indeed a number of mossy saxifrages still met with in old gardens, but long separated from any name, are almost certainly some of the lost cultivars.

Saxifraga 'Rosenzwerg'.
One of the new very
dwarf hybrids.

Saxifraga 'Dartington Double' is one of the very
few double mossy saxifrage hybrids, along with
'Dartington Double White' and 'Ruffles'.

Shortest (stems less than 4 cm): 'Hi-Ace', 'Rosenzwerg', 'Weisser Zwerg'
Very short (less than 10 cm): 'Birch Baby', 'Cloth of Gold', 'White Pixie'
Short (10–12 cm): 'Beechcroft White', 'Cambria Jewel', 'Dartington Double',
    'Densa', 'Elegantissima', 'Findling', 'Flowers of Sulphur', 'Peter Pan',
    'Triumph'
Medium (12–18 cm): 'Apple Blossom', 'Ballawley Guardsman', 'Carnival',
    'Corennie Claret', 'Diana', 'Dubarry', 'Fairy', 'Golden Falls', 'Gold Leaf',
    'Holden Seedling', 'Purpurmantel', 'Silver Cushion'
Tall (20–30 cm): 'Black Beauty', 'Fleece', 'Gaiety', 'James Bremner', 'Knapton
    Pink', 'Pompadour', 'Ruth McConnell', 'Sir Douglas Haig',
    'Wallacei', 'Winston Churchill' and Saxifraga trifurcata and
    S. canaliculata

Saxifraga 'Peter Pan', a small neat
hybrid. Photograph John Howes.

Saxifraga 'Winston Churchill'.

Saxifraga 'James Bremner'.

Flower colour and petal shape

The range of colour in mossy saxifrage hybrids is from pale greenish-cream, through off-white to pure white, and then through a range of cooler and warmer pinks to rich deep pinks, and a range of reds from brightest scarlet-crimson to darkest crimson.

Greenish-cream: 'Flowers of Sulphur', 'White Pixie'
Creamy-white: 'Wallacei'
Pure white: 'Findling', 'Beechcroft White'
Pale pink: 'Knapton Pink', 'Diana', 'Winston Churchill', 'Silver Cushion'
Mid-pink: 'Pixie'
Deep pink: 'Elf', 'Gaiety'
Bright red: 'Holden Seedling', 'Ballawley Guardsman',
    'Sanguinea Superba', 'Gold Leaf'
Deep red: 'Pompadour', 'Corennie Claret'
Very dark red: 'Black Beauty'

Saxifraga 'Corennie Claret'.

Mossy saxifrage flowers—1 (left to right).

Top row: *Saxifraga pubescens*, 'Elegantissima', *S. exarata* subsp. *moschata*.

2nd row: 'Elf', 'Fairy', 'Pixie'.

3rd row: 'Beechcroft White', an old pink hybrid—probably one of the "lost cultivars", 'Findling'.

4th row: 'Winston Churchill', 'Wallacei', 'Holden Seedling'.

Bottom row: An unnamed white hybrid, 'Mrs E. Piper', 'White Pixie'.

Another characteristic of note here is that some of the red and pink cultivars have the whole petal the same colour while others have a much lighter, sometimes white, base to the petal. The white "eye" gives the flowers a very different feel. Examples of cultivars with red flowers which have this white (or very pale) centre include 'Sanguinea Superba', 'Peter Pan', 'Holden Seedling' and 'Red Admiral'.

Mossy saxifrage flowers—2 (left to right).

Top row: *Saxifraga bourgaeana*, 'Pixie', *S. berica*.

2nd row: 'Gaiety', 'Schneeteppich', 'Peter Pan'.

3rd row: 'Alba Grandiflora', 'Corennie Claret', *S. genesiana*.

Bottom row: 'Triumph', 'Fleece', 'Triumph' (another form in circulation).

Among those where the whole petal is the same colour, 'Corennie Claret' is one of the most striking, and 'Black Beauty' is another of the very strongly coloured cultivars without a paler centre. In some cases, such as the very old cultivar 'Triumph', plants in circulation vary, with some clearly showing paler bases to the petals and others with almost the whole petal the same colour. Among those with pink or pale red flowers, the effect of this is less dramatic, and although there are differences between how obvious it is, most of them have a paler eye.

Other factors apart from size and colour determine a flower's appearance, among them petal shape, and the degree to which the petals are separated, touch or overlap. These characteristics are extremely valuable in helping identification, since size may vary with conditions but these remain constant. Cultivars such as 'Elegantissima' have narrow, widely separated petals, while at the other extreme 'Fleece' and 'Wallacei' have petals that overlap so much that the flowers have an almost circular outline.

Petals widely separated: 'Elegantissima'
Petals quite narrow and separated: 'Findling', 'Elf'
Petals just touching: 'Triumph', 'Pixie'
Petals wider, overlapping at base: 'Peter Pan', 'Mrs Piper', 'White Pixie'
Petals broad, clearly overlapping: 'Gaiety', 'Fairy'
Petals very broad, strongly overlapping: 'Fleece', 'Wallacei'

An interesting variation on this basic scheme is that of 'Schneeteppich', with almost circular petals which do not overlap very much since the flowers open very flat.

Foliage colour

Most mossy saxifrage hybrids make soft green cushions, some of which can develop dramatic red anthocyanic highlights in winter, but some very attractive cultivars have foliage which ranges from yellow through variegations of green, grey, yellow, cream and white. In some cases the paler foliage may tinge with pink in winter. Not all are easy to maintain: some plants have large areas of chlorotic foliage (sometimes only at particular times of the year) but as the proportion of non-green foliage increases the ability of the plant to photosynthesize is jeopardized and so is the long-term vigour of the plant.

Saxifraga 'Grace'.

Variegated foliage: 'Bob Hawkins', 'Golden Falls', 'Gold Leaf', 'Grace' or 'Seaspray', 'Hi-Ace', 'Margaret Webster', 'Pearly Gold', 'Silver Cushion', 'Variegata'

Yellow foliage: 'Cloth of Gold'

Proportions—a matter of aesthetics

Mossy saxifrage hybrids vary in their proportions and it is obviously a matter of opinion (or aesthetics) as to what the right proportions are for the ideal plant. So any account seems to depend on personal judgement although, as the Greek mathematicians demonstrated, aesthetics can be mathematically demonstrated in such things as the golden mean.

Among the better proportioned mossy saxifrages, as far as I am concerned, are 'Pixie', which has rosettes 1–1.5 cm in diameter and flower stems 5–7.5 cm

Saxifraga 'Hi-Ace'.

tall, and 'Knapton Pink' with rosettes around 3 cm in diameter and flower stems around 18 cm. These are plants that feel right—they set the standard—and this can be expressed as a ratio of stem height to rosette diameter. In the case of 'Pixie' this ratio is 5 to 1 and in 'Knapton Pink' 6 to 1. To add to this it is worth noting that in the best-proportioned, the individual flowers are about the same size as the individual rosette in plants with only two or three flowers per stem (and rather smaller in those with more flowers per stem). Taken together these factors contribute a sense of balance and poise to the plant.

To pursue this: 'Gaiety' is well-proportioned with rosettes about 3.5 cm in diameter and 20 cm tall (6 to 1), but 'Black Beauty', with rosettes of similar size, has a flower stem up to 30 cm and therefore seems rather too tall (8 to 1). On the other hand 'Wallacei', with rosettes up to 4.5 cm diameter and a flower stem of 20 cm (4 to 1) is obviously rather below the bottom end of what might be seen as well-proportioned, and the exceptionally large flowers add to this effect, making it feel slightly dumpy despite its splendour. There are some cultivars which are much shorter than my suggested ideal, such as 'Weisser Zwerg' and 'Rosenzwerg', even though they may have other qualities. Obviously some of this is affected by where a plant grows—some being more susceptible than others, in terms of height, to the effect of a shaded position.

One might add finally that for plants not to seem too tall, decent-sized cushions need to be grown—the cushion needs to be at least half as big again as the plant is tall. So the minimum size that would be appropriate for 'Pixie', which is up to 7.5 cm tall, would be perhaps 11 or 12 cm across; a cushion of 'Knapton Pink' would need to be around 27 cm across; and a cushion of 'Black Beauty' some 45 cm across. This then can help give an indication of the size that a plant needs to be before it seems right. Cushions larger than these look very nice but ones that are smaller will look undergrown. This should help determine the appropriate plant for a particular place in the garden. Individually some of the tall cultivars are very handsome but should not be confined to too small a niche in a rock garden: much better to choose a smaller cultivar.

As far as flower size and numbers per stem are concerned, typically, 'Pixie' has 3 or 4 flowers per stem, 1.25 cm in diameter with a rosette size of 1–1.5 cm; 'Knapton Pink' has 4 to 5 flowers per stem, 2.4 cm in diameter, against a rosette of about 3 cm; 'Gaiety' has up to 9 flowers per stem, 2.5 cm diameter against a rosette of about 3.5 cm. 'Black Beauty' has 5 or 6 flowers per stem, up to 3.3 cm in diameter against rosettes of 3.5 cm; and in 'Wallacei', with only maybe 2 or 3 flowers per stem, the individual flowers are up to 4 cm diameter against a rosette of up to 4.5 cm.

Branching of the inflorescence

Apart from their proportions, the overall aesthetics of a mossy saxifrage are affected greatly by the way that the inflorescence is branched. In some cultivars branching is largely confined to the upper section with only short individual pedicels. This is true in both 'Pixie' and 'Wallacei', for example, with relatively few flowers on short branching near the top of the flower stem. In the case of both of these branching tends only to be in the top third or even quarter of the inflorescence. 'Knapton Pink' has similar branching in only the top third, while for example 'Gaiety' and 'Black Beauty' will often have branching occurring right from the bottom third.

Growing Hybrid Mossy Saxifrages

Mossy saxifrages are pretty easy to propagate from cuttings. These need be little more than rosettes extracted from a large cushion, stripped of dead foliage at the base and then inserted into a rooting tray of sand and seed compost (or pushed into the garden soil with a thumb). Rooting takes place over a matter of weeks without the need for rooting hormone or heat, and the rooted cuttings can then be potted up. This is best done in a soil-based compost rather than the peat-based composts in which these plants are so often found at garden centres.

Most mossy saxifrages are good at growing into large cushions (in the manner of *Saxifraga trifurcata* or 'James Bremner') and these characteristically make many adventitious roots under the expanding cushion. These are easy plants to divide or from which to extract rooted fragments. A few plants are more difficult because they tend not to root adventitiously. The most extreme is 'Cloth of Gold' which makes very few adventitious roots, if any, and which therefore remains dependent on the roots made by the original rooted stem. This makes it a very difficult cultivar to grow into a large cushion in the open—a plant over 12 cm across is a rarity—but it is easy to take cuttings from it and since it looks very good in a small pot it remains popular.

How well the plants do once planted in the open depends on the particular site, the aspect, shade, soil type, and local weather as well as the nature of the plant itself. The hybrid mossy saxifrages generally like a heavier, more moisture-retentive soil than is normally suggested for a rock garden, where the great need is to provide most of the plants with extra drainage. This tends to mean that borders, and ordinary flower beds, are usually appropriate. If conditions are relatively cool and there is reasonable humidity, rather than a bone-dry atmosphere, mossy saxifrages will do well in a sunny border, but in areas which are drier, or hotter, some light shade may be a great advantage. A soil which tends to hold on to some moisture is needed. Soils high in humus are obviously appropriate but in my own garden we have a heavy clay soil and this seems at least as good.

Cultivars in Cultivation

Date given is earliest known. Quotations are from a wide variety of nursery catalogues. A list of the lost or extinct cultivars is given in an appendix at the end of the volume.

'Ajugifolia' ('Ajugaefolia'). Although often listed as a fancy cultivar name, this is variously used to describe *Saxifraga pedemontana*, *S. wahlenbergii* and *S. praetermissa*.

'Alba Grandiflora' (pre-1913, Arends). Still listed in Austria and in Netherlands.

'Amoena' (ca.1934, Germany, Sündermann). Tiny cushions, pale pink flowers.

'Anceps' (1990s, Germany, Sündermann). Probably a form of *S. hypnoides*.

'Ane Kirstine' (1980s). Believed to have red flowers. May be extinct.

'Ann Parr' (1980s, UK). Good pinkish-red flowers with crimson veins, medium size. Dark red stems to 20 cm. Rare.

'Apple Blossom' (ca.1900, UK, Mrs Lloyd Edwards). One of only a handful of cultivars surviving from this period. Pale pink backs to creamy-white petals. Flowers to 2 cm diameter, dull red stems to 15 cm. Pretty and rather delicate.

'April Blush' (1996, UK, L. Drummond). Pink seedling from *S. granulata*, so tends to die down and care needs to be taken not to lose it.

S. ×arendsii. Used to cover a parental combination rather than an individual cultivar. Now normally used to refer to nothing more than hybrids originating in Germany. Originally the name given to the hybrid mossy saxifrages arising from the multiple cross of *S. exarata* subsp. *moschata* × *S. decipiens* (now *S. rosacea*) × (*S. rosacea* × *S. granulata*). Defined by Engler & Irmscher in 1916 who included the following under this combination: 'Magnifica', 'Blütenteppich', 'Rosea Superba', 'Juwel', 'Pupurmantel', 'Arkwrightii', 'Lady Deane', 'A. Lynes', 'P. W. Hosier', 'Schöne von Ronsdorf', 'Splendens' and 'Spendidissima'.

'Atrosanguinea' (1980s, UK, Holden Clough). Dark red flowers.

'Backhousei' (1926, UK, Backhouse). Still listed by Rogers of Pickering in 1987. "Brilliant red" according to Backhouse catalogues.

'Ballawley Guardsman' (pre-1963, UK). "Carmine" or "velvety crimson-scarlet", 15 cm, not too vigorous.

'Beauty of Letchworth' (pre-1930, UK). Neat, compact cushion. Stems with up to 3 rounded flowers of an "old rose" colour. Sometimes described as "bright rose red". Still being listed in 1990s but may now be extinct.

'Beauty of Ronsdorf' (translation of 'Schöne von Ronsdorf'). Listed under English name by Backhouse in 1930 and still being listed in *Plant Finder* in 1990s.

'Beechcroft White' (ca.1990, UK, C. Kimber). Vigorous, dwarf, free-flowering with white flowers over bright green foliage. Distributed by Beechcroft Nursery in Surrey.

'Biedermeier' (1980s, Germany). White, frilled petals, 12 cm (according to Köhlein). Listed by Eschmann in 1995.

'Birch Baby' (1990s). Originated at Ingwersen's.

'Birch Beauty' (1990s). Rich pink flowers, light centre, 1.8 cm, stems dull red, to 7 cm. Originated at Ingwersen's.

'Black Beauty' (ca.1990). Rosettes about 3.5 cm, stems up to 20–30 cm can be branched from lowest third, with 5–6 flowers, to 2–2.5 cm diameter. Very dark red/crimson flowers with darker veins and stems. Originated at Potterton & Martin. A very impressive cultivar although it can be difficult to site it to show its dark flowers well.

'Black Knight'. Incorrect naming of 'Black Beauty'.

'Blütenteppich' ('Flower Carpet') (ca.1911). Carmine pink, 12 cm. One of the original group defined as belonging to *S. ×arendsii*. Still listed in Germany and Netherlands. Plants under the name 'Flower Carpet' are occasionally on offer in the UK but their provenance is suspect.

'Bob Hawkins' (mid-1970s, UK, Bill Archer). Relatively new with finely divided (more than in other variegated cultivars) cream and rather grey-green variegated leaves in which the tips may be tinged pink. White flowers, 1.2 cm diameter, green stems 9–15 cm. Quite an easy drought-resistant plant which will stand full sun.

'Cambria Jewel' (1980s). Deep pink, pretty, quite small, 10 cm.

'Cardinal'. See 'Kardinal'.

'Carnival' (1960s). Brilliant rose-pink/crimson-rose, sun-resistant, 15 cm.

'Clare Island' (1920s). White, 10 cm. Probably a form of *S. rosacea*.

'Clibranii'. Plants in circulation today under the name 'Clibranii' are identical with 'Elegantissima' and do not match the original drawings of the plant or Clibran's description of "broad expanded petals".

'Cloth of Gold' (ca. 1930). This is a very attractive small cultivar which is easily obtainable. Yellow-foliage form of *S. exarata*. It forms a small dense cushion which varies through the year from yellowish-green through to a rich golden yellow. Flowers are white, 1.2 cm diameter, on dull red stems, to 5 cm. Can be impermanent but easy to propagate—take regular cuttings. The problem stems from the fact that it does not seem to form adventitious roots under the cushion, a characteristic which gives most cultivars a long life. In this case rooting is often confined to the stem of the original cutting. In very favourable conditions additional roots may be made, but I have not experienced this.

'Corennie Claret' (1995). A deep rich red cultivar, stems about 12–15 cm, from Fred Carrie at Tough Alpine Nursery, Aberdeenshire. Originally named 'Glowing Ember'. One of the best of the deep-coloured cultivars, not quite as dark as 'Black Beauty', with large rosettes.

'Cukrák' (ca. 2000). A new cultivar from J. Bürgel in the Czech Republic.

'Cwm Idwal' (1990s). Probably collected form of *S. rosacea* which grows but is very rare, and is now protected, in Cwm Idwal in Snowdonia.

'Dartington' (1990s). Single- not double-flowered, pink.

'Dartington Double' (ca. 1933). Double. Red or deep pink, slow, 5 cm. Usually 9 petals.

'Dartington Double Red' (1939). Now used by some nurseries (incorrectly) for 'Dartington Double'.

'Dartington Double White' (1990s). Semi-double white. Not vigorous.

'Densa' (ca. 1929). Cultivated form of *S. hypnoides* with very dense cushions, which colour well in winter, and have sparse white flowers. An excellent plant and very easy. It has also been used as a synonym for some forms of *S. bronchialis*.

'Densa Compacta' (date unknown). Probably indistinct from 'Whitlavei Compacta' and 'Densa'.

'Diana' (ca. 1929). "White, extra large" (Clibrans 1929). More recently described as pale/light pink, 15 cm, early.

'Donald Mann' (1990s). Very compact cultivar, raised and named by John Tuite, stems less than 10 cm, with deep red flowers.

'Dornröschen' (probably 1980s, Germany, Benary) ('Sleeping Beauty'). Vigorous, red (tinged salmon), 15 cm.

'Double White'. Dartington hybrid similar to 'Dartington Double' but with white flowers usually with 8 petals. Presumably the same as 'Dartington Double White'. See also 'Ruffles'.

Dovedale Moss. Colloquial English name for *S. hypnoides*. Dovedale is in Derbyshire where the species is relatively common.

'Dubarry' (ca. 1930). Large, deep crimson/carmine/rose-red, stems 18–20 cm, late.

'Earl Haig'. Listed under this name by Nightingale Nursery (1939). Correctly 'Sir Douglas Haig'.

'Edie Campbell' (date unknown). Many large rose red-flowers on dull red stems.

'Egemmulosa' (date unknown, Germany). Small form of *S. hypnoides*, synonymous with 'Kingii'. Often, even usually, indistinct from 'Densa'.

'Elegans Rosea' (date unknown). Germany. Listed in Erhardt (*PPP Index* 1997). Probably the same as 'Roseum Elegans' and the name suggests an old cultivar.

'Elegantissima' (1871). Probably the first mossy saxifrage hybrid to appear, *S.* × *elegantissima* arose at Geneva Botanic Garden some time before 1871. Plant now in cultivation (from Sündermann) is dense, low (stems ca. 10 cm), long-lived, sun-resistant, and has very small bright pinkish-red-purple flowers, on very finely divided foliage. It is unlike any other current cultivar and has the characteristics of a very old hybrid—very small flowers with widely separated petals very much in the vein of an "improved" wild *S. exarata* subsp. *moschata*. This plant deserves much wider circulation and accords much more with the spirit of the contemporary rock gardener looking for smaller and more delicate plants than the typical modern hybrid mossy saxifrage.

'Elf' (1980s?). Dwarf, carmine-red/deep pink, pretty, 5–8 cm, late.

Fair Maids of France. Colloquial English name for *S. granulata* 'Flore Pleno'.

'Fairy' (pre-1929). Said incorrectly to be form of *S. exarata* subsp. *moschata*. Compact, white flowers on 7 cm stems, late-flowering. Clarence Elliot refers to pale pink flowers, as do Ingwersen and Prichard catalogues, but plants in cultivation at present have white flowers and are much larger than suggested above. It seems fairly certain that these plants are different to those referred to by Elliott, Ingwersen and Prichard.

'Farbenkissen' ('Colour Cushion') (1990s). Listed by German nursery Frei in 1995—no details. May well be 'Riedel's Farbenkissen'.

'Farbenteppich' ('Colour Carpet'). Rose pink.

'Feuerteppich' ('Fire Carpet'). Red.

'Feuerwerk' ('Firework'). Carmine to rose-pink, 15–20 cm. Early.

'Findling' (1959, Germany). Synonyms 'Findel', 'Foundling'. Deeply cut green foliage, flowers abundant, pure white, 1.8 cm diameter, fine dull red stems 5–12 cm. Long-flowering. Vigorous and easy.

'Fire Carpet'. See 'Feuerteppich'.

'Firefly'. See 'Leuchtkäfer'.

'Firework'. See 'Feuerwerk'.

'Fleece' (1993). Softly hairy grey-green foliage, large white flowers, flower stems tinged slightly red, about 12 cm tall. Scarce.

'Flore Pleno'. *S. granulata* 'Flore Pleno'. Invalid name for double form of *S. granulata*. 'Plena' is also invalid.

'Flower Carpet'. See 'Blütenteppich'.

'Flowers of Sulphur'. See 'Schwefelblüte'.

'Four Winds' (1966). Outstanding. Crimson flowers, darker veins, 2.5 cm diameter, 5 or more flowers per stem, stems crimson, 15–20 cm.

'Gaiety' (1960s?). Rosettes about 3.5 cm, stems 12–20 cm, can be branched from lowest third, with up to 9 flowers, 2–2.5 cm diameter. Deep pink, very early. A splendid plant which flowers very reliably with very full petals. Well worth getting.

'General Joffre' (1933). See 'Marshall Joffre'.

'Glasnevin Beauty' (ca.1930). Round, ivory-white flowers. May be extinct.

'Glassel's Crimson'. Plant in Royal Botanic Gardens Edinburgh, not in commerce.

'Gleborg' (late 1980s, UK). Quite short, strong, darkish red flowers. Sometimes, incorrectly, 'Glenborg'.

'Gloriosa' (1934, Germany). Tiny cushions, red. Very scarce.

'Glowing Ember' (1994, UK). Deep red flowers. Introduced by Tough Alpine Nursery. Now sold as 'Corennie Claret'.

'Gnome' (1970s). Carmine-red/crimson, 7 cm, late.

'Golden Falls' (?1980s). Creamy gold outer margin to otherwise rich green leaves, greenish-white flowers, 1.5 cm diameter, green stems 10 cm. Although not the most dramatic of the variegated mossy saxifrages 'Golden Falls' is an attractive plant in which the variegation highlights the rosettes rather than dominating them. Fairly easy-going in the open border. Raised and named by John Tuite.

'Gold Leaf' (ca.1992). Originally from the Netherlands, introduced in the UK by Steve Furness. Bright red flowers over variegated foliage, quite a bright yellow when flowers are out. Very dramatic in flower, nondescript out of flower. Difficult to maintain.

'Grace'. Two plants have gone under this name. The original plant, now lost, was crimson-pink according to Prichard's 1929 catalogue. The new cultivar (1983) from John Tuite is small, variegated, turns cream in winter, white flowers 1.2 cm, on green 7.5 cm stems. Sport of 'Pearly King'. A very pretty plant but not at all easy to get hold of and quite easy to lose. It may no longer be in circulation. The later 'Seaspray' appears to be identical.

'Guardsman' (1989?). Red, 12 cm. The only reference I can find to this plant is in Reginald Kaye's 1989 catalogue, in which the name 'Ballawley Guardsman' also appears. Probably extinct.

'Harder Zwerg'. See 'Luschtinetz'.

'Hartshorn White' (1980s). May be synonymous with 'Hartswood White'.

'Hartswood White' (1980s). White tinged pink, 15–20 cm.

'Hi-Ace' (1982, UK). Quite new, very small, variegated cream and green (one of the most dramatic), red flowers to 1.2 cm diameter on dull red stems to 3.5 cm. Often on show bench. Difficult to maintain for long periods but well worth the effort.

'Highlander' (?). Red flowers, about 20 cm tall.

'Holden Seedling' (ca.1990). Bright crimson flowers, deeper toward centre, 1.5 cm diameter, medium height, scarlet-crimson stems 15 cm (9 cm above cushion). One of the brightest of all the red cultivars.

'Ingeborg' (1990s?). Large dark red flowers, short and compact.

'Irish' (1980s, UK). Potterton & Martin. Hairy leaves and hairy red flower stems. Flowers pink. 10 cm. Probably originally wild-collected *S. rosacea*. An attractive cultivar.

'James Bremner' (ca.1930). Old, robust (requires lots of space), very large white flowers (about 2.5 cm), 25 cm tall. The comment that it needs regular propagation (Ingwersen says "annually") and that its flowers are "larger than any other mossy Saxifrage" indicates possible confusion with 'Wallacei' at some point.

'Kardinal' (?). Red flowers. May be a corruption of 'Carnival', also sometimes seen as 'Cardinal'.

'Kazín' (ca.2000). Apparently a hybrid between 'Triumph' and *S. cespitosa*. From J. Bürgel in Czech Republic.

'Kingii' (ca.1929). Small variety of *S. hypnoides*, very close to 'Whitlavei Compacta'. Possibly synonymous with 'Egemmulosa'.

'Kingscote White' (1934). Large white (round) flowers, 10 cm. "Particularly neat and tidy".

'Knapton Pink' (1932). Rosettes about 3 cm, flower stems dull red, about 18 cm (14 cm above cushion) branched in top third with 4 or 5 flowers, 2.2 cm diameter. Old. Large rich soft pink flowers. Softly hairy grey-green foliage.

'Knapton Red' (date unknown). Only the name—plant from Waterperry Garden Centre, Oxfordshire.

'Knapton White' (1992 but probably much older). White flowers with veins turning red toward centre, to 2.0 cm diameter, dull red stems 10 cm above cushion.

'Late Vintage'. See 'Spätlese'.

'Leuchtkäfer' ('Firefly') (1980s, Germany). Slow-growing, firm cushions. Flower stems slightly hairy, flowers dark red, not fading in sun. 15 cm. The transliteration 'Firefly' is preferable to, although not as exotic as, Köhlein's reference to 'Luminous Beetle'. The other possibility, 'Glow Worm', does not appeal greatly.

'Luminous Beetle'. See 'Leuchtkäfer'.

'Luschtinetz' (1980s, Germany). Blood-red flowers, reasonable size, short stems, sun-resistant. 'Harder Zwerg' seems to be synonymous.

'Lydia' (1990s). Listed in Erhardt (*PPP Index* 1997) as available in Germany (as *S. ×arendsii* 'Lydia'). Also a name for an indistinct *S. ×hornibrookii* cultivar.

'Manteau Pourpre'. French for 'Purpurmantel'.

'Margaret Webster' (1990s). Variegated form of *S. trifurcata* but not in commerce.

'Marshall Joffre' (1931). Deep red. Sometimes described as bright red. Rarely found. Occasionally and incorrectly as 'General Joffre'.

'Miss Britton' (ca.1933). White ("large cream") flowers.

'Mrs Britten'. See 'Miss Britton'.

'Mrs E. Piper' (pre-1939). Red, 7 cm, but pink according to Backhouse (1939).

'Nona McGrory'. Plant in Royal Botanic Gardens Edinburgh—not in commerce.

'Pearly Gold' (1980s). Creamy-yellow variegated foliage with white flowers.

'Pearly King' (1943). A neat dwarf plant with pure or clear white flowers. 10 cm. Ingwersen. In 1943 Ingwersen referred to the colour as "soft pearl-pink".

'Peter Pan' (1939). Deep rose-red flowers with paler, almost white, eye. Flowers 1.7 cm diameter. Flower stems about 8 cm (5 cm above cushion).

'Pink Queen'. See 'Rosakönigin'.

'Pixie' (1937). Rosettes 1–1.5 cm, flower stems 5–7.5 cm branched only at top of stem, with 3 or 4 flowers, 1.3 cm diameter. Extremely easy-going dwarf hybrid with warm pink flowers.

'Plena' or 'Pleno'. See 'Flore Pleno'.

'Pompadour' (1921). An old, and according to Ingwersen, "giant" mossy. Very large (2.4 cm diameter), round, dusky-crimson flowers on 20–25 cm stems (16 cm above cushion). Will develop an untidy habit unless regularly propagated.

'Priestwood White' (1980s). Only the name. May be extinct.

'Pulchella' (1990s). Form of *S. hypnoides*.

'Purple Carpet'. See 'Purpurteppich'.

'Purple Cloak'. See 'Purpurmantel'.

'Purpurea' (1910). Red flowers. Probably form of *S. exarata* subsp. *moschata*. May be different plants through this period.

'Purpurmantel' (1911, Germany, Arends). ('Purple Cloak'). Quite vigorous with free, long-lasting, deep carmine-red (but colour fades a bit) flowers to 2.1 cm diameter. Stems 10–15 cm. One of the oldest mossy saxifrage hybrids in cultivation.

'Purpurteppich' (1930, Germany, Arends). ('Purple Carpet'). Strong growing. Pale carmine-red flowers. 15–20 cm.

'Queen of the Belgians' (1929). Brilliant crimson, dwarf (Clibrans). Also listed by G. P. Porter 1930/2. I had assumed this was extinct until I found it listed in Erhardt (*PPP Index* 1997) for German nursery Gerhard Rudolf.

'Red Admiral' (ca.1910). An old cultivar from Mrs Lloyd Edwards ("an improvement on *Clibranii* in size and colour") with a neat habit and "splendid" well-rounded red flowers on 10 cm stems. Very free-flowering. Today there appear to be two distinct plants in circulation under this name. The difference seems to be one of scale, with one plant being consistently smaller in foliage and height but with flowers of the same size. This may have given rise to the plant occasionally named 'Red Dwarf' but this is only conjecture. Farrer comments on 'Red Admiral' as one of the smaller cultivars alongside 'Guildford Seedling', 'Craven Gem', 'Stormonth's Seedling' and 'Fergusonii'. This would suggest that the plant we have now, certainly in its larger form, is not what was familiar to Farrer.

'Reidel's Colour Cushion'. See 'Reidel's Farbenkissen'.

'Reidel's Farbenkissen' (1980s?). Deep fire-red, fading to pink, stems to 20 cm. Now often listed as 'Farbenkissen'.

'**Ronsdorf Beauty**' (1930). Originally 'Schöne von Ronsdorf' but listed under the English name by G. P. Porter.

'**Rosea**' (1929). No description. Listed by M. Prichard (1929–39). Erhardt (*PPP Index* 1997) lists *S. × arendsii* 'Rosea' as available from one German nursery.

'**Rose Dwarf**'. See 'Rosenzwerg'.

'**Rose Foam**'. See 'Rosenschaum'.

'**Rosenschaum**' (?). ('Rose Foam'). Pink. 10–20 cm.

'**Rosenzwerg**' (1990s). ('Rose Dwarf'). Deep pink. Compact, dense-growing. 3 cm.

'**Roseum Elegans**'. (Germany). Probably synonymous with 'Elegans Rosea'. Pink. 8 cm.

'**Ruffles**' (1980s?). Flowers double white, tinged pink.

'**Ruth McConnell**' (1980s). Tall plant, stems much branched 14–20 cm, with quite deep rose-red flowers to 2.5 cm diameter, which resist fading quite well.

'**Sanguinea Superba**' (pre-1911, UK). Raised (and named as *S. sanguinea superba*) by Mrs Lloyd Edwards who wrote: "neat, finely cut foliage … I think no redder Saxifrage can be produced". Blood-red flowers (to 1.8–2.0 cm diameter) with a pale central area. Stems 10–15 cm. This is the only hybrid mossy saxifrage still probably in cultivation with an Award of Merit from the RHS and shows the need for a proper trial to be undertaken.

'**Savenake**' (1990, UK). Hybrid of *S. erioblasta* crossed with *S. cebennensis*, with white flowers. Raised by Ron Bass. Rare if not extinct.

'**Schneeteppich**' (1930). Profuse snow-white flowers to 2.2 cm diameter on 15–20 cm stems.

'**Schöne von Ronsdorf**' (ca.1915, Germany, Arends). ('Beauty of Ronsdorf'). Flowers rose-pink, the petals being lighter underneath. I have not seen this cultivar, which appears to be in very limited circulation from a couple of German nurseries. 10–12 cm.

'**Schwefelblüte**' (1934, Germany). ('Flowers of Sulphur'). Flowers pale cream to greenish-yellow, 1.8 cm diameter, dull red stems 8–12 cm. The only mossy saxifrage hybrid with yellow flowers (if you want to call them that).

'**Seaspray**' (1993). Sport of 'Pearly King'. Identical with 'Grace'.

'**Silver Cushion**' (1980s). White and grey-green variegated foliage and pink flowers, flower stems to 7 cm above cushion. Flowers pale pink, to 1.5 cm diameter. Attractive, good in the garden, but unfortunately the pink flowers are really not quite strongly coloured enough to set off the foliage to maximum effect. At its best when the rich reddish buds, which promise deeper pink flowers than finally appear, are well formed.

'**Silver Dome**'. Incorrect name for 'Silver Cushion'.

'**Silver Mound**' Incorrect name for 'Silver Cushion'.

'**Sir Douglas Haig**' (1926). A robust plant with large, circular, deep crimson flowers on 20–25 cm stems. Said to be best in the shade, possibly to lessen fading.

'**Sleeping Beauty**'. See 'Dornröschen'.

'**Snowcap**' (1988). An attractive cultivar (not a hybrid) of *S. pubescens* which received an RHS Award of Merit and which regularly appears on the show bench. Soft, slightly sticky, hairy foliage, flower stem to 4.5 cm, white flowers (more than one per stem) to 1.0 cm diameter. A beautiful plant for the alpine house.

'**Snow Carpet**'. See 'Schneeteppich'.

'**Spätlese**' ('Late Vintage') (1980s, Germany). Pale carmine-red flowers. Flowering quite late—May.

'**Spring Snow**'. See 'Summer Snow'.

'**Sprite**' (1960s?). Flowers carmine-pink/crimson-rose. Late-flowering. 10 cm.

'**Stansfieldii**' (pre-1912) (sometimes as *S. rosacea* 'Stansfieldii'). Flowers warm pink but fading readily but not really accounting for Ingwersen saying "white flowers", and Backhouse in 1913 also referring to it as "white".

'**Summer Snow**' (1990s). White flowers. Not apparently listed widely—may be misnomer.

'**Tapis de Neige**'. French for 'Schneeteppich'.

'**Tinkerbell**' (1989). A variegated plant with red flowers. Presumably related to 'Peter Pan'.

'**Tom Thumb**' (1980s?). Shell-pink flowers on 15 cm stems. Listed in UK.

'**Triumph**' (1920). Arends. Flowers large, dark blood-red. 10–15 cm. Requires slightly moister conditions. Plants in cultivation are very variable and often wrongly named.

'**Variegata**' (date unknown). Variegated form said to be of *S. exarata* subsp. *moschata*. Small, finely divided leaves, white–green variegation, tinged pink in winter.

'**Wallacei**' (pre-1880). Large rosettes up to 4.5 cm, flower stems 20 cm, branched only at top of stem, usually 2 or 3 flowers per stem, to 3.5 cm diameter. Enormous creamy-white flowers of good texture. A wonderful display plant but needs regular propagation. The plant we now have under the name 'Wallacei' is clearly not the plant that some of the early writers refer to. It is, however, so splendid that it is worth considerable effort.

'**Ware's Crimson**' (date unknown). The origins of this cultivar are obscure but the general aspects of the plant seem to indicate that it is probably a very old cultivar, possibly originating around the end of the 19th century from Thomas Ware of Tottenham, from whom Arends obtained *S. Rhei* in 1897. A small cultivar with rounded petals which just touch, starting deep crimson but fading very dramatically to white, with only base and tips (where the main vein terminates) remaining crimson, although the effect can be somewhat more indiscriminate. Not available in the UK, but in circulation in France: I found it in the street flower and plant stalls in Paris in the mid-1990s, and Erhardt (*PPP Index* 1997) lists it as being available in France.

'Wargrave Rose' (1980s). Smallish, pale pink. May be extinct.

'Weisser Zwerg' (1990s) (translated as "White Dwarf"). Very dwarf. White flowers on 1–1.5 cm stems. Attracts attention. Possibly synonymous with 'Schneezwerg'.

'Welsh Dragon' (1980s). A very attractive newish cultivar from Keith Lever at Aberconwy Nursery. Deep red flowers on a neat plant.

'Welsh Red' (1980s). Newish cultivar from Keith Lever.

'Welsh Rose' (1980s). From Keith Lever at Aberconwy.

'White and Wooley' (1990s). White flowers.

'White Christmas' (1999). White flowers on short stems. Listed in USA (Rice Creek Gardens).

'White Pixie' (pre-1970). (Synonym 'Pixie Alba' is invalid.) A neat plant, green stems to 6 cm, with creamy-white flowers to 1.5 cm diameter.

'White Sprite'. Corrupted synonym for 'White Pixie'.

'Whitlavei Compacta' (1930s). Cultivar of *S. hypnoides*. May have disappeared.

'Winston Churchill' (1943). A vigorous plant with large pale pink flowers. 10–15 cm. Described by Ingwersen as "soft pink break from *S. Wallacei*". Sometimes incorrectly as 'Winston S. Churchill' and as 'Sir Winston Churchill'.

'Woodside Ross' (1993, UK, Bernard Thomas). Very dwarf, red, flowers with paler centres. Possibly extinct.

A number of cultivars have been listed in various countries since the 1980s about which no other details are available:

'Adebar' (1990s, Germany). As *S. ×arendsii*.

'Berner Moosteppich' (1990s, Germany).

'Dawn' (1990s). Listed as available in Norway.

'Fire Dragon' (1990s). Listed as available in Belgium.

'Frühlingsschnee' (1990s). Listed as available in France.

'Gladys' (1990s, UK).

'Kelmshott' (1980s?, UK).

'Lammefjord' (1990s). Available in Germany and Netherlands.

'Laura' (1995, Germany). Listed by Feldweber.

'Pike's Primrose' (1980s?, UK?). Probably extinct.

'Pike's White' (1980s?, UK?). Probably extinct.

'Roter Knirps' (1990s, Germany).

'Rubra' (1990s, Germany). As *S. ×arendsii* 'Rubra'.

'Schneewittchen' (1990s). Available in France and Germany.

'Schneezwerg' (1995, Germany). Possibly synonymous with 'Weisser Zwerg'.

'Schwefellicht' (1990s, Germany).

'Spätrot' (1990, Germany).

'Tom's Red' (1980s?, Germany?). Listed by Eschmann.

'White Spire' (1990s, UK).

'Wilson' (1995, Germany). Listed by Longin Ziegler.

'Witham's Compact' (1980s, UK).

15 · Mid- and Late-Flowering Far-Eastern Saxifrages
Section *Irregulares*

The late autumn garden has a limited flora but a distinctive one. Himalayan gentians, a few colchicums, some cyclamen and crocuses, chrysanthemums and Michaelmas daisies will all flower into November and even December. Among the rich colours of the fall, the effects of this late flowering can be especially beautiful—and some of the Far-Eastern saxifrages from section *Irregulares* add an air of dainty elegance. Their flowers have petals which are dramatically exaggerated to the point where they only seem fit for a place in some Darwinian cartoon-strip. The elongated petals catch the eye in the dappled light in which the plants are often found, and then, in the wild, persist as the seeds ripen and the capsules open, and so seem to contribute to seed dispersal by catching the lightest breeze. The foliage, which assumes rich autumn colours, enhances the way in which the plants feel at one with the fallen leaves.

Although there are quite a number of species from this section that appear in the garden of the specialist from time to time, most people are likely to have met only a handful of species. Most saxifrages flower in the first half of the year, but most of these flower much later and they have always had value in the garden. Now, for the first time in many years, interest in them is being re-awakened by new introductions which are distinct, pretty and, equally importantly, available.

Saxifraga rufescens. The red-hairy stems are characteristic of this species.

Botanical History

The saxifrages of this section—now known as *Irregulares*—were for nearly two hundred years known as the *Diptera* saxifrages. Unlike most saxifrages, the flowers of plants in this section are zygomorphic: the petals are not all the same length, with one, or more usually two, being substantially longer than the others.

Recent genetic analysis makes it clear that of other saxifrages the early summer-flowering *Saxifraga mertensiana* (sole member of section *Heterisia*) from western North America is the most closely related to section *Irregulares*.

The nearest ecological equivalents among the European saxifrages are the evergreen *Gymnopera* saxifrages, which inhabit more or less dense deciduous woodland both as woodland floor plants and as cliff dwellers, and the section *Cotylea* species, *Saxifraga rotundifolia* which grows in moist woodland and along stream edges.

In the wild the *Irregulares* saxifrages are found in Japan and far-eastern Russia, Korea, and westward through China to the southeastern reaches of Tibet. This has meant that they came into cultivation in the West only very gradually. The first species introduced into Europe was *Saxifraga stolonifera* (known for many years as *S. sarmentosa*), before 1771 according to Bailey Balfour. This would indicate that it was of Chinese origin since very few plants came from Japan in the period between Kaempfer's visit to Japan in 1693 and Thunberg's in 1776. That *S. stolonifera* was widely grown after its introduction is obvious from the number of common names it has acquired— mother of thousands, roving sailor and wandering Jew—all referring to its stoloniferous habit which helped make it easy to propagate and pass on to other growers. It was some considerable time before the second species, *S. fortunei*, was collected by Fortune in 1863; and *S. cortusifolia* was introduced sometime before 1874 by Veitch & Son (according to Harding), having been collected by Maries or possibly by Fortune and Standish. Wilson collected *S. veitchiana* in 1900, which was also introduced by Veitch, and *S. rufescens* was collected by Forrest in 1906 and subsequently introduced by Bees. The key authors who set about making sense of the material collected up to that point were Balfour in Edinburgh, and Engler in Berlin.

The story is confused: Engler first worked on them, publishing a couple of new species in 1913. Bailey Balfour published his major account in 1916 without obvious knowledge of the 1913 publication and then Engler, with Irmscher, continued his own work in the second half of *Das Pflanzenreich* published in 1919. This last appears to have been done without sight, or presumably knowledge, of Balfour's work, just as Balfour's had been without sight or knowledge of the earlier Engler publication. For some species it is quite easy to disentangle the overlap since, in some cases, they used precisely the same herbarium specimens with different results. For example, *S. mengtzeana* of Engler & Irmscher in 1913 was described by Balfour as two species, *S. aculeata* and *S. henryi*, equating conveniently to var. *cordatifolia* and var. *peltifolia* of Engler & Irmscher. However, all this has left a legacy of confusion which has not served us, or the plants, well.

The *Irregulares* Species

The recent appearance of the English language *Flora of China* (Pan Jintang et al) treatment of the *Saxifraga* has cut through much of the previous confusion, most dating back to the overlapping work of Balfour and Engler & Irmscher. The new delineation of the Chinese species submerges some of those with which we have been familiar, although often only by name, and in one notable case separates a new species, *S. epiphylla*, out from the pre-existing order. This is unique in having plantlets developing in the axil at the base of the leaf blade—technically foliar embryos—which enable the plant to propagate itself vegetatively. It is a fascinating alternative to the embryos found at the tip of the runners in *S. stolonifera* and in *S. cortusifolia* var. *stolonifera*.

Two species are widespread, with both *Saxifraga fortunei* and *S. cortusifolia* found in both Japan and China and also in Korea.

Saxifraga stolonifera

This is distinguished from all other species in the section (with the minor exception of a rare variety of *Saxifraga cortusifolia*) by having thin runners with plantlets at their tips. As these root the plant spreads to make mats of the leafy rosettes in suitably moist or shaded habitats. It can have stems with well over a hundred flowers which come much earlier than do those of many other species in this section. The flowers are white or pale pink with a yellow spot and deep magenta dots on each of the smaller upper petals. I find the ordinary unnamed form hardy in the open garden where it is established among rose bushes as part of the underplanting. The main variation within the species is in leaf colour, and the variegated 'Tricolor', 'Hsitou Silver' (BSWJ1980) with green leaves with broad silver-grey markings, finely netted 'Hime', the dark-leaved 'Kinki Purple' and 'Maroon Beauty', and yellowish 'Harvest Moon' together show the range. It is noticeable that all the plants that are being selected have foliage with some sort of variegation, but plants with very dark green unmarked leaves with red hairs are in cultivation and would make very attractive additions to those already in circulation.

Saxifraga cuscutiformis has now been incorporated within *S. stolonifera* and is probably best treated now as *S. stolonifera* 'Cuscutiformis'. This has small foliage and long, very thin runners and it is worth preserving from a horticultural point of view. *Saxifraga veitchiana* has also been incorporated into *S. stolonifera* and since, like *S. cuscutiformis*, it is currently in cultivation, and since the plant, which has smallish white flowers on a quite short stem, is recognizably

Saxifraga stolonifera 'Harvest Moon'. The colour of the leaves varies through the year. The foliage can be much more yellow in good light in high summer.

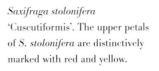

Saxifraga stolonifera 'Cuscutiformis'. The upper petals of *S. stolonifera* are distinctively marked with red and yellow.

different from most plants under the name *S. stolonifera*, it would probably be useful to continue use of the name as a cultivar name: *S. stolonifera* 'Veitchiana'.

Other species names which have over the years disappeared into *Saxifraga stolonifera* include *S. chaffanjoni*, *S. chinensis*, *S. dumetorum*, *S. iochanensis*, and *S. sarmentosa*, which was for many years the normally accepted Latin name for what was known colloquially as the strawberry saxifrage because of the aerial stolons, like strawberry runners. There is a variety in Japan with five equal petals, var. *aptera*.

Saxifraga fortunei

In the wild *Saxifraga fortunei* is a very variable species in terms of size, leaf shape and ecological situation from wooded riverside slopes to rocky clefts in higher mountains. The *Flora of China* gives var. *fortunei*, and var. *koraiensis*, and Japanese texts typically give varieties such as: var. *incisolobata*, var. *obtusocuneata*, var. *minima* (sometimes var. *alpina*), var. *partita* and var. *crassifolia*. A number of botanical forms are in cultivation although they are less commonly met with than some of the named cultivars which are discussed later. Typically plants in cultivation have flower stems about 30 cm tall with often around 30–50 white flowers. The leaves are typically drab to olive-green above, and shiny reddish-purple underneath, and are markedly lobed and toothed. The foliage dies down in winter with the frosts. But if this is the typical form, variation is dramatic. The smallest forms such as var. *minima* are plants which may be no more than 7–8 cm tall and wide, while the largest may be 50 cm tall and 35–40 cm wide. There are also three broad types of leaf form which can be found within *S. fortunei*. In forms easily found in the trade, these equate to those of 'Wada' and 'Mount Nachi', the typical form with markedly toothed and pointedly lobed leaves; 'Cheap Confections' and 'Blackberry and Apple Pie' which have lobes that are much more rounded; and 'Cotton Crochet' which has the most fan-like blade, also thickly textured. In horticultural forms these differences are supplemented by variations in leaf colour, and flower colour and form.

The considerable confusion between *Saxifraga fortunei* and *S. cortusifolia* can be traced back to the contrasting approaches of Balfour and Engler. For Balfour the leaves were the critical feature, those of *S. fortunei* being coloured red or purple on the underside, while those of *S. cortusifolia* are green beneath. For Engler it was the incompleteness of the ring of nectaries around the ovaries that distinguished *S. cortusifolia* from *S. fortunei*, which he treated as a variety of *S. cortusifolia*. And contemporary authors continue to use different characteristics as their key features. Tebbitt cites the presence of yellow spots as the base of the smaller petals in *S. cortusifolia* as characteristic, while Pan, Gornall & Ohba also highlight the serrate margin on the long petals as characteristic of *S. fortunei*, in most varieties at least. A further characteristic that should be added to these is the shape of the small upper petals: narrowly elliptic in *S. fortunei*, broadly cordate or truncate with a narrow haft in *S. cortusifolia*. Taken together these make typical forms of each species quite distinguishable, but difficulties arise with some of the more exotic forms.

Saxifraga fortunei
'Wada' flowers.

Saxifraga fortunei
'Wada'.

Saxifraga fortunei (above) and *S. cortusifolia* (left). The distinguishing characteristics can clearly be seen, with *S. cortusifolia* having yellow spots on the small petals, which are also clawed at the base.

Saxifraga fortunei var. *pilosissima* is one of the most stately varieties of the species.

Japanese and other Species of the Pacific Far East

Saxifraga cortusifolia

This is the most common of the endemic Japanese species from the section, but it is still rather rare; both *Saxifraga fortunei* and *S. stolonifera*, which also occur in China, are more common. The distinctions between *S. cortusifolia* and *S. fortunei* have already been discussed. *Saxifraga madida*, which is also Japanese, was separated originally by thinner leaves, more deeply cut, and possibly rather larger and more hairy, but is now normally included in *S. cortusifolia*. As with *Saxifraga fortunei*, there is a wide range of variability, particularly in leaf colour and form. A rare stoloniferous form is found on Kyushu, but the stolons are usually quite short.

Saxifraga nipponica

Although it is quite a rare plant in the wild, *Saxifraga nipponica* is one of the more straightforward species in the garden, with the evergreen leaves being able to cope with frosts. It is also able to survive drier and more sunny positions than most of the other species. It usually flowers in May rather than in the late summer or autumn, a characteristic which led to it also being named *S. vernalis*. Winton Harding grew the typical form of *S. nipponica* in the open for a number of years and 'Pink Pagoda', which is a new cultivar, has similar bright green hairy leaves which are slightly thickened, with a typically circular outline and a toothed but not lobed margin. It has yellow-spotted pink flowers and clawed petals like those of *S. cortusifolia*. Before it closed, Heronswood Nursery listed 'Yukino Shita', a cultivar with white flowers.

Saxifraga serotina

This is clearly closely related to *Saxifraga nipponica*, with rounded leaves on long pubescent stems and white to pink flowers. It is found on north Japanese islands

Saxifraga nipponica.
Photograph Winton
Harding.

Saxifraga sendaica.

and also in the Primorskiy region of far-eastern Russia, and possibly in Sakhalin, in damp, shaded rocky ground. It flowers in September. Pictures on the internet of plants growing in rocky crevices in the Primorskiy region show flowers which are much less exaggeratedly zygomorphic than in most other *Irregulares* species, and the leaves are apparently short-stemmed.

Saxifraga sendaica

Another rare species, *Saxifraga sendaica* is found on the southern Japanese islands, so it is not surprising that this species is rather tender in the UK. Unlike all other species in the section, *S. sendaica* has erect stems, up to about 10 cm tall, with the large leaves developing fully only toward the top of the stems, and with a complex although quite compact terminal inflorescence. The flowers have jaggedly cut longer petals and the whole plant has a very different air to the other *Irregulares*. A variety with much more cut leaves has been named var. *laciniata*. A very well protected woodland garden or a fairly frost-free, well-shaded greenhouse seem to offer the best chance of success. The leaves are rather larger than in most other species with the circular blade up to about 10 cm long and broad, with a long petiole.

Saxifraga sichotensis

This is a rather obscure species described from Siberia as having affinities with *Saxifraga nipponica*. Its leaves have rounded blades which are broadly and sharply toothed, with both the blade and petiole being hairy. Its flower stem is up to about 20 cm tall with 5–15 flowers—but they lack petals, so diagnosis as an *Irregulares* species is somewhat doubtful and it may in fact belong in *Micranthes*.

Endemic Chinese Species

Saxifraga mengtzeana and S. epiphylla

These two species are quite easily recognized because of the purple-spotted backs to their thickened leaves. *Saxifraga mengtzeana* now incorporates many other previously recognized species, including *S. aculeata*, *S. geifolia*, *S. henryi*, *S. lancangensis* and *S. ovatocordata*. These hide a wide variation in leaf and flower colour, with some described as having red flowers. In general terms it has an oval leaf blade with an acute tip, which is thick, crisp, fleshy and hairy on the upper green surface as well as having a bristly hairy margin. It is now seen as restricted to Yunnan, while *S. epiphylla* is much more widespread in China and is apparently found in Vietnam. Although not recorded as being found in Tibet, this is probably the species that I photographed in the gorge of the Rong-Chu, a tributary of the Tsang Po, growing on the cliffs in a very humid environment where leeches and snakes both flourished. Until recently *S. epiphylla* had not been separated from *S. mengtzeana*. It has very similarly textured leaves with the same purple-spotted backs, but the embryo plantlets at the base of the leaf blade in *S. epiphylla* quite clearly distinguish it. The plantlets are generally formed late in the summer or in the autumn and, where the leaves can lie flat on the ground, they will root and the old blade rot away. This characteristic makes it a very easy plant to propagate and it is likely that it will become much more widespread in the next few years. The plants in cultivation vary quite widely. Various clones have been named by Bleddyn and Sue Wynn-Jones: the first was 'Purple Piggy' (BSWJ4966), and subsequent ones are 'Little Piggy' and 'Precious Piggy'. Heronswood listed what appeared to be same species, possibly from the same Japanese nursery, under the designation "*Saxifraga* sp. (Gotemba)".

Saxifraga epiphylla. The embryo plantlets can be seen on those leaves touching the ground.

This *Irregulares* saxifrage growing on the cliffs of the Tsangpo Gorges, in southeast Tibet (outside the range of *S. stolonifera*), matches the descriptions of *Saxifraga mengtzeana*, apart from the obvious stolons hanging down with plantlets at their tips.

Saxifraga rufescens and S. imparilis

Saxifraga rufescens is distinguished by its characteristic densely red-hairy flower stems with the red colouring often staining the numerous white flowers, which appear in summer rather than autumn. Its leaves are broadly circular or kidney-shaped and may be toothed or cut more deeply. Originally collected by Forrest in Yunnan, this species is also found in Sichuan, Hubei and Tibet. It is rarely cultivated and then, seemingly, with some difficulty, although Bailey Balfour notes that it was hardy in Edinburgh, flowering in July. Effectively a Chinese equivalent of the Japanese *S. cortusifolia*, there are three botanical varieties of which var. *flabellifolia* probably deserves specific status and should then be *S. zhejiangensis*.

Saxifraga imparilis, from Yunnan, is closely related to *S. rufescens* var. *rufescens* and also generally similar to *S. cortusifolia*. Its leaves have a broadly circular blade with 7–11 lobes and it has a loose panicle of flowers very similar to those of *S. cortusifolia*. The capsules are apparently distinct in being truncate rather than having an erect style.

Saxifraga kwangsiensis and S. jingdonensis

Two much rarer species have not come into cultivation. Growing in waterside rock crevices in Guangxi, *Saxifraga kwangsiensis* has white flowers, is about 30 cm tall, and has very distinctive, much narrower leaf blades than in other species, with a cuneate base to the blade and a toothed end. These long leaves are quite unlike those of any of the other species.

The other very rare species is *Saxifraga jingdonensis*, which has recently been described from Yunnan with stems about 10 cm tall and leaves with a blade less than 2.5 cm long. This may turn out to be a small form of *S. mengtzeana*.

Cultivars of *Saxifraga fortunei* and *S. cortusifolia*

For many years the range of *Irregulares* cultivars available to Western gardeners was very limited. In Japan, however, great attention has been paid to collecting and breeding exotic cultivars and the variability of *Saxifraga fortunei* in the wild has been fully exploited. Most of the cultivars available to gardeners in Europe and North America stem from nurseries in Japan and possibly Korea, Taiwan and China, although there have been some collections by westerners, particularly by Bleddyn and Sue Wynn-Jones of Crûg Farm Nursery in north Wales, and Dan Hinckley of Heronswood Nursery in Washington State. These developments have seen the number of species and of cultivars rise dramatically. Already a number of the new introductions have started to make an impact in gardens and on the show bench in the UK, and it is likely that a number of these plants will become firm favourites. It is also clear that a wide range of others, some apparently very pretty, are waiting in the wings. In some cases names are already filtering through and there are signs that others will follow.

As has been outlined, the range of cultivars of *Saxifraga stolonifera* has been extended by a widening of the range of leaf colour, and some cultivars of *S. epiphylla* and *S. nipponica* are also being distributed, but it is in *S. cortusifolia* and particularly *S. fortunei* that there has been most development. There are now far more cultivars of *S. fortunei* than of all the other species in section *Irregulares* put together.

In *Saxifraga fortunei* (and to a lesser extent in *S. cortusifolia*) the range has been extended in four different ways:

Leaf shape. Introduction of forms of *S. fortunei* with more fan-shaped leaves and ones with more rounded outlines, and forms of *S. cortusifolia* with more laciniate leaves.

Leaf colour. Greatly extended with many cultivars with variegated and unusually coloured foliage.

Flower colour. Extended range of colour from white and very pale pink to greenish-yellow and deep pink.

Flower form. Range extended from single flowers to extravagantly doubled flowers and flowers with bracteose petals.

The combined effect has been to make these cultivars among the most exciting of new introductions. Unfortunately, in some cases, the cultivars of *S. fortunei* and *S. cortusifolia* have become somewhat confused in both the general horticultural trade and in the literature. Wherever possible, cultivars are allocated to the appropriate species in the lists below and where there is uncertainty this is noted.

Saxifraga 'Cotton Crochet'.

Older Cultivars

When compared with the spectacular range of plants introduced recently, the list of older cultivars seems very short and rather limited in ambition, with the main variation among the forms of *Saxifraga fortunei* being simply in overall size. The largest of these is 'Wada' with flower stems up to about 45 cm tall and thickened, smooth, dull green leaves dark red-purple underneath, and 'Rubrifolia' is slightly smaller with darker reddish-green foliage which is very similar in texture. The smallest of these older cultivars is the charming 'Mount Nachi', with its thin, dark, deeply cut leaves not thickened at all. All of these have white flowers typical of the species. In 'Wada' the petals are slightly longer and narrower than in the other two. All are attractive plants: 'Mount Nachi' is ideal for a trough, and the larger plants are wonderful in the autumn border. The only old named cultivar of *S. cortusifolia* is the pink-flowered 'Rosea', which is interesting, although rather less dramatic than the normal white-flowered form.

New Cultivars in the UK

Many of the large number of new introductions in recent years from growers in the UK are now on their way to becoming firm favourites, with Bob Brown of Cotswold Garden Flowers being among the most important nurserymen. Two introductions of his into the UK stand out because of their spectacularly elaborated flowers. *Saxifraga* 'Cheap Confections' has dramatically bracteose pink flowers and thickly crispy foliage and is one of the earlier autumn cultivars to flower, with 'Rubrifolia' and 'Wada'.

Left: *Saxifraga fortunei* 'Rubrifolia'. Photograph John Howes.

Right: *Saxifraga* 'Cheap Confections'.

Left: *Saxifraga* 'Black Ruby'.

Right: *Saxifraga* 'Blackberry and Apple Pie'.

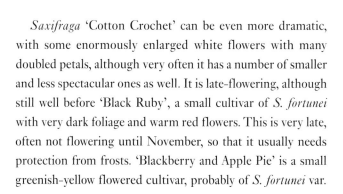

Saxifraga 'Cotton Crochet' can be even more dramatic, with some enormously enlarged white flowers with many doubled petals, although very often it has a number of smaller and less spectacular ones as well. It is late-flowering, although still well before 'Black Ruby', a small cultivar of *S. fortunei* with very dark foliage and warm red flowers. This is very late, often not flowering until November, so that it usually needs protection from frosts. 'Blackberry and Apple Pie' is a small greenish-yellow flowered cultivar, probably of *S. fortunei* var.

incisolobata; 'Crystal Pink' has very small leaves which are heavily variegated with white and pink, especially when new.

Bleddyn and Sue Wynn-Jones have been a source of many of the new introductions of *Irregulares* mostly of their own collections from the wild. Most of these have collection numbers with a BSWJ or BWJ prefix, but they have also introduced *S. cortusifolia* 'Ruby Wedding' and *S. fortunei* 'Fumiko', a distinctive small form of the species.

While others have been introducing plants from the wild or from the Far-Eastern nursery trade, Keith Lever at Aberconwy, again in north Wales, has been crossing forms of *Saxifraga fortunei*. These have been derived from various self-pollinations and crosses using a small form of *S. fortunei* var. *obtusocuneata* and a "pink seedling" raised at the nursery. The resulting cultivars include the white-flowered 'Conwy Snow' and 'Conwy Star' and the pink cultivars 'Pink Cloud', 'Pink Haze', 'Pink Mist' and 'Autumn Tribute'.

New Cultivars in North America

While a number of nurseries in the UK have been involved with bringing in plants from Japan and China, so too have Dan Heims (at Terra Nova Nurseries in Oregon) as well as Daniel Hinckley. Between Heronswood and Terra Nova, some very distinctive cultivars have been introduced. These include cultivars of *S. fortunei*, some with variegated foliage such as 'Five Color' (the Japanese 'Go Nishiki') and 'White Chrysanthemum'; pale green-flowered 'Jade Dragon'; and the *S. cortusifolia* cultivars 'Velvet' and 'Silver Velvet' which is one of the most sumptuous of recent introductions from Dan Heims with nicely scalloped, velvety leaves which are rich grey-purple and pale lilac and it is an extremely attractive plant. Before the closure of Heronswood there were a whole range of other cultivars in their collection, some with cultivar names. Of these *Saxifraga* 'Quadricolor' struck me as particularly attractive.

Japanese Cultivars

Most of the plants in cultivation in Europe and North America stem from Japan, but a whole range of Japanese cultivars have yet to reach the West and it is possible to find information about many of these through the internet. In some cases they have been described, in others pictured. Some have been posted under Japanese names, some under English ones. The following list at least provides some pointers for the adventurous web-gardener. Among those with white flowers are 'Shiraito-no-Taki' and 'Ucho-no-hikari' and the spectacularly pretty 'Shima-no-Shiraito'. With creamy-green flowers there are 'Apple Snow' and 'Momo Henge' ("Plum Symphony") and among the pink and red cultivars there are 'Cherry Pie', 'Aya', 'Tamayura' and 'Beni Fuji'. An enormous range of Japanese cultivars has yet to reach the Western horticultural trade although Jürgen Peters in Germany has a remarkable list of new introductions on his nursery website.

Saxifraga 'White
Chrysanthemum'.

Saxifraga cortusifolia
'Silver Velvet'.

A possible area of confusion is the use of Japanese names for the species and
these are given at the end of the list of species descriptions but apart from these
there are many more Japanese cultivars. Apart from those listed at the end of the
chapter, about which I have been able to assemble some information, there are
other Japanese names which must conceal between them other wonderful plants,
with 'Hanamatsuri' being a flower festival celebrating the Buddha's birth, 'Hino-
tsukasa' seeming to mean "maple" and 'Nishikikujaku' meaning "azalea". 'Yama-
biko' refers to the Hokkaido highlands.

'Ayanishiki'	'Hiten'	'Senhime'
'Benikujaku'	'Kizakura'	'Shichihenge'
'Buko'	'Miyaki'/'Miyuki'	'Shiranui'
'Daiuchu'	'Momo-Benkei'	'Shirohohoh'
'Hagoromonomai'	'Nachinohanabi'	'Tamamushi'
'Hanaguruma'	'Nishikikujaku'	'Tenho'
'Hanamatsuri'	'Ryokuho'	'Togen'
'Hien'	'Ryokuo'	'Yaguruma'
'Hiho'	'Ryokusen'	'Yamabiko'
'Hinotsukasa'	'Secchubai'	'Yamato'

Plants in Cultivation

The three species that are most likely to be met with in cultivation are *Saxifraga
fortunei*, *S. cortusifolia* and *S. stolonifera*, which may still be found under the very
old name *S. sarmentosa*, and into which have also been incorporated the well-
known *S. cuscutiformis* and *S. veitchiana*. This list may seem extremely abbreviated
but the range is obviously greatly extended, particularly in recent years, by introductions of cultivars of these species from a number of sources.

   A number of the other species are brought into cultivation occasionally. None
seems impossible to grow, although some from warmer and more humid regions,

such as the Tsangpo Gorges in Tibet at the far west of their range, or in particular the southern Japanese islands, can prove tender in Britain. Although few of the species are widely available, some such as *S. epiphylla* are likely to become so, and there are others in the specialist trade and these deserve attention. What is clear however is that in recent years it has been the proliferation of named cultivars, particularly of *Saxifraga fortunei*, which is leading to a revival of interest.

Most of the introductions which stem from the Japanese horticultural trade have been given English-language trade designations such as BLACKBERRY AND APPLE PIE or SUGAR PLUM FAIRY when they appear in Britain or North America, although they already have Japanese names. These are given where known in the discussion below: they are the proper cultivar epithets. For example, there is a *Saxifraga fortunei* cultivar which has the Japanese cultivar name, when transliterated into Western script, *S. fortunei* 'Toujya'. This is the same plant which in the European trade has been given the trade designation *S. fortunei* SUGAR PLUM FAIRY. This can be further confused because in some cases the trade designation is a translation of the Japanese name but in many cases it is not. 'Toujya' can be translated as "plum happiness", so it is possible that the plant could also be found with labels to this effect. Although trade designations should be orthographically distinguished, for example by the use of small capitals, as in *Saxifraga* SUGAR PLUM FAIRY, this can only be done consistently if it is clear which plants are being treated in this way. Failing this I have chosen here to treat all the names as normal cultivar names. Lewis Carroll would have loved this, and so presumably would the Reverend Dodgson.

Growing *Irregulares* saxifrages

The *Irregulares* saxifrages are generally quite straightforward to grow given a bit of shelter from the most extreme cold. *Saxifraga fortunei* and *S. cortusifolia* are herbaceous and non-persistent, dying right back as and when the frosts catch them, but some species such as *S. epiphylla*, *S. stolonifera* and *S. nipponica* are normally evergreen, with *S. epiphylla* being rather less hardy than the other two. I have found them to be resistant to most pests except vine weevils which enjoy the fleshy bases of the stems. This is a problem if they are grown in pots but not generally with open-ground plants. I have also been told by some people that *Irregulares* saxifrages are susceptible to slugs, but although I have a range of small but voracious slugs I have had no such problem.

Most of the plants met with regularly can be grown in pots. A leafy or peaty soil seems to suit them very well although unfortunately peat mixtures also suit the vine weevil and if such composts are to be used then it may be necessary to use a pesticide or a biological control. A compost using a loam-based mix with quite a bit of added sand and some grit can be helpful, although weaning the plant from its original peat-based compost is not always easy. Great care needs to be taken to ensure that plants which are bought in are pest-free. Since they are usually grown in a peat-based compost it can be difficult, but it is well worth the effort.

The main decision as to whether they are plants for the open garden involves factors such as scale (some are very small), shelter, and having a spot which does not dry right out. The most obvious species for the open are *S. cortusifolia*, *S. nipponica* and *S. fortunei* (particularly in its standard unnamed state and in its larger cultivars such as 'Wada'). Forms much smaller than 'Wada', such as 'Rokujo' or 'Mount Nachi', or the newer cultivars from Keith Lever, really need to have rather more attention focused on them because they can otherwise be overwhelmed. This can obviously be done in an appropriate raised bed or in a small shaded corner of a rockery. In general terms, in the open garden the larger forms can be seen and treated as plants for the woodland garden and the smaller ones, which often originate at higher altitudes, as ones for the rockery. I have to add leaf mould to our clay soil to open it up (in the same way I would for *Meconopsis* for example) for *S. fortunei* and *S. cortusifolia*. Plants grown in the open garden seem to last longer than those in pots if the right situation can be found.

Most saxifrages can be propagated by taking cuttings, but that is not an option with these plants. For the gardener, the primary method with *Irregulares* saxifrages has to be division, which works very well. It is quite straightforward to cut a plant into pieces, or tease it apart, so that each piece still has some of the root system. In the trade, many of these plants have been propagated using cell culture, micropropagating plants which would otherwise have taken many decades to become widely circulated although this approach produces surprising levels of variability.

It is possible to grow *Irregulares* saxifrages from seed. The difficulty, apart from the fact that the seed is extremely fine, is that very few plants ever set seed in the UK so seed is rarely available. The seed is small and should be surface-sown. I have raised *Saxifraga stolonifera* and *S. fortunei* from seed and there seems no particular reason why others should not be equally possible if seed is obtainable.

Saxifraga 'Five Color'. The variation between individual plants produced by micropropagation is seen clearly in this batch of plants.

Section *Irregulares* Haworth

Species

Except in *S. sendaica* leaves are basal and inflorescence generally pyramidal.

Saxifraga cortusifolia Siebold & Zuccarini (1843) [incl. *S. madida* (Maximovich) Makino (1892)]. Stems to 35 cm. Leaves to 15 cm, thinner than in *S. fortunei*. Flowers with 2 long, 3 short petals. Short petals usually with yellow (or very occasionally red) spot and clearly clawed at base. Japan.

var. *stolonifera* (Makino) Koidzumi. Short stolons produced with leafy embryos at tip. Only stoloniferous *Irregulares* not included in *S. stolonifera*. Japan: Kyushu.

Note: Before it was included here, *S. madida* was distinguished from *S. cortusifolia* by thinner leaves, more deeply cut, possibly larger and more hairy.

Saxifraga epiphylla Gornall & H. Ohba in Gornall et al (2000). Distinguished from *S. mengtzeana* by presence of embryos at base of leaf blade. Variable. Stems to 35 cm, up to 30 flowers. Leaves thickened, ovate to kidney-shaped, variously lobed and toothed, base cordate with foliar embryo developing in autumn, to 10 × 8.5 cm, margin hairy, petiole to 12 cm, quite brittle. Leaves are mottled purple beneath, plain green or sometimes with lighter green markings above. Petals white, longest to 30 × 7.5 mm, shortest 3–4.5 × 2.2 mm. 800–3800m, China: Sichuan, Yunnan, Guangxi, Guangdong, Vietnam.

Saxifraga fortunei J. D. Hooker (1863). Very variable. Stems 5–40 cm, typically 25–40 cm. Leaves thin, fleshy or crisply thickened, variously kidney to fan-shaped, 3 × 4 cm to 16 × 20 cm, glabrous to hairy or with warts, margin roundly or deeply sharply lobed and toothed. Flowers white or pink. Longer 2 petals to 17 × 2–5 mm, shorter 3 petals to 4.1 × 1.7 mm, rounded not clawed at base. Many varieties described, many forms based on differences in foliage, with status of the taxa often arguable:

var. *fortunei*. Petals with glandular-hairy margin. 2200–2900m, Hubei, Sichuan.

var. *alpina*. Japan.

var. *crassifolia*. Leaves thickened, long-hairy, broad, shallow lobed. Japan: Honshu islands.

var. *incisolobata*. Large more or less hairless leaves, roundly lobed leaf blade. Japan. Most of the spectacular new cultivars derive from this variety.

var. *koraiensis*. Petals glabrous, entire. China (Jilin, Liaoning), Korea.

var. *minima*. Very small, leaves to 0.5–1.6 cm, base slightly cordate or truncate. Japan.

var. *obtusocuneata*. Leaf base cuneate. Variable in size. Japan.

var. *partita*. Deeply divided leaves, base broadly cordate. Elongated petals particularly long. Japan.

var. *pilosissima*. Very large leaves on short-hairy petioles. Large broad, many-flowered inflorescence. May fall within var. *crassifolia*. Korea.

Saxifraga imparilis I. B. Balfour (1916) [*Saxifraga martinii* H. Léveillé & Vaniot (1917)]. Stems to 17 cm, with up to 16 flowers. Leaves kidney-shaped, cordate, lobed and toothed, to 4 × 5 cm, petiole to 10 cm. Petals white, 2 longer, longest to 15 × 1 mm, shorter to 4 × 1 mm, shortly clawed. Close to *S. rufescens* var. *rufescens*. 1800–4000m, Yunnan.

Saxifraga jingdonensis H. Chuang (2001). Stems to 10 cm, 4–6 flowers. Leaves broadly ovate, thickened, to 1.8 × 1.6 cm, margin 5–8-toothed. Flowers white, longest petal to 10 × 2 mm, shorter 4 petals to 5 mm long. 2300m, Yunnan. Status unclear, possibly belongs to *S. mengtzeana*.

Saxifraga kwangsiensis Chun & How ex C. Z. Gao & G. Z. Li (1983) [*S. longshenensis* J. T. Pan (1991)]. Distinctive narrow leaves, elliptic-oblong to 6.5 × 2.2 cm, apical margin serrate, apex acute, petiole to 7.5 cm. Stems 20–40 cm, 5–16 white flowers, 2 long petals to 20 × 2.2 mm, 3 short petals to 2.3 × 1.2 mm with claw. Leaves elliptic-oblong. 800m, Guangxi.

Saxifraga mengtzeana Engler & Irmscher (1913) [*Saxifraga aculeata* I. B. Balfour (1916); *S. geifolia* I. B. Balfour (1916); *S. henryi* I. B. Balfour (1916); *S. lancangensis* Y. Y. Qian (1995); *S. ovatocordata* Handel-Mazzetti (1931)]. Leaves peltate to broadly ovate, apex acute, to 7.5 × 6 cm, thickened, margin bristled, dark spotted below, petiole to 1.2 cm. Flower stems to 25 cm, 10–30 white flowers. Longest petal to 19 × 3.5 mm, shortest to 3.5 × 2.2 mm. 1100–1900m, China: Yunnan.

Saxifraga nipponica Makino (1901) [*S. vernalis* Y. Jinuma (date unknown)]. Thick, hairy leaves with reniform-circular, finely crenate blade to 6 × 8 cm, cordate base, petiole 7–15 cm. Flower stems to 40 cm.

Flowers white or pink, unspotted, longer 2 acuminate petals to 20 mm, shorter 3 × 2 mm. Early-flowering (May, June). Japan.

Saxifraga rufescens I. B. Balfour (1916) [incl. *S. zhejiangensis* Z. Wei & Y.B. Chang (1989)]. Flower stems 16–40 cm, typically 10–30 white or pink flowers, thin branches with 2–4 flowers. Stems and inflorescence with long red glandular hairs. Leaves reniform, cordate, truncate or cuneate, variously cut margin with 9–11 lobes. Longest petal(s) to 19 × 1.3–4.6 mm with entire margin, shortly clawed and often with extended narrow apex, short petals to 4.5 × 2.3 mm. 600–4000m.

> var. *rufescens*. Leaves cordate at base. Petals with glandular-ciliate margin, multi-veined. 1000–4000m, Sichuan, Yunnan, Tibet, Hubei.
>
> var. *flabellifolia* (*S. zhejiangensis*). Cuneate-truncate leaf base. Petals multi-veined. 600–2100m, Sichuan, Yunnan.
>
> var. *uninervata*. Cordate leaf base. Petals with hairless margin, single-veined. 2400m, Sichuan.

Saxifraga sendaica Maximovich (1872). Fleshy leaves, leaf bases and stems. Stems are thickened to 20 cm, with thickened bases to unformed leaves lower down and of large leaves above. Foliage glabrous, leaves broadly and finely toothed, blade to 10 × 7 cm, petiole to 10 cm. Inflorescence is terminal to about 10 cm, a many-flowered, broad rather than elongated cyme. Petals white, longer ones to 20 mm, deeply cut, shorter to 4 mm. Frost-tender. Mountains, Southern Japan. A form (f. *laciniata*) has deeply cut leaves.

Saxifraga serotina Siplivinsky (1977). Plain green, glabrous, circular, roundly lobed leaves, cordate at base. White flowers, longer petals about 2–3 times as long as wide, and twice length of shorter. Seems to be closest to *S. nipponica*. Far-eastern Russian (Primorskiy and possibly Sakhalin), Japanese islands.

Saxifraga sichotensis Gorovoj & N. S. Pavlova (1970). Described as close to *S. nipponica* but with no petals, minor differences to the calyx, and seeds. 2000m, Siberia (Khabarovsk province).

Saxifraga stolonifera Curtis (1774) [*S. chaffanjoni* H. Léveillé (1911); *S. chinensis* Loureillo (1790); *S. cuscutiformis* Loddiges (1818); *S. dumetorum* I. B. Balfour (1916); *S. iochanensis* H. Léveillé (1916); *S. sarmentosa* Linnaeus (1780); *S. veitchiana* I. B. Balfour (1916)]. Leaves coarsely hairy, slightly lobed, toothed, kidney-shaped to circular to 9 × 9 cm, petiole to 10 cm, blade usually dark, rather reddish, green with lighter markings, dark purple-red below. Stems to 45 cm,

broadly pyramidal inflorescence, up to 100 flowers with 3 short petals to 4.5 × 2 mm, short-clawed, spotted yellow and magenta, 2 longer unspotted petals to 20 × 4 mm. 400–4500m, China (very widespread but absent from Tibet), Japan, Korea.

Japanese names for species

Dai-Monji-So. *Saxifraga fortunei*.
Haru-Yuki-No-Shita. *Saxifraga nipponica*.
Hoshizaki-Yuki-No-Shita. *Saxifraga stolonifera* var. *aptera*.
Izu-No-Shima-Dai-Monji-So. *Saxifraga fortunei* var. *crassifolia*.
Jinji-So. *Saxifraga cortusifolia*.
Kaede-Dai-Monji-So. *Saxifraga fortunei* var. *partita*.
Sendai-So. *Saxifraga sendaica*.
Tsuru-Jinji-So. *Saxifraga cortusifolia* var. *stolonifera*.
Uchiwa-Dai-Monji-So. *Saxifraga fortunei* var. *obtusocuneata*.
Yuki-No-Shita. *Saxifraga stolonifera*.

Cultivars

Saxifraga cortusifolia cultivars

'Rosea'. Old pink-flowered cultivar of the species.
'Ruby Wedding'. Dark reddish-purple leaves with light grey-green bars along the veins. B. & S. Wynn-Jones. UK.
'Silver Velvet'. Scalloped velvety leaves. Rich purple with extensive grey and pale lilac marking. White to pale lilac-pink flowers. USA (Dan Heims).
'Velvet'. Deep purple-green overlaid with rich grey-brown. Flowers slightly off-white or very pale pink with a yellow spot on each of three smaller petals. USA (Dan Heims).

Saxifraga epiphylla cultivars

'Little Piggy'. Small round-leaved, "wavy-edged" form. UK.
'Precious Piggy'. (BWJ7750). Round slightly crenate leaves, smaller than 'Purple Piggy', light markings on darker leaves. Leaf embryos small and produced less readily. UK.
'Purple Piggy'. (BSWJ4966). Green lobed leaves, leaf embryos readily produced. UK.

Saxifraga fortunei cultivars

'Apple Snow'. Clean pale green-yellow flowers, petals more rounded than many of this colour. Shiny green leaves. Japanese name not traced.

'Autumn Tribute'. Small mid-pink cultivar with very dark foliage from Aberconwy Nursery. UK.

'Aya'. Deep pink, extra petals, petals toothed to laciniate.

'Ayako'. Similar to 'Cheap Confections' but with more petals which are deep pink.

'Beni Fuji' ("Red Flames"), **'Beni-fuzi'** and **'Red Jacket'** are probably all names for the same new Japanese plant which has deep shocking-pink or red flowers with broad petals. Leaves with bristly surface, red backs, pale veins and pink-red petioles.

'Beni Fuusha' or **'Beni Fusha'** ("Red Windmill"). Deep shocking-pink flowers. Flowers often with all petals long. Long petals narrow, slashed toward tip. This may be the same as 'Beni Fuji' ("Red Flames"), 'Beni-fuzi' and 'Red Jacket'.

'Beni Komachi'. Japanese. Compact with deep pink flowers with broadened petals.

'Benikujaku' or **'Beni Kujyaku'**. Pink flowers, petals deeply cut. Flowers like less exaggerated 'Cheap Confections', foliage like 'Blackberry and Apple Pie'.

'Beni shishi'. Extraordinary flowers like rich pink starburst. Some flowers may have many dozens of narrow petals.

'Blackberry and Apple Pie'. Flowers small, greenish-yellow. Stamens coral pink. Petals slightly bracteose. Deep green leaves, rounded outline, stained deep red at base of indents and tips of rounded lobes. In autumn foliage turns deep red.

'Black Forest Gateaux'. Red flowered cultivar from Long Acre Plants, Somerset, UK.

'Black Ruby'. Small very dark foliage, extremely deep purple-brown on both surfaces, which can colour bright red in autumn. Flowers rich warm red but very late and often caught by frosts. Japanese name apparently means "black leaf". UK.

'Cheap Confections'. Pale warm pink bracteose flowers. Individual petals broad with deeply laciniate margin. Anthers coral pink. Foliage quite large, thick, fleshy, green with rounded outline, green on reverse. Unclear whether this is a cultivar of *S. fortunei* or *S. cortusifolia*. UK.

'Cherry Pie'. Deep pink flowers, foliage deep green with dark marks at the base of the leaf lobes (like 'Blackberry and Apple Pie').

'Conwy Snow'. Similar to 'Mount Nachi' but with extra petals. From Aberconwy Nursery, UK.

'Conwy Star'. Small white-flowered cultivar from Aberconwy Nursery, UK.

'Cotton Crochet'. Flowers white and doubled and some flowers are spectacularly enlarged although very often also having smaller ones. Thickened leaves, green on both surfaces. Late flowering.

'Crystal Pink'. Small, pale green and white leaves during the growing season, but variegated white, green and pink when new. It very rarely flowers, but if it is kept away from the frosts then it may flower in December. UK.

'Five Color'. This is the Japanese cultivar 'Go Nishiki' which translates literally as 'Five Color'. USA.

'Fumiko'. (BSWJ 6124). Dwarf alpine form with normal-sized white flowers. Leaves are much more rounded than in other very small forms of the species in cultivation. Collected on Yakushima, Japan.

'Gashikifu'. Foliage dramatically variegated. Similar and possibly identical to 'Quadricolor'.

'Go Nishiki'. Japanese cultivar. Foliage variegated green, grey, white and pink. White flowers. In USA as 'Five Color'.

'Jade Dragon'. Small glossy, rich green leaves, deep red-purple undersides, deep red, quite long petioles. Flowers pale green. USA.

'Kokaku'. This is very similar, and may be identical, to 'Blackberry and Apple Pie'.

'Maigrün'. Very similar to 'Wada'. Slightly shorter and leaves green rather than purple beneath.

'Maiko'. Pale to mid-pink flowers. Dark foliage. Petals broadened with roundly toothed margins. Sometimes with extra petals.

'Miyabi', **'Miyaki'** or **'Miyuki'**. Flowers with up to about ten narrow petals. Longer petals may be deeply lobed. Petals deep pink toward tip, paler toward base.

'Momo-Benkei'. Very similar to 'Cheap Confections' and may be identical.

'Momo Henge' ("Plum Symphony"). Pale biscuit-coloured flowers with pink flush. Medium-sized scalloped leaves.

'Momo Tarou'. Flowers with broadened but not doubled petals. Cream to creamy-pink.

'Mount Nachi'. Collected by Professor Rokujo. Small, pretty, old cultivar with quite deeply cut, toothed, dark reddish leaves with stems of pure white flowers. There is a smaller green-leaved plant in circulation under the same name.

'Pink Cloud'. Small pink-flowered cultivar from Aberconwy Nursery, UK.

'Pink Haze'. Small pink-flowered cultivar from

Aberconwy Nursery, UK.

'Pink Mist'. Small pink-flowered cultivar from Aberconwy Nursery, UK.

'Purpurea'. See 'Rubrifolia'.

'Quadricolor'. Attractive multi-variegated foliage. Probably *S. fortunei*. USA (Heronswood) but not introduced before nursery closure and may have been lost, although 'Gashikifu' is similar and possibly identical.

'Red Flames'. See 'Beni Fuji'.

'Red Jacket'. See 'Beni Fuji'.

'Red Windmill'. See 'Beni Fuusha'.

'Rokujo'. Very similar to 'Mount Nachi' (and probably collected by Professor Rokujo at the same time) but with warmer mid brown-purple foliage. Flowers look white but are the palest of pinks when set alongside those of 'Wada'. Stamens coral.

'Rubrifolia'. Old, middle-sized cultivar with dark reddish-green foliage, turning dramatic orange-red in autumn. Flowers pure white. There are also plants in circulation as 'Purpurea' with darker red foliage but otherwise the same.

'Ryokubai'. Petals broadened, not doubled, light green tinged pink. Foliage dark-green with dark red tinge.

'Sakuragari'. Deep pink, some extra petals, not much broadened, cut toward tip.

'Shima-no-Shiraito'. Extremely desirable with numerous pure white flowers, petals very elongated and doubled. Leaves are roundly scalloped (like those of 'Blackberry and Apple Pie'), mid-green with a complex of broad and discrete cream veins. Japan only.

'Shiragiku'. Flowers of normal form (not doubled or brateate) but very cool white, ovary light clear green, foliage.

'Shiraito-no-Taki' ("White Cotton Waterfall" or "White Thread Waterfall"). White flowers with multiple and elongated petals. The name refers to an actual waterfall in Japan. 'White Chrysanthemum' may be **'Shiraito-no-Taki Variegata'**. Japanese.

'Spinners Snow-storm'. A white-flowered cultivar from Spinners Garden, Lymington, Hants, UK.

'Sugar Plum Fairy'. Pale cream-pink petals toothed rather like 'Cheap Confections' but lower petals clearly longer than upper. Leaves large and pale green. Original Japanese name is 'Toujya'.

'Tamahime'. Broad rich pink petals, doubled and deeply cut.

'Tamayura'. Sugar-pink flowers and dark red stems. Dark leaves with red undersides. Probably very similar to 'Black Ruby'.

'Toujya'. Japanese cultivar (name meaning "plum happiness") in UK trade as 'Sugar Plum Fairy'.

'Ucho-no-hikari'. Very similar to 'Blackberry and Apple Pie' but with white flowers with notched petal tips.

'Wada'. Old cultivar. Largest form of species common in cultivation (var. *pilosissima* is bigger) and one of first to flower. Deep rather olive-green leaves, red beneath, flowers white with petals longer and narrower and generally not toothed. Stamens white or very pale cream.

'White Chrysanthemum'. Leaves very variegated, green with white splashes, and thickened as in var. *crassifolia*. Flowers white with many extra petals, long and short, but of normal width, unlike 'Cotton Crochet'. May equate to 'Shiarito-no-Taki' or 'Shiarito-no-Taki Variegata'. USA.

Saxifraga nipponica cultivars

'Pink Pagoda'. Form of species with pink flowers. UK from Japanese trade.

'Yukino Shita'. Cultivar with white flowers previously listed by Heronswood Nursery, USA.

Saxifraga stolonifera cultivars

'Cuscutiformis'. Previously as *S. cuscutiformis*. Small foliage, very long and thin stolons. Most commonly grown as a house plant.

'Harvest Moon'. Light yellowish-green foliage, smaller than typical. Apparently derived from 'Eco Butterfly' about which I have no other information. USA.

'Hime'. Normally green leaves with a network of much finer light veins. Japan.

'Hsitou Silver'. (BSWJ1980). Green leaves with broad silver-grey markings on the upper surface. UK.

'Kinki Purple'. (BSWJ4972). Dark purple leaves, particularly on the lower surface. UK.

'Maroon Beauty'. Dark leaves, somewhat smaller than typical. UK.

'Tricolor'. An old cultivar with variegated foliage, mid-green, markedly bordered by irregular creamy-white splashes and often having pink tinges to areas.

'Veitchiana'. Previously as *S. veitchiana*. Small plants, white flowers.

16 · Smaller Sections
Sections *Cymbalaria, Odontophyllae, Cotylea* and *Heterisia*

Some of the sections of *Saxifraga* have more than a hundred species in them, and most have a dozen or more, but a few species are in different ways sufficiently distinct from the others as to sit outside these larger groupings. The genetic research discussed in Chapters 2 and 4 has helped clarify the position of some of these within the genus, although not all.

Section *Cymbalaria* has just four species in it, three centred on the Mediterranean, with one outlying species in Ethiopia. They are closer to section *Ciliatae* than any other section, although they look very different from the *Ciliatae* species, and life-cycles are dissimilar.

Section *Odontophyllae* has just a single species from the Himalaya. This is quite distinct from the species in other sections. Genetic research has so far not explored this species, so that its position is uncertain, although it seems likely that it will sit near section *Saxifraga*.

Section *Cotylea* is a European section with two species. The flowers can be seen to be similar to those of section *Trachyphyllum*, but the general morphology of tall leafy flower stems is very unlike the small needle-leaved mats in that section. The genetics suggest that this is not at all closely allied to any other section, but lies somewhere between the section *Saxifraga* grouping and the section *Irregulares* grouping.

Section *Heterisia* has a single North American species which looks in many ways like a *Micranthes*. In fact it is clearly a *Saxifraga* species, and is most closely related to the species in section *Irregulares*.

Perhaps surprisingly, given the obvious oddities of the species in these small sections, species from three of the four sections find a place in gardens. Only section *Odontophyllae*, is not represented in the garden flora since the sole species, *Saxifraga odontophylla*, has not been introduced into cultivation.

Saxifraga mertensiana. Clusters of axillary bulbils.

Section *Cymbalaria*

The saxifrages of section *Cymbalaria* are small African and Mediterranean plants but the eponymous *Saxifraga cymbalaria* has a place in the garden as a charming self-seeding annual which has escaped into the wild in various parts of the world. The usual plant found in cultivation is *Saxifraga cymbalaria* var. *huetiana*: at its best it fits well among the mossy saxifrage hybrids and can form cushions much the same size, covered in starry warm yellow flowers.

Whereas *Saxifraga cymbalaria* can make a rather nice little mound with lots of yellow flowers, *S. hederacea* can be very insignificant, often rather diffuse with the leaves and flowers on rather straggling stems growing in shady spots among rocks. I saw it in Turkey in cracks on a shady cliff and this is typical of the general habitat. Apparently *S. hederacea* is as amenable in the garden as *S. cymbalaria*, and *S. sibthorpii* could also be successful, although I have no direct experience to confirm this assertion of Webb & Gornall. *Saxifraga hederifolia* from the mountains of Ethiopia has not been collected.

Section *Odontophyllae*

Saxifraga odontophylla as it was named by Wallich—or *S. asarifolia*, as it is sometimes called to avoid confusion with Piper's subsequent use of the same name for what is now *Micranthes odontoloma*—is the only species in this section of the genus. It is a plant of the southern watershed of the Himalaya where it can be found among rocks or on cliffs from about 2800 metres up to about 4600 metres. The general appearance is very similar to *S. granulata* from section *Saxifraga*, with roundly kidney-shaped leaves, mainly basal, and flower stems with up to a dozen vase-shaped white flowers. These are much the same size and shape as those of *S. granulata*, but often have red streaks or shading at the throat.

Various characteristics seem to warrant its lonely status in a section of its own.

Saxifraga odontophylla Wallich (*S. asarifolia* Sternberg). Thanks are due to the Department of Botany, Natural History Museum, London, for allowing me to photograph these specimens.

Close-up showing the flowers of *Saxifraga odontophylla* with the red marks (showing blueish-purple) at the base of the petals.

It lacks bulbils and, unlike the section *Saxifraga* species, it has underground rhizomes. Engler & Irmscher, with some hesitation, thought it might be linked with the *Micranthes*, but the flowers are unlike those of *Micranthes* in appearance and are much closer to the flowers of section *Saxifraga* and section *Mesogyne*. The structure of the ovary is very similar in appearance to that of section *Saxifraga* species such as *S. granulata*, except that it is superior and the ripe capsule looks very similar.

It has not yet come to the attention of the contemporary researchers into the genetics of the *Saxifraga* and *Micranthes*, but it will be interesting when it does. Until then its proper place must remain an intriguing speculation.

One area of confusion in the past has been that many descriptions have followed Engler & Irmscher in describing the underside of the leaf as purple. In herbarium specimens the leaves can appear purple beneath, but collectors' notes make it clear that at least some live specimens have leaves that are "glossy," "whitish" or "silvery" beneath. Observation of further live specimens would be valuable in clarifying this since it may be that the purple underside of the leaf is an artefact of dried material.

Saxifraga rotundifolia.
Maritime Alps.
Photograph John
Howes.

Section *Cotylea*

In shady spots in the woods of southern Europe anywhere up to about 2000 metres the saxifrage most likely to be found is *Saxifraga rotundifolia*. It occurs all the way from the eastern Pyrenees to the shores of the Caspian Sea and prospers on shady banks or in shallow runnels. It can often be found at the side of roads cutting through the mountain woodland.

Section *Cotylea*—section *Miscopetalum* as it used to be—is somewhat remote from any other section, probably as close to section *Saxifraga* as any, although the spotted petals in section *Cotylea* are similar in pattern to those in sections *Gymnopera* and particularly to section *Trachyphyllum*. The section is distinguished by the species having superior ovaries and leafy flower stems, and they also have underground rhizomes.

If the right spot in the shade garden can be found, *Saxifraga rotundifolia* is a very pretty plant which well deserves its place. In a cool leafy soil it can make wonderful clumps with handsome, toothed, circular leaves and masses of starry white flowers on stems up to 90 cm tall on large plants. In the wild this plant is most often found in mountain woodland. The starry white flowers are seen at their best in dappled shade where the flowers catch the eye in the patches of sunlight. Close-up the flowers can be seen to have spotted petals, heavily spotted in some cases, with yellow spots toward the base, then orange and red further out along the petal. In the wild it is very variable but the only named

Flowers of *Saxifraga rotundifolia*. Although quite remote from species in section *Trachyphyllum*, the flowers show the same pattern of dots.

variety in cultivation is likely to be found as "*S. chrysosplenifolia*". This usually has leaves with a more crenate edge, often wavy as well as crenate, and seem usually to belong to *S. rotundifolia* subsp. *chrysosplenifolia* var. *chrysosplenifolia*.

Saxifraga taygetea is a much smaller species than *S. rotundifolia* and inhabits much higher open sites. Confined to the Balkans from Greece to Montenegro, it has flower stems which are up to about 25 cm tall, with leaves proportionately smaller than those of *S. rotundifolia*, but with the petals spotted with dark red.

Section *Heterisia*

Saxifraga mertensiana is unmistakable when it is in flower. The widely branched inflorescence has only small white flowers, but bunches of cherry-red bulbils in the axils of the branches. These bulbils are its main means of propagation, falling off as the stem withers and growing on to flowering size in the next two or three years. Very often it will build up large colonies where all of the individual plants are genetically identical because they have come from asexual bulbils rather than from sexually produced seed. For the gardener this intriguing production of bulbils is extremely helpful as they propagate themselves as efficiently in the damp or shaded garden, as they do on damp shaded cliffs in the Cascades or the Olympic Mountains. In the Cascades I have found it alongside *S. vespertina* by the Crest Trail in northern Oregon on an almost vertical mossy bank with the sun only catching it aslant. In the Cascades, looking for the Olympic endemic saxifrage *Micranthes tischii*, I found it growing in a vertical north-facing gulley along with *M. nelsoniana* subsp. *cascadensis*.

Saxifraga mertensiana on a shady cliff (with out-of-focus *S. vespertina* behind) in the Cascades in Oregon.

Until recently *Saxifraga mertensiana* was seen as being close to some of the *Micranthes* saxifrages in particular those from subsection *Calthophyllum*. Most obviously the leaves, with their long petiole and round toothed blade, seemed to fit well with such as *Micranthes odontoloma* and *M. nelsoniana*. The flowers of *S. mertensiana* are also not dissimilar to these *Micranthes* having small round white petals narrowed or even clawed at the base, and stamens broadened filaments. Among the North American saxifrages it seems an obvious connection, but the phylogeneticists have now demonstrated that this is illusory and that it is much more closely aligned with the east Asian section *Irregulares* many of which have similar leaves and broadened filaments. The most obvious differences which distinguish *S. mertensiana* from these new first-cousins are the fact that its petals are all similar, and the presence of inflorescence bulbils. Some

Saxifraga mertensiana with the clusters of pink bulbils clearly visible.

plants can be found without bulbils, but these do not seem to have taxonomic significance.

It is possible to get *Saxifraga mertensiana* from nurseries, but it is easy to grow from the bulbils that are offered regularly by specialist seed exchanges. Seed may be produced, but it is not what is collected. The bulbils should be sown immediately in exactly the same way as seed. Once established a plant will regularly "seed" itself, shedding its bulbils into its surroundings, and masses of the simple palmate leaves of the young plants will be found. If it is grown in a pot in a frame, young plants of *S. mertensiana* will soon appear in surrounding pots. These occur in great numbers, and show the benefit of immediate sowing, but the bulbils from seed exchanges have plenty of life in them.

Species in sections *Cymbalaria, Odontophyllae, Cotylea* and *Heterisia*

Section *Cymbalaria* Grisebach

Saxifraga cymbalaria Linnaeus (1753). Annual. Loose stems 10–25 cm, 2–6 flowers. Small tufts of foliage with leaves having palmate, ivy-shaped blade, usually 5–9 acute to rounded lobes. Petals bright yellow to 6 mm. Ovary superior or almost so. Sea-level to 2300m. Turkey, Caucasus, northern Iran. Also isolated in Lebanon, Algeria and Romania.

> **var.** *cymbalaria*. Most leaves alternate, lobes acute, petals to 5 mm. Ovary superior. Throughout range.
> **var.** *atlantica*. Most leaves alternate. Narrow petals to 6 mm. Ovary almost superior. Algeria.
> **var.** *huetiana*. Some leaves opposite, 5–7 rounded lobes. Petals to 5 mm. Ovary superior. Asian part of range.

Saxifraga hederacea Linnaeus (1753). Winter annual. Stems from 5–25 cm, with small palmate lobed leaves, blade renate, typically to 1.5 cm, petiole and pedicels slender, 1–4 flowers, white or pale yellow, petals to 3 mm. Ovary almost wholly superior. 1600–2000m or higher. Southern Turkey, northern Iran, Iraq, Lebanon, Israel, Greece, Croatia, Sicily, Libya.

Saxifraga hederifolia Hochstetter ex A. Rich (1847). Closely related to *S. cymbalaria* but petioles have swollen bases and the ovary is more or less inferior. The most southerly species outside South America. 3300–4600m, Northern Ethiopia.

Saxifraga sibthorpii Boissier (1843). Usually biennial. Tufted, flower stems to 8 cm, single flowers. Basal leaves to 1.5 × 1.5 cm, usually 3–5, sometimes 7, rounded lobes, usually short. Petals to 7 mm, orange-yellow. Sepals reflex after flowers open. Ovary superior. 1700–2400m, Greece; one population in western Turkey.

Section *Odontophyllae* Gornall

Saxifraga odontophylla Wallich (1828) (not of Piper) [*S. asarifolia* Sternberg (1831)]. Underground rhizomes. Flower stems typically to 30 cm, branched near the top, 7–12 flowers (normally about 7–9). Stems covered with long hairs, petioles densely so. Leaf blade reniform-circular to 5 cm, green and long-hairy above, silvery-white (or purple) below. Leaf margin broadly crenate, with 7–15 closely spaced lobes, broadly oblong (wider than long), sometimes slightly mucronate, stem leaves with shorter or no petioles. Flowers white with obovate petals 9–15 × 8 mm, often streaked or spotted red toward their base, sometimes forming a ring at the throat. Ovary superior, filaments light green, anthers pink-orange. 2900–5000m, Himalaya: northwest India to Bhutan.

Section *Cotylea* Tausch

Saxifraga rotundifolia Linnaeus (1753) [*S. coriifolia* (Sommier & Levier) Woronow (1921)]. Very variable with many subtaxa described. Forms clumps of shoots, leaves mainly basal, flower stems typically to 70 cm, many flowers in a loose inflorescence. Leaves with more or less circular/reniform blade to 5 × 8 cm, cordate base, margin hairy or translucent, toothed or crenate with up to more than 20 teeth or crenate lobes, petiole to 18 cm. Flower stems (often with more than 20 flowers) with up to 5 stem leaves similar to basal but progressively smaller up stem. Flowers white usually with yellow spots at petal base and red spots above. Petals to 6–11 × 2.5–5 mm. Widespread in southern Europe: eastern Pyrenees continuously to Caucasus and Iran. North to Slovakia, south to Corsica, Sicily and Cyprus. Plants from the Caucasus and Iran have been described as *S. coriifolia*.

subsp. *rotundifolia*. Leaf blade with translucent border and petiole narrowing to top.

var. *rotundifolia*. Flowers starry, narrow petals, lightly spotted, to 9 mm. Throughout range.

var. *apennina*. Robust, petals heavily spotted, 11 mm. Southern Apennines.

var. *heucherifolia*. Flowers cup-shaped, broad petals, heavily spotted, to 11 mm. Balkans at higher altitudes and southern Carpathians.

subsp. *chrysosplenifolia*. Leaf blade usually with hairy margin, petiole expanded just below leaf blade. Aegean and Balkans.

var. *chrysosplenifolia*. Leaves crenate, petals unspotted. More southerly.

var. *rhodopea*. Leaves finely toothed. Petals spotted. More northern.

S. taygetea Boissier & Heldreich (1849). Small clump, flower stems to 25 cm, typically up to about 10 flowers. Leaves, mainly basal, with circular-reniform blade to 1.3 × 2.3 cm, margin 5–9 broadly crenate, petiole to 7 cm. Flowers white with dark red spots, petals to 9 × 3 mm. 1800–2400m, Greece, FYR Macedonia, Albania, Montenegro. Hybrids are formed with *S. rotundifolia* and there is a putative garden hybrid with *S. cuneifolia* (*S. ×tazetta* Hort.), but Gornall views this as merely a variant of *S. cuneifolia*: it has spathulate untoothed leaves with a more distinct petiole than in latter species with flowers not unlike *S. taygetea*.

Section *Heterisa* (Rafinesque ex Small) A. M. Johnson

Saxifraga mertensiana Bongard (1832). Tuft or clump of round or reniform toothed leaves, flower stems to 40 cm, many flowers. Leaf blades are thickened, to 8 cm diameter, with a margin shallowly lobed and the lobes toothed, petioles to 30 cm. Inflorescence is widely branched, usually with clusters of bulbils in the axils of the inflorescence branches. Flowers are small, white, petals roundly obovate, narrowed at base, to 5 mm. North America: Alaska to California; east in Cascades to Montana and Idaho.

Part 3 · *Micranthes*

17 · *Micranthes* Saxifrages

Sections *Merkianae, Intermediae, Micranthes, Arabisa* and *Calthophyllum*

Various trips in search of the North American saxifrages have taken me to the Blue Ridge Mountains of North Carolina and Virginia, the woodlands of New Jersey, the Rocky Mountains around Denver and Yellowstone National Park, the Cascades and the Olympic Mountains, and to Alaska. Most of the North American saxifrages were members of genus *Saxifraga* when I was last there in 2006, but now the bulk of them have been separated into genus *Micranthes* and there are some glorious species here.

There are *Micranthes* which are quite straightforward to grow, that have allowed themselves to be tamed by gardeners, but many of the others remain suicidal, stubborn or at best reluctant in the garden. Perhaps it is this untameable quality which makes me fond of them—they retain their wild heritage. The only way to see some plants is to seek them out in the places where they grow wild, and that is why I travel so far and spend so much time trying to photograph them. Only a handful of *Micranthes* are found in Europe, and only two in Britain, but there are around forty species in Asia and the same sort of number in North America.

The species in genus *Micranthes* vary considerably in general appearance. A small number of species make a mat of foliage, but the vast majority have a rosette or tuft of leaves and a single leafless flower stem carrying a more or less complex inflorescence. The flowers of this latter type are often very small individually, but the inflorescence may be very densely flowered so that the effect of the whole is much more important as a signal to insects than the impact of the individual flower

Micranthes nelsoniana var. cascadensis. Obstruction Point, Olympic Mountains, Washington.

in much the same way as in the *Heuchera*. Most grow either in the high mountains, some up to 5700 metres, or in the Arctic where the high latitude is the equivalent of high altitude. The niches in which the various species are found are indicated by their morphology. In most of the species the slightly thickened leaves lie pretty flat to the ground and generally these are plants found in open conditions such as rocky ground, high-altitude meadow or arctic tundra. But there are some, usually with longer leaves that stand up, which are plants of much damper conditions, growing in rank meadow or marshland, and some species, usually with larger and thinner leaves, are found in damp woodland. Very often species growing in these conditions have much more diffuse inflorescences so that there is a greater chance that at least some of the flowers will catch the dappled sunlight. In general the genus *Micranthes* species flower in summer rather than spring and many do not flower until August.

Taxonomy of Genus *Micranthes*

The *Micranthes* were first separated as a genus by Haworth in 1803, but since then most botanists have treated them as a section within genus *Saxifraga*. However, the most recent work by Richard Gornall, in two papers, one with Hideaki Ohba on the Old World species and one with Luc Brouillet on the New World species, has led to the reinstatement of the genus and a new taxonomy within it. Richard Gornall gave me sight of both papers, as they stood, in advance of publication and both he and Luc Brouillet, who gave me sight of his intentions for the *Flora of North America* treatment, have made it possible for me to reflect the latest thinking. Any areas of confusion are mine.

Genus *Micranthes* Haworth
    Section *Merkianae* (Engler & Irmscher) Gornall
    Section *Intermediae* (Engler & Irmscher) Gornall
    Section *Micranthes* (Haworth) Gornall
    Section *Arabisa* (Tausch) Gornall
        (*Saxifraga* section *Micranthes* subsection *Stellares* (Engler & Irmscher) Gornall)
    Section *Calthophyllum* (A. M. Johnson) Gornall
        (*Saxifraga* section *Micranthes* subsections *Rotundifoliatae* A. M. Johnson and *Cuneifoliatae* A. M. Johnson)

The separation of the sections and subsections depends on a series of characteristics at microscopic level, including whether the glandular hairs on leaves and stems are made up of a single column of cells (uniseriate), the nature of the seed surface, and the texture of the cuticle. Fortunately these can be equated to broader morphological characters and these generally allow recognition of which section a *Micranthes* species belongs to without examining the seeds and hairs under a microscope. Leaf shape, flower structure and the form of the inflorescence are all useful characteristics.

Sections *Merkianae* and *Intermediae* each have a single mat-forming species: *Micranthes merkii* and *M. tolmiei*. At different times they have been in two separate sections (the approach of Engler & Irmscher), or together in a single section (the approach of Webb & Gornall). The latest view is that these two species have less in common than has recently been supposed and in fact that *M. merkii* may not in fact sit well in either genus *Micranthes* or genus *Saxifraga*.

Most of the other species that have been treated as *Micranthes* fit well enough in sections broadly on lines long established, although it is not really clear at present in which section *M. nudicaulis* sits.

Micranthes merkii.
Kamchatka. Photograph
Vojtěch Holubec.

Section *Merkianae*

The one member of this section, *Micranthes merkii*, is found from Kamchatka down to Japan, in bare rocky habitats. It makes mats of leaves, the leaves flattened and usually entire, although sometimes with a lobed apex. The flowers are solitary and are usually described as off-white. The ovaries are large, fully superior and more or less spherical.

Section *Intermediae*

Micranthes tolmiei is a North American species, at home in the mountains of the Cascades as far south as California and as far north as southern Alaska. The only species in the section,

Micranthes tolmiei. The broadened, clavate filaments are easy to see.

Micranthes tolmiei on Mount Rainier in the Cascades.

it is typically found on fairly bare ground, usually near late patches of snow, with the prostrate stems of small fleshy, almost translucent, cylindrical leaves often making mats up to a foot or more across. The white flowers are often solitary, but sometimes there are up to four per stem, and the surface of the petals looks crystalline, reflecting large amounts of light. The petals are supplemented in their effect by the broadened filaments, almost like extra petals.

Section *Micranthes*

Across North America this is the most important and most numerous group of any among the saxifrages. From the Blue Ridge Mountains and the Ozarks up the Appalachians to Canada, and from Mexico up to Alaska there are species in this section. The leaves usually do not have a separate petiole, although the blade may narrow abruptly at the base. The blade varies considerably in shape and is often shallowly toothed and in some species the leaves can be large (*Micranthes micranthidifolia*), but in most cases the leaves are no more than 8–10 cm long and may be considerably shorter, with some no more than 2–3 cm long.

In most of the species in this subsection it is not so much the individual flowers as the inflorescence as a whole which is the signal flag for insects. Only at close range do the individual flowers come into focus. The flowers are often densely clustered, sometimes in a globular or pyramidal head, sometimes in a column of flowers not unlike that of the *Heuchera*, to which they have obvious connections. The shape of the inflorescence is a great aid to identification. This is a large and complex group of species, almost all of them North American, which has been divided into three series:

Micranthes micranthidifolia. North Carolina.

Series *Aulaxis*—superior ovaries and carpels only united at base
Series *Micranthes*—ovaries inferior to semi-inferior, broad nectary disc
Series *Dermasea*—ovaries semi-inferior to superior, carpels more or less free to base

Series *Aulaxis*

Micranthes micranthidifolia, the mountain lettuce of the Appalachians, from New Jersey right the way down to Georgia, is the sole species in series *Aulaxis*. It is typically found among damp rocks or at the side of streams. The demotic name refers to the leaves which are thin, light green, narrowly oblong with a slightly toothed margin, up to about 40 cm long. They look very similar to those of cos lettuce and can, apparently, be used as a salad leaf or even cooked as greens. Rather sadly, despite knowing its common name (another name is deer-tongue), I neglected to taste the leaves when I found it in North Carolina, so cannot comment on its qualities in this respect. It can grow to about 75 cm tall and has a very diffuse inflorescence of tiny white flowers. This might well find a home in a shady damp garden.

Series *Micranthes* and series *Dermasea*

While series *Aulaxis* is obviously the odd-man-out in the section, both the other series have many more species and have at least one species that is circumboreal: *Micranthes hieracifolia* in series *Micranthes*, and *M. nivalis* and *M. tenuis* in series *Dermasea*. These then are the species which may well represent the ancestral stock from which these two series have individuated, and the two are very easy to distinguish.

Micranthes hieracifolia is typically found in subArctic tundra and has a solid flower stem up to 45 cm tall with clusters of deep red-brown starry flowers. Its leaves are typically up to about 7–8 cm long, ovate and slightly toothed, and stand up rather than lie flat.

Micranthes nivalis, on the other hand, is typically found in rocky habitats, is no more than 15 cm tall and has a dense cluster of white flowers held above a flat rosette of red-backed, slightly leathery, toothed leaves. It is one of the two genus *Micranthes* species (the other is *M. stellaris*), that are native to the British Isles and although rare it can be found in Snowdonia growing in horizontal cracks on large boulders.

Series Micranthes

In series *Micranthes*, along with *Micranthes hieracifolia*, is one eastern American species and a lot more from the west, and all apart from *M. hieracifolia* have white or pale green flowers. The one species from eastern America is *M. pensylvanica*, which has strong flower stems up to about 60 cm tall and clusters of pale green flowers. To my mind the most attractive of the western species is the snowball saxifrage, *M. rhomboidea*, from high up in the Rockies, with a dense head or ball of white flowers. In mid-June a good place to find it is at high altitudes around Denver, where it can be found along with *Saxifraga chrysantha*.

A species growing up to around 60 cm tall is *Micranthes oregana*, which grows in damp meadows and bogs from California and Oregon across to the Rocky Mountains of Idaho, with a column or loose conical inflorescence of white flowers often clustered in short-stemmed groups. In the Yellowstone area this is supplemented by the closely related and equally tall *M. subapetala*, the Yellowstone saxifrage, in which all the petals have

Micranthes hieracifolia. Seward Peninsula, Alaska.

Micranthes nivalis. Kangerlussuaq, Greenland. Photograph Ian Bainbridge.

Left: *Micranthes rhomboidea*. Mount Evans, Colorado.

Micranthes oregana in cultivation in Oregon.

Micranthes subapetala. Yellowstone National Park.

been lost and the inflorescence is a pale green dense-flowered poker, the flowers often having purple-stained stamens.

Most of the other species in the series are rather smaller. One of the more widely spread is *Micranthes integrifolia*, which is found from California up to British Columbia. It has off-white flowers and forms small basal bulbils which help it survive dry conditions, and also help survival from year to year in the dry garden. *Micranthes nidifica* and *M. fragosa* are found east of the Cascades and are similar, with smoother, more rhomboid leaves. A couple of other small species have much more limited distribution: *M. aprica* in California and adjoining Nevada, and *M. tempestiva* from western Montana, centred on the Anaconda Range. More impressive than these is *M. californica*, which has a flower stem up to 20 cm or so tall and is rather like a smaller *M. pensylvanica*.

Micranthes nidifica. Bald Mountain, Oregon.

Series *Dermasea*

Micranthes nivalis and the very close *M. tenuis* are the circumboreal representatives of the *Dermasea* series, most of which are found in North America, with *M. virginiensis* being the best known of the species from the Appalachians. Further south is the large-leaved *M. caroliniana* and, slightly smaller, *M. careyana*, and then further west there is the Ozark endemic *M. palmeri*, and down from Missouri through the Ozarks to Texas there is *M. texana*. In the West there is a quite separate set of species, with *M. occidentalis* from the northern and central Rockies being typical. This has toothed leathery leaves and a loose conical inflorescence

Micranthes virginiensis.
New Jersey.

of white flowers up to around 20 cm tall. *Micranthes rufidula* from the Cascades has very similar foliage, but with a flat-topped inflorescence. Further north, to southern Alaska and the Yukon, *M. reflexa* is again similar but may be up to 60 cm tall, although usually quite a lot less.

Other species in this series include *Micranthes marshallii*, *M. howellii* and further south *M. eriophora* from Arizona and *M. mexicana* from the Sierra Madre Occidental in Mexico. All the species here have small white, or pale yellow-green, flowers. There are also four Asian species of which the best known is *M. sachalinensis*.

Among the rarest of all saxifrages, *Micranthes tischii*, from the Olympic Mountains and a few sites on Vancouver Island, is an intriguing species only growing in the most exposed of north-facing sites, typically on bare rocky ledges, at higher altitudes. This was only recognized during the 1980s and described in 1988. It is a very diminutive species, usually no more than 3 cm tall, with just a few flowers with greenish-yellow persistent petals. Photographing *M. tischii* in company with Steve Doonan, on a narrow ledge facing out over a sheer drop with an uninterrupted view north to Vancouver Island, was one of the high-points of my trip to North America in 2005.

Section *Arabisa*

Most of the seven species are subArctic species of Europe and America, varying very considerably in size and general appearance, but with a number of distinctive and shared characteristics. In some species the five petals are of two different sorts, some clawed and spotted, some plain and unclawed. But all species have at

Micranthes rufidula. Crest
Trail, Lolo Pass, near Mount
Hood, Oregon.

Micranthes reflexa. Savage
River, Denali, Alaska.
Photograph Ian Bainbridge.

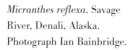

Micranthes tischii. This plant, typically for the species, was no more than 3 cm tall. Klahhane Ridge, Olympic Mountains, Washington.

The back of this shaded, sloping, north-facing ledge (foreground) is typical of the habitat of *Micranthes tischii*.

least some of the flowers with large yellow spots towards the base of the petals. The flower stem usually has stem leaves, which are particularly large in some species, and the inflorescence may be widely branched.

The most widespread species is *Micranthes stellaris*, which is found primarily in Europe, from the Pyrenees and Alps northward, but it also crosses over the Atlantic through Iceland to Greenland and Arctic Canada. It is normally a species of damp habitats in the mountains, often growing at the edge of streams, and hence more common over acid rocks rather than limestone. Although often quite a small plant, it can form substantial mats in prime habitats. Typically it is up to 15 cm tall, with the leaves being anything from narrowly oblong to broadly rounded, with two or three fairly distinct teeth toward the tip; the inflorescence of 5 to 15 flowers is fairly lax with small bracts at the base of the branches. The flowers are usually fairly regular with the white petals being narrowly ovate, all of them narrowed at the base to a "claw", and all of them having two yellow spots toward the base, although these are not as conspicuous as in a number of other species. Although the petals are white, the first impression might be that they are pink, because the prominent ovary, standing above the petals, is a strong pink. *Micranthes stellaris* is a variable species with Engler & Irmscher recognizing over a dozen varieties, but one that is of interest is var. *prolifera* from the Alps of eastern Austria, in which many of the flowers are replaced by leafy buds which can give rise to clonal colonies of asexually reproduced plants. This we found growing in running water, where it seemed wholly to replace the normal form, although in drier habitats in the same area plants exhibited far less of this adaptation.

The most closely related species to this is *Micranthes foliolosa*, not taller but rather more spindly, with most of the flowers replaced by leafy buds. While *M. stellaris* spreads down through the European mountains as far as Spain and Portugal, Bulgaria and Romania,

Micranthes stellaris. Maritime Alps, France. Photograph John Howes.

Close-up of leafy buds of
Micranthes redofskyi.

Micranthes redofskyi.
Wooley, Seward
Peninsula, Alaska.

M. foliolosa is essentially a pan-Arctic (or circumpolar) plant of damp cold conditions, although outlying isolated populations have been recorded as far south as Colorado and Mongolia. It has solitary rosettes and smaller bracts than *M. stellaris*, and the leafy bulbiliferous buds replace most of the flowers in the more or less unbranched inflorescence. *Micranthes redofskyi*, treated by some authors as a variety of *M. foliolosa*, has a more robust and more branched inflorescence and rather more flowers, typically one at the end of each branch of the inflorescence, although still with most of the flowers replaced by bulbils. This seems only to be found at coastal sites in the extreme west of Alaska and into far-eastern Siberia.

Micranthes ferruginea. It is unusual
to find quite such tall plants with so
many flowers. Olympic Mountains,
Washington.

Micranthes ferruginea.
Olympic Mountains,
Washington.

I found just two specimens near Wooley Lagoon on the coast of the Bering Straits, where it was growing in sea-level shingle with the much more abundant *M. nudicaulis*.

Micranthes bryophora is a further species with most of its flowers replaced by leafy buds. Until recently this was considered a purely Californian species, but a variety (var. *tobiasiae*) has been identified in the Payette National Forest, Idaho. This has been described as annual and it had previously been considered to be *M. foliolosa*. The branches of the inflorescence tend to bend downwards. *Micranthes laciniata* from Japan and Korea has flowers like those of *M. stellaris* but has very distinctive leaves with a very sharply slashed apical margin.

The remaining three species in this subsection are *Micranthes clusii*, *M. petiolaris* (*Saxifraga michauxii*) and *M. ferruginea*. All these have flowers which normally have the two distinct sorts of petals, three clawed with yellow basal spots, the other two unclawed and unspotted. The flowers are often quite clearly zygomorphic, with the two unclawed petals as a pair separated from the others, although this three-plus-two arrangement is not invariant. *Micranthes ferruginea* is quite common in the Cascades and Rocky Mountains and is found in habitats which are often dry, certainly in summer. This is a very variable species, typically with light green, soft hairy leaves. In Alaska I was shown a plant collected near Anchorage which was no more than 10 cm tall with no more than perhaps six flowers, while in the Olympics we found a stand of plants that were at least 55 cm tall with hundreds of flowers per stem.

Micranthes ferruginea. This specimen has more hairy leaves and larger flowers and bracts than most of those I have seen in the wild.

Perhaps the most intriguing species in this subsection is *Micranthes petiolaris* (*Saxifraga michauxii*) from the southern Appalachians, where it is at home in extremely damp locations, happily growing on rock faces down which water is pouring. It is immediately recognizable with its dramatically toothed leaves (and inflorescence

Micranthes petiolaris (Saxifraga michauxii). The only thing staying dry in the picture is the surface of the leaves. Blue Ridge, North Carolina.

Micranthes petiolaris (Saxifraga michauxii) starting into flower. Blue Ridge, North Carolina.

Micranthes nelsoniana var. *nelsoniana*. Anvil Mountain, Nome, Alaska.

Flowers of *Micranthes nelsoniana* var. *nelsoniana*.

bracts), the leaves having a water-repellent surface, presumably due to surface architecture. This can give it the air of a strange marine creature on the wet rock face. The overall effect with the large bracts and leaves is impressive, although the individual flowers are not. Similar in broad outline, although rather less dramatic, *M. clusii* is found in damp often shady habitats in the mountains of southern France, northern Spain and Portugal. The only species it might be confused with is *M. stellaris*, but typically it is quite distinct with larger, more toothed leaves which are light green and hairy, with more leafy inflorescence bracts, and with flowers having the three-plus-two arrangement with only the three petals having yellow spots. It is about 15–20 cm tall, although it can vary substantially.

Micranthes nelsoniana var. *cascadensis*. Obstruction Point, Olympic Mountains, Washington.

Section *Calthophyllum*

The old classification of the plants in this section was to divide them between subsections *Rotundifoliatae* and *Cuneifoliatae*, based primarily on the shape of the leaves. It is likely that some of the species which have previously been seen as belonging in these subsections (now making up the *Calthophyllum*) may be misplaced. However, I have chosen here to discuss these species based on the old morphological approach, since that is helpful for recognition, although the species are integrated in the list at the end of the chapter.

The old *Rotundifoliatae*

The eight or nine species that were in the *Rotundifoliatae* are very distinctive. As their old name suggests, they have a round leaf blade

Micranthes lyallii near
Anchorage, Alaska.

Micranthes odontoloma.
Mount Rainier,
Washington.

(with the exception of *Micranthes lyallii*), and this is carried on a narrow petiole. The blade has a toothed margin, in some cases looking almost like a circular-saw blade. The flowers are generally quite small and the inflorescence may be quite diffuse (as in *Micranthes odontoloma*) or more or less capitate (as in *M. manchurienis* and some subspecies of *M. nelsoniana*). These are species which are found in western North America and eastern Asia so that geographically these form a bridge between the species that had previously been in subsection *Cuneifoliatae* in Asia and subsection *Micranthes* in North America.

Flowers of *Micranthes
odontoloma.*

    Micranthes nelsoniana is a good example of a species from this group. It is widespread from northern European Russia across Siberia through Alaska and British Columbia as far as the Cascades and Coastal Range of Washington, but as one might suspect with such a wide range it is very varied and about half a dozen varieties

Micranthes spicata.
Photograph Forrest
Baldwin.

Micranthes spicata. Western
Alaska. Photograph Forrest
Baldwin.

Micranthes manchuriensis.

Micranthes purpurascens
in cultivation.
Photograph Finn Haugli.

have been described. The leaves have a round, toothed blade on a narrow petiole which is as much as four times the length of the blade, but the size and form of the inflorescence varies. One extreme is represented by plants with a tight head of flowers such as the dwarfed var. *insularis* with thickened leaves from the Aleutian Islands, and at the other extreme is the lax, thin-leaved var. *cascadensis*, which is found in the Olympic Mountains and Cascades.

Two other species take the place of *Micranthes nelsoniana* away from the far northwest of North America. *Micranthes odontoloma* is the brook saxifrage of the Rocky Mountains and it is the only one of the section extending any great distance south of the Canadian border, getting as far south as New Mexico and the Sierra Nevada of California. It is a rather lax plant with very small white flowers on very diffuse stems, found growing, as its common name suggests, in or at the edge of creeks or runnels where it can make large patches. Very closely related is *M. lyallii*, which is found from northern Washington and Montana up to southern Alaska, and which hybridizes with *M. odontoloma* where the two species overlap. Again it has few small white flowers and again it grows in running water, often in large patches, but it is atypical of the old *Rotundifoliatae* in having cuneate or spathulate leaves: and it is such anomalies that have led to the new overarching section *Calthophyllum*.

The only other round-leaved American species is the much larger *Micranthes spicata*, found only up in the very far northwest of Alaska. This is substantially larger than most of the other species in this section with the thickened hairy leaves having a large ovoid or circular blade which has a very toothed margin. The flower stem is up to around 70–75 cm tall with numerous white flowers in a tall narrow inflorescence. This species was the type species for Sternberg for what is now section *Calthophyllum*, although both the leaves and the tall narrow inflorescence are atypical in the section.

In Asia there are another five or so round-leaved species of which *Micranthes manchuriensis* from Korea and Russia is the best known because it is occasionally listed by specialist nurseries and is sometimes obtainable from the seed exchanges. It has a flower stem up to about 45 cm tall with a compact head of white flowers and the typical rounded, toothed leaf blade.

The remaining Asian species are *Micranthes purpurascens*, and *M. fusca* and *M. japonica*, both of which come from Japan. *Micranthes japonica* has flower stems up to 60 cm tall with numerous yellow-spotted white flowers and kidney-shaped leaf blades up to about 10 cm on 50 cm petioles. This grows in damp conditions, as does

M. fusca, which has similarly shaped leaves but is a somewhat smaller plant whose name derives from its starry flowers with dusky red petals not unlike those of *M. hieracifolia*. It seems likely that *M. purpurascens* will be submerged in *M. fusca*. It has both flowers and particularly stems stained bright red. This has been successfully grown by Ole Olsson in northern Norway where winters are long and definite, quite unlike the weather in England, and where summer gives 24-hour-long sun.

The old *Cuneifoliatae*

This group has around 25 species in it, of which about 20 are Asian, and 5 or so spread as far as Alaska. They vary sufficiently to have been split by Gornall, in his 1987 revision, into three series: *Birostris* (type *Saxifraga birostris*), *Melanocentrae* (type *S. melanocentra*) and *Astasianthes* (type *S. pallida*). The latest taxonomy may yet separate *Astasianthes* as a section from the remainder.

These species are generally small plants with a basal rosette of often leathery leaves which tend to be broader than in other subsections. In general terms the outline of the leaf is cuneate, but a number of the Chinese species in this group have a distinct petiole. According to Webb & Gornall, one of the distinguishing characteristics is in the texture of the seed, which has "ribbon-like ribs and a finely striate cuticle", and it may be that further taxonomic work will produce further revision. In some species there are only solitary flowers, but much more normal is for a stem of maybe 5 to 15 flowers in a more or less open inflorescence.

Some of the species in this section are clearly attractive with large dark purple or black ovaries surrounded by a dark nectary disk and white or red petals with yellow spots. The flowers vary quite considerably in size, the largest being over 1 cm in diameter. The petals are usually clawed, even if the claw is very short, and all five petals, which are usually white, are similar (unlike some of the species from section *Arabisa*). The effect of the flowers is enhanced in some species such as *Micranthes calycina* by the filaments in the same way, although to a lesser extent, as those of *M. tolmiei* in section *Intermediae*.

Typically these are plants that are found in rock crevices or on very open or stony ground and in open alpine meadow. There are some attractive species in this group so it is unfortunate that all of them seem to be difficult to grow even if seed is available.

Perhaps the most desirable of all the species is *Micranthes melanocentra*, which can have flowers over 1 cm in diameter, with broad petals, usually white with two large yellow basal spots, and with dramatic smoothly shiny black ovaries which may be over 1 cm high. The typical image of this Sino-Himalayan species is of a fairly stocky plant with up to about five white flowers, but in the *Flora of China* a broader approach to the species is taken. The broad approach contentiously incorporates two other species, *M. gageana* (which has rich red petals) and *M. paludosa*, and uncontentiously incorporates the previously separate *S. pseudo-pallida* (which applied to plants that were taller and had slightly smaller flowers than the typical

form of *M. melanocentra*). Apparently *M. melanocentra* varies with geography, with possible hybridization in Nepal with *M. pallida*, and has widely varying chromosome counts. *Micranthes pallida* is another variable species which ranges over the whole of the Himalaya and on into China. It is described as having an inflorescence anything from 3.5 to 33 cm tall carrying 4–13 white flowers with dark ovaries, and *M. davidii* from Sichuan and Burma is similar.

More restricted species in China are *Micranthes clavistaminea* (Yunnan and Sichuan), *M. parvula* (Yunnan), *M. atrata* (Gansu and Qinghai), *M. zekoensis* (Qinghai), as well as *M. divaricata* (Tibet, Qinghai and Sichuan) and *M. dungbooii* (Tibet and Sikkim). In the Himalayan region there are two more species: *M. pluviarum* (Sikkim), and *M. rubriflora* (Bhutan), which is like a small *M. gageana*.

In Siberia there are a handful of other species—*Micranthes astilbeoides*, *M. brachypetala*, *M.davurica*, *M. melaleuca* and *M. tilingiana*—which do not spread across to North America, as well as those trans-Bering species *M. nudicaulis*, *M. calycina* and *M. unalaschensis*.

In Alaska, *Micranthes calycina* and *M. unalaschensis* can be found growing together on the tundra of the Seward Peninsula, one of the only places where this occurs, and intermediate plants can be found. Nevertheless the distinguishing characteristics are quite clear in general. They both have a rosette of rather leathery, deeply toothed leaves, but those of *M. calycina* are narrower and pointed while those of *M. unalaschensis* are broader and blunter. This same general characteristic is carried through to the flower stem, which has narrower upward-facing branches in *M. calycina* and much more right-angled stems in *M. unalaschensis*. Finally the capsules are narrower in *M. calycina* and broader in *M. unalaschensis*. This was consistent

Left: *Micranthes gageana*. Photograph Vojtěch Holubec.

Micranthes unalaschensis. Seward Peninsula, Alaska.

Micranthes calycina. Seward Peninsula, Alaska.

On the Seward peninsula in Alaska plants intermediate between *Micranthes calycina* and *M. unalaschensis* are found.

Micranthes nudicaulis.
Closeup of flowers.

in the plants we examined, with broad-leaved plants having broadly branched inflorescences and broad capsules, and narrower-leaved plants having narrower inflorescences and capsules, with only some plants falling in the middle. In northeast Alaska and in the northern Yukon these two species give way to *M. razshivinii*, the new name for *M. davurica* var. *grandipetala*, although this may be no more than a variation of *M. calycina*.

Micranthes nudicaulis

My favourite species within the genus *Micranthes* has to be the slightly anomalous *M. nudicaulis*, with its charming display of white flowers with bright pink ovaries. Although it was previously safely tucked into the *Cuneifoliatae*, it seems to fit uneasily there and it may well be that it will find itself in a section of its own so that it will be in a similar position to *M. merkii* and *M. tolmiei* and hence it is dealt with separately here. This is a plant which crosses the Bering Straits but it is pretty restricted to the immediate area on either side. It is quite distinctive in its habit because rather than the simple rosette of leaves, *M. nudicaulis* has running stems which root at the nodes in the damp conditions in which it flourishes. The leaves may have rounded or pointed lobes around the margin. This can be seen

Micranthes nudicaulis. This beautiful specimen has particularly sharply pointed lobes along the margin of the leaves. Wooley, Seward Peninsula, Alaska.

Micranthes nudicaulis forming extensive mats in sphagnum bog near Nome–Council road, Seward Peninsula, Alaska.

easily in the upland sphagnum bog with streams running through where the saxifrage can form mats, rooting as it grows in the sphagnum. It also grows in the gravel fringes of coastal pools and on the tundra, but in neither of these habitats is growth so luxuriant, and plants tend to remain as tufts rather than extensive mats.

Growing *Micranthes*

The *Micranthes* are not everyone's idea of garden saxifrages, but they include a range of species of nonchalant charm and there are some that are positively desirable. With many groups of saxifrages there are many species which can be grown quite easily, but this is much less clearly so in the *Micranthes*. Very few species are grown even by the specialist. This seems to me to be a pity since it is quite straightforward to grow some species from three subsections (*Micranthes*, *Arabisa* and *Calthophyllum*) and they form a nice, if unshowy, addition to the wild garden or naturalistic rock garden. In the last few years there has been an enormous growth in interest in members of the *Heuchera* group within the *Saxifragaceae*, in particular with *Heuchera* and *Tiarella* and the hybrids between them all exciting interest. Wild *Micranthes* vary far more widely than do the *Heuchera* and some of the American species seem to offer scope for the gardener. Like the *Heuchera*, they may even offer scope to hybridizers.

Micranthes integrifolia. In cultivation.

In general terms I have found that there are more American species which are easily grown than there are Asian ones, although this could be a function of the range of collections made which are never very extensive and are positively scarce in relation to most of the Chinese and Himalayan species.

It is not difficult to grow many of the species from the Rockies and the Cascades to flowering size. The biggest limitation is that seed is rarely collected. This is not to say that I am advocating large-scale collection of seed from the wild (which would anyway be pointless given the lack of demand). In general, seed of the Cascades and Rocky Mountain species is fairly easy to germinate. During 2005 I had *Micranthes integrifolia* and *M. occidentalis* flower after one year from seed, and the former seems to have established itself on a dry rockery with a number of other American alpines. Most desirable is the more showy *M. rhomboidea*, which would make a handsome addition to a native-plant rock garden, but as yet I have failed to obtain seed in order to try it.

Micranthes ferruginea is another of the American species which is straightforward from seed and usually flowers in the second year. It is very variable in the wild, however, and may be anything from a couple of inches tall with a handful of flowers to a couple of feet tall with hundreds of flowers. From eastern North America both *M. virginiensis* and *M. pensylvanica* are easy to grow from seed. The former is a plant which is found at its best in similar conditions to stands of *Anemonella* as an early spring plant in light woodland, while the latter is a much larger, more robust plant which can survive in the damp garden or border. Another eastern species is *M. micranthidifolia*, which is listed by a British nursery and which I have seen in cultivation in the United States.

Micranthes tolmiei is one plant that most rock gardeners would love to grow. Seed is often collected and will germinate, but I have failed to get any plant to grow bigger than about 0.5 cm diameter before it has died. Dry conditions are a killer for this, like so many other snowmelt plants. Equally nice is *M. merkii*, but although seed can be obtained (from Dr Alexandra Berkutenko in Magadan for one) and I have done so twice, I have not yet succeeded in germinating it.

The European species *Micranthes nivalis* is not difficult to grow from seed. It survives for a few years in tufa but is not large enough to make much of a show.

Most of the Alaskan *Micranthes* tend to be difficult. Germination can be what is referred to as a "challenge," which usually means that it is nearly impossible, although keeping seed in damp kitchen towels in a fridge for six months before sowing produced results with *M. calycina*. Among the Asian species the two that have given me most success are *M. sachalinensis* and *M. manchuriensis*. One of the only other *Calthophyllum* species in cultivation is *Micranthes fusca*, which is listed by one North American nursery. The others are the preserve of seed exchanges: seed of *M. purpurascens* that I got from a seed exchange last winter germinated, and I now have a handful of seedling plants.

As the poor relations within the genus *Saxifraga*, the species which are now seen as belonging to genus *Micranthes* rarely attracted much attention from the gardener, but I hope that their separation and the new recognition of them as a distinct genus with a great North American bias will attract the specialist gardener. My own experience suggests that the range of species that might be grown is much wider than we have so far generally recognized and there is no particular reason why these will not join the range of genera which take their place in the wild rock garden.

Genus *Micranthes*

Almost all the species here have now been, or are being, given names as *Micranthes*. The few that have not are either obscure or disputed, or in a few cases quite new. Within each grouping the listing is alphabetical by specific name whether under *Micranthes* or *Saxifraga*, and thus, for example, *Saxifraga benzilanensis* takes its place between *Micranthes atrata* and *Micranthes brachypetala*.

Section *Merkianae* (Engler & Irmscher) Gornall

Micranthes merkii (Fischer ex Sternberg) Gornall & H. Ohba (2008) [*Saxifraga merkii* Fischer (1822)]. Mat of ovate, spathulate or cuneate leaves to 1.5 × 0.4 cm, margins hairy. Plants with trilobed tip to leaves are distinguished as **var**. *idzuroei*. Flower stems 3–6 cm with 1–4 flowers. Petals off-white to with clawed base. Globose yellow-green ovary. To 3000m, Kamchatka, Sakhalin, Japan and Kuril Islands. Unfortunately, seed being distributed through seed exchanges as var. *idzuroei* is clearly little more than a section *Saxifraga* hybrid.

Section *Intermediae* (Engler & Irmscher) Gornall

Micranthes tolmiei (Torrey & A. Gray) Brouillet & Gornall (2008) [*Saxifraga tolmiei* Torrey & A. Gray (1840)]. Mats of stems with thickened, fleshy, cylindrical linear leaves to 1.0 cm. Stems 2.5–12 cm with 1–4 flowers. Petals white with crystalline surface, to 6 mm. Clavate white filaments with black anthers. Large globose ovary often finely streaked purple. Usually associated with snowmelt. 1000–3000m, western North America: southern Alaska south to Utah and California.

Section *Micranthes* (Haworth) Gornall

Series *Aulaxis* (Haworth) Gornall

Superior ovaries, carpels only united at base.
Micranthes micranthidifolia (Haworth) J. K. Small (1903) [*Saxifraga micranthidifolia* (Haworth) Steudel (1821)]. Mountain lettuce. Long, light green, slightly toothed leaves, to 20 cm. Flower stem to 75 cm with very diffuse inflorescence of tiny white flowers, petals 1.5–3 mm. Moist habitats. Appalachians.

Series *Dermasea* (Haworth) Gornall

Ovaries semi-inferior to superior, carpels more or less free to base.
Micranthes careyana (A. Gray) J. K. Small (1903) [*M. tennesseensis* Small (1903), *Saxifraga careyana* A. Gray (1843)]. Leaf blade to about 10 cm. Flower stem to 30 cm with fairly loose inflorescence. Petals white, unspotted, about 3 mm. Edges of streams. Southern Appalachians.
Micranthes caroliniana (A. Gray) J. K. Small (1905) [*M. grayana* (Britton) Small (1903), *Saxifraga caroliniana* A. Gray (1848)]. Finely toothed leaf blade to 14 cm with distinct petiole. Flower stem to 50 cm with loose branches. Petals white, unspotted, 3–4 mm. Stream sides and wet ground. Southern Appalachians.
Micranthes eriophora (S. Watson) J. K. Small (1905) [*Saxifraga eriophora* S. Watson (1882)]. Leaf blade to 1.5 cm tapering to petiole. Flowers in loose flat-topped inflorescence. Petals pinkish to 4 mm. 2700m, Arizona: Santa Catalina mountains.
Micranthes gormanii (Suksdorf) Brouillet & Gornall (2008) [*Saxifraga gormanii* Suksdorf (1923)]. Distinguished from *M. occidentalis* by the stiffly branched inflorescence and regularly toothed leaf margins. Petals white, unspotted, about 3 mm. Oregon: Coast Range and lower Columbia River Gorge.
Micranthes howellii (Greene) J. K. Small (1905) [*Saxifraga howellii* Greene (1897)]. Leaf blade to 2 cm, red hairy below. Inflorescence loose with small clusters of flowers with unspotted petals 2.5–4.5 mm. Damp ledges. To 900m, Oregon to California.
Micranthes idahoensis (Piper) Brouillet & Gornall (2008) [*Saxifraga idahoensis* Piper (1900)]. Often treated as a subsp. of *M. marshallii*. Leaves ovate to 3 × 2.2 cm rather than oblong. Petiole only 1.5 times length of blade. Petals white with 2 yellow spots, 2.5–4.5 mm. Open moist rocks. To 2500m, Oregon to Idaho and Montana.
Micranthes marshallii (Greene) J. K. Small (1905)

[*Saxifraga marshallii* Greene (1888)]. Ovate to oblong blade 3 cm with petiole up to 3 times as long. Flower stem to 20 cm. Pyramidal inflorescence with scattered flowers with petals white with 2 yellow spots, 2.5–4.5 mm. Deep shade. 100–1500m, Oregon to California.

Micranthes mexicana (Engler & Irmscher) Brouillet & Gornall (2008) [*Saxifraga mexicana* Engler & Irmscher (1916)]. Crenate or toothed leaf blade 3–6 cm tapering to broad petiole. Flower stem to 20 cm. Inflorescence cylindrical with clustered flowers, petals to 4 mm. 2000–3000m, Mexico.

Micranthes nivalis (Linnaeus) J. K. Small (1905) [*Saxifraga nivalis* Linnaeus (1753)]. Rosette of red-backed toothed leaves up to 4 cm. Flower stem 5–20 cm with a terminal ball of white flowers, petals 2–3 mm. Rocky places. Circumboreal.

Micranthes oblongifolia (Nakai) Gornall & H. Ohba (2008) [*Saxifraga oblongifolia* Nakai (1909)]. Ovoid, slightly toothed, thin leaves 8 × 4 cm with petiole up to 8 cm. Flower stem to 20 cm with diffuse many-flowered inflorescence of small white flowers. Rocky ledges and gorges. Said to be found in Korea and China but not referred to in the *Flora of China* so there must be doubts about the status of this species.

Micranthes occidentalis (S. Watson) J. K. Small (1905) [*M. allenii* Small (1905), *M, saximontana* (E. Nelson) Small (1905), *M. lata* Small (1905), *Saxifraga occidentalis* S. Watson (1888)]. Rosette of slightly leathery ovate, distinctly toothed, leaves typically 3 cm long with abrupt narrowing to petiole. Flower stem typically 20 cm branched to form conical inflorescence of white flowers, petals unspotted, 2–3.5 mm. Meadows and rocky ground. Rocky Mountains: British Columbia to Wyoming.

Micranthes palmeri (B. F. Bush) Brouillet & Gornall (2008) [*Saxifraga palmeri* B. F. Bush (1928)]. Similar to *M. virginiensis* but with entire leaves and less hairy inflorescence. Flowers white, petals unspotted, 3–6 mm. Rocky glades. Ozarks.

Micranthes reflexa (Hooker) J. K. Small (1905) [*Saxifraga reflexa* Hooker (1833)]. Leaf blade to 2 cm with broad petiole. Flower stem 10–60 cm tall with loose flat-topped inflorescence. White, yellow-spotted petals, 2–3 mm. Tundra and open ground, Alaska to British Columbia.

Micranthes rufidula J. K. Small (1905) [*M. aequidentata* J. K. Small (1905), *Saxifraga rufidula* (Small) Macoun (1906)]. Slightly leathery ovate, distinctly toothed blade to 3 × 2 cm with abrupt narrowing to petiole, often densely red-hairy below.

Flower stem 12 × 20 cm branched to form flat-topped inflorescence of white flowers, petals unspotted to 3.5 mm. Cascades.

Micranthes sachalinensis (Fr. Schmidt) Hara (1939) [*Saxifraga sachalinensis* Fr. Schmidt (1868)]. Small obovate leaves with toothed blade to 3 × 2 cm and 2 cm petiole. Flower stem 20–30 cm typically with 20 white flowers on ascending branches towards top. Exposed cliffs and stony slopes near sea. Sakhalin, Kuril Islands.

Micranthes tenuis (Wahlenberg) J. K. Small (1905) [*Saxifraga tenuis* (Wahlenburg) H. Smith ex Lindman (1918)]. Small version of *M. nivalis* with leaf blade up to 1.5 cm and flower stem to 12 cm. Circumboreal Arctic.

Micranthes texana (Buckley) J. K. Small (1903) [*Saxifraga texana* Buckley (1861)]. Broad leaf blade to 2 × 1 cm. Flower stem to 15 cm with compact inflorescence sometimes with more than one cluster with white flowers, petals 2–3.5 mm. Sandy or rocky ground. Missouri and Kansas to Texas.

Micranthes tischii (Skelly) Brouillet & Gornall (2008) [*Saxifraga tischii* Skelly (1988)]. Rosette of red-backed, toothed leaves up to about 2 × 1 cm. Flower stem to 3 cm with up to 5 or 6 greenish-yellow persistent petals, 3 × 1.5 mm. Very rare and very local. Shaded north-facing sites at high altitudes. Olympic Mountains and Vancouver Island.

Micranthes virginiensis (Michaux) J. K. Small (1903) [*Saxifraga virginiensis* Michaux (1803)]. Basal rosette of rhomboid-bladed, slightly toothed, leaves, up to about 8 cm. Flower stem 6–50 cm with branched terminal cluster of pure white flowers, petals 3–6 mm. May be found in very large numbers. Woodland. Eastern North America.

Saxifraga yezoensis (Franchet) Engler (1916). Obovate, irregularly toothed, thin-textured leaves up to 5 × 3 cm with short petiole. Flower stem 5–30 cm with branched inflorescence, petals white, clawed, to 4 mm. Japan, Kuril Islands, Sakhalin.

Series *Micranthes*

Ovaries inferior to semi-inferior, broad nectary disc.

Micranthes apetala (Piper) J. K. Small (1905) [*Saxifraga apetala* Piper (1900)]. Ovate leaves 2–5 cm with petiole. Flower stem 6–15 cm. Ovoid or cylindrical cluster of flowers. Petals usually absent. Wet places. 600–2800m, Washington and Montana.

Micranthes aprica (Greene) J. K. Small (1905) [*Saxifraga aprica* Greene (1896)]. Obovate or elliptic leaves 2–5 cm with petiole. Flower stem 6–15 cm. Capitate cluster of flowers. Narrow white petals to 3 mm. Meadows and rocky places. 1700–4500m, Oregon, California and Nevada.

Micranthes californica (Greene) J. K. Small (1905) [*M. napensis* J. K. Small (1905), *M. fallax* (Greene) J. K. Small (1905), *M. parvifolia* (Greene) J. K. Small (1905), *Saxifraga californica* Greene (1889)]. Crenate or toothed, ovate leaf blade 2–5 cm with petiole of similar length. Flower stem 10–25 cm with white flowers in loose inflorescence, petals 2.5–4.5 mm. Damp or shady sites. Oregon and California.

Micranthes fragosa (Suksdorf) J. K. Small (1905) [*Saxifraga claytoniaefolia* Canby ex Small (1896)]. Similar to *M. nidifica* in which it is sometimes included but with a looser conical inflorescence, very slightly larger flowers. Grows on wet cliffs or hillsides. Washington and Oregon.

Micranthes hieracifolia (Waldstein & Kitaibel ex Willdenow) Haworth (1821) [*Saxifraga hieracifolia* Waldstein & Kitaibel (1799)]. Cluster of upright elliptic leaves up to 6 × 3 cm tapering toward base. Flower stem typically 20–35 cm with clusters, or column, of starry dark red flowers, petals narrow, often pointed, to 3 mm. Damp ground and tundra. Circumboreal subArctic and Arctic.

Micranthes hitchcockiana (Elvander) Brouillet & Gornall (2008) [*Saxifraga hitchcockiana* Elvander (1984)]. Elliptic leaf blade 4–10 cm, usually broadly toothed, narrowing to broad petiole. Flower stem to 15 cm with flat-topped inflorescence. Flowers white, petals 2–5 mm. Ledges and wet rocks. Northwest Oregon.

Micranthes integrifolia (Hooker) J. K. Small (1905) [*Saxifraga integrifolia* Hooker (1833)]. Rosette of oval to round leaves to 4 × 3 cm with flower stem to 20 cm with a terminal cluster of flowers in variable inflorescence. Petals white, to 4 mm. Bulbiliferous. Moist places. British Columbia to California.

Micranthes nidifica (Greene) J. K. Small (1905) [*M. montana* Small (1905), *Saxifraga columbiana* Piper (1900), *Saxifraga nidifica* Greene (1893)]. Rosette of thick rhomboid-bladed leaves to about 3 cm. Flower stem to 20 cm with small, dense, terminal cylindrical cluster of very small white flowers, petals to no more than 2 mm. Open meadows in pine woods. Cascades.

Micranthes oregana (Howell) J. K. Small (1905) [*M. montanensis* (Small) Small (1905), *Saxifraga oregana* Howell (1895)]. Cluster of narrow oblong upright leaves 10–25 cm. Densely flowered inflorescence up

to 60 cm, broadly columnar, but with some branches lower down. Flowers in clusters with narrow petals, white, to 4 mm. Marshes and meadows. Widespread in Rocky Mountains.

Micranthes pensylvanica (Linnaeus) Haworth (1821) [*Saxifraga pensylvanica* Linnaeus (1753)]. Rosette of untoothed, narrowly ovate, light green leaves typically 12 cm long. Tall strong flower stem, up to 75 cm with clusters of small pale green flowers, petals to 3 mm, with brown stamens. Eastern North America.

Micranthes rhomboidea (Greene) J. K. Small (1905) [*Saxifraga rhomboidea* Greene (1898)]. Leaf blade rhomboid or broadly ovate, 1–3 cm with short petiole. Flower stem to 20 cm. Small white flowers in dense small head, petals to 4 mm. Rocky Mountains from Montana south.

Micranthes subapetala (E. E. Nelson) J. K. Small (1905) [*Saxifraga subapetala* E. E. Nelson (1899)]. Yellowstone saxifrage. Cluster of upright elliptic leaves up to 12.5 × 2.5 cm. Dense column of flowers up to about 45 cm. Individual flowers usually without petals but with obvious nectary disc. If present then pink-purple, no more than 2 mm. Bogs and damp meadow. Idaho, Wyoming and Montana.

Micranthes tempestiva (Elvander & Denton) Brouillet & Gornall (2008) [*Saxifraga tempestiva* Elvander & Denton (1976)]. Rosette leaves up to 1 cm tapering to broad petiole Flower stem 3–8 cm with small terminal cluster of very small white flowers, petals about 1 mm. Local in Rocky Mountains centred on Anaconda Range.

Zhmylev also maintains as separate species *M. fallax* (Greene) Small and *M. parvifolia* (Greene) Small which are here included in *M. californica* Greene; and he also maintains *M. ×ursina* Siplivinsky (1976) (*M. hieracifolia* × *M. nivalis*).

Section *Arabisa* (Sternberg) Gornall

(*Saxifraga* section *Micranthes* subsection *Stellares* (Engler & Irmscher) Gornall)

Micranthes bryophora (A. Gray) Brouillet & Gornall (2008) [*Saxifraga bryophora* A. Gray (1865)]. A small species from California close to *M. foliolosa* with some flower buds replaced by leafy ones. Flowers white, petals with 2 yellow spots, to 5 mm. An annual var. *tobiasiae* has been identified in the Payette National Forest, Idaho. Previously ascribed to

M. foliolosa. Branches of the inflorescence tend to bend downwards.

Micranthes clusii (Gouan) Gornall (2008) [*Saxifraga clusii* Gouan (1773)]. Similar to *M. petiolaris* (*S. michauxii*) with toothed, narrowly oblong or cuneate, light green leaves. Flower stem typically 15–20 cm, with many-flowered, usually lax inflorescence. The flowers are typical of the subsection with 3 clawed and spotted petals and 2 unspotted and unclawed, petals to 7 × 2.5 mm. France and Spain.

Micranthes ferruginea (Graham) Brouillet & Gornall (2008) [*Saxifraga ferruginea* Graham (1829)]. Very variable in size. Leaves typically 2–5 cm usually softly hairy, light green, oblong with broadly toothed apex. Flower stem from 10–50 cm with 10–100 flowers. Flowers with 3+2 arrangement of white petals, 3 clawed with two yellow spots and 2 unclawed and unspotted, petals to 5 mm. Easy from seed. Moist and rocky places. Cascades and Rocky Mountains.

Micranthes foliolosa (R. Brown) Gornall (2008) [*Saxifraga foliolosa* R. Brown (1823)]. Close to *M. stellaris* but with solitary rosettes, smaller bracts, and leafy bulbiferous buds replacing most flowers except terminal one. Petals narrower than in *M. stellaris*. Pan-Arctic and Rocky Mountains.

Micranthes laciniata (Nakai & Takeda) Gornall & H. Ohba (2000) [*Saxifraga laciniata* Nakai & Takeda (1914)]. Wedge-shaped leaves typically up to 3 cm long and 0.5–1.0 cm wide and deeply slashed around the broad tip. Inflorescence up to about 15 cm with 5–8 flowers. White, yellow-spotted, clawed petals about 6 × 2.5 mm. Meadows and rocks. 2300–2600m, Japan and Korea.

Saxifraga michauxii. See *Micranthes petiolaris*.

Micranthes petiolaris (Rafinesque) Brouillet & Gornall (2008) [*Saxifraga michauxii* Britton (1894), *S. leucanthemifolia* Michaux (1803)]. Basal leaves and bracts on the flower stem are dramatically toothed with the basal leaves being around 8 cm long. The leaves have a water-repellent surface. The inflorescence can be multi-branched, broadly pyramidal, with lower branches quite widely angled from the main stem. Flowers white with 3+2 arrangement. Petals white, yellow-spotted, to about 3 mm. In a large specimen there may be up to around 100 flowers in an inflorescence. Dripping rocks. Southern Appalachians.

Micranthes redofskyi Adams (1834). Treated by some authors as *M. foliolosa* var. *multiflora*, this is rather taller, and has a more branching stem with a fully developed terminal flower on each branch. Found in coastal sites on either side of the Bering Straits.

Micranthes stellaris (Linnaeus) Galasso, Banfi & Soldano (2005) [*M. engleri* (Dalla Torre) Galasso, Banfi & Soldano (2005), *Saxifraga stellaris* Linnaeus (1753)]. Starry saxifrage. Mats or tufts of oblong leaves to 7 × 2 cm , with 2 or 3 teeth at apical margin. Flower stem up to 15 cm with 5–15 white flowers. All 5 petals usually similar, clawed, white, with two yellow spots at bases, to 8 × 3 mm. Pink ovary often makes flowers look pink from a distance. European mountains (including Britain) to arctic Canada. Usually by running water over acid rocks. Among many subtaxa which have been described and seem still to be supported are:

subsp. *stellaris* var. *gemmifera*
subsp. *engleri* (Dalla Torre) Gornall (subsp. *alpigena*, subsp. *robusta*)
subsp. *alpigena* var. *prolifera*

Section *Calthophyllum* (A. M. Johnson) Gornall

(Includes *Saxifraga* section *Micranthes* subsections *Rotundifoliatae* A. M. Johnson and *Cuneifoliatae* A. M. Johnson)

Micranthes astilbeoides (Losinskaja) Gornall & H. Ohba (2008) [*Saxifraga astilbeoides* Losinskaja (1939)]. Obscure. Russian Far East.

Micranthes atrata (Engler) Losinskaja (1928) [*Saxifraga atrata* Engler (1883)]. Leaves with ovate crenate blade up to 2.5 × 1.8 cm on petiole up to 2 cm. Flower stem 7–23 cm with cylindrical inflorescence of 7–25 flowers. White petals clawed, overlapping, 3.2 × 2 mm. Meadows and rocks. 3000–4200m, China (Gansu & Qinghai).

Saxifraga benzilanensis H. Chuang (2001). Stems 15–25 cm, up to 10 flowers. Leaves ovate to 3 × 2.5 cm, margin crenate, upper surface white hairy, glabrous below, petiole to 5 cm. Petals white or pink 2.0 × 0.5 mm. 3200m, Yunnan.

Micranthes brachypetala (Malyschev) Gornall & H. Ohba (2008) [*Saxifraga brachypetala* Malyschev (1960)]. Leaves have broadly elliptic blade 0.4 × 0.2 cm narrowing to petiole at base. Stem, 1–3 cm, has 2–5 slightly nodding flowers up to 3 mm long with pale to pink reddish-violet petals slightly shorter than sepals. Eastern Siberia.

Micranthes calycina (Sternberg) Brouillet & Gornall (2008) [*Saxifraga calycina* Sternberg (1831)]. Leaves obovate-cuneate up to 4.5 × 1.2 cm, with coarsely toothed apex, narrowing at base to broad petiole. Flower stem 3–15 cm with flowers on simple branches in narrowly conical inflorescence. Flowers are white to pink with petals up to 2.5 mm. Narrow capsules. Siberia and Alaska.

Micranthes clavistaminea (Engler & Irmscher) Losinskaja (1928) [*Saxifraga clavistaminea* Engler & Irmscher (1912)]. Spathulate, serrate, leaves, oblong-ovate, 2.2 × 1.5 cm. Flower stem 4–6 cm with inflorescence of 2–3 flowers with white, short-clawed, petals with 2 yellow and 3 purple spots, 4.5 × 2 mm. Clavate filaments. Forests and rocky valleys. 2300–2600m, China: Sichuan, Yunnan.

Micranthes davidii (Franchet) Losinskaja (1928) [*Saxifraga davidii* Franchet (1886), includes *S. birostris* Engler & Irmscher (1914)]. Spathulate, serrate leaves up to 8 × 4 cm. Flower stem 7.5–30 cm with inflorescence of 7–30 flowers. Petals white with yellow spot, 3.4 × 1.4 mm, with brown anthers and clavate filaments. Rock crevices. 1500–2400m, China (Sichuan) and Burma.

Micranthes davurica (Willdenow) Small (1905) [*Saxifraga davurica* Willdenow (1799)]. This species has been much confused with *M. calycina* and *M. unalaschensis* but it has smaller flowers with petals only 3 × 1.5 mm, smaller and narrower than in the North American species. Confined to eastern Siberia.

Micranthes divaricata (Engler & Irmscher) Gornall & H. Ohba (2000) [*Saxifraga divaricata* Engler & Irmscher (1914)]. Height 3.7–10 cm. Leaves with ovate blade, which may be serrate, up to 2.4 × 1.3 with petiole up to 3 cm. Inflorescence 5–14 flowers, spreading branches. Petals white, 2.6 × 1.3 mm, anthers and ovaries purple, filaments subulate. Damp meadows and marshes. 3400–4500m, China (Qinghai, Sichuan) and Tibet.

Micranthes dungbooii (Engler & Irmscher) Gornall & H. Ohba (2000) [*Saxifraga dungbooii* Engler & Irmscher (1914)]. Leaves with oblong entire blade up to 1.5 × 0.7 cm on petiole up to 3 cm. Flower stem 8–12 cm with inflorescence with 3–7 white flowers. Petals short-clawed up to 7 × 3.5 mm. Filaments subulate. Ovary dark purple. China, Tibet, Sikkim.

Micranthes fusca (Maximovich) Hara ex Gornall & H. Ohba (2008) [*Saxifraga fusca* Maximovich (1872) and includes *S. kikubuki* Sennen (ca.1933) and S. ×*tolmatchevii* Zhmylev (1995)]. Crenate reniform blade 3–6 cm on 7–18 cm petiole. Flower stem 8–20 cm tall with a branched conical inflorescence up to 5

cm across with small, dusky red (*fusca*), starry-petalled flowers, sometimes very numerous. Damp ground. To 2800m, Japan. Two varieties have been described: var. *kikubuki* and var. *kiusiana*.

Micranthes gageana (W. W. Smith) Gornall & H. Ohba (2000) [*Saxifraga gageana* W. W. Smith (1911)]. Height 2–8 cm. Leaves with ovate blade up to 3 cm on petiole up to twice as long. Up to 3 flowers on the stem. Red petals up to 3.5 × 3.5 mm. Anthers and ovary purple. 4200–4750m, Sikkim and probably Tibet.

Micranthes japonica (de Boissieu) Hara (1939) [*Saxifraga japonica* de Boissieu (1897)]. Serrate leaf blade up to 9 × 10 cm on petiole to 50 cm. Flower stems to 60 cm with an inflorescence of upward-facing branches in top 20 cm. Small white flowers, white petals with yellow basal spot(s). Wetlands. Japan.

Micranthes lyallii (Engler) J. K. Small (1905) [*Saxifraga lyallii* Engler (1869)]. Cuneate-spathulate leaves up to 4 cm with broad petiole about 4 cm. Blade with forward-facing teeth making leaves appear fan-shaped. Flower stem to 30 cm with small flowers, held rather awkwardly on stiff branches. Rounded white petals, to 5 mm, clawed, with two green or yellow basal spots. Ovaries dark red towards tip. Running water or bog. Alaska and Yukon to Montana and Washington.

Micranthes manchuriensis (Engler) Gornall & H. Ohba (2000) [*Saxifraga manchuriensis* (Engler) Komarov (1904)]. Circular blade to 8 cm on petiole to 30 cm. White flowers with stamens longer than petals, to 5.5 mm, in compact inflorescence on stem up to 40 cm. Meadows and rocks. Korea, Russia.

Micranthes melaleuca (Fischer) Losinskaja (1928) [*Saxifraga melaleuca* Fischer (1808)]. Leaves with broadly ovate blade up to 2.3 × 1.8 cm, dentate at apex with narrow petiole twice length of blade. Flower stem 10–23 cm with inflorescence of 5–10 flowers on short branches. Petals are white, up to 4 × 1.8 mm. Ovary dark purple. SubArctic Asia.

Micranthes melanocentra (Franchet) Losinskaja (1928) [*Saxifraga melanocentra* Franchet (1896), *S. pseudopallida* Engler & Irmscher (1914), *S. sulphurascens* Handel-Mazzetti (1929)]. Very variable. Leaf shape and size varies up to 4 × 2 cm. Flower stem 3.5–22 cm with 2–17 flowers. Petals broad, overlapping, clawed, usually white (sometimes red) with 2 large yellow spots at base, 3 × 2 mm to 6 × 5 mm. Ovary large and black. Meadows, crevices, bogs. 3000–5300m, China, Bhutan India, Nepal. The variability probably includes two other taxa, *M. gageana* W. W. Smith and *M. paludosa* J. Anthony.

Micranthes nelsoniana (D. Don) J. K. Small (1905) [*Saxifraga nelsoniana* D. Don (1821), *S. reniformis* Ohwi (1931)]. Leaf blade more or less circular from 2 × 3 cm to 8 × 9 cm with roundly toothed margin. Petiole up to 4 times longer than blade. Flower stem to 30 cm with head of pure white flowers, rounded petals about 3 × 2 mm, with green ovary and red-brown anthers on clavate white filaments. Leaves vary in size, thickness and hairiness in different varieties, as does the form of the inflorescence. Alpine tundra, rocky ground, shaded damp rocks. Siberia to Cascades.

var. *nelsoniana*. Thickened pubescent leaves and dense flower head. Siberia and northern Alaska.

var. *aestivalis*. Looser inflorescence. Northern European Russia to Alaska.

var. *carlottae*. Queen Charlotte Islands.

var. *cascadensis*. Larger thinner leaves, much looser inflorescence. Cascades and Olympic Mountains.

var. *insularis*. Smaller leaves. Aleutian Islands.

var. *pacifica*. Small leaves. Gulf of Alaska.

var. *porsildiana*. Very small thicker leaves. Eastern Alaska and Yukon.

var. *reniformis* [*S. reniformis*]. Usually treated as a variety of *M. nelsoniana*. Rocky ground. Sakhalin, Kuril Islands.

var. *tateyamensis*. Japan.

Micranthes odontoloma (Piper) A. A. Heller (1912) [*Saxifraga odontoloma* Piper (1901)]. Leaves with round toothed blade typically 5 cm diameter on 15 cm petiole. Scattered small flowers on diffuse inflorescence up to 60 cm, with white, greenish-yellow-spotted, circular, clawed, petals which are often swept back, 2–4 mm. Hybridizes with *M. lyallii* where they overlap. Stream edges and wet rocky slopes. Cascades and Rocky Mountains south to California and New Mexico.

Micranthes pallida (Wallich ex Seringe) Losinskaja (1928) [*Saxifraga pallida* Wallich ex Seringe (1828), *S. clavistamineoides* T. C. Ku (1989), *S. leptarrhenifolia* Engler & Irmscher (1914), *S. pallidiformis* Engler (1922)]. Very variable. Leaves are oblong-ovate. Flower stem 3.5–35 cm tall with 4–13 flowers with white petals, 4 × 2 mm with two yellow spots. Stamens purple, clavate filaments. Clearings, meadows, crevices. 3000–5000m, China, India, Nepal, Bhutan.

Micranthes paludosa (J. Anthony) Gornall & H. Ohba (2000) [*Saxifraga paludosa* J. Anthony (1933)]. Height up to 5 cm. Entire lanceolate leaves with blade 0.7 × 0.3 cm and petiole as long as blade. Solitary flowers with obovate white petals, 5 × 3 mm, with two yellow spots at base. Anthers coral-red. China: Yunnan.

Micranthes parvula (Engler & Irmscher) Losinskaja (1928) [*Saxifraga parvula* Engler & Irmscher (1912)]. Height 2.7–4 cm. Oblong-ovate leaves, 2.7 × 1.2 cm. Usually one flower per stem. White short-clawed petals with 2 yellow spots at base, 3.2 × 2.5 mm. Clavate filaments, ovary tinged purple. Meadow and crevices. 3800–5700m, China: northwest Yunnan.

Micranthes pluviarum (W. W. Smith) Gornall & H. Ohba (2008) [*Saxifraga pluviarum* W. W. Smith (1913)]. Leaves with ovate-elliptic blade, may be slightly dentate, up to 1.5 × 0.8 cm narrowing to petiole. Flower stem up to 7 cm with branches carrying a solitary very small white flower and 4–8 very small green or purple bulbils. Sikkim. Note: the bulbils are uncharacteristic of species in section *Calthophyllum* and suggest that it may be misplaced here.

Saxifraga pseudoparvula H. Chuang (2001). Flower stem 3–6 cm, 1–3 flowers. Ovate or triangular-ovate leaves 0.5 × 0.4 cm, margin slightly serrate, densely softly hairy, petiole to 1.0 cm. Petals white to 2 mm, short-clawed. 3800–4700m, Yunnan.

Micranthes purpurascens (Komarov) Komarov (1929) [*Saxifraga purpurascens* Komarov (1914)]. Round toothed blade typically 4 × 3 cm on 12 cm petiole. Stem 10–30 cm with 10–80 flowers on widely branched inflorescence. Flowers and whole inflorescence stained bright red. Open and rocky ground. 900–1500m, Russian Far East: Kamchatka, Sakhalin.

Micranthes razshivinii (Zhmylev) Brouillet & Gornall (2008) [*Saxifraga razshivinii* (Zhmylev (1990)]. Close to *M. unalaschensis* with larger flowers and capsules than in *M. calycina*. Replaces these two species in northeastern Alaska and Yukon.

Micranthes rubriflora (Harry Smith) Gornall & H. Ohba (2008) [*Saxifraga rubriflora* Harry Smith (1960)]. Like a small *M. gageana*, no more than 2 cm high with a dense rosette of broadly cuneate leaves about 0.7 cm broad and long. Solitary flowers on stems less than 1 cm. Petals 2.5 × 1.5 mm, and the whole flower (calyx, corolla and ovaries) is rich red. Bhutan.

Micranthes spicata (D. Don) J. K. Small (1905) [*Saxifraga spicata* D. Don (1821)]. Leaves with rounded, thickened, hairy blade up to 15 cm with petiole to 30 cm. Flower stem 15–70 cm with a narrow inflorescence (like a spike) of white flowers, petals to 4.5 mm, yellow spotted. Tundra and among rocks. Alaska and Yukon.

Micranthes tilingiana (Regel & Tiling) Komarov (1929) [*Saxifraga tilingiana* Regel & Tiling (1859)]. Leaves with ovate blade up to 2.0 × 1.6 cm, may be slightly toothed at apex, petiole twice as long as blade. Flowers on many-flowered stem, 15–22 cm tall, with 4 or 5 branches carrying 3–8 flowers. Petals white up to 4 × 2 mm. Siberia.

Micranthes unalaschensis (Sternberg) Gornall & H. Ohba (2008) [*Saxifraga unalaschensis* Sternberg (1831), *M. flabellifolia* (R. Brown) Small (1905)]. Differs from *M. calycina* in having broader leaves, broader inflorescence with wide branching and much fatter capsules. Flowers pink-white. Western Alaska and Aleutian Islands.

Micranthes zekoensis (J. T. Pan) Gornall & H. Ohba (2000) [*Saxifraga zekoensis* J. T. Pan (1978)]. Leaves with ovate serrate blade with acute apex up to 3 × 1.4 cm with petiole up to 2.5 cm. Flower stem to 19 cm with 21–29 flowers with white-pink clawed petals up to 3 × 1.3 mm. Ovary dark purple. Meadows. 3000m, China: Qinghai.

Sectional placing unclear

Saxifraga jamalensis Zhmylev & Razzhivin (2000). Described from arctic Siberia as a allopolyploid hybrid species deriving from *M. nivalis* × *S. aestivalis*. This is fascinating if correct as the parental species are in different sections, *M. nivalis* in section *Micranthes* and *S. aestivalis* (*M. nelsoniana* subsp. *aestivalis*) in section *Calthophyllum*, and this is the first such recorded hybrid species.

Micranthes lumpuensis (Engler) Losinskaja (1928) [*Saxifraga lumpuensis* Engler (1922)]. Ovate serrate leaves up to 2.5 × 2.1 cm on petiole up to 5 cm. Inflorescence cylindrical on stem 5–27 cm with 11–56 flowers with bracts up to the size of the basal leaves. Petals red/purple, short-clawed, lanceolate, 3.4 × 1.0 mm. Filaments subulate. Description and illustration suggest this is not unlike *M. hieracifolia* but with petiolate leaves and leafy bracts. Meadows and

clearings. 3500–4100m, China: Gansu, Sichuan.

Micranthes nudicaulis (D. Don) Gornall & H. Ohba (2008) [*Saxifraga nudicaulis* D. Don (1822)]. Very distinctive with running stems which root at nodes in its very damp habitat. Thick, prominently toothed, semicircular leaf blade with narrow petiole. Flowers on branched inflorescence up to about 10 cm with perhaps 4–10 flowers. Pretty flowers have white petals, 4 × 2 mm, and white ovary which turns pinkish-red on pollination. Siberia to Alaska.

Saxifraga svetlanae Voroschilov (1977). Stems to 15 cm, leaves to 3 × 2 cm, petioles twice as long. Petals pale yellow 2 × 1.5 mm. Russia: Kabarovsk.

Obscure species

Saxifraga cismagadanica Malyschev (1988). Probably section *Calthophyllum*. Russian Far East.

Micranthes gaspensis (Fernald) J. K. Small (1918) [*Saxifraga gaspensis* Fernald (1917)]. Probably best included in *M. nelsoniana*.

Micranthes kermodei (Harry Smith ex Wadhwa) Gornall & H. Ohba (2008) [*Saxifraga kermodei* H. Smith ex Wadwha (1983)]. Burma. Probably section *Calthophyllum*.

Saxifraga korshinskii Komarov (1900). Excluded by Zhmylev (1996).

Saxifraga lamashanensis Hao (1936). Type specimen lost—may be *Saxifraga* section *Ciliatae* species *S. tangutica*.

Saxifraga punctata. As used by Linnaeus this is *Micranthes davurica*; as used by Sternberg it refers to *M. nelsoniana*. Such confusion means that its use should be consigned to history.

Saxifraga selemdzhensis Gorovoi & Voroschilov (1966). Excluded by Zhmylev (1996).

Saxifraga sichotensis Gorovoj & N. S. Pavlova (1970). Discussed in chapter on *Saxifraga* section *Irregulares* but may be properly placed here.

Saxifraga sieversiana Sternberg (1831). Excluded by Zhmylev (1996) as not belonging to *Micranthes*.

Saxifraga staminosa Schlotg. & Voroschilov (1972). Probably section *Calthophyllum*. Eastern Siberia.

Part 4 · Gardening with Saxifrages

18 · Saxifrages in the Garden

With the exception of one or two species which can be found in subtropical zones or in the southern hemisphere, saxifrages come from across the temperate and alpine zones of the northern hemisphere. So they fit very well into the gardens of American, European, and Japanese gardeners: most of our garden plants have a similar heritage. But gardens vary dramatically in the conditions they naturally offer plants. Year-round temperature variation, day–night variation, rainfall levels and pattern, all come together with soil types, latitude and light levels to form the particular environmental context. But for the gardener, this is just a starting point. And just as gardens come in all sorts of shapes and sizes, so to do gardeners.

At one end of the spectrum are people who garden in their allotted space, with its natural limitations, fitting in saxifrages as and where they can within the constraints of the existing conditions; at the other end are the enthusiasts who will move earth (if not heaven) to accommodate all the saxifrages they possibly can. These people will be preoccupied with all the minutiae of hardiness zones, soil type, rainfall, exposure, watering, drainage and winter protection. They're the ones most likely to provide increasingly artificial growing conditions: from pots and troughs through raised beds, sand-beds, tufa walls and rock gardens. They will want an alpine house to keep off the rain. Fanatics may set the alpine house down into the ground so that the temperature of the material in the plunge beds is buffered against extremes and fluctuations of temperature, and might even have a refrigerated bench. These are collectors rather than gardeners—if they don't have the right habitat they build it. Whether it blends in with the wider garden is not important: it's not constructed to blend in, it's constructed for the plants.

Most enthusiastic gardeners fall somewhere between these two extremes: after all, any garden is an artificial construct where we adapt the natural world to suit our own needs and tastes.

Saxifrages in the tapestry of the author's rock garden. The mossy saxifrage *Saxifraga* 'Wallacei', with its enormous and luscious flowers, and silver saxifrage *Saxifraga* 'Esther', together with sedums, erodium and campanula in the background.

The Saxifrage Calendar

The saxifrage year is a long one: in temperate England it is possible to have a collection of saxifrages flowering right through the calendar from January to December—plants for all seasons. The five most common types are, in order of flowering: section *Porphyrion* (dwarf cushion saxifrages) from late January to April; section *Saxifraga* (mossy saxifrages) from April onwards; section *Ligulatae* (silver saxifrages) flowering in May and June; section *Gymnopera* (London pride saxifrages) in July, and section *Irregulares* (autumn-flowering saxifrages) completing the season. The earliest of these *Irregulares*, *Saxifraga nipponica*, is in flower during May but others will flower in late summer and into autumn, with the very latest being various forms of *S. fortunei*, which may not come into flower until late November or early December. Others from the genus such as *Saxifraga rotundifolia*, which flowers at the same time as London pride saxifrages, contribute to the garden flora, as do many from the wider saxifrage family, but these five types make a wonderful starter. The *Porphyrion* and *Irregulares* are less often grown by the beginner, but they extend the season dramatically, and contain some of the great beauties of the saxifrage world—while specialists, of course, can get hooked on anything. In most years there is a winter break between the last of the *Irregulares* to flower and the first of the *Porphyrion*, but it is far from a dead season.

Saxifrages serve the winter garden well. Even in the coldest winters, while there are reminders of the old season, special rewards are reserved for winter. The evergreen cushions of silver and dwarf cushion saxifrages have their naturally encrusted foliage dramatized by frosts, while the rosettes of mossy saxifrages are disclosed in a new clarity. And then, from the heart of winter, there is the renewed promise of the fresh season—saxifrages do furnish the year.

Last year's silver saxifrage seed heads poking out through the snow.

Frost emphasizes the variety of form among a group of silver and dwarf cushion saxifrages.

Questions of Hardiness and Location

Although the saxifrage year can be a long one, the exact timing of flowering, and the plants which can be grown in a particular garden, will depend on a number of things and local conditions are one of these. The particular habitats available in the garden will provide a variety of conditions of shade, sun, moisture and drainage which need to be considered, but the climate of a particular locale is obviously significant.

Most saxifrages can be classified as hardy perennials. Many can survive very low temperatures, long winters and months of snow-cover. More problematic for many species will be excess heat or drought, and their survival can be enhanced by judicious choices and intelligent gardening. Summer shading, watering systems and provision of cooling are all possible strategies.

The USDA Plant Hardiness Zones are concerned with average annual minimum temperature as the critical factor. This gives:

z9 minimum temperatures +20°F to +30°F (−6.6°C to −1.2°C)
z8 minimum temperatures +10°F to +20°F (−12.2°C to −6.7°C)
z7 minimum temperatures 0°F to +10°F (−17.7°C to −12.3°C)
z6 minimum temperatures −10°F to 0°F (−23.3°C to −17.8°C)
z5 minimum temperatures −20°F to −10°F (−28.8°C to −23.4°C)
z4 minimum temperatures −30°F to −20°F (−34.4°C to −28.9°C)

Calculated for continental North America, these ratings work less well in other places—such as Britain with its maritime climate.

East Yorkshire, where I garden, is rated as equivalent to z9. This means that it has mild winters, moderated by closeness to the sea, and it also has cool summers—although this is all offset by its being a low-rainfall area. It is rather startling to find that in North America z9 areas are Florida, southern coastal Texas, and western California, all of which have much hotter summers than mine. It is also important to recognize that for most saxifrages summer maxima will be at least as important as winter minima. Most of Britain is z8, as are Belgium and the Netherlands; most of Germany, Denmark and coastal Scandinavia are classified as z7; most of the Czech Republic and Slovakia are z6. And all of these are countries in which saxifrages are grown very successfully. In southern Europe, the Mediterranean coasts are generally classified as z10: only the most drought-adapted of the bulbous mossy saxifrage species would be found in such areas, and even then only rarely.

Saxifrages can be grown from z4 to z9— not all of them in all the zones, but many of them in most of the zones. In the colder zones protection may be needed in winter, although snow cover will often provide that protection. In summer, however, temperatures above +90°F (+32°C) will prove difficult for saxifrages, particularly if they are sustained and if night-time temperatures are not much lower.

Two geographical features have great effects on this picture: maritime influences and altitude. In high mountains temperatures may be high during the day but, with thinner air, fall dramatically at night. This drop may be moderated or exaggerated by the closeness or remoteness of sea or ocean, more continental climates usually having a greater fall in temperature from day to night than maritime ones. This day–night temperature gradient has a number of effects: rainfall may be a common afternoon phenomenon in high mountains, and the rapid cooling of the ground may lead to heavy dew at night. Both will greatly ameliorate the stresses of high daytime temperatures.

Exposure (aspect and shade), soil make-up and precipitation each play a part in contributing to the overall health of a plant. Plants that are fully exposed at high altitudes may well need to be planted out of full day-long sun at lower altitudes, or be given some summer shading, to lessen heat stress. They may also need enhanced watering in the evening, which will itself also help cooling.

Another consideration is that although saxifrages can cope with long cold winters, they may cope far less well with long wet winters. Some groups such as London pride saxifrages and many mossy saxifrages have no problem with winter wet. However others, such as the silver saxifrages and the dwarf cushion saxifrages, will suffer unless given enhanced drainage. Growing plants in tufa also helps avoid waterlogging. Unfortunately, giving a plant a well-drained spot, to deal with excess wet, can also entail the need to water during summer. While many growers use a hose or watering-can, the more dedicated may construct elaborate computerized watering systems with individual watering points, or a leaky hose.

Garden Habitats for Saxifrages

Most people think of saxifrages as rock-garden plants and many of them are just that—plants from mountain areas, often small, and usually spring-flowering. But lots of saxifrages can flourish in quite other parts of the garden: shaded borders, open flower beds, lawns and damp spots. Each of these echoes a natural habitat—a couple of shrubs and a small tree is a mini-woodland; a lawn replicates grazed grassland; longer grass around a tree mimics a tiny patch of ungrazed meadow; a rockery creates a tiny piece of mountain rock-face or alpine pavement—and each can provide a niche for saxifrages.

Some people, of course, already have particular habitats—wooded areas crying out for drifts of American native woodland saxifrages, or a damp patch by a stream where *Saxifraga aquatica*, *S. hirculus* or *Micranthes stellaris* might be possible. But this outline starts by considering the average gardener and the "average" garden— usually a more-or-less rectangular plot adjacent to the house. Our back garden is about 50 feet by 70 feet (15 metres by 20 metres), and our front garden is much smaller and mostly drive and hard-standing. So this is very much the kind of space that many people have available. Our previous garden was less than a quarter of the size. But saxifrages are small plants that are well suited to small gardens.

Shade

The conditions in the shady border mean that the saxifrages that are happy there will usually be plants from deciduous woodland or woodland margins. In the wild they may get reasonable amounts of light in winter when there are no leaves on the trees (saxifrages do not usually grow in coniferous forests) but they will spend most of the year quite well shaded, or perhaps in dappled light. This may not be the case in the garden. In our own garden the border that gets most shade is in the lee of a conifer hedge at the northern boundary of our neighbours' garden. In winter the ground sees no sun for around six months, but from spring through summer the sun rises so much earlier and gets so much higher in the sky that it gradually reaches over the hedge to the border below. It is worth being conscious that areas shaded in winter may be exposed in summer when plants may need shade most.

Most of the saxifrages you might grow in shady parts of the garden tend to prefer dappled shade, or sun for only part of the day, rather than the very dark corners in full shade. They tend not to flower very early (the preserve of woodland bulbs and a few small trees), usually flowering around April to June in the case of the London pride saxifrages. These will cope with quite heavy shade, and a selection of forms will provide contrasting foliage. Then later the *Irregulares* saxifrages flower on until the frosts cut them down.

You can extend the range with some leafy species from North America. *Saxifraga mertensiana*, for example, with its leathery leaves and fascinating branched flower stems with white flowers and tiny red bulbils, is hardly typical, but can set the grower off in a whole new direction. *Micranthes virginiensis* is another species at home on shady woodland banks. From European woodlands *Saxifraga rotundifolia* can prosper in these conditions, and among the wider family plenty of others can be added to this list, some of the *Heuchera*, *Tiarella* and *Tolmiea* among them.

Open beds and borders

An enormous range of plants are suitable for the open border—which can be planted in a range of styles reflecting different tastes, traditions and local conditions. The borders in our garden have as little earth bare as possible. One reason is to suppress weeds, but also our ground is quite heavy clay which bakes hard and gets very hot in summer if exposed directly; the other main reason is that we can never resist buying something new. At the back of the border are shrubs up to a couple of metres in height and tall perennials such as delphiniums, verbascums and hollyhocks, with clematis growing up the fence behind. None of the saxifrages proper (*Saxifraga* species) can compete with these, although some of the saxifrage

Saxifraga hostii.

Rodgersia podophylla in the gardens
at Mount Usher, Wicklow, Ireland.

family—such as *Rodgersia*, with their large dramatic leaves—can provide great contrasts in the middle ground of a border. At the front of the border saxifrages can take their place.

Mossy saxifrages and the London pride saxifrages are extremely effective as edging plants, forming ground-covering mats of foliage gently scalloping the otherwise straight edge of a path or lawn. Flowering is primarily late spring and early summer, which attracts attention before the taller plants of late summer further back in the border take precedence.

Of the silver saxifrages only *Saxifraga hostii* is really appropriate in the border. It likes a good rich soil, flowering better here than it would in a leaner soil such as that of a rockery or raised bed, and seemingly not worried by the lack of sharp drainage.

The damp garden

The damp garden may be a bog garden, the edge of a stream, a patch of permanently damp ground or just a large container with its base in a pond, but any of these can provide a habitat for some saxifrages. Few of us can manage the sphagnum bog over running water needed by species such as *Saxifraga aquatica*, or the cold running water of a high mountain rill in which the starry saxifrage, *Micranthes stellaris*, is at home. But the damp garden can provide a great home for *M. pensylvanica*, and the bog garden or pond edge would suit *M. oregana* and its close relatives. Among the wider family *Darmera peltata* is one species which will flourish in moist soil—but it will become a pretty big clump—and *Rodgersia* and *Astilbe* can also do well.

Lawns

Most gardens have some patch of grass. Some people aspire to bowling-green smoothness, but for most of us the lawn is something rather less perfectionist, grazed rather than shaved by the weekly mowing. Daisies and other weeds may have a hold but are tolerated, even enjoyed, rather than eradicated. At the base of the flowering cherry there may be some longer grass not strimmed to oblivion, as my neighbour suggests. Some saxifrages, primarily meadow plants, allow themselves to be naturalized in grass. The most obvious of these (and the one that I succeed with) is *Saxifraga granulata*, the British native meadow saxifrage. In the wild this is a plant of unimproved meadows, flowering in May and then later dying back to resting bulbils which lie dormant among the bases of the grasses. Except when the plant is nearing flowering time, the leaves sit pretty much at ground level. Seedlings from one year may be large enough to introduce into grass at the end of the following summer, although if they seem a bit small it is probably better to wait until the following spring, in other words when they are two years from seed. For most of the year the plant sits happily below the reach of the mower, but in late spring the flower stems emerge and need to be avoided. Once the plant has finished flowering and setting seed it is possible to mow over it as long as the blades are not set too low at first.

Saxifraga continentalis in drought-adapted state in late summer.

Saxifraga continentalis in flower—the same plant two years later, in spring.

The dry garden

The dry garden is of increasing interest for gardeners faced with drought, water shortages or restrictions. And some saxifrages certainly enjoy dry Mediterranean conditions. Even though we garden in a low-rainfall area I have built a sand-bed where the specifically Mediterranean *Saxifraga carpetana*, a very close relative of *S. granulata*, seems happy. *Saxifraga continentalis* is also very much at home, and a small group of *Micranthes integrifolia* seems to be establishing itself. This is essentially no more than a heap of coarse sharp sand restrained by a couple of low walls, with stones embedding the surface to help retain moisture. Another possible approach is to develop a dry gravel garden, a style that has gained great popularity in England recently, with the gravel helping minimize surface evaporation and suppress weeds. Although this has appeal, it is primarily a habitat for plants of the Mediterranean, and most of the plants that will colonize the gravel successfully will be more aggressive than saxifrages.

The rock garden

The rockery is the garden habitat for a great range of saxifrages. Raised above the general level of the surrounding garden, the rockery has better drainage; the soil should be rather leaner, and rocks provide micro-habitats with cool root-runs, shelter and shade. Small, low and slow-growing, many saxifrages need the help which such a rockery gives to survive against the quicker-growing plants that would, if given a free hand, take over. In the wild the harshness of mountain climates inhibits the growth of some plants but in most lowland gardens it is the harshness of the gardener that must serve as a substitute.

Although most mossy saxifrages can be grown in a rockery, the hybrids may prefer a fuller, less well-drained soil. Among the species, however, *Saxifraga cuneata* and *S. continentalis* are both excellent on the rock garden.

The silver saxifrages are often thought to be naturals for full sun, but most prefer some respite, particularly from direct afternoon sun. Their habitats vary widely and it is often necessary to provide rather more shade than one might expect—they are not like sempervivums, which relish full sun at any time. Among the most amenable silver saxifrages are most forms of *Saxifraga paniculata*, *S. longifolia*, the hybrids 'Carniolica' and 'Whitehill', and *S. hostii*.

The *Porphyrion* saxifrages are in many cases too small, and some too pernickety, for the open rockery, but some are magnificent rockery plants. Among the yellow-flowered hybrids the old *Saxifraga ×apiculata* cultivars such as 'Gregor Mendel' and 'Albert Einstein', some of the more robust *S. ×paulinae* cultivars such as 'Winton',

A saxifrage rock garden in central Wales in late winter.

A rock garden with silver saxifrages in early summer.

and any of the *S. ×elisabethae* cultivars are excellent plants, forming vigorous mats of foliage rather than the tight buns of many others of this type. For a brighter yellow, any of the very similar cultivars of *S. ×eudoxiana* would be suitable. Among the white-flowered hybrids, *S. ×salmonica* and *S. ×petraschii* provide some great plants, and the white *S. ×apiculata* 'Alba' is always successful. The pink-flowered cultivars need a more shaded site.

Bergenia ciliata in the rock garden.

From the wider family I particularly like *Bergenia* species (the hybrids are usually too vigorous), which grow really well at the base of a rock wall.

Rock gardens can be constructed from almost any rock. Traditionally limestone, waterworn if possible, was seen as the ideal, but today this is protected. Anyway, it confers little benefit as far as the plants are concerned, and rarely retains even the faintest hint of the magnificent limestone pavements from which it was untimely ripped. Sandstone is often used in large-scale rock gardens, such as that at Kew, and has a massy solidity, but the best approach is to use the local stone. This is the rock that can be seen in the local countryside, this is the rock which matches the local soil, this is the rock which will look most natural.

Extending the Range

While general garden habitats provide many opportunities to grow saxifrages, most people who get enthusiastic about saxifrages will find other ways to enhance their success and pleasure. Containers, specialist materials such as tufa, a specialized alpine house and automated watering systems are all part of this extended gardening toolkit.

Raised beds, and troughs

Large specialist collections of *Porphyrion* or *Ligulatae* saxifrages are best kept in raised beds, troughs or pots. All of these can provide highly adapted habitats in which to grow plants. Raised beds, at least 30 cm deep (or perhaps two or three times as much), function much like a rockery, but it is not the aesthetics of well-laid rock that are of interest, but the special conditions provided. They allow the gardener to provide plants with extra drainage, and a thick layer of grit or chippings helps prevent evaporation from the surface. Plants grown in a raised bed with free-draining soil need a lot of watering to help establish them initially, but will develop very extensive root systems which help them resist even strong direct summer sun. One of the snags of a thick layer of gravel or chippings, say 5 cm or more, is that it can be difficult to establish small plants at all, particularly if you knock surplus soil off before planting. In the short run this means that the plant will need more

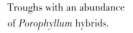

Concrete trough
planted with *Saxifraga*
×*poluanglica* seedlings.

Troughs with an abundance
of *Porophyllum* hybrids.

watering to get established, but seems in the long run to lead to healthy plants. In general I will plant new saxifrages in the raised bed in winter or very early spring. The root systems are at their most active in the spring, so I try and give them the maximum time before the summer without having too much time in the winter wet. Another approach is to build in various automated watering systems, something I keep promising myself, but have yet to do.

My favourite way of growing saxifrages, particularly the *Porphyrion* and smaller *Ligulatae*, is in troughs. For their size they provide a wonderful home for all or part of a collection. Stone troughs are great but I find the cost prohibitive, so I've now settled on shallow stoneware sinks as my favourite. I prefer those with a light brown or buff glaze, or a decorated surface. Some people cover plain old sinks with hypertufa to disguise them. Whatever the appearance of the trough, it must have a drainage hole in the bottom.

Planting up a trough is a nice combination of aesthetic and horticultural considerations. I will often lay an upturned turf in the bottom of a sink to retain moisture (in our low-rainfall area drying out is often a greater problem than getting waterlogged). My current recipe is a mixture of a proprietary loam-based compost combined with some added sand (perhaps 2:1) and then mixed about 50:50 with a sharp grit. I use a lot of rock in a trough, and wherever possible top-dress with smaller pieces of the same rock. It tends to be easier to plant while you are arranging a trough, making sure each plant is properly secure as you go rather than trying to plant them once all the rocks are in place. Planted troughs do well for quite a few years but sooner or later they will need replanting, although an annual feed of a fertilizer high in trace elements will prolong their life substantially.

Pots

Pots are the home for many saxifrages—particularly perhaps for those of us who end up with very large collections. Individual plants can be grown in a pot appropriate to their size, generally one in which they have room for at least two years' growth before repotting is needed. Each plant has its own little micro-habitat which can be fine-tuned, and the plant can be moved around—outside in the open during the summer; inside a glass-house or frame in winter; they can be moved to capture the appropriate conditions for the time of year: extra light in winter, extra shade in summer.

Those who like to plunge pots in a plunge-bed usually choose clay pots, but I find that the plant ends up with a net of fine roots over the inner surface of the pot and far fewer in the middle. I'm sure this is a result of the watering regime I employ, but it makes repotting difficult. Normally I use plastic pots; some people prefer square, but I use round ones.

I start freshly rooted cuttings in standard 5 or 6 cm pots, still known by the old sizes as 2½ inch pots, and move them up to 9 cm (3½ inch) pots. I prefer pots with round holes in the bottom rather than slots, but I have no good reason for this.

Alpine House

An alpine house—an unheated greenhouse with a lot of extra windows for ventilation— is an essential for the dedicated saxifrage grower. Pots can be kept on benches or plunged in sand. The main advantage is that the plants are sheltered from excess moisture in winter. That goes for the gardener too, who can enjoy close-up views of plants in comfort as well as having a sheltered place to work in winter. But the plants need constant watering in summer if they are kept inside. An

Pots of *Porophyllum* saxifrages in the alpine house.

A bench behind the alpine house with another part of a collection.

An alpine house need not be enormous, but it does need plenty of ventilation.

alpine house is a luxury; most saxifrages are quite happy—and many do much better—outside, but some need the protection from winter, or possibly summer, rain and some benefit from the extra shading which can be given during the summer. Various saxifrages gain from such treatment. Plants with delicate flowers which might be spoilt by the weather, such as some of the *Porophyllum* saxifrages in subtle pastel shades, can be brought into the alpine house to flower. Some of the smaller mossy saxifrage species with soft sticky-hairy foliage, such as *Saxifraga pubescens,* which can be difficult to grow in the open, are quite straightforward in the alpine house.

Tufa

Tufa is an exceptional way to maintain difficult, and otherwise often short-lived, plants. It provides a well-buffered environment where plants are able to develop root systems much more akin to those that they would make in a wild habitat, the roots following the grain in the obviously porous rock, tracking the water gradient. In general terms, the larger piece of tufa the better, and since it is lightweight it is possible to move large pieces if they can be sourced, but tufa which is too soft is very difficult to use since it will often continue to flake away for a considerable time. Tufa can be built up in different ways, in rockeries or as a tufa wall, but the most significant extra that can be added when building such a thing is some form of automatic or semi-automatic watering within the tufa.

Tufa is highly appropriate for most *Porphyrion* saxifrages, although I would exclude the *Oppositifoliae,* which seem to want a more extensive root run. Plants

Tufa is a wonderful medium for growing saxifrages. Part of the National Collection of *Porphyrion* saxifrages managed by Adrian Young at Waterperry Gardens, near Oxford.

A spectacular tufa wall in Harry Jans's garden in the Netherlands.

are best grown in small holes drilled in the tufa and will grow slowly but in character, hard and healthy. My own preference is to insert rooted cuttings in small-diameter holes, just about the width of a pencil and only about 5 cm deep, using a matchstick to poke them in with a bit of thin potting mix and the tufa-debris drilled from the hole, while Adrian Young at Waterperry Gardens in Oxfordshire makes a hole about 1.5–2 cm in diameter and slightly deeper than my 5 cm and uses slightly bigger plants. Water them in well—say half a watering can for a single cutting—and repeat that regularly over the first few weeks. At some point your attention will pass to something else, but by then the rooted cutting should have started to get established.

Peat

Peat is excellent as part of a mixture for rooting cuttings. Mixed with an equal portion of sand, and not allowed to dry out, it helps provide a homogenous medium, low in nutrients but easy for the newly developing root-hairs of the cutting to penetrate. In a peat-based compost young plants quickly make a mass of very fine cottony roots rather than the stronger roots they make in a loam-based compost. But if left too long in peat-based composts, young plants often fail to grow out of the original compost properly when the time comes to plant them out. This is a major problem with saxifrages bought from garden centres (small nurseries are much better), as the horticultural trade often uses peat-based composts for convenience. Plants will grow well in such composts as long as they are fed and watered on a regular basis, but they are likely to severely disappoint the ordinary gardener once they reach home. Often the only thing that can be done with plants grown in peat-based composts is to turn them into cuttings, and this is my normal practice. Cuttings should be moved on into a mix of loam-based compost, grit and sand earlier rather than later.

Propagating Saxifrages

Saxifrages from cuttings

Most of the garden saxifrages, including the hybrids, can be propagated by cuttings, except the *Irregulares* which have to be divided (or micropropagated if you are a professional) either by gently pulling a plant apart, or by carefully cutting through the clump with a sharp knife. In some cases such as the London Pride saxifrages, the process can be as simple as breaking off a rosette and pressing the broken end of the rhizome into the earth. This can be done in a pot or a tray, but they will root successfully in a shady patch of earth. Likewise the hybrid mossy saxifrages are often rooted easily if a few rosettes are detached and their broken ends thumbed into the ground rather than being laid out in pots or trays. Among the silver saxifrages *Saxifraga hostii* can also be treated like this, but with the remaining *Ligulatae* species, with the *Porphyrion* saxifrages, and with the section *Saxifraga* species, the best method is to take single-rosette cuttings and root them in trays.

A saxifrage cutting from a healthy, vigorous plant will generally root well within a few weeks, with no need for rooting hormone if prepared properly. Cuttings should be small, usually a single rosette or shoot, and the lower leaves should be peeled away until the little cutting has only fresh material at the bottom. This can then be placed in a pot or tray of peat and sand, or potting compost and sand, with a layer of sterilized sand on the top—the exact mix is not critical as long as they are kept fairly cool and not allowed to dry out. I often add vermiculite to the basic mix to aid this, particularly if I do not have peat to hand. Grit is unnecessary as the cuttings root well in a fairly even mix. I water each cutting in with a pipette full of water as I go to ensure each cutting is well settled in the sand. When I have a whole tray of cuttings I stand the pot or tray in a tray of water until the water reaches the surface of the sand. Keep the tray covered with a transparent plastic cover for a week or two to let the cuttings settle and then you only need to keep them protected from heavy rain, which might wash the cuttings out before they are rooted. No heat is needed at any time. The cuttings will take different lengths of time to root, depending on the species, the state of the plant used for cuttings and the time of year.

The usual advice is to take cuttings immediately after flowering, or as a second best in September or October. In fact cuttings can be taken at almost any time of the year. The plants are probably at their most vigorous in the spring, forming new shoots after flowering from which cuttings can be taken. These may be small, even very small, but are likely to root rapidly. Cuttings taken at other times take longer to root but will usually do so. The only time I normally avoid is the summer months when high temperatures are something of a problem. In general cuttings can be taken whenever you have the time. It should not need to be said that each batch or row of cuttings should be labelled as you go—in a standard seed tray I line out about 200 cuttings of up to around 40 different cultivars, so it becomes vital to be methodical.

Saxifrages usually do much better if small cuttings are taken.

Saxifrages from Seed

Most saxifrages are quite straightforward from seed. If seed is fresh, sown straight from the newly opened capsules, then germination can be pretty much immediate, with the first pair of tiny leaves showing in less than 14 days, but if seed is not fresh than it will be slower and can be erratic.

Saxifrage seed is small and this dictates how it should be treated. I use a very well-draining mix of equal parts compost (loam- not peat-based), coarse sand and small grit, which I tamp down and then add a little more of the mix (with some additional sand) and gently tamp it. If you don't have loam-based compost available, then garden soil sterilized and sieved will be perfectly good when mixed with the sand and grit. Unless great attention is going to be paid to the seedlings it is a good idea to add a thin layer of small grit. In either case I sprinkle a small amount of silver sand over the surface of the compost or grit and then sow the seed directly on this. I stand the pot in water until the grit can be seen to dampen and immediately remove it to a frame and cover it. This is pretty standard for small seed of alpine plants and works equally well for other genera. Other growers will refine this method, but in general saxifrage seed is easier than might be expected.

The usual approach is to leave pots for a year or so while the seedlings get to a size when they are fairly easy to handle, but young seedlings are also much tougher than might be expected. It is possible to prick out seedlings immediately after germination—although it requires sharp-pointed tweezers, care and a steady hand to lift the seedling at such an early stage. The rest of the pot can be left to germinate in the fullness of time.

Sourcing Saxifrages

Saxifrages are readily available. But if you want to extend a collection beyond the normal handful of mossy saxifrages, silver saxifrages and London pride that you are likely to find in your local garden centre, you need to start looking at more specialist sources. Specialist nurseries extend the list of plants very dramatically, in particular with greater ranges of *Porphyrion* and *Irregulares* saxifrages. The *RHS Plant Finder*, the directory of garden plants and sources in the UK and Ireland (now online as well as in book form) currently lists sources for over 800 saxifrages. Up until the late 1990s there was a similar publication, *PPP Index*, for nurseries on the European mainland, but this seems to have died away although apparently it is incorporated in the professional version of the Plant Finder CD (with all sorts of other goodies on it as well, but rather too expensive for most of us).

Today of course the internet is the key resource for the obsessive gardener, greatly extending the range of nurseries whose catalogues become accessible. Throughout Europe and North America the access to nursery lists has never been easier, although the same cannot yet be said of nurseries in Japan and other coun-tries in eastern Asia.

Many nurseries have catalogues, many do mail order, many of the best are happy to deal with export orders and the appropriate phytosanitary certificates, and many also have small quantities of unusual things which never get as far as their cata-logues. Visiting obscure nurseries is a delight and the person who gets to know nurseries only through mail order is missing a treat. There's the same joy driving up to a previously unvisited nursery that there is going into a newly discovered second-hand bookshop. With some it's love at first sight, but others are like second cousins twice removed— great fun, but definitely odd; or dodgy uncles—down at heel or gone to seed.

Saxifrages are great value. A dozen years ago I wrote that it was not easy to pay much above £5 for a plant in the UK—the price of an everyday bottle of wine. Little has changed. A handful of plants break through this sort of figure, but only a handful— and if you buy plants from Switzerland it is possible to push through this price-barrier. In North America the current top price seems to be about US$20, but $5–$10 is more typical. For mail order you can often add £10 ($20) or so to cover postage, but it's great fun getting a box full of plants through the post and it makes it worth ordering at least ten or so to get as much as possible at the basic postage rate.

Seed Exchanges and Collectors

One way of building a collection of more obscure saxifrages from the wild is to get involved with growing them from seed. The seed exchanges of the Alpine Garden Society, Scottish Rock Garden Club, North American Rock Garden Club and other such clubs usually have great lists of donated seed you can apply for. The Saxifrage Society also has a seed exchange for members and is a great source for specialist and obscure saxifrages. It's just about the only way to get some plants. I've grown some obscure things from seed obtained this way and I still remember my delight when I discovered that the seed of *Saxifraga cinerea* which I'd managed to get, then germi-nate, and finally flower had originally been donated by Winton Harding.

If you get completely hooked then there are specialist suppliers. I've had seed from a number of them and got seduced by wild-collected peonies, dionysias, androsaces and gentians at the same time. This is not necessarily a cheap way to get plants. It is quite common to pay something like US$5 for a single packet of seed: usually the quantity is not wildly different from that in an average packet from one of the big seed exchanges. So this is an acquired taste. Don't bother getting into this till you've cracked growing saxifrages from seed from the seed exchanges—at least that's cheap—and wild-collected seed is no more likely to germinate, and often less likely.

The other thing to remember about growing from seed is that you only have the collector's opinion as to what the thing is. Almost anything about it could be wrong. If it is seed from a garden, then the original plant could have been wrongly labelled. If it's from the wild, then there is no label and by the time the seed is ready there is no flower to help with identification. Very careful labelling of pots is helpful to try and make sense later of what you've got with information such as date sown, source or location of seed, and if the seed has one, the collection number (so that reference back to the original seedlist or collection notes is possible).

Specialist Societies

The most obvious way of extending your opportunities to get hold of plants is to join up with other specialists. As well as their seed exchanges the three large specialist rock gardening clubs (the Scottish Rock Garden Club, Alpine Garden Society, and North American Rock Garden Society) all produce excellent journals, and all have a network of local groups which have regular meetings. These have a programme of talks from visiting specialists and there is usually some sort of bring-and-buy members' stall which can have wonderful treasures.

The Saxifrage Society is much smaller but it does bring together an amazing amount of expertise. It is based in the UK although it has a wide international membership. It has twice-yearly general meetings in the UK, a website with a brilliant online database, and an annual *Saxifrage Magazine*. It has also established a pattern of four-yearly conferences (Holland in 2000, the Czech Republic in 2004, Scotland in 2008) and field trips to the European mountains visiting the Maritime Alps in 2002 and Austria in 2006. If a saxifrage is in cultivation, the chances are high that a member of the Society is growing it.

The Saxifrage Society
Saxifrage Society, The Gardens, 12 Vicarage Lane, Grasby, Barnetby, North
    Lincolnshire DN38 6AU, UK (www.saxifraga.org)

Rock-garden societies
Alpine Garden Society, AGS Centre, Avon Bank, Pershore, Worcs WR10 3JP, UK
    (www.alpinegardensociety.org)
North American Rock Garden Society, Box 67, Millwood NY 10546, USA
    (www. nargs.org)
Scottish Rock Garden Club, 145 Stonehill Avenue, Birstall, Leicester LE4 4JG, UK
    (www.srgc.org.uk)
The Rock Garden Club of Prague, Klub skalnickaru Praha, Marikova 5, 162 00
    Praha 2, Czech Republic (www.skalnicky.cz)

Suppliers and nurseries

Some of these nurseries are open to the public, some are mail order only, some have no mail order.

England

Mendle Nursery, Holme, Scunthorpe, North Lincolnshire DN16 3RF, UK (www.Mendlenursery.com)

Pottertons Nursery, Moortown Road, Nettleton, Caistor, Lincolnshire LN7 6HX, UK (www.pottertons.co.uk)

West Acre Gardens, West Acre, King's Lynn, Norfolk PE32 1UJ, UK (0(044) 1760 755562)

W. E. Th. Ingwersen, Birch Farm Nursery, Gravetye, East Grinstead, W. Sussex RH19 4LE, UK (www.ingwersen.co.uk)

Scotland

Ian Christie, Downfield, Main Road, Westmuir, Kirriemuir, Angus DD8 5LP, UK (www.christiealpines.co.uk)

Ron McBeath, Lamberton Nursery, No. 3, Lamberton, Berwickshire TD15 1XB, UK (www.lambertonnursery.co.uk)

Wales

Aberconwy Nursery, Graig, Glan Conwy, Conwy LL28 5TL, UK (0(044) 1981 240419)

Crûg Farm Plants, Griffith's Crossing, nr. Caernarfon, Gwynedd LL55 1TU, UK (www.crug-farm.co.uk)

North America

Mt Tahoma Nursery, 28111 112th Ave. E., Graham, WA 98338, USA (www.backyardgardener.com/mttahoma)

Wrightman Alpines, RR 3, Kerwood, ON Canada N0M 2B0 (www.WrightmanAlpines.com)

Pacific Rim Native Plant Nursery (www.hillkeep.ca)

Europe

Ger van den Beuken, Zegerstraat 7, 5961 XR Horst (L), Netherlands (gervandenbeuken@wanadoo.nl)

Jacob Eschmann, Waltwil, CH-6032 Emmen, Switzerland

Sun Valley Nursery, Bart & Hannelore Moerland, Bilderdijkstraat 129, 7442 VK Nijverdal, Netherlands (www.alpigena-saxifrages.nl)

Studengärtnerei Alpine Raritäten, Jürgen Peters, Auf dem Flidd 20, D-25436 Uetersen, Germany (www.alpine-peters.de)

F. Sündermann, Botansicher Alpengarten, Aeschacher Ufer 4, 88131 Lindau(B), Germany (www.alpengarten-suendermann.de)

Seed suppliers
There are many seed collectors, but these regularly list seed of rare *Saxifraga*:

Chris Chadwell, 81 Parlaunt Road, Slough, Berks SL3 8BE, UK
   Seed-collecting expeditions to the Himalayas.
Alexandra Berkutenko (www.meconopsis.st/Berkutenko.html or berkuten@ online.magadan.su)
   Seed collections in the Russian Far East.
Josef Halda Seeds, PO Box 110, 50101 Hradec Králové 2, Czech Republic (jjhalda@jjh.cz or www.jjh.cz)
   Seeds collected in mountain areas of Europe, the Caucasus, Central Asia and China.
Vojtěch Holubec, Sidltni n210, CZ-165 00 Praha 6, Czech Republic (holubec@ vurv.cz)
   Wild-collected seed from expeditions in Asia and Europe.
Josef Jurasek, Lamacova 861, Prague 5, 152 00, Czech Republic. (www. jurasekalpines@atlas.cz)
   Wild-collected seed from expeditions in Asia and Europe.

Trough with saxifrages planted between diagonally placed rocks.

19 · 100 Saxifrages Mixed

Years ago my father passed a seed catalogue from Thompson & Morgan on to me. He pointed out that under *Saxifraga* they offered packets of "100 Saxifrages Mixed"—but each packet contained only 50 seeds. This was not only amusing but intriguing. Exactly which species and hybrids were included in any year would obviously depend on what seed was available—but it was also intriguing to speculate as to just what selection of the original "100" any individual customer might get, or would choose for themselves. So it seemed appropriate here to try and list the hundred saxifrages that would provide the beginner with plants from across the whole genus. If only the most choice *Micranthes* were easier to obtain and grow, they would have forced their way on to the list—*Micranthes nudicaulis, M. gageana, M. petiolaris* and *M. purpurascens* among others, are all plants I keep hoping to succeed with one day.

Any selection of species and hybrids will inevitably attract criticism from other specialists who might wonder why I left out their particular favourite, but this is my selection of plants from the different sections of genus *Saxifraga*. I could have easily chosen twice as many instead of a mere handful more than that precise one hundred. I had no hard and fast criteria, although most of the plants are reasonably straightforward (the odd ones that are not easy are signalled). They are all distinct and unmistakable. These are the plants I would choose and would replace if I lost them. One or two are difficult to get (and I have indicated which), but the nurseries and seed exchanges listed in Chapter 18 will, between them, provide all the others.

Mossy saxifrage hybrids

This is a selection with some smaller and some taller cultivars and just a few very old, historic hybrids.

Historic cultivars

It seems wonderful that some of the original hybrids from Mrs Lloyd Edwards and Georg Arends are still in cultivation so, as a tribute, I would pick a small historic group of plants:

Saxifraga 'Winton's Dream'.

1. **'Elegantissima'**. If this cultivar is still the same as the original plant it is a bit of a miracle, but anyway this is a tribute to it. Small red flowers and happy on the rockery.
2. **'Apple Blossom'**. One of Mrs Lloyd Edwards's early hybrids.
3. **'Wallacei'**. The most spectacular large flowers, but needing regular attention.
4. **'Triumph'**. An early hybrid from Arends which still looks good, although plants in circulation do vary.

More modern mossy saxifrage hybrids
5. **'Corennie Claret'**. Deep red with dark red stems.
6. **'Fleece'**. A strong white-flowered cultivar with hairy, rather greyer foliage.
7. **'Gaiety'**. Large rich pink flowers with overlapping petals, quite tall.
8. **'Holden Seedling'**. Very bright, rich red, sun-resistant flowers.
9. **'Knapton Pink'**. Pale pink flowers over hairy foliage, quite tall.
10. **'Pixie'**. Much smaller, with light red flowers. Very easy-going.
11. **'Weisser Zwerg'**. With white flowers on very short stems.

Mossy saxifrages with variegated or coloured foliage
12. **'Golden Falls'**. The foliage is nicely patterned with slightly golden variegation. White flowers.
13. **'Hi-Ace'**. A beautiful, very small variegated cultivar with deep red flowers. Not easy.
14. **'Silver Cushion'**. More pointed foliage, silver and grey-green. Flowers are a disappointing pink after richer pink buds.

Some other great plants could be recommended here, including 'Grace', 'Gold Leaf' and 'Cloth of Gold', but these are variously almost unobtainable or can be very difficult.

Mossy saxifrage species
15. *S. canaliculata*. Stiff, finer foliage than the garden *S. trifurcata*, and not quite such large cushions. Good in the open.
16. *S. continentalis*. Drought-adapted self-seeding species with white flowers. Excellent on the rock garden.
17. *S. exarata* **subsp.** *moschata*. An excellent small species for a trough. Neat cushions and small dull yellow flowers.
18. *S. granulata*. Very nice and can be naturalized in grass. Not good in a pot. Good from seed.

Saxifraga continentalis.
Photograph John
Howes.

19. *S. granulata* **'Flore Pleno'**. A splendid double form, again best grown in grass.

20. *S. latepetiolata*. Spectacular biennial species.

Silver saxifrages

This is a very abbreviated list. Despite the obvious attractions of *S. callosa* and *S. cotyledon*, the Southside Seedling Group and some of the other forms of *S. paniculata*, I have settled on:

21. *S. longifolia*. On the list because of its stunning rosettes.

22. *S. paniculata* **'Correvoniana'**. Very reliable and flowers well.

23. *S. kolenatiana*. Not so easy but such a wonderful flower colour.

24. *S. hostii* subsp. *hostii*. Wonderfully easy. Good flowers on tall stems in ordinary garden soil.

25. *S. cochlearis*. Usually as 'Minor', this is the most charming of the silver saxifrages.

26. *S. ×burnatii* **'Emile Burnat'**. One of the great saxifrages, with arching sprays of flower.

27. **'Carniolica'**. Narrow leaves, beaded at the edge: this is one to grow for its foliage.

28. **'Whitehill'**. Another to grow for foliage: grey leaves with deep red staining at the base.

29. **'Tumbling Waters'**. Spectacular, but needs attention.

London pride saxifrages

30. **'Dentata'**. Saw-toothed, round-bladed leaves with long stems. Flowers pale pink.

31. **'Miss Chambers'**. Flowers deeper pink than London pride, and leaves dark green with purple tinge.

32. **London pride**. This is such an easy-going plant that it can easily be overlooked. Plant it at the front of the border or along the edge of a path.

Section *Ciliatae*

Of the handful of species which are grown occasionally, this is the best:

33. *S. candelabrum*. Interesting rosette. Great tiger-striped custard-yellow flowers. Grow from seed.

Section *Trachyphyllum*

Although others such as *S. cherlerioides* could be recommended, the best to me seems to be:

34. *S. aspera*. Easy from seed. Flowers with strong yellow spots.

Section *Cymbalaria*

35. *S. cymbalaria*. Charming little annual with ivy-shaped leaves and yellow flowers. Will self-seed.

Section *Irregulares*

36. *S. fortunei* 'Mount Nachi'. An old collection, smaller than many, but well worth its place.

37. *S. fortunei* var. *pilosissima*. A splendid, handsome, robust form of the species with large leaves on very short stems and a magnificent stem of flowers.

38. *S. nipponica* 'Pink Pagoda'. Evergreen foliage and lots of pink flowers in May.

39. *S. fortunei* 'Fumiko'. A small discreet rather than demonstrative cultivar, which I think is charming.

40. *S. epiphylla*. The plantlets on the leaves make this an intriguing species. 'Purple Piggy' is the cultivar which shows this characteristic best.

41. *S. cortusifolia* 'Silver Velvet'. Glorious foliage, deep velvety red with silvery grey bars on the leaves.

42. *S. sendaica*. Frost-tender but a very distinctive species, unmistakable.

43. *S. fortunei* 'Beni shishi'. Amazing pink starburst flowers.

44. *S. fortunei* 'Shima-no-Shiraito'. I have only seen a picture of this on the internet, but it is very beautiful. It is a plant which has yet to reach the western nursery trade, but it is just so pretty that it has to be recommended.

Section *Heterisia*

45. *S. mertensiana*. Easy North American species with diffusely branched stems of small white flowers with bunches of bright pink bulbils in the axils of the pedicels. Readily self-seeds. Great fun.

Section *Porphyrion—Oppositifoliae*

46. *S. oppositifolia* **'Theoden'**. Simply the best—of *S. oppositifolia,* at least.

Section *Porphyrion—Porophyllum* hybrids

47. **'Alba'**. White-flowered sibling of 'Gregor Mendel'. Excellent on open rockery.

48. **'Albert Einstein'**. An old *S. ×apiculata* cultivar, probably from Franz Sündermann, with stronger yellow flowers than 'Gregor Mendel'.

49. **'Aldo Bacci'**. A handsome yellow-flowered Milford Group cross from Sergio Bacci.

50. **'Allendale Bravo'**. A brilliant small cultivar with bluish-purple flowers, from Ray Fairbairn.

51. **'Alpenglow'**. A lovely old cultivar. Tall with buff flowers, from Lincoln Foster.

52. **'Becky Foster'**. Very good *S. ×borisii* cultivar with multiple flowers. From Lincoln Foster.

53. **'Beinn Eighe'**. A new cultivar from John Mullaney with luxurious pale pink flowers very like those of 'Beinn Alligin', but with tighter foliage.

54. **'Bohemia'**. Best of the orange-flowered hybrids for the open rock garden, from Mirsolav Kraus.

55. **'Bridget'**. An old hybrid with pale pink flowers on tall stems with dark red calyx. Excellent still, having originated in Ireland in the 1930s.

56. **'Citronella'**. Tall, stately, yellow-flowered, from Winton Harding.

Saxifraga 'Citronella'.

57. **'Coningsby Queen'** or **'Riverslea'**. Two classic *S. ×hornibrookii* crosses with very deep red-purple flowers. 'Coningsby Queen' from Geoffrey Gould has bigger flowers but is less easy to get than Prichard's 'Riverslea'.

58. **'Coolock Kate'**. New. Striking pink flowers, small neat cushion, from Jim Almond.

59. **'Cranbourne'**. One of the best-flowering and easiest of Russell Vincent Prichard's classic *S. ×anglica* cultivars.

60. **'Cumulus'**. Free-flowering white hybrid of *S. ramsarica* from Ron Beeston.

61. **'Faldonside'** or **'Nottingham Gold'**. Two classic *S. ×boydii* cultivars. 'Faldonside' from John Brack Boyd must take precedence, but 'Nottingham Gold' from Geoffrey Gould is a great plant.

62. **'Gold Dust'**. My favourite of the *S. ×eudoxiana* cultivars, this one from Adrian Bloom. They all have small bright yellow flowers. Very good on the open rockery.

63. **'Gothenburg'**. An exceptional small Himalayan-style cultivar with small yellow flowers tight in the cushion. History slightly obscure, but apparently originated in Gothenburg Botanic Gardens.

64. **'Gregor Mendel'**. A *S. ×apiculata* hybrid from Franz Sündermann. One of the first (1894) and still one of the best hybrids.

65. **'Iris Prichard'**. Buff-pink flowers with bright red nectary ring. Flowers early. A Russell Vincent Prichard hybrid. 'Penelope', from Rob Dunford, with larger flowers has some of the same qualities.

66. **'Karel Čapek'**. Still the best of the *S. ×megaseaeflora* cultivars, from Frantisek Holenka. Large flowers with soft pink petals.

67. **'Kaspar Maria Sternberg'**. This is a *S. ×petraschii* cultivar with typical good white flowers. It was a toss-up between this very old cultivar from Sündermann and 'Mrs Helen Terry' from Valerie Finnis.

68. **'Krasava'**. With almost white flowers flushed warm pink at the base, this *S. ×megaseaeflora* cultivar from Frantisek Holenka flowers early.

69. **'Lismore Pink'**. Very small deep pink hybrid from Brian Burrow. More generally popular is 'Lismore Carmine' with deeper red flowers, but I prefer the edgy combination of poised pink flowers set against the almost perfectly complementary green foliage.

70. **'Marc Chagall'** or **'Claude Monet'**. Two recent hybrids from Karel Lang involving *S. kotschyi*, with red buds and red-orange flowers over neat cushions.

71. **'Maria Louisa'**. Very early, compact *S. ×petraschii* cultivar from Johann Kellerer. White flowers, grey foliage.

72. **'Marianna'**. An old *S. ×borisii* hybrid with very well-shaped yellow flowers from Karel Stivin.

73. **'Mary Golds'**. Lovely white flowers with pink backs to petals. A very nice cultivar from Tim Golds which flowers well.

74. **'Moai'**. An intriguing and nicely simple new hybrid from Karel Lang with buff-pink flowers.

75. **'Mollie Broom'**. White-flowered sister seedling to pink 'Meg' and 'Amy' from John Mullaney.

76. **'Naarden'**. Very attractive with yellow orange-flushed flowers. Exceptional newer cultivar from Karel Lang.

77. **'Nancye'**. Winton Harding's cross of *S. cinerea* and 'Winifred' with deep red-pink flowers.

78. **'Peach Blossom'**. Older cultivar with warm, pale pink flowers with a darker centre from Lincoln Foster.

79. **'Peach Melba'**. New, accidental cultivar with unique colouring, from David Victor.

80. **'Pluto'**. A beautiful *S. ×megaseaeflora* cultivar with pink flowers that are beautifully vase-shaped. From Frantisek Holenka.

81. **'Primrose Dame'**. Nearly all the *S. ×elisabethae* cultivars are good rock-garden plants. This is my favourite. It is from Russell Vincent Prichard but there are many others, such as 'Carmen' from Sündermann and 'Foster's Gold' from Lincoln Foster, which are good.

82. **'Robin Hood'**. The original *S. ×megaseaeflora* cross from Russell Vincent Prichard. The *S. ×irvingii* cultivar 'Timmy Foster' is similar but more difficult.

83. **'Silver Edge'**. Variegated foliage, very pale pink flowers from John Good.

84. **'Tábor'**. My favourite *Engleria* cross with small orange flowers, from Radvan Horný.

85. **'Tvůj Úspěch'**. One of Jan Bürgel's *S. ×poluanglica* cultivars with pink flowers.

86. **'Věcerní Hvězda'**. Sister seedling to 'Naarden'. Clear light yellow multi-flowered hybrid from Karel Lang.

87. **'Verona'**. Named for the 2004 Saxifrage Society International Seminar in Beroun. From Karel Lang.

88. **'Vladana'**. One of Kraus's *S. ×megaseaeflora* cultivars with pale buff-yellow-orange flowers with bright red-orange nectary ring. 'Galaxie' is similar but smaller; 'Jupiter' similar but not so well proportioned.

89. **'Walter Irving'**. The original cultivar to involve *S. lilacina*, this has small cushions of spiny leaves and very light pink flowers. Smaller than the more common 'Jenkinsiae', which has the same parentage. Bred at Kew by Walter Irving and given his name later.

90. **'Winifred'**. The classic *S. ×anglica* cultivar which has contributed so much to many of the modern pink and red hybrids. From Geoffrey Gould.

91. **'Winton'**. A robust yellow-flowered *S. ×paulinae* hybrid with spiny foliage. One of Winton Harding's best.

92. **'Winton's Dream'**. A hybrid by Winton Harding of *S. media*, with lilac-pink flowers, named posthumously. Not unlike 'John Byam-Grounds' from Karel Lang, but taller.

Saxifraga dinnikii has the largest flowers of any *Porophyllum* saxifrage species.

Section *Porphyrion—Porophyllum* species

All the *Porophyllum* species have their own charms, but some are difficult. To my mind the best are:

93. *S. burseriana*. Dark red stems over spiny grey foliage with single white flowers. Very attractive, some forms with very large flowers. My favourite is 'Crenata', with neatly scalloped petals.
94. *S. corymbosa*. A small *Engleria* species with yellow rather than dark red flowers. Will seed itself.
95. *S. federici-augusti*. A strange beast of a plant with a dragon's head of small flowers tucked into hairy red calyces. Fascinating and not difficult from seed.
96. *S. marginata*. Many forms, all of them nice and fairly weather-resistant. My favourite is 'Balkan', which has large flowers with recurved petals.
97. *S. ramsarica*. A beautiful species from Iran with large single white flowers which flush pink as they age. Irresistibly pretty.

Saxifraga 'Dora Ross'.

Saxifraga [Vanessa Group] 'Cio-Cio-San'.

98. *S. stribrnyi*. Reliable *Engleria* which forms small cushions of large rosettes and has a branched inflorescence and small dark red–purple flowers.

And finally two exquisite new introductions from the wild:

99. *S. dinnikii*. Only recently in cultivation. From the Caucasus, with spectacular large lilac-purple flowers.

100. *S. pulchra*. This is so pretty and so unlike anything else that it is a must.

A Personal Offering

I have not included any of my own hybrid crosses in the list above but here are just a few of mine which seem to be distinctive and liked by others as well as myself:

101. '**Alice**'. A Milford Group hybrid with good yellow flowers which lift their heads once fully open. A handsome plant.

102. '**Cio-Cio-San**'. Vanessa Group cross with small, very pretty, pale pink flowers with serrated margins. Easy to propagate in damp sand.

103. '**Maria Callas**'. An early-flowering *S. ×poluanglica* cultivar with slightly serrate flowers of a distinctive sometimes fugitive warm red-pink-mauve.

104. '**Omar Khayyam**'. Large pink flowers on short stems. Round buds, neat cushions. A cross between *S. lilacina* and *S. ramsarica*.

105. '**Honeybunch**'. A small yellow multi-flowered cultivar. The only cross involving *S. meeboldii*, it has inherited the faintest of scents.

106. '**Dora Ross**'. Deep pink, reliable cross of *S. stolitzkae* and *S.* 'Winifred'.

20 · On The Road Again

Outat-Oulad-el-Haj is very much an Arab town, far from the old centres of French colonial rule, in the east of Morocco in the long strip of arid semi-desert between the Middle and High Atlas. We have come to look at what it would take to find *Saxifraga luizetiana*, one of the mossy saxifrages which only grow in Morocco, and like *S. werneri* only known from one collection more than 75 years old. There is very little French spoken in Outat, even by *le patron*, with whom I share a loaf and a dish of olive oil at seven in the morning. More like something out of a road movie than a botanical trip, the cafe is fly-blown and the customers sit facing the door. Upstairs the rooms have three beds apiece, but since they have not been made or changed in memory, sleeping on top of the blankets seems the best bet. And they are the only beds in the only hotel: Outat is a lunch stop if you must, not a destination. Out of the door you can look straight across the gently rising plain to the southeastern foothills of Jbel Bou Naceur. The mountain rises about 2400 metres from the plain and at its highest is 3340 metres. Any approach to the higher parts of the mountain (and *Saxifraga luizetiana* was found at about 3000 metres) probably has to be from the north ridge, and from many miles away we can see that in just a few high gullies on the north-facing slopes there is standing snow in late May, most unlikely from down in the baked plain. On the maps there used to be a road up to a col, but now we find that it has disappeared under the arid sands, abandoned to the wind and the scavenging raptors, black kites, buzzards and eagles, the scattered flocks of goats and the occasional group of camels. There are other roads but over the next three days none will get us close enough. *Saxifraga luizetiana* would be a fascinating plant to find but it will take another trip in which it is the major objective, and which has dealt with logistical requirements not obvious in advance; a guide speaking Arabic (or a term or two of an evening class in Arabic) would seem to be a minimum requirement, and horses would be helpful. For the moment, therefore, *S. luizetiana* remains known from a single collection. But we were much more successful with our other targets.

It was in the 1870s that Mr Baker took J. D. Hooker to see *Saxifraga maweana* high above Tetouan on Beni Hosmar in the Rif mountains, but it is not easy to follow them since Beni Hosmar is not on the maps. Having tried a series of different and, from the point of view of our search for *S. maweana*, unrewarding roads we

Looking across to the northern face of Jbel Kraa, western Rif.

find a deeply rutted track leading high up into the mountains south of Tetouan. Where the goats have failed to reach, in deep narrow fissures in the eroded limestone, some unbrowsed plants of *S. maweana* are immediately identifiable from the drawing in Maire's *Flore de l'Afrique Nord*—very much like *S. maderensis*, but with the summer-dormant buds in the leaf axils. That this is Beni Hosmar is confirmed by a young shepherd whose flock of goats is browsing on the mountain; he suddenly smiles and points to the ground when we mention its name.

Another of the endemic saxifrages we are looking for is *Saxifraga embergeri*, which we find in the Monts des Zaian, hundreds of metres down, baking in the gorge of the Oued Agenour near the source of the mineral water Sidi Ali at Oulmès des Thermes. On the rocks at the base of the north face of the gorge *S. embergeri* is well into its summer state by the third week in May, with most of the cushions of tiny foliage crisped already by the heat, sharing the rocks with such other plants as dwarf fan palms, much less surprising inhabitants of such a habitat.

There are various reasons why the saxifrages of northern Morocco are so little known. *Saxifraga embergeri* and *S. luizetiana* live far from the main areas where botanists usually go in Morocco, and they are even farther off the tourist trails. And yet the Rif mountains, home to *S. maweana* and *S. werneri*, start immediately south of Tangier, just across the straits from Gibraltar, before stretching eastwards all the way into Algeria, where they finally expire in Constantine province. These are fascinatingly varied mountains close to Europe but with a fearsome reputation. This was the Barbary Coast from where 18th-century pirates raided the coasts of Europe for slaves. Now the Rif is famous because it is a centre of the drug trade, with Ketama district being an area in which up to 90 percent of the arable crops in some areas are *kif*, the local name for cannabis, and there are plenty of the bright green fields, and large modern villas surrounded by high walls built on the back of the trade. Usually I have no problem finding companions to travel with, but when I started planning the trip to Morocco for the second half of May 2007 (poring over what maps I could get, rereading Maire and so on, checking flight times and car hire possibilities) I did have some difficulty, so I must thank Kathryn Hart from the Royal Horticultural Society Gardens at Wisley, and David Victor, vice-president of the Saxifrage Society, who came with me. We were helped by our multilingual guide (English–French–Arabic–Berber), who acted as our flag of convenience in the Rif.

Our base in the Rif was Chefchaouen, famed for the blue-washed walls and blue-painted doors of the houses and passageways of the old medina. From here we could get to Tetouan to look for *Saxifraga maweana*, and we could get up into the massif behind Chefchaouen and to Jbel Kraa, the highest mountain of the western Rif at 2150 metres, and the place where *S. werneri* was collected in the 1920s.

I had arranged by email to have a four-wheel drive vehicle, a driver and a guide for a couple of days, but it was not inspiring to start the first day with half an hour at the tyre repair shop to pick up a spare wheel for our Land Rover (they are all

Land Rovers in Chefchaouen) and even less inspiring the following day when the spare wheel suddenly went flat without ever having been used—obviously not much of a repair.

The road to Bab Taza is quite a drag out of Chefchaouen up though the cork oaks and cistus on the way to Ketama. Turning off up through dusty Bab Taza the road turns to track, and gladioli and *Muscari comosum* in the fields of the lower hills gradually give way to *Saxifraga globulifera* on the rocks and stands of *Paeonia coriacea* flowering in the dappled shade. And above us, almost enchanted, hanging in the heat, Jbel Kraa—the bald mountain—with its top bare of trees.

The ridge of the mountain runs parallel with the four-wheel drive track, and our guide has no knowledge of the path, so a direct approach up the eastern slope seems as likely to be as productive as any. We duck under the barbed wire by the side of the track—there to stop the flocks of goats and sheep, which nibble everything to the ground if they are not restrained. From here the mountain slopes up, steepening progressively, with stands of big conifers *Pinus halepensis*, *Cedrus atlantica* and

One of the extraordinary blue-washed passages in Chefchaouen.

Abies marocana, the Moroccan equivalent to *Abies pinsapo* of Andalucia, punctuating the smaller trees, which in turn give way to the well-eroded limestone of the mountains, bare, sun-baked. On the way up in the Land Rover we had seen outcrops of rock but most of these were in the shade of trees. Up here it is more open: outcrops, boulders, scree bleached wood-ash grey. And, on all the barest rock, *Saxifraga werneri*—not a handful of plants tucked in a crack near the summit, but thousands of plants, scattered across scree and outcrop alike, the flowers pure white against the rock.

And the dry botanical descriptions become a plant, the reddened foliage with the glandular tips of the villose hairs like pinpoints across the surface, the complex inflorescence an elegant posy showing off to the world.

Gradually it is the detail we notice, how the plants differ from the descriptions as well as meet them. No plants form the loose cushions Maire described. Almost every plant consists of a single rosette of leaves, rather like a single rosette of *Saxifraga exarata* or *S. pubescens*. But even though they only have a single rosette, perhaps the size of a finger- or thumb-nail, they are beautiful. The single flower stem is intricately branched and although most plants have from 10 to 25 flowers, larger plants have about 35 to 40 flowers, and the largest has twice this.

And what of the petals, "blancs, puis bientôt purpurin-clair" in Maire's words? The pictures say it—as the pure white flowers are pollinated the petals turn clear pink-purple as they go over, the colour that they turn in *S. marginata*, but they also close and furl their blushing petals, almost like the buds of an oxalis. And the stems and the foliage turn from clear green to foxy red in the strong Moroccan sun, and

then with the swelling capsules, on to deepening crimson-lake, standing out against the pallid rock.

Before we went to Morocco I had hoped that we would find at least some of our four target plants. In fact we found three: in itself a great reward for the efforts. But one of these went beyond any expectation. Botanical detail overtaken by beauty, *Saxifraga werneri* transcended the dry formal descriptions: this was a plant to be seduced by—a plant to fall in love with …

… and there are always places to go: Bulgaria, the Caucasus, the mountains of Sakhalin, the Sierra Madre Orientale in Mexico … and there are always new plants to grow …

Saxifrages are some of the most beautiful small garden plants: poised and charming. Their poise stems from their classical proportions: with five petals, the ratios

of the distances between the tips of the petals are another example of that mysterious golden section which brings together nature, mathematics and our sense of beauty. That so many flowering plants have five petals, far more than have four or six, even raises the intriguing question of whether insects have the same aesthetic preference for the golden section that we do. The charm of saxifrages is that, like some horticultural Tess of the D'Urbervilles, they retain the qualities of the places from which they come: the meadows of lowland Europe, and the high rocks and screes of mountains across the northern continents; shady damp woodland, and streamsides and bogs, and the high slopes of the Himalaya; the tundra of the far north; the ashen limestone of the western Rif.

Saxifraga werneri. This is the first time since the 1920s that this plant has been seen, and the first time it has ever been photographed. Jbel Kraa, western Rif, Morocco.

Appendix of Lost Cultivars

Gardeners and botanists view cultivars in very different ways. For a botanist a hybrid cultivar is merely a named selection of a particular cross. The loss of a particular cultivar might be regrettable, but unlike the extinction of a species, it represents no permanent loss of genetic diversity. For the gardener the hybrid cultivar is a unique combination with an individual history of human intervention: whether the crossing was intentional or accidental, its selection and naming were deliberate. For it to disappear is to lose a unique piece of horticultural heritage, although it would be silly to claim that every cultivar has great value. Some perhaps deserve to disappear because they have faults or are overtaken by a newer plant. These might not be lamented, but some losses are much more unfortunate.

Most of the losses among the silver saxifrages have been of named collections from the wild. Many collectors brought back more or less unusual forms and gave them names relating to the location where they were found or to some characteristic of a particular plant. Few of these offer significant losses. Most losses among the silver saxifrages have been of such named collections as 36 forms of *Saxifraga paniculata*, three of *S. callosa*, and four of *S. cotyledon*. A similar situation is seen with *S. oppositifolia* from section *Porphyrion*. Over 20 cultivars are probably still in cultivation, but nearly as many again have been lost. Among the London pride saxifrages about a dozen hybrid cultivars from the London Pride Group have disappeared, and just a couple of *S. cuneifolia*.

Apart from the mossy saxifrage hybrids, the major losses have been among the dwarf cushion *Porophyllum* hybrids. Around 70 named cultivars have disappeared, about half of them known crosses, and about half plants whose parentage was unknown. In some cases these were probably only ever distributed in very small numbers. Of these, 24 stem from Russell Vincent Prichard (around the same number of his hybrids are still in cultivation) and were introduced after Russell emigrated to Australia around 1930 by the Riverslea Nursery run by Maurice Prichard. These include: *Saxifraga* ×*anglica*: 'Aubrey Prichard', 'Brenda Prichard', 'Brilliant', 'Delight', 'Desire', 'Elysium', 'Exquisite', 'Prichard's Glorious', 'Priory Jewel', 'Sparkling', 'Valerie Keevil' and 'W. Reeves'; *S.* ×*petraschii* 'Ada'; *S.* ×*hornibrookii* 'Laurent Ward' and 'Sonia Prichard'; and various other cultivars whose parentage is unknown: 'Adela', 'Amenity', 'Bayswater', 'Cream Rock', 'The Duke', 'E. D. Doncaster', 'Kenneth Rogers', 'Tangerine', 'Thorpi' and 'Unique'. The cultivars of his that do survive suggest that these evocative names must represent some valuable plants. Another lost cultivar, from Maurice Prichard's nursery in the 1960s, was *S.* ×*elisabethae* 'White Dame', apparently a white sport of 'Primrose Dame', which would have been an attractive plant.

Mossy Saxifrage Hybrids now Lost or Extinct

Apart from the Prichard cultivars, the losses in groups other than the mossy saxifrages do not have any great significance. With the mossy saxifrage hybrids of section *Saxifraga*—discussed in detail in Chapter 14—this is far from the case. Many of these cultivars were instrumental in the development of the plants we grow today. Some were lost early, some between the two world wars, but the bulk disappeared during or immediately after the Second World War.

Not all the plants on this list are necessarily extinct. Some are likely still to be in cultivation, but if so then they are among the old hybrids sometimes found in gardens but without names. Brief descriptive quotes are given to aid possible identification of plants still in cultivation. Where possible the earliest and latest dates traced are given. Where only the name of the nursery occurs in the list below, plants were originally listed without a description.

'Alba' (1882). Probably synonymous with 'Grandiflora Alba', in which case it may still be the plant in circulation. Also used for Section *Porphyrion* cultivar *S. ×apiculata* 'Alba'.

'A. Lynes' (1909–13, UK, Bakers of Wolverhampton). "Rosy-crimson blossoms" (Bakers); "Flesh pink" (Prichard, 1912); "large flowering … opening deep rose, changing to pale rose" (Backhouse, 1913). Probably one of Mrs Lloyd Edwards's hybrids.

'April Joy' (1929–39, UK, Prichard). "Crimson with white centre".

'Arkwrightii' (1909–25, UK, Bakers of Wolverhampton). A free-flowering plant with 1 in. (2.5 cm) white flowers, buds, stems and calyx tinged pink. RHS Award of Merit (AM) by 11 votes to 3. "Pure white" (Backhouse, 1913). Probably one of Mrs Lloyd Edwards's hybrids.

'Aureole' (1920s, UK, Prichard). "White with crimson centre".

'Avoca Gem' (1960s, Ireland?). "Finest pink, strong grower" (Kaye's).

'Bakeri' (1920s, UK, Pritchard). "Rich carmine".

'Bathoniensis' (pre-1911–39, UK). "Large rosy-scarlet flowers" (Prichard, 1912); "fine red shade" (Prichard, 1929); "very fine, large-flowered, crimson, rapid grower" (Backhouse, 1913). Listed by Bakers of Codsall 1925. Prichard, 1939.

'Best of All' (1935, UK). Probably synonymous with 'Wenlock Best of All'.

'Bickham's Glory' (1920s, UK). No details.

'Birch Crimson' (1930s, UK, Ingwersen). "Beautiful crimson".

'Brightness' (1920s, UK, Prichard). "Blood-crimson".

'Brilliant' (1920s–30s, UK). As *S. muscoides* (*moschata*) 'Brilliant' (Prichard and G. P. Porter).

'Brilliant Rose' (pre-1920). No details.

'Buff Queen' (ca.1931–47, UK). Strong-growing, large pink to buff. Listed in 1930s by Ingwersen, G. P. Porter and Stuart Boothman. Last listing found: Nightingale Nursery, 1947.

'Cerise Queen' (1929, UK, Prichard). "Cherry-rose" (Prichard). Note: at some later point the name appears to have got transferred to the *Porphyrion* cultivar we now call 'Christine'.

'Chez Nous Pink' (1930s, Chez Nous Nurseries).

'Chez Nous White' (1930s, Chez Nous Nurseries).

'Clare Island Pink' (1970s, UK). Only the name—listed by NCCPG as on Pink Book search list.

'Clibranii' (1909–29, UK, Mrs Lloyd Edwards). Presented to the RHS in 1909 by Messrs Clibrans, Altrincham: "Flowers large, deep lilac, very free, reddish stems, 4″ high. Ovary rather conspicuous. AM, 11 votes to 5." "Brilliant red, dense green tufts" (Prichard, 1912). According to Clibrans (still listing it in 1929) it had "broad expanded petals, rich crimson intensified at base" and was "The finest single crimson-flowered saxifrage. The individual rich crimson colour is intensified at the base . . . several flowers on each stem . . . which are rich blackish-crimson colour" (Clibrans, 1913/14). Originally called 'Ruby'. Confusion occurs because of the use of this as a name for a group of crosses in the binomial *S. × Clibranii* which contained 'Apple Blossom', 'Rose Beauty', 'Sanguinea Superba' and probably 'Red

Admiral' and 'Rosea Superba'. Plants in circulation today under the name 'Clibranii' are identical with *S.* × *elegantissima* and do not match the drawings or Clibrans's description of "broad expanded petals".

'Codsall Brilliant' (ca.1930–38, UK, Bakers of Codsall). Red flowers.

'Codsall Gem' (1920s–ca.1941, UK, Bakers of Codsall). "Deep red, large" (Backhouse, 1941).

'Codsall Maid' (1938, UK, Bakers of Codsall). Pale pink.

'Colour Carpet'. See 'Farbenteppich'.

'Comet' (1912, UK). "Charming cross of *S. granulata* with a good red mossy variety—large white flowers, stems 9" high arising from a tuft of vigorous foliage. AM, 7 votes for" (*JRHS*, 1912). Plate looks quite like *S. granulata*. One of the original cultivars defined in *S.* × *Edwardsii*.

'Corby Dream' (1980s, UK, Heybridge Alpines of Eastleigh).

'Craven Gem' (1913–?, UK, Craven Nursery). Synonym *S. decipiens* (*rosacea*) 'Craven Gem'. Small, red ("brilliant dark crimson").

'Crimson King' (1930s, UK). Said to be of neat habit with large rose-coloured flowers "of neat form". "Deep crimson" (Ingwersen, 1934).

'Dainty Maid' (1933/4, UK, Bakers of Codsall).

decipiens. Old name for *S. rosacea*.

decipiens Bristoliana (1913). *JRHS*, 1913. Mr Kitley of Bath.

decipiens Colstonii (1909). *JRHS*, 1909. Mr Kitley of Bath.

decipiens Grandiflora (pre-1911). Probably hybrid of *S. rosacea*.

decipiens hybrida grandiflora (pre-1909). *JRHS*, 1909. Mr Kitley of Bath. Crimson variety of *S. decipiens* (*S. rosacea*). AM unanimous. *The Garden*, 1 May 1909: "The largest of the coloured Saxifrages we have seen." Mrs Lloyd Edwards records that it was seed under this name, from Thomson & Morgan, from which she raised the seedling 'Ruby', later 'Clibranii'.

decipiens Lutescens (pre-1930). Probably hybrid of *S. rosacea*.

'Ditton Crimson' (pre-1909). Very similar to *S. decipiens grandiflora*.

'Draycott Beauty' (1947, UK). "New giant rosy red, 'one of the best'" (Prichard).

× *Edwardsii*—used to cover a parental combination (like *S.* × *Arendsii*) rather than an individual cultivar. Originally contained 'Comet' and 'White Queen'. The cross was given by Engler & Irmscher as *S. exarata* subsp. *moschata* × *S. rosacea* × *S. granulata*. Current

usage render this invalid and equivalent to *S.* × *arendsii*.

'Feltham Queen' (1948–53, UK, Ingwersen). "Palest soft pink flowers, 4"".

'Fergusonii' (pre-1906–31, UK). "Rosy pink" (Backhouse, 1913); "rosy red" (Prichard, ca.1914).

'Garnet'. Only a name on an Alpine Garden Society seedlist (1994).

'Glasnevin Red' (?, Ireland?). Only mention is in NCCPG Pink Book search list.

'Glasnevin White' (?, Ireland?). Only mention is in NCCPG Pink Book search list.

'Grace'. Two plants have gone under this name. The original plant, now lost, was crimson-pink according to Prichard's 1929 catalogue. A newer cultivar (1983) from John Tuite is small, variegated, turns cream in winter, with white flowers 1.2 cm, on green 7.5 cm stems.

'Grandiflora Alba' (1912–13). Older, reliable, vigorous, white, 20 cm. See also 'Alba Grandiflora'.

'Grenadier' (1920s, UK, Prichard). "Amaranth".

'Greystones' (1920s, UK, Prichard). "Light pink".

'Guildford Seedling' (1902–39, UK, Upton). RHS AM 1902. "One of the first and best red flowered mossies. Compact foliage. Flowers bright crimson, 7--10 cm stems, very free-flowering".

'Harlequin' (ca.1929–32, UK). "Blush striped pink" (Prichard and G. P. Porter).

hirta. As used by Mrs Lloyd Edwards probably a form of *S. exarata* subsp. *moschata* or *S. rosacea*.

'Holgate Gem' (1926–66, UK, Backhouse). New to Backhouse in 1926: "vigorous, pale pink 9"". Still listed by Kayes, 1966–67.

'House's Variety' (1912–30, UK). As *decipiens* (*rosacea*) House's variety (Prichard, 1912) with large pale pink flowers, but "compact red" according to Backhouse (1926).

'J. C. Lloyd Edwards' (1916–39, UK, Mrs Lloyd Edwards). *JRHS*, 1916: "Dwarf mossy with large bright rose flowers having a yellow green eye. Flowers are borne about 4 inches above foliage. AM unanimous". AM again 1919. Listed 1929–30 by Clibrans and described as "rose, beautiful, very free".

'Jewel' ('Juwel') (1912–13). Low-growing. Red flowers.

'J. F. Tottenham' (1912, UK, Mrs Lloyd Edwards). AM 1912. Possibly same as 'Mrs J. F. Tottenham'.

'Juwel'. See 'Jewel'.

'Lady Dean(e)' (1909–30, UK). Bakers of Wolverhampton: "Most vigorous—flowers suffused slightly with rose". Listed still in 1925. White flowers with pink centre (Prichard, 1913). Listed by G. P. Porter, 1930. Tall—20 cm—stout stems.

'Lady Eveline Maud' (1929–39, UK). "Rich blood red" (Clibrans, 1929).

'Lindsiana' (?1912–35). "Very small, white".

'Magnifica' (1912–13). Listed as *S. × arendsii* by Engler & Irmscher.

'May Queen' (1935, UK, Prichard).

'Miss Willmott' (ca.1900–1960s, UK, Bakers of Codsall). "A pretty free-flowering cultivar with large creamy flowers, blotched chocolate at the base of the petals." (*JRHS*, 1909). Bakers: "Much like 'Arkwrightii' but more decided tone of colour. Rachis and pedicels, tinged purple, glandular hairy. Flowers white marked with purple. Buds tinged reddish purple, make effective contrast with white flowers. AM unanimous". *The Garden*: "large and well-formed flowers being of a blush pink shade, with somewhat deeper colouring at the base." Listed by Clibrans from 1929 to 1939/40 as "white with chocolate markings". Still listed by Ingwersens 1962/3. May still exist.

'Monica' (1920, UK, Mrs Lloyd Edwards). Large-flowered, individual flowers at least 2.5 cm across, deep rose-red in bud, but a much paler pink when fully open. AM (1920), 21 for, 3 against.

'Mother of Pearl' (pre-1956). "Shell-pink" flowers. This name duplicates that of section *Porphyrion S. ×irvingii* cultivar.

'Mrs J. S. Baker' (ca.1920, UK). Listed by Prichard in catalogue no. 24.

'Mrs Donaldson Hudson' (1912–29, UK). "[New] dark red flowers, rich green foliage" (Prichard, 1913); "rose, early" (Prichard, 1929). Sometimes as 'Mrs D. Hudson'.

'Mrs Lloyd Edwards' (1930, UK). Flowers red. Habit of 'Guildford Seedling'. Listed by G. P. Porter.

'Mrs Rudd' (ca.1920, UK, Prichard).

'Mrs J. F. Tottenham' (1912, UK). *JRHS*, vol. 38: "Cross as 'Comet' (*S. granulata* × good red mossy variety). White flowers, hairy stems 6″ high. Exquisite pink colouring of unopened buds. More compact than 'Comet'."

'Mrs R. T. Wickham' (1916, UK, Mrs Lloyd Edwards). *JRHS*: "Very free flowering, dark stems, large rose-coloured flowers streaked with deeper shade, height about 8 inches. AM 7 for, 3 against." Correct name for 'P. T. Wickham'.

'Oculata Rosea' (1916). *S. × Edwardsii* cross.

'Picture' (1930, UK). Listed by G. P. Porter.

'P. T. W(h)ickham'. Corruption of 'Mrs R .T. Wickham'.

'P. W. Hosier' (pre-1909, UK, Bakers of Wolverhampton). *Gard. Chron.*, 1909. Robust but not very tall with rich crimson flowers.

'Queen of the Carpeters' (1930). Listed as such by G. P. Porter, otherwise generally listed as 'Teppichkönigin'.

'Red Dwarf' (1919–30, UK, Mrs Lloyd Edwards). AM 1919: "Very free flowering, deep reddish scarlet flowers. Height 3 to 4 inches." (*JRHS*).

'Rev. Wilcox' (1930, UK). Listed by G. P. Porter.

'Reyeri'. See 'Rheyeri'.

'Rhei' (1889–1930s?). Listed by Prichard from 1907: "soft pink" (Ingwersen 1934). A synonym of 'Laxa' according to Ingwersen (1956).

'Rhei Coccinea' (1910). As *S. muscoides* (*moschata*) Rhei coccinea (*Gard. Chron.*, 21 May 1910).

'Rhei Improved' (1902, UK, Craven Nursery).

'Rhei Superba' (1904–?, UK). Listed by Prichard from 1907; "deeper colour than Rhei" (Ingwersen 1934).

'Rheyeri' (1912–33, Germany, Arends). Sometimes as *S. × reyeri*.

'Rob Roy' (1929–30, UK, Prichard). "Fine rich red".

'Robusta' (1935). Listed by M. Prichard.

'Robusta Grandiflora' (1935). Listed by M. Prichard.

'Rosakönigin' (1938, Germany, Arends). (Transl. "Pink Queen"). Later-flowering. Pure pink flowers on rather loose cushions, 15 cm.

'Rosea Grandiflora' (1935). No description (M. Prichard).

'Rosea Superba' (1912, UK, Mrs Lloyd Edwards). As *S. rosea superba*: "a very fine, free flowering early variety with dark stems and red buds".

'Rose Beauty' (1913–39, UK, Mrs Lloyd Edwards). "Beautifully shaped flowers with small centres which flowers very late." Still listed by Clibrans in 1939. "Bright rose, late" (Clibrans, 1929).

'Rosy Gem' (1931, UK, Bakers of Codsall). "New—rose pink".

'Ruby' (1909, UK, Mrs Lloyd Edwards). Original name given by Mrs Lloyd Edwards to plant subsequently introduced by Messrs Clibrans as 'Clibranii'. Further details under 'Clibranii'.

'R. W. Hosin'. Mistranscription of 'P. W. Hosier'.

'Sanguinea (Prichard's)' (1939, UK). Listed by M. Prichard without description.

'Scarlet Gem' (ca.1910–?). A very fine crimson-scarlet variety, free-flowering.

'Splendens' (1912). No details.

'Splendissima' (1912). No details.

'Stansfieldii Rosea'. Only the name, but given the fact that 'Stansfieldii' is pink today, probably synonymous.

'Stormont(h) Seedling' (pre-1905–33, UK). An old cultivar with rosy-pink flowers on 5 cm stems.

'S. T. Wright' (1925–30, UK, Bakers of Codsall). "Cream. The nearest approach to yellow to date. Rather erratic in flowering, some of the plants not flowering until late summer." Also listed by G. P. Porter.

'Tapis Rouge' (pre-1913–20s). Quite small, 3 in. "pink, very pretty" (Clibrans). Listed by Prichard ca.1920.

'Teppichkönigin'. Reference in Correvon (1930).

'Twynham Beauty' (1929). Glowing rose (Prichard).

'V.A.D.' (pre-1929–39, UK). "Late red" (Prichard); also described as "beautiful rich crimson".

'Vivid' (pre-1920–38, UK). Listed by G. P. Porter.

'Webbiana' (1906, UK, Craven Nursery).

'Wenlock' (1930s, UK). May be an abbreviation of 'Wenlock Best of All' or 'Wenlock Peach'. Kaye's catalogue referred to it as having "large rosy flowers".

'Wenlock Beauty' (ca.1918, UK). "New pink" (Prichard).

'Wenlock Best of All' (1913–39, UK, Lady Milnes Gaskell). *JRHS*, 1914. "Very fine salmon-pink, large flowers" (Backhouse, 1926). New in Clibrans 1913–14—raised by Lady C. Milnes Gaskell, 5/-. Also raised *Dianthus* 'Wenlock Incomparable', also 5/-. Listed till 1939/40; also listed by G. P. Porter in the late 1930s.

'Wenlock Peach' (1926–34, UK). "Large in growth, and flower, spreading to form large tufts. fl. stem 9 in. Flowers peach-coloured. Spring. Needs frequent top-dressing or division to keep neat." Listed by Ingwersens in 1934—"large round pink flowers", 6 in. "Pale pink" (Prichard, 1929).

'Wenlock Sanguinea' (1920s, UK, Bakers of Codsall).

'White Empress' (1929–39, UK). "Pure white" (Prichard).

'White Queen' (pre-1916). One of the originally listed *S. × Edwardsii* cultivars in Engler & Irmscher.

'Wild Rose' (1931–46, UK). Small ("wee and dainty"), 5–7 cm high, pale pink flowers. Listed by Ingwersen.

'Wolley Dod' (1907, UK). Red flowers.

'Wonder' (1931, UK, Mrs Lloyd Edwards). Only a name.

Conversion Table

Millimetres	Centimetres	Metres	Inches	Feet
1 mm			0.04 in	
2 mm			0.08 in	
2.5 mm			0.1 in	
5 mm			0.2 in	
10 mm	1.0 cm		0.4 in	
15 mm	1.5 cm		0.6 in	
25 mm	2.5 cm		1 in	
	5 cm		2 in	
	10 cm		4 in	
	20 cm		8 in	
	30 cm		12 in	1 ft
	50 cm		20 in	
	60 cm		24 in	2 ft
	75 cm		30 in	
	100 cm	1m	39 in	3.25 ft
		2m		6.50 ft
		5m		16.50 ft
		10m		33 ft
		100m		330 ft
		500m		1650 ft
		1000m		3300 ft
		2000m		6600 ft
		3000m		9900 ft
		4000m		13,200 ft
		5000m		16,500 ft

Kilometres	Miles
10 km	6.25 miles
16 km	10 miles
50 km	31 miles
80.5 km	50 miles

Bibliography

Balfour, I. B. 1916. Saxifrages of the Diptera Section with Description of New Species. *Transactions of the Botanical Society of Edinburgh*.

Bland, B. 2000. *Silver Saxifrages*. Alpine Garden Society.

Brochmann, C., Q-Y. Xiang, S. J. Brinsfeld, D. E. Soltis and P. S. Soltis. 1998. Molecular evidence for polyploid origins in *Saxifraga* (Saxifragaceae): the narrow arctic endemic *S. svalbardensis* and its widespread allies. *American Journal of Botany* 85 (1).

Brouillet, L. 2008. *Saxifraga* and *Micranthes*. *Flora of North America* 8.

Brouillet, L. and R. J. Gornall. 2008. New combinations in genus *Micranthes* (a segregate of *Saxifraga*, Saxifragaceae) in North America. *Journal of the Botanical Research Institute of Texas* 1: 1019–1023.

Brown, B. 2003. Saxifrages with longer-season appeal. *The Garden* 128.

Bürgel, J. 1996. *S. karadzicensis* and *S. ×karadzicensis* Bürgel. *Saxifrage Magazine* (Journal of the Saxifrage Society) 4.

Bürgel, J. 1998. Reports on saxifrages in Central Nepal, Albania and Macedonia. *Saxifrage Magazine* (Journal of the Saxifrage Society) 6.

Bürgel, J. 2004. Dhaulagiri Experience. *Alpine Gardener* (Bulletin of the Alpine Garden Society) 72 (1).

Bürgel, J. and R. A. Fairbairn. 2004. Saxifrages of Central Nepal. *Saxifrage Magazine* (Journal of the Saxifrage Society) 12.

Calder, J. A. and D. B. O. Saville. 1959. Studies in *Saxifragaceae*. II: *Saxifraga* Sect. *Trachyphyllum* in North America. *Brittonia* 11.

Calder, J. A. and D. B. O. Saville. 1960. Studies in *Saxifragaceae*. III: *Saxifraga odontoloma* and *lyallii*, and North American subspecies of *S, punctata*. *Canadian Journal of Botany* 38.

Chuang, H. 2001. New Taxa of Saxifragaceae from Yunnan. *Acta Botanica Yunnanica* 23 (2).

Conti, E., K. Arroyo and F. Rutschmann. 2003. Phylogenetic relationships and molecular dating of the rare *Saxifraga florulenta* Moretti: Implications for biogeography and the evolution of monocarpy. Poster, abstract ID 55, Botany 2003 Conference.

Conti, E., D. E. Soltis, T. M. Hardig and J. Schneider. 1999. Phylogenetic Relationships of the Silver Saxifrages (*Saxifraga*, Sect. *Ligulatae* Haworth): Implications for the Evolution of Substrate Specificity, Life Histories, and Biogeography. *Molecular Phylogenetics and Evolution* 13 (3).

Dashwood, M. and B. Bland. 2005. Silver Saxifrages. *RHS Plant Trials and Awards* 9.

Elvander, P. E. 1984. The taxonomy of *Saxifraga* (Saxifragaceae) section *Boraphila* subsection *Integrifoliae* in western North America. *Systematic Botany Monographs* 3. American Society of Plant Taxonomists.

Elven, R., B. Jonsell, D. F. Murray and B. A. Yurtsev. 2005. An Operational Species Concept for the Panarctic Flora. Pan Arctic Flora website (www.binran.spb.ru/projects/apf/papers/sp_concept).

Engler, A. and E. Irmscher. 1916 and 1919. *Das Pflanzenreich IV.* 117: *Saxifragaceae-Saxifraga*. Leipzig.

Erhardt, A and W. 1997. *PPP Index*. Verlag Eugen Ulmer, Stuttgart (Hohenheim).

Esteban, J., I. Martínez-Castro, P. Vargas and J. Sanz. 1999. Chemosystematic study on leaf volatile compounds of *Saxifraga* L. series Ceratophyllae (Saxifragaceae). *Biochemical Systematics and Ecology* 27.

Gao, C. Z. and G. Z. Li. 1983. New Species of Saxifragacae [sic] from Guangxi. *Guihaia* 3: 20.

Gornall, R. J. 1987. An outline of a revised classification of *Saxifraga* L. *Botanical Journal of the Linnean Society* 95.

Gornall, R. J., H. Ohba and Pan Jintang. 2000. New Taxa, Names, and Combinations in the *Saxifraga* (*Saxifragaceae*) for the *Flora of China*. *Novon* 10: 375–377.

Gornall, R. J. and H. Ohba. Paper in preparation. Resurrection of the genus *Micranthes* (Saxifragaceae): new combinations for some Asiatic and European taxa.

Gorovoi, P. and V. Voroschilov. 1966. Species Nova Generis *Saxifraga* L. e Provincia Amurensi. *Novitates Systematicae Plantarum Vascularum URSS*.

Grierson, A. J. C., and D. G. Long. 1987. *Flora of Bhutan*. Royal Botanic Garden, Edinburgh.

Hara, H. 1976. New or noteworthy flowering plants from Eastern Himalaya (17). *Journal of Japanese Botany* 51 (1).

Harding, W. 1970. *Saxifrages: the Genus Saxifraga in the Wild and in Cultivation*. Alpine Garden Society.

Harding, W. 1992. *Saxifrages: A Gardener's Guide to the Genus*. Alpine Garden Society.

Harding, W. 1994. *Saxifraga*. In K. Beckett, ed. *Encyclopedia of Alpines* 2. Alpine Garden Society.

Harvey, J. H. 1974. The Stocks held by Early Nurseries. *The Agricultural History Review*, 22 (1): 18–35.

Hegi G. 1975. *Illustrierte Flora von Mitteleuropa*. [Revision of the 1923 edition].

Holubec, V. 2003. Occurrence of *Saxifraga columnaris, S. dinnikii* and *S. scleropoda* hybrids in upper Balkaria, Caucasus (Russian Federation). *Saxifrage Magazine* (Journal of the Saxifrage Society) 11.

Holubec, V., and P. Křivka. 2006. *The Caucasus and its Flowers*.

Horný, R., and K. M. Webr. 1985. *Nejkrásnější lomikameny*.

Horný, R., K. M. Webr and J. Byam-Grounds, 1986, *Porophyllum Saxifrages*. Stamford, UK.

Ingwersen, W. E. T. 1951 (2nd ed. 1956). Saxifraga. In F. J. Chittenden, ed. *Dictionary of Gardening*, Royal Horticultural Society.

Irving, W., & R. Malby. 1914. *Saxifrages or Rockfoils*. Headley, London.

Jalas, J. 1999. *Atlas Florae Europaeae notes* 14: Nomenclatural adjustments in *Hylotelephium* (Crassulaceae) and new combinations in *Saxifraga* (Saxifragaceae). *Annales botanici fennici* 36, Helsinki.

Kamelin, R. V. 1989. Novyi vid Saxifraga L. iz Zapadnogo Pamira. *Doklady Akademii Nauk Tadzhikskoi SSR* 32 (12).

Kitamura, S. 1955. Flowering Plants and Ferns. *Fauna and Flora of Nepal Himalaya (Land)*.

Köckinger, H. 2003. *Saxifraga styriaca* spec. nova (*Saxifragaceae*): ein Endemit der östlichen Niederen Tauern (Steiermark, Österreich). *Phyton* 43 (1).

Köhlein, F. 1984. *Saxifrages and Related Genera*. B. T. Batsford, London.

Lang, K. 2004. Red Porphyrion Saxifrages. *Alpine Gardener* (Bulletin of the Alpine Garden Society) 72 (1).

Maire, R. 1980. Saxifragaceae. *Flore de L'Afrique Nord* 15.

Malyschev, L. I. 1988. Novyi vid Roda Saxifraga (Saxifragaceae) iz Yakutii. (A New Species of the genus *Saxifraga* (*Saxifragaceae*) from Yakutia). *Botanicheskii Zhurnal (Nauk Ukrainskoi RSR)* 73 (1).

Malyschev, L. I. 1960. Species Nova Generis *Saxifraga* L. *Notulae Systematicae Herbario Instituti Botanici Acadamiae Scientarum URSS* 20.

Maximova, M. 1970. Nova Species Generis Saxifragae L. e Sochondo Minoris. *Novitates Systematicae Plantarum Vascularum URSS* 6.

McGregor, K. 1994. Mossy Saxifrage Hybrids. *Saxifrage Magazine* (Journal of the Saxifrage Society) 2.

McGregor, K. 1995. Flowering Times, *Saxifrage Magazine* (Journal of the Saxifrage Society) 3.

McGregor, M. 1992. Mossy Saxifrages. *Journal of the Saxifraga Group* 2.

McGregor, M. 1995. *Saxifrages: The Complete Cultivars and Hybrids* (1st edition *International Register of Saxifraga Cultivars*). Saxifrage Society.

McGregor, M. 1997. Kabschia Saxifrage Species from the Caucasus. *Saxifrage Magazine* (Journal of the Saxifrage Society) 5.

McGregor, M. 2001. *Saxifrages from Scratch*. Saxifrage Society.

McGregor, M. 2003. *Saxifrages: The Complete Cultivars & Hybrids* (2nd edition *International Register of Saxifraga Cultivars*). Saxifrage Society.

McGregor, M. 2005. North American Saxifrages. *Saxifrage Magazine* (Journal of the Saxifrage Society) 13.

McGregor, M. 2005. Spring Jewels. *Journal of the Scottish Rock Garden Club* 114.

McGregor, M. 2005. Autumn Glories. *Journal of the Scottish Rock Garden Club* 115.

McGregor, M. 2006. Report on Andalucian Saxifrages. *Saxifrage Magazine* (Journal of the Saxifrage Society) 14.

McGregor, M. 2006. Searching for Saxifrages: Part 1: Alaska. *Bulletin of the North American Rock Garden Society* 64 (3).

McGregor, M. 2006. Searching for Saxifrages: Part 2: Northwest and Rocky Mountains. *Bulletin of the North American Rock Garden Society* 64 (4).

McGregor, M. and W. Harding. 1998. *Saxifrages: the complete list of Species*. Saxifrage Society.

McGregor, M., D. Victor and J. Howes. 2003. *Saxifraga cotyledon* in a new location. *Saxifrage Magazine* (Journal of the Saxifrage Society) 11.

Miyabe, K. and M. Tatewaki. 1938. Contributions to the Flora of Northern Japan XI. *Transactions Sapporo Natural History Society* 15 (4).

Ohba, H. and S. Akiyama, 1992. The Alpine Flora of the Jalajale Himal, Eastern Nepal. *The University of Tokyo, Nature and Culture* 4. The University Museum, Tokyo.

Ohba, H. and M. Wakabayashi. 1984. Notes on the Himalayan Saxifraga (1). Two new species in the sect. Hirculus. *Journal Japanese Botany* 59 (12).

Ohba, H. and M. Wakabayashi. 1987. Three new species in the section Ciliatae. Notes on the Himalayan Saxifraga (2). *Journal Japanese Botany* 62 (6).

Pan Jintang. 1992. *Flora Reipublicae Popularis Sinicae* 34 (2).

Pan Jintang, R. J. Gornall and H. Ohba. 2001. *Saxifraga*. Flora of China 8: 269–452. (available online free at www.efloras.org).

Peters, J. 2006. *Saxifraga cortusifolia* Herbsteinbrech. Staudengärtnerei, Jürgen Peters, Uetersen.

Reiche, K. 1897. Familia Saxifragáceas. *Estudios Críticos Sobre la Flora de Chile* 3.

Roberts, T. 2004. Nepalese saxifrages, an Ongoing Appraisal. *Alpine Gardener* (Bulletin of the Alpine Garden Society). 72 (1).

Siplivinsky, V. 1971. Generis *Saxifraga* L. Species Asiaticae e Sectione *Trachyphyllum* Gaud. *Novosti sistematiki vysshikh rastenii (Novitates Systematicae Plantarum Vascularum)* 8.

Siplivinsky, V. 1982. Sect. *Porophyllum* Gaudin in the USSR. *Phytologia* 51 (3).

Skelly, R. J. 1988. A new species of *Saxifraga* (Saxifragaceae) from the Olympic Mountains, Washington, and Vancouver Island, British Columbia. *Madroño* 35 (2).

Smith, H. 1958. *Saxifraga* of the Himalaya: I. Section *Kabschia*. *Bulletin of the British Museum (Natural History)* 2 (4).

Smith, H. 1960. *Saxifraga* of the Himalaya: II. Some New Species. *Bulletin of the British Museum (Natural History)* 2 (9).

Soltis, D. E., R. K. Kuzoff, E. Conti, R. Gornall and K. Ferguson. 1996. MATK and RBCL Gene Sequence Data Indicate that *Saxifraga* (Saxifragaceae) is Polyphphyletic. *American Journal of Botany* 83 (3).

Stearn, W. T. 1999. Early introductions of plants from Japan into European gardens, *Taxonomy of Cultivated Plants*. Royal Botanic Garden Kew.

Tebbitt, M. 1999. The cultivated species of *Saxifraga* section *Irregulares*. *New Plantsman* 6 (4).

Vargas, P. 1997. *Saxifraga*. In Castoviejo, S. et al. *Flora Iberica* V: *Ebenaceae—Saxifragaceae*. Real Jardin Botanico, CISC.

Vargas, P., and G. N. Feliner. 1996. Artificial hybridization within Saxifraga pentadactlyis (Saxifragaceae). *Nordic Journal of Botany* 16 (3).

Vargas, P., C. M. Morton and S. L. Jury. 1999. Biogeographic patterns in Mediterranean and Macronesian species of *Saxifraga* (Saxifragaceae) inferred from phylogenetic analyses of ITS sequences. *A,merican Journal of Botany* 86 (5).

Voroschilov, V. M. 1977. Novyi Kamnelomkakh. *Byulletin Galvnogo Botani-Cheskogo Sada (Moscow)* 103.

Wadhwa B. M. 1986. A new species of *Saxifraga* from Bhutan. *Kew Bulletin* 41 (1).

Webb, D.A., and R. J. Gornall, 1989, *Saxifrages of Europe with Notes on African, American and some Asiatic Species*. Bromley: Christopher Helm. Published in the USA as *A Manual of Saxifrages and Their Cultivation*.

Young, A. 1993. The Pyrenean Notomorphs. *Saxifrage Magazine* (Journal of the Saxifrage Society) 1.

Young, A. 2005. Saxifraga catalaunica. *Bulletin of the North American Rock Garden Society* 63 (4).

Zhmylev, P. Y. 1988. Eamtki o Kamnelomkakh (*Saxifraga* L.) Sektsii *Trachyphyllum* Gaud. (Note on Rockfoils (*Saxifraga* L.) of the Section *Trachyphyllum* Gaud.). *Byulleten' Moskovskogo Obshchestva Ispytatelei Prirody, Otdel Biologicheskii* 93 (1).

Zhmylev, P. Y. 1990. Novaya Kamnelomka (*Saxifraga* L.) s Territorii Yukona (A new *Saxifraga* L. from the Yukon). *Byulleten' Moskovskogo Obshchestva Ispytatelei Prirody, Otdel Biologicheskii* 95 (3).

Zhmylev, P. Y. 1991. Novyye Nazvaniya Kitayskikh Kamnyelomok (*Saxifraga* L.) I Z Syektsii *Hirculus* (Haw.) Tausch. (New Names for *Saxifraga* L. species belonging to *Hirculus* (Haw.) Tausch). *Byulleten' Moskovskogo Obshchestva Ispytatelei Prirody, Otdel Biologicheskii* 96 (3).

Zhmylev, P. Y. 1992. *Saxifraga codyana* - new saxifrage from North America. *Byulleten' Moskovskogo Obshchestva Ispytatelei Prirody, Otdel Biologicheskii* 97 (1).

Zhmylev, P. Y. 1995. K Taksonomii Kompleksa *Saxifraga nelsoniana* L. *Byulleten' Moskovskogo Obshchestva Ispytatelei Prirody, Otdel Biologicheskii* 100 (3).

Zhmylev, P. Y. 1996. Rockfoils of the Subgenus *Micranthes* (Haw.) H. G. L. Reichenbach. *Byulleten' Moskovskogo Obshchestva Ispytatelei Prirody, Otdel Biologicheskii* 101 (6).

Zhmylev, P. Y. 1997. Systematical Review of Rockfoils (*Saxifraga* L.) of Russia and Contiguous Territories: Subgenera *Micrant[h]es*, *Diptera* and *Hirculus*. *Byulleten' Moskovskogo Obshchestva Ispytatelei Prirody, Otdel Biologicheskii* 102 (3).

Beyond these a large range of nursery catalogues have been used in the research for various chapters. These include catalogues from Aberconwy Nursery (1988-2005), G. Arends (1912, 32, 38, 41), Backhouse & Sons (1926, 30, 39, 41), Bakers of Codsall (1925, 31, 33, 38); Beechcroft nursery (1995); Ron Beeston (1994, 95); Ger van den Beuken (2000–2006); Brambling House Nursery (1990); Clibrans Nursery (1880, 82, 1913, 29, 39); Cotswold Garden Flowers (1999, 2000–2002 and website); Craven Nurseries (1902, 05, 06, 13); Edrom Nurseries (1992); Eschmann (1995, 2001, 03, and online catalogue 2007); Greenslacks Nursery (1993–94);

Hartside Nursery Gardens (1989); Hillview Hardy Plants (1990, 94); Holden Clough (1988, 89, 91, 92); C. G. Hollett, Sedburgh (1977); Ingwersen's (1931, 31 supplement, 37, 39, 43, 46, 50, 53, 61, 63/4, 64, 67, 68, 92); Inshriach Alpine Plant Nursery (1993/4); Jouet (Thierry) (2002 e-catalogue); R. Kaye, Waithman Nurseries (1933, 66); Kuroishi Wildflower Farm Ltd. (2002 e-catalogue); Lissadell Nursery (1913); Lochside Alpine Nursery (1991, 92); Nightingale Nursery (Stuart Boothman) (1939, 47, 63); Norden Alpines (1986–89, 91, 92, 95); G. P. Porter Alpine Nursery (1930 (as R. M. Prichard's), 32, late 30s (probably 38)), Potterton & Martin (1990); M. Prichard & Sons (1910, 29, 35, 39, 47, 63); R. M. Prichard (1930); Rice Creek Gardens (2001/2 e-catalogue); R. V. Roger Ltd. (1987, 88, 93, 94); Six Hills Nursery (Clarence Elliott Ltd.) (1931); Sündermann (1994/5, 2007 e-catalogue); Thuya Alpine Nursery (1986, 94); Tough Alpine Nursery (1994–5, 1998). Beyond these are various volumes of the *RHS Plant Finder* (1989–90, 92–93, 2000–01, 01–02, 03-04, 06-07) and the 3rd edition of the European equivalent *PPP Index* (1997), and the journals of the Saxifrage Society.

Index

Page numbers in bold signify main list entry; numbers in italic indicate an illustration. Names in brackets are to help the reader to find entries, particularly in the alphabetic lists of taxa at the end of chapters. For instance the entry "*Saxifraga* 'Gregor Mendel' (*S.* ×*apiculata*)" indicates that *Saxifraga* 'Gregor Mendel' is a cultivar of the cross *S.* ×*apiculata* and may most readily be found under that entry. Other cases deal with changes in nomenclature: thus in "*Saxifraga apetala* (*Micranthes apetala*)" the *Saxifraga* epithet is a synonym of the *Micranthes* epithet but the page number will take you to an instance where the *Saxifraga* epithet appears.

Common (rather than botanical or horticultural) names are indexed alphabetically as if they had a *Saxifraga* prefix, so that "Dovedale moss" appears between "*Saxifraga* 'Double White'" and "*Saxifraga doyalana*".